D1433724

CHAMPION
TREES

CHAMPION TREES

OF BRITAIN & IRELAND

Ed. Dr Owen Johnson

Foreword by Her Grace, the Duchess of Devonshire
Introduction by Thomas Pakenham

The Tree Register
of the British Isles

TREE REGISTER

Whittet Books

Frontispiece: Champion Oriental Plane at Rycote, Oxfordshire.

First published 2003
Copyright ©2003 by The Trustees of the Tree Register of the British Isles

Whittet Books Ltd, Hill Farm, Stonham Rd, Cotton, Stowmarket, Suffolk IP14 4RQ

Cataloguing in publication data
A catalogue record for this title is available from the British Library.

ISBN 1 873580 61 4

Acknowledgments

The Trustees of the Tree Register would like to thank Dr Owen Johnson for his dedication and hard work in editing this book; also David Alderman, the Registrar of the Tree Register, and the tree recorders who, together with Dr Johnson, are responsible for the data in the book. The Trustees also gratefully acknowledge the financial support provided by The Royal Horticultural Society and The Friends of Westonbirt Arboretum towards the costs of publication. Thanks are also due to those who kindly provided the photographs included in this book and to landowners who granted our recorders access to their land.

Picture credits

The author and publishers gratefully acknowledge the following for pictures on the pages mentioned: David Alderman, pp. 32, 42, 48, 52, 60, 61, 62, 71, 80, 92, 103, 108 (above), 114, 116, 128, 131, 149, 164, 171; David Arscott, pp. 5, 8, 14, 30, 36, 41, 46, 83, 98, 100, 102, 108 (below), 111, 141, 142, 157; Bicton Park Botanical Garden, pp. 27, 65; B Cheasley, p. 84; A W Farrell, p. 88; Aubrey Fennell, p. 50; Den Gregson, p 68; Charles Henderson, pp. 18, 175; Tim Hills, pp. 105, 106; Derrick Holdsworth, pp. 44, 75, 109, 121; Pamela Johnson, pp. 51, 76; Alan Mitchell, pp. 70, 72, 118, 135, 173; David Mitchell, pp. 39, 90, 180; Andrew Morton, p. 151; Thomas Pakenham, p. 10; Jim Paterson, pp. 21, 28; A D Schilling, pp. 2, 53, 78, 120, 123, 167, 177; John Simmons, pp. 20, 96; Pamela Stevenson, pp. 12, 168; Tower Hamlets Borough Council, p. 59; Steve Young, pp. 17, 34, 56, 87, 125, 127, 138, 154, 159.

Printed in Hong Kong by Wing King Tong

Foreword by
The Duchess of Devonshire

There is a great and growing interest in all things natural and trees, in particular, are loved and appreciated as never before. The temperate climate of these islands, about which we continually grumble, is of inestimable benefit to foresters and gardeners. It provides a big difference of rainfall from the northwest of Scotland to the southeast of England, and the same goes for the geological formations below ground. This means an enormous variety of trees, both native and those introduced in the last four hundred years, grow successfully. They are one of the glories of this country and are of first importance in the landscape.

Once an interest in trees is aroused it stays with you and makes the shortest journey in this country a pleasurable experience, identifying the favourites and looking for the unusual on the way. This eagerly awaited book will fuel this. It satisfies the curious and answers our questions, providing new information on this fascinating subject. We are told where the best specimens are to be found, the grandest, the tallest, those of massive girth, the oldest and rarest in woods, fields, parks and gardens – the champions of the land. With the gazetteer we can go in search of them and perhaps add to their number by our own discoveries.

It is an honour for me to be Patron of the Tree Register of the British Isles and to have the chance of commending to the reader this unique record of champion trees, unavailable to us till now. I like to think how much it would have pleased our co-founder, Alan Mitchell, as well as the wider audience who will enjoy it and learn from it.

Chatsworth, February 2003

The Queen Elizabeth Oak (Sessile) at Cowdray Park, W Sussex.

Contents

Introduction by Thomas Pakenham

Why take trouble to make lists of prodigious trees? The question goes echoing back across the centuries, from today's enthusiastic 'tapers' (The Tree Register's team of tree measurers) in their jeans and sweat-shirts, back to 17th century gentlemen like John Evelyn measuring his parkland oak trees in wig and tricorne hat.

It was Evelyn who published in 1664 his book *Sylva*, a six-hundred-page compendium of tree scholarship and tree enthusiasm, which included the first list of British tree prodigies. Three hundred and forty years later most of us would agree with his answer to that question, why it was worth the trouble: because trees are one of the most undervalued wonders of nature.

Ironically, Evelyn, one of Charles II's principal advisers on the arts and sciences, had been commissioned to write a practical guide to timber production. This was in the early 1660s and the newly restored royal government found itself threatened by a naval war with Holland. There was a panic about the shortage of planking timber (especially oak) available for the British navy. The full title of Evelyn's mighty tome is *Sylva: or a Discourse of Forest-Trees and the Propagation of TIMBER in his Majesty's Dominions.* But the book is about far more than mere timber production. It's a passionate argument for planting ornamental trees and for conservation of trees of all kinds, including the new exotics. And, astonishingly, it struck a chord among his fellow landowners, the lumping gentry of the shires! In fact no book on trees has ever been more influential in Britain and beyond. Of course Evelyn was a man of letters as well as a man of the trees. His book ran to four editions in his own lifetime, the last with additions written when he was in his 85th year and still hale and hearty enough to plant trees with his own hands. (Evelyn was now waiting, as he put it, 'for Him to transplant me into those glorious regions above, the Celestial paradise, planted with Perennial Groves and Trees bearing immortal fruit.') The book is a scientific account of the various forest trees then recognised to be suitable for planting in England – not so different from a list we would draw up today. There were native Beech, Oak, Elm and Ash; naturalised Sweet Chestnut, Walnut, Sycamore, Norway Spruce and Scots Pine; and the new exotics like Cedar, Larch and Silver Fir. It's also a *discourse* – a passionate, witty, rambling, erudite plea for his fellow countrymen to plant trees and to value them as the prodigies they often are.

Evelyn lists the great trees of the world that, over the centuries, have stirred men's hearts: the Olives of Hesiod and Homer, the Plane of Herodotus (which Socrates swore by), the giant trees of the East, like the Fig under which Buddha found enlightenment. He then asks the question: how would Britain's own ancient prodigies have compared to these celebrated foreigners? The Druids, he says, kept no records of their prodigious trees. More's the pity. But he's convinced that, despite the current neglect of trees, and despite the infamous hurricane of 1703 (he was writing this the next year in a note to the fourth edition) 'the remains of what are yet in being … may stand in fair competition with anything that antiquity can produce'.

He then lists just over forty trees in Britain that he considers prodigious, and gives the heroic size of many of them. It's an important list – indeed you could call it the first published list of champion trees growing throughout Britain. (Earlier that century, local antiquarians, like Dr Plot in Oxfordshire and Staffordshire, had published lists of local champions, and it was by consolidating these and adding to them that Evelyn produced the first national list.) Today we would be glad to include many of Evelyn's giants in our list of current champions. Sadly, only a couple have survived the vicissitudes of the last 350 years. The first is a native, the 'Crowhurst yew' (Did Evelyn mean the Yew of Crowhurst, Surrey, or Crowhurst, Sussex (see p.105). It makes no odds, as both have survived.) The second is an introduced tree, the great Sweet Chestnut of Tortworth (see p.42) or Tamworth, which Evelyn, rather naively, believed was then the oldest tree in Britain. We now know that it is Yews, not Chestnuts or Oaks, that are the Methuselahs of our world. Yew wood is the most durable. So it is Yews that live much longer lives, whole millennia longer in fact, than any other living creature in Europe.

After listing these wonders Evelyn explains why he believes trees have always fascinated discerning men. It is because we feel they resemble us. He contrasts the enormous size and strength of the mature tree with the frail and almost invisible seed from which it springs. Buried 'in the moist womb of the earth' the seeds are transformed into trees that can 'render asunder whole rocks of stone … (able) even to remove mountains.'

The Howletts Chestnut near Canterbury is a product of the enthusiasm for planting parkland trees at the turn of the 18th century. Its great octopus of limbs may originally have been trained to support a tree-house.

He continues: 'our tree, like man, (whose inverted symbol he is) being sown in corruption, rises in glory, and by little and little ascending into an hard erect stem of comely dimensions, becometh a solid tower, as it were! And … this which but lately a single ant would easily have borne to his little cavern, should now become capable of resisting the fury, and braving the rage of the most impetuous storms'.

In 1776 Evelyn's original list of British champions was marginally amplified by an amateur naturalist, a professional doctor called Alexander Hunter. He added one tree that is alive today, the tree some people believe is the oldest tree in Europe: the crumbling ruin of a Yew at Fortingall, Perthshire (see p.105). The material was published by Hunter in a sumptuous new illustrated edition (entitled *Silva* not *Sylva)* produced with the blessing of the great and the good in the botanical world of the period – Carl Linnaeus, Joseph Banks and Philip Miller. Dr Hunter also listed, and illustrated, the tree that can claim to have been the largest oak ever known to have grown in Britain, the Cowthorpe Oak (see p.93). The prodigy was then 78 feet in girth close to the ground (750 cm diameter), 48 feet at three feet above (460 cm diameter at 90 cm). (Sadly it collapsed and died in the mid-nineteenth century.)

But it was not until 1835 that Evelyn's pioneering list of champions began to be replaced by a much more systematic and comprehensive work. In that year the Scottish encyclopaedist and journalist, John Claudius Loudon, launched in monthly issues what would by 1838 become an astonishing 2,694 page, 8-volume encyclopaedia of trees and shrubs, illustrated by 2,500 engravings and 400 separate plates: the *Arboretum et Fruticetum Britannicum*. Loudon lacked the literary gifts and psychological insights of an insider like Evelyn. Today his prose seems rather solemn. But given his handicaps – a self-educated farmer's son from Lanarkshire, with his left arm crippled, his right amputated, for years in such constant pain that he needed twice daily doses of laudanum, and the very real danger of bankruptcy – he was a prodigy himself. The *Arboretum* covers in detail an amazing range. It was based on 30 years' research and correspondence with literally *thousands* of the botanists, dendrologists and tree enthusiasts of the era. In 1834 he sent out 3,000 questionnaires to be completed by his correspondents; many of their names are given in the text of the *Arboretum*. The full title of the great work is a 62-word mouthful but only hints at the good things inside. It's *Arboretum et Fruticetum Britannicum or The Trees and Shrubs of Britain Native and Foreign, Hardy and Half-Hardy, Pictorially and Botanically*

Delineated, and Scientifically and Popularly Described; with Their Propagation, Culture, Management, and Uses in the Arts, in Useful and Ornamental Plantations, and in Landscape Gardening; Preceded by an Historical and Geographical Outline of the Trees and Shrubs of temperate Climates throughout the World.

Like Evelyn before him, Loudon believed that landowners greatly undervalued the rich variety of trees available for planting in temperate Europe. Of course the list had now grown by leaps and bounds. By Loudon's own reckoning there were only 84 foreign woody plants available for cultivation in England by the end of the 16th century, and a further 170 introduced in the next century. But in the first three decades of the 19th century Loudon estimated that 786 shrubs and trees had been brought in, many of which were exotic trees from North America collected by explorers like David Douglas, John Fraser and John Lyon. It was this cornucopia of new trees that Loudon wanted to see growing in the plantations and pleasure grounds of the 'gentlemen of landed property'. And one of the main ways to encourage them was to list outstanding specimens of the new exotics growing in Britain and beyond.

So Loudon compiled lists of thousands of individual trees scattered over Britain and Europe – and far beyond. Unfortunately Loudon's gifts for collecting and publishing data about trees exceeded his ability to organise it, edit it and – above all – to index it fully. So, for the historian, the *Arboretum* remains a gold mine of a book, teeming with ore, but difficult to exploit. I doubt whether any tree historian has ever counted the individual trees measured and recorded in the *Arboretum*. My guess is that the total listed for Britain and Ireland exceeds 3,000. Evelyn had listed just over 40 prodigious trees in Britain. Loudon lists the measurements for over 221 specimens of native oak trees alone, of which 92 would be considered exceptional today, that is, they were at least 100 feet (30m) high or 25 feet in girth (240cm in diameter). (Some have miraculously survived till the present. I have encountered and photographed 11 of these giants myself.) Sadly, the book effectively killed him. He died in 1843, worn out and nearly bankrupt, and the second edition, in 1844, was edited by his long-suffering wife, Jane.

It was a further 70 years before anyone dared to tempt fate with an encyclopaedia describing and listing exceptional trees on this heroic scale. In 1906, Henry Elwes and Augustine Henry threw down the gauntlet. Elwes was a Gloucestershire landowner of independent means, Henry a medical doctor from Northern Ireland and an amateur naturalist famous for his plant discoveries in the wilds of China. Both men were fascinated by trees as well as other plants. Together they produced a seven-volume work, *The Trees of Great Britain and Ireland*, which was privately printed in Edinburgh in 1906 to 1913. This remains in many ways the most sumptuous and well-informed book exclusively on trees ever published. However, despite its professionalism and scholarship, its scope is much smaller than Loudon's – and so are its lists of champions. (Compare Elwes and Henry's 43 listed current specimens of *Fagus sylvatica* with Loudon's astonishing total of 71.) Both Elwes and Henry were widely travelled and widely respected. Their book is richly illustrated with monochrome photographs professionally taken. Though Elwes expressed himself disappointed with his photographers (and what photograph can combine the body of an accurate record with the soul of a work of art?), the illustrations have much historical value. As for the lists of champion trees, they were in their time a unique record of the size to which all the different species – native, naturalised and exotic – could grow in these islands. *In their time.* Of course, only too soon the Elwes and Henry records were overtaken by storms, and by old age itself, and passed into history. And this brings us, in a century wide leap, to the Tree Register's admirable new book of champions.

This new book uses the up-to-the minute records of the Tree Register of the British Isles and Ireland. These originated as the records compiled by Alan Mitchell while he was working as a research scientist for the Forestry Commission. Alan saw himself in direct line of descent from Elwes and Henry's records. He once said that, if he lived long enough, he would like to visit and check the record of every tree in their book. And perhaps he did. Certainly Alan collected in his life time nearly 100,000 separate records of exceptional trees. In due course he helped create the Tree Register and handed on his own card index. The records, greatly amplified since Alan's day, are now fully computerised. To bring them up to date and keep them that way has involved a large team of volunteers under the leadership of David Alderman. I think Alan would be delighted by the progress (though he might pretend to be shocked by the number of purple-leaved cultivars, his *bêtes noires*, that have found their way onto the register).

Let's now return to the question with which we began: what's the point of bothering with records of champion trees?

I'm impressed by the answers given by Owen Johnson in his text in this book. He cites a number of practical reasons for identifying, measuring and recording outstanding trees. We must identify the regions and soils of Britain and Ireland where particular species will do best – and worst. (Don't expect a champion

Ginkgo to grow in the cool bogland of Ireland, or a champion Silver Fir to spring up on the greensand of Sussex. Put the Ginkgo in the greensand and the Silver Fir in the bogs, not vice versa.) Of course the aim is to encourage diversity in new planting (and here we go back to both Evelyn and Loudon). We must also try to help to protect and preserve specimens reckoned outstanding for age, size and rarity (these themes, too, are implicit in Evelyn and Loudon). We must also protect species threatened in their own natural habitats in the third world – species like the monkey puzzle and *Fitzroya* in the Andes – by giving specimens sanctuary, known as 'ex situ conservation', here in the first world.

Can I conclude with a short canter on a hobby horse of my own. For me there's one overwhelmingly strong argument for this book of champions. It shows how many hundreds of different species and thousands of varieties of tree will grow marvellously well in Britain and Ireland. Yet this stunning richness in our flora – native and naturalised and recently introduced – is now under threat from a strange new disease. I call it *nativitis*, and it's spreading. The buzzword is 'biodiversity' but the result is the precise opposite – at least as far as trees are concerned. For years conifers and other exotics have been out of fashion among the smart set of ecologists. Now they have begun to deride as 'aliens' species of trees like Beech that have long been naturalised in Britain – and have been welcome guests outside the regions of England to which they are native. In the name of biological purity these ecologists now cut Beech down and re-plant with Oak, Ash and other native species. Famous Beech trees have been hacked down in Scotland in pogroms of this kind. In Ireland landowners are encouraged by extra-generous state grants to cut down young Beech and prevent any more Beech regenerating naturally. The official policy is that 'Beech don't belong in Ireland.' It is beginning to be treated like an invasive alien – as if it threatened the environment like the invasive aliens of South Africa and Australia. So these trees, that reach record dimensions and suit the landscape so well, and in fact have been the crowning glory of Irish demesnes for hundreds of years, must be replaced, little by little, with alder, willows and native scrub. In Belgium the situation is even more threatening. Landowners have been warned that it will be illegal for them to plant exotic shrubs and trees if their properties fall in certain designated regions. Perhaps I am being an alarmist. But can we be sure that this fashion for banning exotics and naturalised trees – a form of ethnic cleansing – will not spread to Britain?

How incomprehensible this zeal for native purity would seem to Evelyn and Loudon, struggling to persuade their contemporaries not to take trees for granted. How will it all end? Many plant hunters, like David Douglas, gave their lives to enrich our flora. Let's not make a mockery of their sacrifices by letting the Talibans into our plantations and pleasure grounds.

Metasequoia glyptostroboides – the Dawn Redwood – a genus only discovered in China in the 1940s and now widely planted in Britain and Ireland. Evelyn and Loudon would have approved.

Champion Trees

A 'champion tree' is the tallest example of its kind known in a given region, or the example with the thickest trunk. This book draws on the definitive database of rare, exceptional and historic trees maintained by the Tree Register to list 3,500 champions of 2,020 different kinds of tree in Britain and Ireland. It can be used as a guide to visiting rare, ancient and spectacular trees; as a list of what trees have been planted and are growing in these islands; and as a summary of the growth potential of any species.

The book has two main parts. The Directory lists alphabetically all the kinds of trees represented here by mature or substantial examples, and gives the sizes of the champions. The Gazetteer arranges these champions alphabetically by country, county and site, and provides details on how to find them. No generally agreed definition of a 'tree' exists. This book confines itself to free-standing plants (out of doors) with a woody stem at least 25cm thick.

Today, tree-watching is perhaps at about the stage which bird-watching was in the time of Gilbert White. It is still easy for anyone with a little time to spare to discover new species of (introduced) tree which are established in Britain and Ireland, and, by simple but painstaking observation, to make important discoveries about their life-cycles and distribution. In fact, it is astonishing, if not disquieting, to realise just how little we do know about these most massive and dominant features in our environment. Presumably their overwhelming presence and sheer obviousness is what has militated against trees and led people to assume that, as a subject, they must long ago have been studied to exhaustion. A few are famous for their size, age or colourful history; these are much photographed, feature repeatedly in books and TV programmes, and are regular stations on the tourist trail or even objects on Ordnance Survey maps. But other individuals equally magnificent or remarkable are still being 'discovered' by dedicated volunteers, and are described or portrayed in this book for the first time.

This is a considerably more ambitious volume than the booklet *Champion Trees in the British Isles*, last published by the Tree Register in association with the Forestry Commission in 1994. It is, in effect, the first modern attempt to produce a Tree Flora for Britain and Ireland, detailing even the rarest forms and assessing their frequency, growth potential and distribution.

Interest in the subject is burgeoning, and, by the time that you read these words, more recorders will have filled in more of the gaps in our understanding of the trees around us. In recent years, people have begun in particular to study the trees in public parks, streets, cemeteries and churchyards, and the smaller ornamental forms which have come to dominate urban tree populations, and have found these almost as fascinating and as unexpectedly varied as the trees of well known arboreta. In 1999-2000, the Tree Council of Ireland and the Irish Tree Society funded the Tree Register of Ireland project, and the records of notable Irish trees (a central part of the pool of available information since Elwes' and Henry's work) were greatly extended. The Tree Register is now also working with the Woodland Trust's Ancient Tree Campaign to record and map much more of Britain's unique heritage of 'veteran trees': living history books which play host to a wealth of often rare lichens and fungi, of insects which feed on their decaying wood and of birds which nest in their cavities.

Alan Mitchell, VMH, 1922-1995.

As a 14-year-old, it seemed to me the obvious course of action to begin to identify and to record the sizes of the trees which dominated the public park opposite my home. (I was peculiarly fortunate in that these gardens – Alexandra Park, in Hastings – have turned out to grow perhaps the widest spectrum of very rare and very big trees of any public park in the country.) Another place I was able to explore as a teenager was Beauport Park on the outskirts of the town – two kilometres of rampant rhododendron and dense secondary woodland, concealing rare and huge trees planted by the Lamb family, some from the original consignments of seed sent back to this country by pioneering 19th century plant-hunters. To glimpse such a tree on the skyline and patiently to work towards it, or suddenly to be confronted with giant leaves and improbable blossoms, was to experience, in miniature, something of these adventurers' original sense of triumph and discovery.

These teenage explorations put me in touch with the late Alan

Mitchell, whose role in stimulating dendrology through the second half of the twentieth century has been described by Thomas Pakenham in his Introduction. The principal inspiration for many if not all of today's 'tapers' was Alan's immense breadth of knowledge and his almost boundless enthusiasm. I vividly remember recording with him the trees in a part of the grounds of Chilham Castle in Kent which was then devoted to a small zoo: inside one of the enclosures, we spotted what seemed likely to be a new champion Hybrid Bean Tree. We couldn't see the cage's official occupant, but Alan didn't stop to check what it was: he simply vaulted over the safety-barrier, tape measure in hand. (The Bean *was* a champion, and remains one to this day.) I was particularly impressed since our next appointment was due to be at Howletts Zoo, famed for its tigers.

Why record trees?
Seeing the trees for the wood

Trees are easily viewed as soothing background greenery, or as mere scaffolds for birds to perch and minibeasts to feed on. But if you really look at them you will soon find yourself fascinated by their endless diversity, and you may begin to record and measure particular examples.

Trees are exquisitely responsive to their environment; indeed, for all their abundance, they are perhaps the most 'individual' of life-forms. Anyone can tell a fox from a badger, but recognising the individual fox, or the individual badger, is far harder. Many people, by contrast, will recognise individual trees they pass on their way to work, without being able to say what kind they are. A measurement of height and trunk thickness stands as the tree's 'signature', and can speak volumes about its appearance and its surroundings.

In addition to the inherent excitement of hunting 'champions', visiting gardens not open to the general public, and continually meeting new species in bizarre places, recording specimen trees can bring important benefits.

• Revealing trees' role in the landscape

Across most of Britain and Ireland, the presence and variety of trees defines our response to a landscape as much as the topography or the buildings; half of what we are looking at is tree. Scenes with many trees at least 30m tall – the views across many old parklands in lowland England, or the deep valleys of the eastern Highlands – foster a sense of unbroken history, even of peace and well-being, which will be absent whenever poor soils or exposure limit the height of the trees to 15m or 20m; property prices will be raised simply by the presence of trees which are both big and old. Quantifying the extremes of size, age and vigour is one way to gain a clearer idea of how our environment and our appreciation of it would be changed if we planted more trees, or felled more trees, or allowed more trees to grow. Even apparently trivial data about the growth, health and distribution of common trees may come to fascinate and inform future generations.

• Protecting trees and gardens

Collections such as the National Arboretum at Westonbirt are widely known, and revered, for their wealth of historic and champion trees. What too few people realise is that their local public park or cemetery is quite likely to have at least one tree which is just rare and historic, or which has outgrown every other known example. These community sites, often under-funded and neglected, may become more widely cared for once the quite remarkable arboreal heritage common to so many of them is more fully appreciated.

Rare trees often long outlive the gardens they were planted in. Today, many champions survive incongruously in school grounds or the waste ground behind industrial estates. No legislation exists to protect trees and tree-collections in the way that buildings or historic landscapes can be listed. (Tree Preservation Orders tend only to be placed on trees of scenic importance or ones that are visible from public land.) However, to learn that your tree is the only one of its kind known locally, or is the largest example in the country, can encourage you in protecting it, while businesses can easily turn the potential publicity to their advantage.

The landscape historian Oliver Rackham has pointed out that one 500-year-old oak tree has a greater conservation value, and can tell us more about our past, than 500 century-old oaks will. But an oak that took five centuries to grow and which 20 generations have preserved and managed can now be chainsawed in ten minutes. The presence of any planted tree is a triumph of long-term survival and a monument to the vision and hard work of whoever established it – seldom the individual currently responsible for its management.

• Informing gardeners and foresters

The data now maintained by the Tree Register has long provided nurseries, foresters and local authorities with essential information on how large a certain tree species will grow and what conditions it prefers. 'Safe', tough trees are often chosen by planters who may not realise that beautiful and fascinating but much scarcer alternatives have been found to thrive under the conditions in question.

• Conserving endangered species

Trees that we easily take for granted, such as Monkey Puzzle and Dawn Redwood, may have only tiny and vulnerable wild populations. A picture of their distribution and genetic diversity when planted in Britain and Ireland can be of international importance to conservation.

• Providing data on how to age trees

It is often the longevity of a tree that most excites and inspires people. A series of measurements provides an effective way of estimating a tree's age, and is the only way to do so once the growth rings towards the centre have rotted away and documentary evidence has been lost. Alan Mitchell was able to use his accumulated data to suggest that trees of most kinds in open conditions add an average of one inch in girth for each year of their lives. Young examples will tend to exceed this rate and older ones to fall below it; a few extra vigorous species regularly surpass it for long periods, while a tree growing in dense shade will grow at no more than half this rate.

• Locating trees with exceptional genes

The champions of commoner trees will tend to have exceptional genes; they will be the best individuals to propagate, not only for forestry use but for anyone wanting to grow a particularly fine specimen.

Influences on tree growth

Why is the distribution of Britain and Ireland's champion trees so patchy? Why do Scottish glens bristle with tall, fast-growing conifers, and why can you find so many huge and ancient field oaks along the Welsh Marches?

Demographic

As 98% of the trees in this book are neither native nor thoroughly naturalised, a map of champion trees inevitably highlights urban areas (or at least the wealthier towns and those with tourist-based economies where the planting of ornamental trees has long been a priority, such as Bath or Cheltenham). It also reveals the regions where a hundred or more years ago people wealthy enough to grow rare trees chose to live. These tended to be scenic areas which were also conveniently close to a metropolis: Perthshire, or the Wicklow Mountains, or the Surrey hills. (Hilly countryside tends to grow fine trees, while the presence of tall trees contributes in turn to a landscape's attractions.) Growing conditions which were known to be exceptional were the more direct reason for the establishment of so many notable gardens along the south coasts of Cornwall and Cork, and in the High

Today it is impossible to get a flavour of the Wildwood – the great forest that covered Britain and Ireland before the first stone-age farmers began to fell the trees. The nearest approximation may perhaps be lightly-grazed deer-parks like Knole in Kent. The trees are much taller, bigger and older than those in the countryside at large, having grown up in competition and never been cropped; this Sessile Oak is the national champion for height (note the figure at the base). Dead and rotting timber is everywhere – gardens for fungi and goldmines for myriad insects. Banks of bracken and pockets of sapling growth make an intricate patchwork with open, grazed lawns.

14

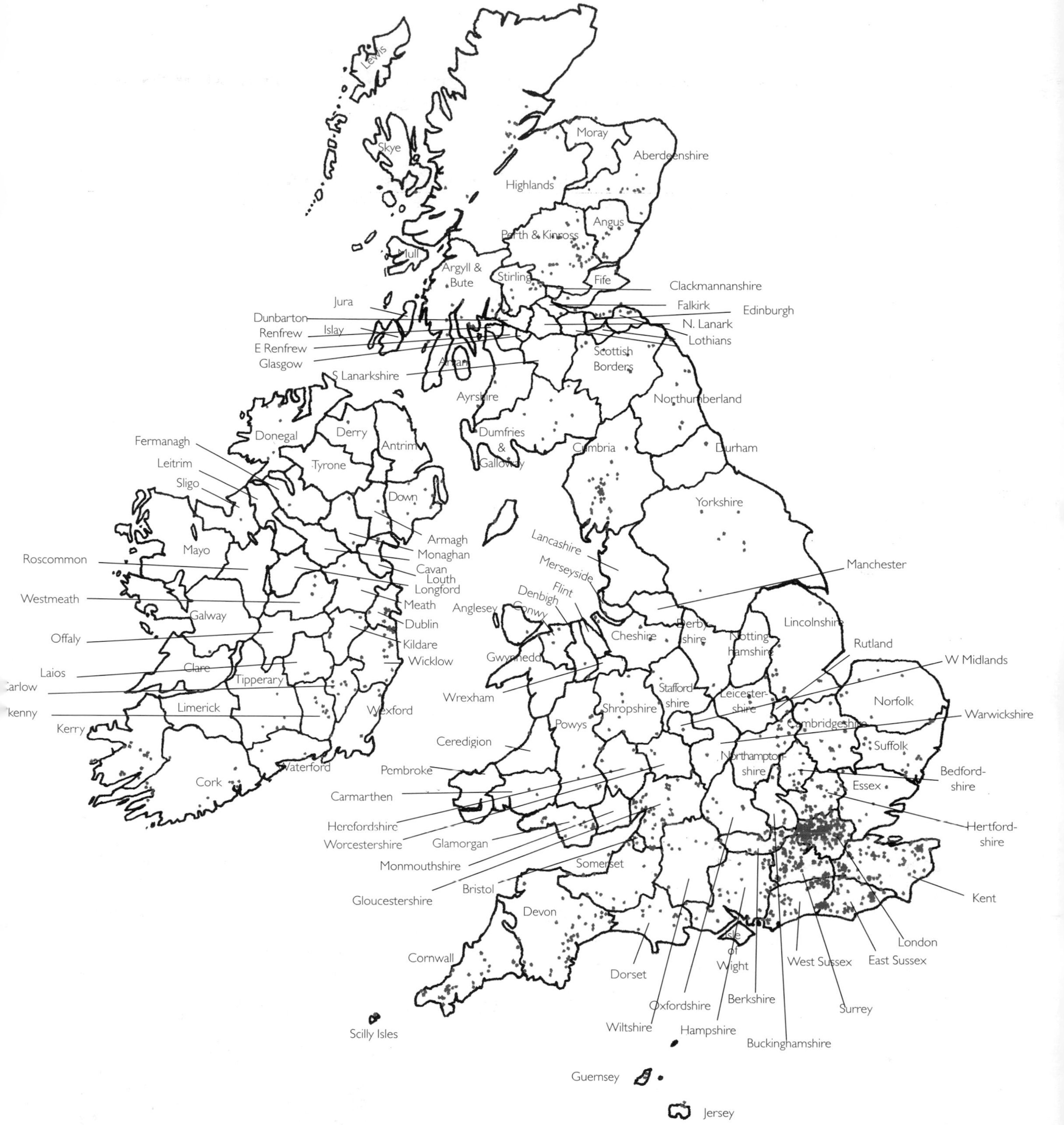

Lewis
Skye
Moray
Aberdeenshire
Highlands
Angus
Perth & Kinross
Mull
Argyll & Bute
Stirling
Fife
Clackmannanshire
Jura
Falkirk
Edinburgh
Dunbarton
Renfrew
Islay
N. Lanark
E Renfrew
Lothians
Glasgow
Scottish Borders
S Lanarkshire
Arran
Ayrshire
Northumberland
Donegal
Derry
Antrim
Fermanagh
Dumfries & Galloway
Cumbria
Durham
Leitrim
Tyrone
Sligo
Down
Yorkshire
Armagh
Lancashire
Mayo
Monaghan
Roscommon
Cavan
Merseyside
Louth
Manchester
Longford
Flint
Denbigh
Westmeath
Meath
Anglesey
Conwy
Galway
Dublin
Derbyshire
Lincolnshire
Offaly
Cheshire
Kildare
Nottinghamshire
Rutland
Wicklow
Gwynnedd
Laios
Clare
W Midlands
Tipperary
Stafford shire
arlow
Wrexham
Leicester-shire
Norfolk
Limerick
Wexford
Shropshire
kenny
Cambridgeshire
Warwickshire
Powys
Kerry
Suffolk
Ceredigion
Northampton-shire
Waterford
Pembroke
Bedford-shire
Cork
Essex
Carmarthen
Hertford-shire
Herefordshire
Worcestershire
Glamorgan
Somerset
Monmouthshire
Kent
Bristol
Gloucestershire
Devon
London
Isle of Wight
Cornwall
West Sussex
East Sussex
Dorset
Oxfordshire
Berkshire
Surrey
Wiltshire
Hampshire
Scilly Isles
Buckinghamshire
Guernsey
Jersey

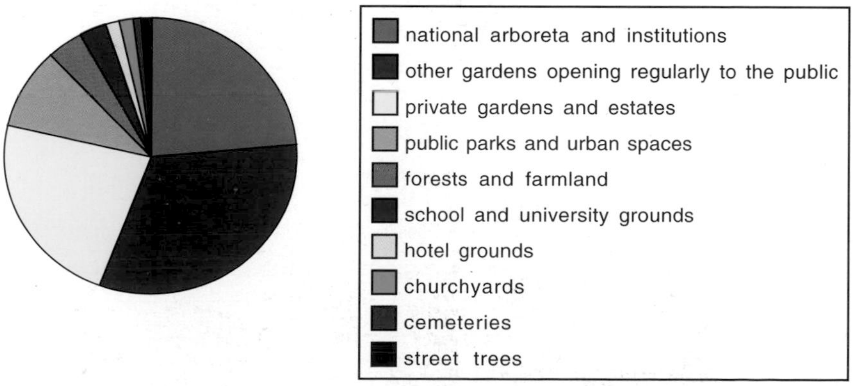

national arboreta and institutions
other gardens opening regularly to the public
private gardens and estates
public parks and urban spaces
forests and farmland
school and university grounds
hotel grounds
churchyards
cemeteries
street trees

Each dot represents one or more champion trees (above). Left: the current distribution of champions.

Weald of West Sussex. More recently, the gravitation of wealth towards London has enhanced the concentration of champions in south-east England.

Land use in the wider sense also affects the growth of trees to champion size. Many champions are concentrated in estates where traditions of arboriculture were in place before today's trees germinated; the most wooded areas, such as the New Forest or Forest of Dean, also grow particularly fine specimens. Most trees are gregarious, luxuriating in the sheltered, milder micro-climate created by their kind, whilst a sapling growing in competition will make a taller, straighter tree than one exposed to potentially damaging and permanently dehydrating winds: it takes several tree-generations to grow the long, straight trunks of a good beech-wood. Vital too to a tree's well-being are the associations formed between its rootlets and the mycorrhiza or feeding filaments of many fungi species, which are present in greater diversity in woods or old parks than they are in farmland or new gardens. The constant removal by foresters of the tallest and straightest trees in their reproductive youth also means that trees in the countryside at large tend to be the descendents of their less illustrious peers; policies of planting the seeds only of particularly fine specimens will have contributed to the relatively outstanding growth of the trees in many old estates.

Climatic

• It is Britain and Ireland's largely mild and temperate climate that allows us to grow such a range of trees, but there are many local variations. For native trees, adapted to these general parameters, such variations have little measurable effect (though Strawberry Tree and Holly are not reliably hardy in the coldest parts of Scotland; Wild Service and Small-leaved Lime are at the edge of their natural range even in southern England in that today's summers are seldom long or hot enough for their seeds to ripen, but they still grow happily when planted here, or indeed further north). Most cultivated trees, however, come from climates which are very much milder, hotter or harsher than ours, so that local fluctuations can mean the difference between a happy life and a slow, miserable death.

Our climate is most anomalous for how cool its summers are and for how seldom the sun shines. Light and heat are central to a plant's metabolism, and growth peaks at a specific temperature. For most trees, this point comes higher than the average maxima even in the warmest parts of Britain (the Midlands, and southern England away from the coast). Sunlight is essential to photosynthesis, and while, because of their high latitude, Britain and Ireland enjoy long daylight hours during the growing season, there is bright sunlight for less than half of this time. As the temperature in sun exceeds the shade temperature, districts like Cornwall whose summers are sunny but not very warm tend to grow heat-loving trees at least as well as hotter but less sunny areas (such as East Anglia).

Most trees' need for prolonged periods of heat and bright sun is the main explanation for the map's most striking feature: the concentration of champions in the south and south-east, like currants in a badly mixed fruit cake. Summers are longest and warmest of all in London, which also enjoys plenty of sun, and the champions of the most heat-demanding trees, such as Catalpas, are nearly all found here. The relatively warm summers of lowland Perth and Kinross, and of south-east Ireland, also contribute to the high proportions of regional champions in these areas.

Many conifers, in contrast, are adapted to montane conditions with high rainfall or humidity. Relative humidity declines rapidly with increasing temperatures, while a greater proportion of the rainfall recorded in areas with warm summers falls as sudden thunderstorms rather than day-long drizzle. The Sussex Downs receive up to 1,000mm of rain in an average year but are less humid, and therefore less suitable for conifer growth, than the valleys even of the eastern Scottish Highlands (whose 800mm is a quarter of what the west coast can receive). Conifers from the western seaboard of North America, or from the cloud forests of the southern Andes, are happiest as a result in the west and north, but local microclimates have an important part to play here: rainfall increases dramatically with altitude, and deep shelter – from surrounding hills or other trees – can raise the humidity, so that (while large London Planes, Pin Oaks or Weeping Willows are entirely absent from Scotland), favoured hillsides in south-east England can still grow the odd champion Spruce or Silver Fir.

Some conifers, such as the Coast Redwood, like both high humidity and high summer temperatures. As these conditions are mutually exclusive here, the distribution of champions among these trees becomes less predictable: north Wales and south-east Ireland often seem to offer the best compromises. Other conifers (like Santa Lucia Fir) are adapted to wet winters but very dry summers during which they derive most of the water they need from snow-melt, or fog. Again, these conditions are provided nowhere in Britain or Ireland, but such trees are generally found at their best here in cool, humid districts.

Perhaps the most exciting thing about trees is that they are, simply, so big. They are among the very few living things which are larger and longer-lived than we are, and which - in an age of central heating, cellophane-wrapped steaks, zoos and insect repellents – remain in some important ways beyond our control. Confronting a veteran or champion tree can become a salutary experience, bringing home to us how vast and unmalleable is the real ecological context in which we live. The Canford Sweet Chestnut, Dorset.

• Intense winter cold is endured by many trees, especially in central Asia, but is not in itself a requirement for good growth (though it may play an important role in reducing populations of insect pests). Some, however, are used to springs which arrive suddenly and reliably, so that after a few mild days they can break their buds without risking frost-damage. When grown here, these trees tend to leaf out during mild spells in winter, only to get repeatedly cut back, and are the ones that often survive best in the harsher conditions of eastern England.
• The diversity of trees, as with all other life-forms, increases exponentially towards the tropics. (The paucity of temperate tree species is largely due to the disruptions of three million years of Ice Ages, which have impoverished the native tree flora of Britain and Ireland as much as they have anywhere in the world.) Due to the influence of the North Atlantic Drift (the 'Gulf Stream'), Britain and especially Ireland are today almost sub-tropical in the mildness of their winters, and this is the principal reason why we can grow such a huge diversity of trees. Most species whose natural range lies much further south are hardy even in eastern Scotland, while many more trees can be and have occasionally been grown in gardens in the milder west of the country (or in central London where the urban 'heat-island' has much the same effect as the warmth of the Atlantic). The tenderest, such as Blue Gum (*Eucalyptus globulus*), are confined as large old trees to the Isle of Man and the coasts of Ireland; they come through most winters in south-east England, but England is more vulnerable to incursions every decade or so of very cold air from the near continent. However, as most tender trees also appreciate high light levels and summer warmth, most are found at their best in the gardens of southern Cornwall.
• Our climate is a windy one, though this does not necessarily affect the height to which trees can grow. Trees that are accustomed to stormy conditions respond by developing thicker stems and branches, and are perhaps less vulnerable to windthrow than those in more sheltered districts where intense thunderstorms can bring

Britain and Ireland's tallest tree: Douglas Fir at the Hyslop Arboretum, Argyll.

the occasional violent squall. Most of the world's tallest trees grow in windy regions; they rely on the shelter offered by steep youthful mountains but even more on the protection created by others of their kind. Britain has no comparably tall trees, because species such as Douglas Fir, capable of exceeding 100 metres, have only been grown here for a century and a half and never in sufficiently large groups to continue to assist each other upwards. Exposure does however mean that, in the north and west, most champions cluster in valleys towards sea-level and the higher hills are almost treeless, while in the warmer and more sheltered south it is typically the highest ground (with lighter soils and higher humidity) that grows the most and the tallest trees.

In some ways, the 'average' climatic conditions of a spot somewhere in the centre of these islands ought to be most suited to the widest range of trees, and there are certainly arboreta full of fine examples in the English Midlands. However, these trees are always likely to be slightly outgrown by specimens in corners of the country which find one or other climatic extreme more to their taste.

Geological

An extraordinary range of strata are jumbled together in Britain and Ireland. No tree grows well in all of the soils derived from them; exotics tends to be choosiest, as they will already tend to be under stress through the imperfect match of the local climate with their growth requirements. Heavy clays are often the least conducive to tree-growth, as roots find them hard to penetrate and they are alternately waterlogged and desiccated; even species such as the Wild Service Tree which are adapted in the wild to clay tend to grow slightly faster when planted on lighter loams. It is not always the case that trees grow largest in fertile sites: many conifers, adapted to rocky, mountainous conditions, get by happily on very few nutrients and in fact shun a deep, soft soil.

Toxins and pathogens

The current effects on tree growth of air pollution are unclear. Some trees (notably silver firs and spruces) are known to be very susceptible to the sulphur dioxides which are by-products of the burning of fossil fuels, and also to the soot and smoke particulates which can clog their resinous foliage; these trees have always done best in the far west and north of Britain, but as these areas of clean air are also those with the most suitable climates, the extent to which their growth has been limited by pollution is unclear. Until 45 years ago, however, central London was too polluted even for trees such as English Oak and Beech to grow properly, whilst clean air legislation is now making the city as a whole the richest place in Britain for champions. Lower levels of pollution, from vehicle exhausts and power stations, are meanwhile coming to affect large parts of the country.

The first generations of tree introduced to a new country often grow exceptionally well, because they have been allowed to escape all but the more generalised and widespread of their pathogens. Native trees can generally be recognised as such by the diversity of the galls on their leaves and the holes left by innumerable munching insects, and all of these predations have a tiny but cumulative effect on their growth. Fungal rusts, which can defoliate a tree, are climatically triggered: wet springs foster Brown Rot in flowering cherries, so that most champion cherries (and most commercial orchards) are in the areas with the driest springs, notably northern Kent. Winter cold, if it does not account for the tree itself, can kill off many of the insects which would otherwise eat its leaves or spread fungal diseases next summer.

Currently, most champion elms are confined to the Disease Control Zone established in the South Downs by East Sussex County Council in 1969.

The champion trees of tomorrow

Human activity has for thousands of years influenced the kinds of tree growing in Britain and Ireland, and the sizes they are allowed or are able to reach. In future, it seems inevitable that we will accidentally introduce diseases almost as destructive as Elm Disease, and that global warming will run its course. A warmer climate should, in itself, promote the growth of most trees here, though at the expense of montane conifers. (The cool wet summers of the mid 20th century seem to have suited the trees of Victorian pineta across lowland England, while increasingly hot dry conditions in the last twenty years have hastened their demise, so that many of these taxa are now rarer in cultivation than they were a century ago.) If the warmth brings with it more prolonged and intense droughts, many shallow-rooting species will be severely challenged in the south (including natives such as Silver Birch and Beech); if it brings wetter, stormier conditions, the frequency of destructive storms like those of October 1987 and January 1990 in southern England will increase. Milder winters would greatly enhance the range of species that could be grown – Canary Palms and Tree Ferns are already becoming popular along the south coast. However, the warm Atlantic currents which we depend on to grow this range of trees were blocked during each glaciation, and could quite suddenly fail again.

With ever-advancing urbanisation, more and more people will surely appreciate the value of trees, which mask eyesores, cool and sweeten the air in summer, deflect winter gales, soak up dust and fumes, and baffle the noise of traffic. There are already probably more trees growing in Britain than at any time in the last 500 years, and the declining profitability of agriculture and increases in leisure time and in funds available for tree-planting are bound to further the trend towards more extensive and adventurous planting.

Tree planting may also be used as a conservation tool: many species are endangered in their natural habitats and gardeners here can become the custodians of an important gene pool. Monkey Puzzle is already represented in Britain and Ireland in a diversity at least as great as the remaining wild populations', though unfortunately other species, such as the threatened Patagonian Cypress, have until very recently been distributed by nurseries only in a narrow range of clones.

The start of the 21st century is an exciting time for plant-hunting. Many new trees are being introduced, and the most ornamental and successful may become garden staples in a few decades.

Expanding our knowledge

The Tree Register's data, however extensive, is a product of the enthusiasm of a relatively tiny number of recorders. It remains easy for newcomers both to remeasure trees which have not been checked for many years, and to discover brand new champions.

For the best-studied counties (south-east England, Cumbria and the Isle of Man), 90-95% of today's champion trees have probably been found. The Gazetteer's county introductions, and the map of champions on p.15, suggest places where the percentage will be much lower than this. (Areas that are known to grow outstanding trees tend to be those that attract further attention from recorders, at other regions' expense.) For permission to record and revisit trees, the Tree Register's volunteers also depend on the goodwill of estate owners and land agents, though it is heartening how regularly this is forthcoming.

Sorbus gonggashanica – one notable recent introduction.

Trees are constantly growing or dying, and part of the Tree Register's fascination is that its data are so fluid. An average of two to three champions die or are felled each week – in practice the deaths are concentrated in periods of drought and high wind. It would have been impossible, even if it were desirable, to confirm that every tree featured here was still alive as the book went to press. (The failure of several recorders to relocate a tree may simply mean that it survives in a very out-of-the-way place.) Sixty-nine per cent of the champions featured in the last edition of *Champion Trees of the British Isles* in 1994 have already been superseded by recent discoveries, or have been found to require substitution; more than 1,000 of the trees in this book also represent newly measured taxa.

The huge range of trees in cultivation, their tendency to hybridise, and the small numbers of experts studying them, mean that positive identification is sometimes impossible. As the alternative would have been to skate over some of our most puzzling and interesting trees, this book includes a number whose identity is open to question, and tries in each case to suggest the degree of doubt.

The Tree Register unreservedly accepts records from all sources. The appendix 'How to record and measure trees' (see p.180) shows how easy it is to over-record a tree's height, or to imply that a trunk is much more impressive than it is by failing to make clear that the measurement has been taken underneath low branches or a fork. Selecting a list of champions also has the effect of concentrating any misprints. In general, the champions for trunk thickness are presented here with more confidence than those for height. The tallest trees, however, have nearly all been measured using the latest laser-based technology, or by climbing them.

Since 90% of the trees in this book are introductions or selections which have been grown here for less than two centuries, today's champions rather seldom represent the limits of a species' stature or lifespan; many are still growing fast and several candidates can compete closely. Most champions are also rare trees rather than big ones – in these cases the champions list should be read as an inventory of the conditions in which such and such a tree will at least prosper. Of the forms distinctive or large-growing enough to feature here, at least 20% are probably represented in Britain and Ireland by fewer than ten examples, and 60% by fewer than a hundred. (No more than 15% can be considered 'common', and only 95 are native or thoroughly naturalised.)

This book omits several hundred taxa which are known here only as young plants; many of these should reach 'tree' size in due course, but their current dimensions are not informative. (The RHS's *Plant Finder* can be used as a more nearly comprehensive list of such trees in commerce.) Perhaps another 1,000 named ornamental selections, and 2,000 fruiting forms, have also been excluded because they are practically inseparable in the field, and because it would be misleading to select as champions the odd examples in accurately labelled collections. Hundreds more plants could have been included by broadening the definition of a 'tree'. At least another thousand species and cultivars have been described in Britain and Ireland by W. J. Bean, or in *Hilliers' Manual of Trees and Shrubs*, but there are no recent records for their cultivation.

No big tree is more impressive than 'Majesty', one of a trio of named ancient English Oaks on the site of Fredville House in Kent. It looms out of the secondary woodland, with a trunk like a windmill and a stately galleon of high limbs. Only one old wound high on the east side shows that the vast trunk is actually hollow and that half the tree must have ripped out in some remote catastrophe – perhaps the great storm of 1703.

Record-Breaking Trees

Trees featured here are located more precisely in the Gazetteer.

The oldest tree

As many as 85% of northern Europe's 'veteran trees' grow in England and Wales. Oldest of all – and among the world's longest-lived trees – are several hundred Yews, nearly all of them in churchyards. The biggest almost certainly stood there before the site was consecrated; their sheltering presence could have been what persuaded early congregations to gather at that spot, while they may have retained a sacred role from earlier periods. Recent estimates of the age of the Fortingall Yew (Perth and Kinross), based on measured growth-rates of old Yews, range from 3,000 to 9,000 years.

The oldest oaks are about 1,000 years old; one of the biggest (at Fredville Park, Kent), can be aged from successive measurements at only 500-550 years. It is likely that today's Tortworth Chestnut in Gloucestershire is the same as 'the Great Chestnut of Tamworth', already an ancient tree in the 12th century – the place name having changed more than the tree. Coppice stools (and suckering trees) can survive almost indefinitely; a Small-leaved Lime stool in Silk Wood (Westonbirt National Arboretum), now a circle of stems 14.5m across, may be up to 6,000 years old. Ireland's ancient trees, meanwhile, have almost all been lost; only a few relatively small veteran Yews survive, on private estates.

The earliest documented planting dates are AD894 and 1136 for Yews at Buttington church (Powys) and Dryburgh Abbey (Scottish Borders). More entirely reliable is the 1550 planting date of a big Sweet Chestnut at Castle Leod (Highland).

The most massive tree

Before the current epidemic of Elm Disease, most of our largest trees were elms. A Wych Elm felled at Field, Staffordshire, was reported by eight witnesses in 1636 to have been 37m tall with a trunk 490cm thick where it was felled – larger by far than any tree recorded since. A Hybrid Elm planted around 1610 at Magdalen College, Oxford was 43m tall with a trunk 274cm thick when it blew down in 1911.

Today, our biggest trees are Giant Sequoias (which is the world's biggest tree but was only introduced from California in 1853). The most massive is probably one at Castle Leod (Highland), 51m high and with a trunk 283cm thick in 2002; it was planted, from the first consignment of seed, to mark the first birthday of the future Earl of Cromarty. One rival is 'The Monster' Common Silver Fir in the Ardkinglas Woodland Garden, Argyll, 46m high and with a trunk 298cm thick: as long ago as 1910 this was described by the 10th Duke of Argyll as 'undeniably the mightiest conifer if not the biggest bole of any kind in Europe'.

The tallest tree

All the trees in Britain and Ireland more than 45m tall (nearly 800 have been measured, with many more in some plantations) are conifers; except for a few Common Silver and Caucasian Firs and Norway Spruces, all are from western North America, and most are less than 130 years old. They do best in high humidity and in the shelter of mountains.

The tallest known examples have all been measured precisely in recent years: Douglas Firs in the Hyslop Arboretum, Argyll, and Reelig Glen Wood, Highland, were 62m tall in 2002 – the height of a 22-storey tower-block. They are now adding height very slowly. A Grand Fir in the Ardkinglas Woodland Garden, Argyll, died back 2.5m in 1993 but has since recovered and, at a good 61m by 2002, seems to be overhauling its rivals again. Another Douglas Fir at the Hermitage, Perth, is sometimes considered the tallest as its height from the lowest exposed roots on the river side is about 64m (but only 59m from ground level on the top side in 2002). The tallest tree known in Wales is a Douglas Fir at Lake Vyrnwy, Powys, 61.5m in 2002; in England a Douglas Fir at Cragside, Northumberland, 57m in 2002; in Northern Ireland a Sitka Spruce at Caledon Castle, Tyrone, 57m in 2001; and in the Irish Republic a Douglas Fir at Powerscourt, Wicklow, 56.5m in 2000.

In future, the tallest trees will be in sheltered Scottish stands of Douglas Fir and Sitka Spruce – such as the one at Benmore, Argyll, where many trees have already passed 55 metres.

Among wild broadleaves, Ash, Common Lime and English Elm have each been reliably recorded to 45m.

The thickest trunk

As trunks grow bigger they tend to split and decay in ways which make comparisons impossible. The oldest Yew, at Fortingall, retains two pieces of a bole which when complete seems to have been at least five metres thick at the base – larger than a double garage. An 'immense super annuated Eugh' at Brabourne church in Kent (destroyed by 1889) was given an even larger measurement by John Evelyn in 1664, and the elm at Field (see 'the most massive tree') must have been comparable. The trunk of the Canford Sweet Chestnut at Canford School in Dorset, 433cm thick in 1992, is much swollen by burrs and side-limbs. The trunk thickness of the Marton Oak in Cheshire, 426cm in 1992, was recorded only by stretching the tape around two fragments; at least three oaks of very similar stature collapsed and died in the 19th and 20th centuries.

The largest smooth, untapered trunk is not in doubt: 'Majesty', an English Oak at Fredville Park, Kent, has a bole 385cm thick, lightly branched for six metres.

Forty-five tree species and hybrids in Britain and Ireland (14 of them conifers) have so far grown single trunks at least 2m thick. They are European Silver Fir, Grecian Fir, Grand Fir, Sycamore, Horse Chestnut, Hornbeam, Sweet Chestnut, Deodar, Cedar of Lebanon, Monterey Cypress, Blue Gum, Beech, Ash, Black Walnut, Tulip Tree, New Zealand Christmas Tree, Sitka Spruce, Monterey Pine, Oriental Plane, London Plane, Wild Black Poplar, Hybrid Black Poplar, Douglas Fir, Chestnut-leaved Oak, Turkey Oak, Lucombe Oak, Holm Oak, Sessile Oak, English Oak, White Willow, Crack Willow, Coast Redwood, Giant Sequoia, Yew, Western Red Cedar, Small-leaved Lime, Common Lime, Broad-leaved Lime, Western Hemlock, Wych Elm, Smooth-leaved Elm, English Elm, Hybrid Elm, Dutch Elm, and Caucasian Elm.

The most spreading tree

Trees spread most when allowed to rest their branches on the ground so that they take root – and this is one category where broadleaves outperform conifers. An Oriental Plane at Corsham Court, Wiltshire, planted in 1757, now has an average spread of 64m and is as big as a football pitch, while the original Weeping Beech at the Knaphill Nursery, Surrey, has formed a grove of stems about as wide. The King Oak (Charleville, Westmeath) has an average spread of 50m, with some branches propped. The Sweet Chestnut at Kateshill House, Worcestershire, has a branch 23m long resting on the ground, and one Yew on the north edge of the ancient grove at Kingley Vale, West Sussex, has spread its branches nearly 30m towards the open downland. Suckering plants, like Blackthorn and Aspen, can develop genetically identical stands more than 100m across.

Fastest height growth

Eucalypts are the fastest-growing trees in most tropical countries, though they fail to sustain their early rates here; Blue Gum (*Eucalyptus globulus*) has reached 15m in 6 years in Kerry and Silver Top (*E. nitens*) 19.5m in 9 years in Argyll. (A good oak would take 40 years to reach this height.) The hybrid Poplar 'Androscoggin' grew 24m in the 14 years from 1978 to 1992 at Glendurgan, Cornwall; a Grand Fir in a plantation near Keltie, Perth and Kinross, blown in 1953 when about 53 years old, was 51m tall.

Fastest trunk growth

Giant Sequoias show the fastest increases in trunk thickness, though their flared boles tend to exaggerate the measured girth. The trunk of one original planting at Castle Menzies, Perth and Kinross, was 200cm thick after 48 years and 250cm thick in 72 years – by which time the tree was dying of Honey Fungus (and perhaps exhaustion). More impressive in being perfectly cylindrical was the 120cm-thick bole of a 34-year-old Coast Redwood in Tilgate Park, W Sussex, in 2001, while a Bat Willow trunk at Boreham, Essex, was 174cm thick when felled, aged 53. These rates are almost four times the universal average of 'an inch of girth a year'.

The rarest tree

Many of the world's trees have only one example in cultivation in Britain or Ireland. Ley's Whitebeam, however, grows nowhere except in the Taff Valley in Glamorgan. A mere 16 wild examples are currently known.

NATIVE TREES

Because of the depredations of the Ice Age and the narrow window of opportunity between the retreat of the ice and the formation of the English Channel, Britain and Ireland have surprisingly few truly 'wild' trees. The 62 *bona fide* native species which grow big enough to feature in this book are:

Field Maple *Acer campestre* (England), p.30.
Common Alder *Alnus glutinosa*, p.36.
Strawberry Tree *Arbutus unedo* (SW Ireland), p.38.
Silver Birch *Betula pendula*, p.39.
Downy Birch *Betula pubescens*, p.39.
Box *Buxus sempervirens* (SE England), p.40.
Hornbeam *Carpinus betulus* (SE England), p.40.
Dogwood *Cornus sanguinea* (England, Wales and Ireland), p.47.
Hazel *Corylus avellana*, p.47.
Midland Thorn *Crataegus laevigata* (S England), p.48.
Hawthorn *Crataegus monogyna*, p.49.
Spindle *Euonymus europaeus*, p.55.
Beech *Fagus sylvatica* (S England, S Wales), p.55.
Common Ash *Fraxinus excelsior*, p.57.
Sea Buckthorn *Hippophae rhamnoides* (E coasts of England and of S Scotland), p.59.
Holly *Ilex aquifolium*, p.60.
Juniper *Juniperus communis*, p.62.
Crab Apple *Malus sylvestris*, p.67.
Scots Pine *Pinus sylvestris* (Scottish Highlands), p.76.
White Poplar *Populus alba*, p.78.
Black Poplar *Populus nigra* ssp.*betulifolia* (England and Wales), p.79.
Aspen *Populus tremula*, p.81.
Wild Cherry *Prunus avium*, p.81.
Bird Cherry *Prunus padus* (N Britain and Ireland), p.84.
Plymouth Pear *Pyrus cordata* (SW England; very rare), p.86.
Wild Pear *Pyrus pyraster* (England; very rare), p.86.
Sessile Oak *Quercus petraea*, p.93.
English Oak *Quercus robur*, p.93.
Purging Buckthorn *Rhamnus cathartica* (England, Wales and Ireland), p.94.
White Willow *Salix alba*, p.95.
Goat Willow *Salix caprea*, p.96.
Grey Sallow *Salix cinerea* ssp.*oleifolia*, p.96.
Crack Willow *Salix fragilis*, p.96.

Salix myrsinifolia (N Britain and Ireland), p.97.
Bay Willow *Salix pentandra* (N Britain and Ireland), p.97.
Purple Osier *Salix purpurea*, p.97.
Almond Willow *Salix triandra*, p.97.
Common Osier *Salix viminalis*, p.97.
Elder *Sambucus nigra*, p.97.
Sorbus anglica (SW England, Wales and Kerry), p.99.
Whitebeam *Sorbus aria* (S England; Ireland), p.99.
Sorbus arranensis (N Arran), p.99.
Rowan *Sorbus aucuparia*, p.99.
Bristol Service *Sorbus bristoliensis* (Avon Gorge), p.99.
French Hales *Sorbus devoniensis* (SW England and SE Ireland), p.101.
True Service *Sorbus domestica* (Wales), p.101.
Sorbus eminens (Wye Valley and Avon Gorge), p.101.
Sorbus hibernica (central Ireland), p.101.
Sorbus lancastriensis (S Cumbria), p.101.
Ley's Whitebeam *Sorbus leyana* (Taff Valley, Wales), p.101.
Sorbus minima (near Crickhowell, Wales), p.101.
Sorbus porrigentiformis (N Devon, the Mendips and S Wales), p.102.
Arran Service *Sorbus pseudofennica* (N Arran), p.102.
Cliff Whitebeam *Sorbus rupicola* (limestone uplands), p.102.
Exmoor Service *Sorbus subcuneata* (Exmoor), p.102.
Wild Service *Sorbus torminalis* (England and Wales), p.102.
Sorbus vexans (N Devon), p.102.
Common Yew *Taxus baccata*, p.104.
Small-leaved Lime *Tilia cordata* (England and Wales), p.107.
Broad-leaved Lime *Tilia platyphyllos* (England and Wales), p.109.
Wych Elm *Ulmus glabra*, p.110.
Field Elm *Ulmus minor* (England), p.112.

Directory

How to use this book

The directory is ordered alphabetically (by botanical name); nomenclature is largely as suggested in the current RHS *Plant Finder*. The information for each taxon includes:

• Approximate area of origin and date of first cultivation in Britain or Ireland (if known).

• Frequency in Britain and Ireland:

abundant: locally ubiquitous and likely to be found in most places.

frequent: present in small numbers in most areas.

occasional: individuals in many large gardens or towns but absent from the majority of parks or woods.

rare: absent from many counties and found in only a few parks and gardens in others.

For some species, the Tree Register's records allow a rough estimate of the numbers in cultivation. When the frequency is not given, the measured examples are the only known mature trees.

• Specimens. The first is the example with the thickest known trunk. Examples are preferred which have single trunks (measurable at or about 1.5m from ground level). Trees whose trunk thickness is inflated by forks or low limbs may be added as alternatives – but specimens from these different categories should not be directly compared. The tallest known example follows (when trees tie, the one with the thicker trunk is generally preferred). Regionally exceptional trees are sometimes appended. The trees' planting dates ('p.1900') are included when documented. When a tree known or assumed to have been lost is much bigger than any recorded recently, this is included (in brackets).

The locations of each tree are given by site and county. Sites are listed (alphabetically by country and by county) in the Gazetteer, where you will find more details of each tree's location. In the Directory, the 15 sites with most champions are abbreviated:

• **Bedgebury NP**: Bedgebury National Pinetum, Bedgebury Forest, Goudhurst, Kent.
• **Birr Castle**: Birr Castle Demesne, Offaly.
• **Borde Hill**: Borde Hill Gardens and park, Haywards Heath, West Sussex.
• **Caerhays**: Caerhays Castle Garden, Gorran, Cornwall.
• **Cambridge UBG**: The University Botanic Garden, Cambridge.
• **Castlewellan NA**: Castlewellan National Arboretum, Down.
• **Edinburgh RBG**: The Royal Botanic Garden, Edinburgh.
• **Glasnevin NBG**: The National Botanic Gardens, Glasnevin, Dublin.
• **Hergest Croft**: Hergest Croft estate, Kington, Herefordshire.
• **Hillier Gardens**: The Sir Harold Hillier Gardens and Arboretum, Ampfield, Hampshire.
• **Kew RBG**: The Royal Botanic Gardens, Kew, London.
• **Wakehurst Place**: Wakehurst Place, Ardingly, West Sussex.
• **Westonbirt NA**: Westonbirt National Arboretum, Tetbury, Gloucestershire.
• **Windsor**: Windsor Home Park and Great Park (including the Savill Garden and the Valley Gardens), Berkshire and Surrey.
• **Wisley**: The Royal Horticultural Society Gardens, Wisley, Surrey.

Entries take this form:

31[1]x165[2]@1.3m[3]+142[4] (2003 Jane Smith[5])

[1] The tree's height (in metres, from the ground on the trunk's upper side to the highest live, woody growth). Figures in brackets are estimates, or have been amended, or are considered unreliable.

[2] Its trunk thickness (in centimetres). See p.180 for a full explanation.

[3] The height the trunk thickness was measured at (1.5m from ground level unless stated).

[4] The thickness of any additional trunks.

[5] The year the measurement was made and who by.

Initials are used for some prolific recorders:
AFM – Alan Mitchell
AF – Aubrey Fennell
DGA – David Alderman
DH – Derrick Holdsworth
HPG – Hatton Gardner
JP – Jim Paterson
JW – John White
OCJ – Owen Johnson
PJB – Peter Bourne
TROI – Tree Register of Ireland project
VES – Victoria Schilling

Other abbreviations used throughout this book:
BG   botanic garden(s)
CP   country park
DED   Dutch Elm Disease
f.   forma
FC   Forestry Commission
NA   National Arboretum
NBG   National Botanic Garden(s)
NGS   National Gardens Scheme
NP   National Pinetum
NT   National Trust
NTS   National Trust for Scotland
p   planted (in)
RBG   Royal Botanic Garden(s)
RHS   Royal Horticultural Society
SGS   Scottish Gardens Scheme
ssp.   subspecies
UBG   University Botanic Garden(s)
var.   variety

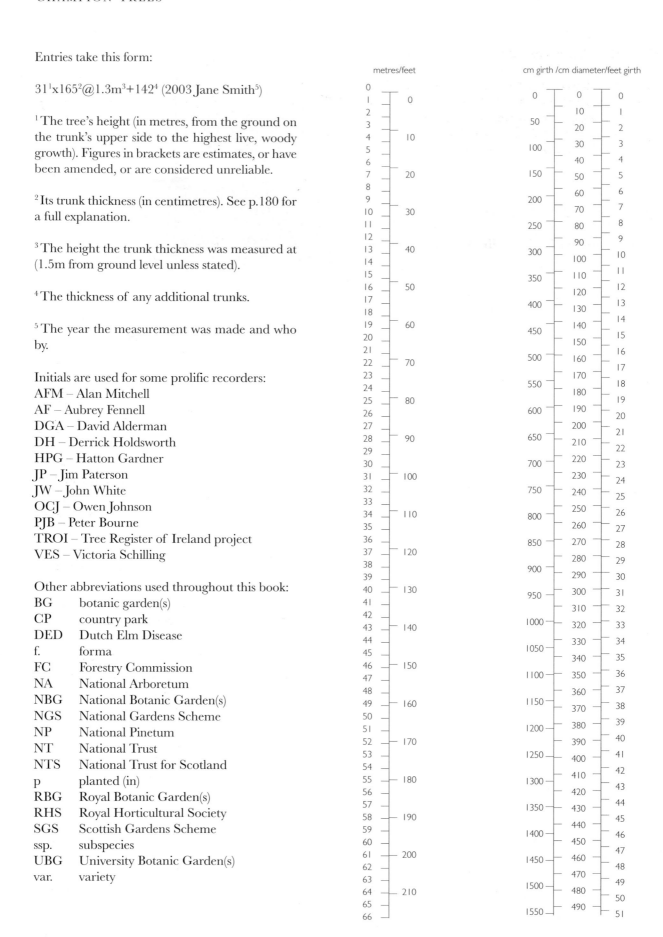

Conversion scales

Abies Silver Firs

***Abies alba* Common Silver Fir** Mountains of C Europe; long grown here and locally frequent. Ardkinglas, Argyll ('The Monster') 46x298 around 'waist' (1994 VES); Abercairney, Perth (40)x203 (1986 AFM) – forking at 4.5m; Raehills, Dumfries & Galloway (40)x201 on good bole (1984 AFM) p1790?; Tullynally Castle, Westmeath 45x189 (1996); Thirlmere, Cumbria 46x186 ('The Giant') and 50x148 (1995 DH); Armadale Castle, Highland (50)x164 (1988 AFM); Benmore, Argyll (50)x127 (1991 AFM).

f. *pyramidalis*. Tregrehan, Cornwall 27x62 (2002 Tom Hudson).

***A. amabilis* Pacific Silver Fir** W N America, 1830. About 100 trees in collections; particularly temperamental. Charleville, Wicklow 36.5x143 (2000 TROI); Leckmelm, Highland (?) 40x77 (1986 AFM).

***A. balsamea* Balsam Fir** N America, 1696. A handful, never thriving. Headfort, Meath 14.5x29 (1980 AFM), p1925. (Saltoun House, E Lothian 20.5x77@3m (1891) – original, swept away by a flood in 1891.)

A. beissneriana An unconfirmed example of this obscure W Chinese fir at Durris, Aberdeen: 17x49 (1987 AFM).

***A. borisii-regis* King Boris's Fir** Balkans. Perhaps 50 trees. Stonefield House, Argyll 36x155 (1992 AFM) – straight to its tip; Rossylongan, Donegal (?) 38.5x109 (2000 TROI).

***A. borisii-regis* x *bornmulleriana*.** Hillier Gardens 18x59 (2001 Harry James).

***A. bornmulleriana* Bornmuller's Fir** Asia Minor. Perhaps 50 trees. Fulmodeston Severals, Norfolk 37x132 (1992).

***A. bracteata* Santa Lucia Fir** California, 1852. Rare. Seems to appreciate summer warmth. Althorp House, Northants. (35)x137 under fork at 1m (1983 AFM); Exeter University, Devon 16x118 (2001 OCJ) – good bole; cut back. (Eastnor Castle, Herefords. 36.5x152 (1969 AFM) – p1865; died of honey fungus 1975.)

***A. cephalonica* Grecian Fir** S Balkans, 1824. Occasional in old parks: thrives in the driest regions, though there is a bias towards the west among the biggest trees (incorporating var. *graeca/apollinis*). Culcreuch Castle Hotel, Stirling 35x229@1m among branches (1984 AFM); Dalemain, Cumbria 28x201 (1995 DH); Bicton Park, Devon 41x128 (2001 OCJ) – slightly leaning narrow spire after removal of side limbs.

***A. cephalonica* x *nordmanniana*.** Bedgebury NP 26x69 (1999 OCJ), p1925.

***A. chengii* Cheng Fir** C China. Young trees are in some collections. Hillier Gardens 19x72 (2001 Harry James), p1952; Westonbirt NA 20x56 (2002 OCJ; ?).

***A. chensiensis* Salween Fir** C China, 1907. A handful in collections. Tannadyce, Angus x50 (1998) – ssp. *salouenensis*?

***A. cilicica* Cilician Fir** Asia Minor to Syria, 1855. 50-100 trees? Speech House, Glos. 26x98 (1988 AFM), p1916; Glenapp, Ayr 33x74 (1989 AFM).

***A. concolor* Colorado White Fir** 1873. The type is rare and probably happier in warm dry regions; no very

With boles like temple columns and needles etched with precious metals, silver firs are aristocrats among trees. Choosy about conditions, slow to establish and particularly sensitive to air pollution, they tend to be ornaments of the largest parks - though recently the cheerful little Korean Fir has become a 'flowering shrub' in many small gardens, its massed cones like Fabergé eggs.

The taste for these dark, reserved trees was supremely a Victorian one, and, because they are short-lived in dry, warm lowland areas, they are one of the few groups of trees that tend to be represented in less diversity than a century ago. Today, they are found at their best in the Scottish Highlands.

Abies cephalonica, from the Greek mountains, is one of the toughest silver firs. It often grows heavy limbs like a cedar: the champion at Bicton Park is notable for its graceful spire-shape as well as its great height.

big trees are now known. (Cragside, Northumberland 47.5x117 (1974 AFM).)

var. *lowiana* Low's White Fir W N America, 1851. Occasional; thrives in high humidity. Durris estate, Aberdeen x159 (1987 AFM) – dying back from 52m.

f. *violacea* Blue Colorado Fir 1875 Occasional garden tree everywhere, in selections such as 'Candicans' and 'Wattezii'. Ardross Castle, Highland 15x99+72 (1989 AFM); Sotterley Hall, Suffolk 27x61 (1985 AFM), p1936.

A. delavayi Nomenclaturally confused group of Chinese

Firs: see *A. fabri, A. forrestii*. Identifications here may not all be correct.

var. *smithii* (var. *georgii*) W. China, 1923. About 50 trees. Castlewellan NA 12x84 (1991 AFM); Headfort, Meath 21.5x61 (1980 AFM).

***A. densa* Sikkim Fir** A handful in collections. Benmore, Argyll 26x69 (1991 AFM).

***A. fabri* Faber Fir** China, 1901. In a few collections. Benmore, Argyll 28x80 (1991 AFM), p1937.

ssp. *minensis* China, 1910. 50-100 trees. Stourhead, Wilts. (?) 21x66 (1992 AFM), p1924; Dawyck BG, Scottish Borders 23x56 (1997).

***A. fargesii* Sichuan Fir** (incorporating *A. sutchuenensis*) China, 1901. Perhaps 100 trees. Castlewellan NA 20x59 (1994 VES); Burnside, Angus (24)x33 (1990 AFM), p1929.

A. faxoniana – see *A. fabri* ssp. *minensis*.

***A. firma* Momi Fir** Japan, 1861. Rare. Ardnamona, Donegal 25x133 (2000 TROI). (Balfour Manor, Devon 31x113 (1979 AFM).)

***A. forrestii* Forrest's Fir** W China, 1910? Very occasional. Cortachy Castle, Angus 19x93 and 26x84 (1992 AFM).

***A. fraseri* Fraser Fir** Mountains of SE USA, 1811. A handful, seldom thriving. Vivod, Denbigh 19x51 (1988 JW), p1952.

***A. gamblei* Gamble Fir** A few dozen trees. Durris, Aberdeen 13x81 (1987 AFM) – broken; Cawdor Castle, Highland 28.5x74 (1994 JP).

A. georgii – see *A. delavayi* var. *smithii*.

***A. grandis* Grand Fir** W N America, 1830. Frequent. Lochanhead Hotel, Dumfries & Galloway 41x232 (1993 VES) – rough, windswept tree; Balmacaan, Highland 51x225@1.8m over low limbs (2002 John Miller) – rough top; Murthly Castle, Perth 53x226 (1993) – impressive bole; Ardkinglas, Argyll 61x195 (2002 DGA), p1875; died back in 1993 and regrowing with twin leaders; Leighton Hall, Powys 60.5m (1994 Mike Kemp) – tallest in 1888 plantation, measured by climbing.

***A. holophylla* Manchurian Fir** 1908. Perhaps 50 trees. Westonbirt NA 20x71 (2002 OCJ), p1930?; Tannadyce, Angus x69cm (1998); near Welshpool, Powys 21x38 (1981 AFM).

***A. homolepis* Nikko Fir** Japan, 1859. Occasional; does quite well in dry and polluted areas. Taymouth Castle, Perth 34x120 (1990 AFM); Ardnamona, Donegal 24x122@1.2m (2000 TROI).

***A. kawakamii* Taiwan Fir** A handful in collections. Headfort, Meath 13x76 (1980 AFM) – 1931 original; top lost; Crarae, Argyll 16x50 (1994 VES).

***A. koreana* Korean Fir** 1905. Frequent in dwarf forms in small gardens for its 'flowering' display. Dunira, Perth 6.5x57 (2002 DH); Hergest Croft 17x37 (1995 VES), p1929.

***A. lasiocarpa* Subalpine Fir** W N America. A few dozen in collections: thriving only in the drier side of N Scotland. Invermay Castle, Perth 22x81 (1988 AFM) – superb tree.

var. *arizonica* Cork Fir 1903. A few dozen plants; thrives nowhere. Pitcarmick, Perth 17x53 (1986 AFM). (Highclere Castle, Hants. 23x48 (1978 AFM).)

The Common Silver Fir (*Abies alba*) was one of the first trees grown here to reveal a flair for gigantism. A specimen at Kilbryde, Argyll, 55x200 in 1960, was for long our tallest tree; planted around 1680, it was finally blown down in 1975, when almost dead. Susceptible to attack by Spruce Aphids, Common Silver Fir has now been thoroughly eclipsed by its cousins from western North America. However 'The Monster' in the Ardkinglas Woodland Garden, Argyll, is still the biggest fir in Britain, and the buttresses supporting its four enormous stems are still adding timber fast – which like the shape itself is very unusual in such an old fir. Specimen conifers like this were sometimes deliberately beheaded in their youth to create a more spreading and imposing habit.

'Compacta' Nominally dwarf. Hillier Gardens 10x27 (2002 Harry James).

A. *magnifica* Red Fir W N America, 1851. Rare. A beautiful but temperamental tree, thriving for long only in the north. Blair Castle, Perth 38x159 (1995), p1878; Taymouth Castle, Perth 44x113 (1990 AFM) – shapely to its tip.

A. *mariesii* Maries' Fir Japan, 1879? A few dozen in collections. Dawyck, Scottish Borders 23x64 (1992 AFM), p1910; growing new tops.

A. *nebrodensis* Sicilian Fir, 1940? A handful in collections (one of the world's rarest trees in the wild). Hillier Gardens 17x72 (2002 Harry James).

A. *nephrolepis* Khinghan Fir NE Asia, 1908. About 50 trees; thrives nowhere. Bedgebury NP 14x39 (1999 OCJ), p1925. (Wakehurst Place 25x48 (1971 AFM).)

A. *nordmanniana* Caucasian Fir W Caucasus, 1840. Rather occasional; a handsome tree everywhere but longer lived in the west and north. Endsleigh, Devon 32x164 (1990 AFM); Cragside, Northumberland 48x112 (2002 DGA).

A. *numidica* Algerian Fir Mt Babor, Algeria; 1861. Rather rare. Will grow in dry areas but still shows a slight preference for the north and west. Charleville, Wicklow 34.5x119 (2000 TROI).

A. *pardei* An old tree of this putative N African hybrid at Headfort, Meath: 18.5x58 (1980 AFM).

A. *pindrow* Pindrow Fir W Himalayas, 1837? Rare. Inchmarlo, Aberdeen 21x128 (1987 AFM) – much died back; forks at 2m; Monk Coniston, Cumbria 33x110 (1998 DH); Aldourie Castle, Highland 36x100 (1992 AFM).

var. *brevifolia* – see *A. gamblei*.

A. *pinsapo* Spanish Fir Sierra de Ronda, Spain, 1839. Occasional. Does well in drier areas but the largest still tend to be in the north. Harestanes, Scottish Borders 19x141 (1999 Donald Rodger); Balmacaan, Highland 33m (2002 John Miller) - forking.

ssp. *marocana* Morocco. Young plants in collections. Hillier Gardens 15.5x47 (2002 Harry James).

A. *procera* Noble Fir W USA, 1830. Rather occasional; growth is best sustained in the far north. Many big trees are the grafted clone 'Glauca'. Taymouth Castle, Perth 47x187 (1990 AFM); Glenferness, Highland 39x187 (1987 AFM); Ardkinglas, Argyll (50)x115 (1994 VES).

A. *recurvata* Min Fir W China, 1910. A few dozen in collections. Abbotswood, Glos. 22x50 (1983 AFM), p1916.

A. *religiosa* Sacred Fir Mexico, Guatemala, 1838. A handful in southern collections. Hillier Gardens 18x48 (2000 H M Brown), p1968. (Tregothnan, Cornwall 23x79 (1931).)

A. *sachalinensis* Sakhalin Fir N Japan to the Kuriles, 1878. About 50 trees. Westonbirt NA (as label) 24x46 (2002 OCJ).

A. *sibirica* Siberian Fir 1820. A tree adapted to intense cold and reliable springs: only one has reached 'tree' size here. Abbeyleix, Laois 14.3x30 (2000 TROI) – in poor condition.

A. *spectabilis* Himalayan Fir 1822. Rare; short-lived away from the west. Kilmacurragh, Wicklow (24)x134 (1992 AFM) – branchy; Gosford Castle, Armagh (25)x134 (1999) – branchy and rough. (Powerscourt, Wicklow 33x86 (1980 AFM), p1867.)

var. *brevifolia* 1879. A few dozen trees. Taymouth Castle, Perth 35x98 (1990 AFM) – slender.

A. *squamata* Flaky Fir W China, 1910. A handful in collections. Durris, Aberdeen 18x40 (1987 AFM).

A. *sutchuenensis* – see *A. fargesii*.

A. *veitchii* Veitch's Fir C Japan, 1879. Rather rather; short-lived everywhere. Dunira, Perth 18.5x97 (2002 DH); Dochfour, Highland 24x92 (1992 AFM) – three stems towards top; Hopetoun House, W Lothian 28x61 (1984 AFM).

A. *vejari* Vejar Fir Mexico. A handful in southern collections. Hergest Croft 14x29 (1995 VES) – 1964 original.

A. x *vilmorinii* Vilmorin's Fir (*cephalonica* x *pinsapo*, 1867) A handful remain. Powerscourt, Wicklow (*A. recurvata?*) 21.5x61 (2000 TROI); Farleigh School, Hants. 23x59 (1982 AFM).

***Acacia baileyana* Cootamundra Wattle** New South Wales, 1888. Rare; tender. Scarcely to tree size.

A. *dealbata* Mimosa SE Australia, Tasmania, 1820. Frequent in mild areas; blows down and can be killed by cold except in the far south-west. Kells House, Kerry 22.5x38 (2001 AF); Chelsea, London (13)x51 (2003 Roy Lancaster).

A. *decurrens* SE Australia. Scarcely seen as a tree. (Garinish, Kerry 16.5x58 (1966 AFM).)

A. *implexa* Hickory Wattle SE Australia. Scarcely seen as a tree. (Trengwainton, Cornwall 16x29 (1979 AFM).)

A. *melanoxylon* Blackwood Acacia SE Australia, Tasmania, 1808. A vigorous tree in very mild areas. Fassaroe, Wicklow 15x97 (2002 AF); Parknasilla Hotel, Kerry 19.5x45 (2001 AF). (Rossdohan, Kerry 25x75 (1966 AFM).)

Acer Maples

Acer acuminatum W Himalayas. A handful in collections. Westonbirt NA 13x58@0.2m (2002 OCJ), p1943; bushy; Westonbirt School, Glos. 10x41 (2002 OCJ) – shapely; ?

A. *amplum* – see *A. longipes* ssp. *amplum*.

A. *argutum* Japan, 1881. A handful in collections; usually a bush. (Hollycombe, W Sussex 11x38@1m (1984 AFM).)

A. x *bornmuelleri* (*campestre* x *monspessulanum*). Hillier Gardens 12x43 (2002 H M Brown).

A. *buergerianum* Trident Maple E China, Japan, by 1890. Rare. The best are in warm areas. Norham End, Oxon. 16x57 (1983 AFM).

A. *caesium* Grey Maple Himalayas. No mature trees now known. (Edinburgh RBG 14x32 (1967 AFM).)

A. *campbellii* Campbell Maple E Himalayas to China, 1851? A handful in collections. Caerhays 15x33 (1991 AFM).

ssp. *flabellatum* Fan-leaved Maple C China, 1907. In a few collections. Hergest Croft (?; 'Laciniatum') 12x48 (1995 VES).

ssp. *flabellatum* var. *yunnanense* In a few collections. Hillier Gardens 12x42@0.5m (2001), from Forrest 9509; Trewithen, Cornwall 15x32 (1985 AFM).

Looking up into the great dome of the champion Field Maple (*Acer campestre*) at Chilston Park, Kent.

A. campestre Field Maple Native to England and Wales. Abundant. Fairlawne, Kent 17x148@0.7m on short, slanting, burred bole (1995 OCJ); Downham church, Essex x141@? (1992 John Hunter) – pollard; Chilston Park, Kent 17x133 on 3m bole (1999 OCJ) – shapely and broad; Kinnettles House, Angus (25)x81 (1986 AFM) – 8m bole.
f. fastigiata Occasional as a young municipal planting in clones such as 'Elsrijk'. Warnham Court, W Sussex (a sport?) 18x74 (1997 OCJ).
'Pulverulentum' Very rare and tending to revert. National Stud, Kildare x34@1.4m (1998 DGA).
'Schwerinii' Very rare. Westonbirt NA 10x34 (2002 OCJ); Hillier Gardens 11x32 (2001).
A. capillipes Red Snake-bark Maple Japan, 1892. Occasional. Windsor (Valley Gardens) 12x49 (2000 OCJ); Winkworth Arboretum, Surrey 16x28@1m (2000 OCJ).
A. cappadocicum Cappadocian Maple Caucasus to China, 1838. Frequent; thrives everywhere. Many are grown as 'Rubrum'. Burrswood, Kent 20x112@1m on short bole (1999 Philip Webb); Munches, Dumfries & Galloway (26)x68 (1985 AFM).

'Aureum' Golden Cappadocian Maple Occasional. Pinkney Park, Wilts. 12x92@0.9m (2002 OCJ) – branchy and decaying; Kew RBG 17x85@1m under graft (2001 OCJ); Sydney Gardens, Somerset (?) 16x81 (2002 OCJ); Leeds Castle, Kent 22x51 (1995 OCJ) – slender.
var. sinicum China, 1901. A few dozen in big gardens. Kew RBG 14x57 (2001 OCJ), from Wilson 1358 (1914); Westonbirt NA (f. *tricaudatum*) 22x40 (2002 OCJ) – good slender tree.
A. carpinifolium Hornbeam Maple Japan, 1879. Rare. Westonbirt NA 10x39@1m on knobbly bole (2002 OCJ), p1944; spread 17m.
A. caudatifolium Taiwan. Bushes in a few collections. (Rowallane, Down 9x47@0.5m (1976 AFM).)
A. circinatum Vine Maple W N America, 1826. Very rare; generally bushy. Mary Bassett School, Beds. 8x46@0.75m (1995 DGA) – broad dome.
A. cissifolium Vine-leafed Maple Japan, by 1870. Rare. Westonbirt NA 12x67@0.3m (p1925), and 5x46 (2002 OCJ) – both very broad; Knocklofty House, Tipperary 13.5x23 (2000 TROI).
A. x coriaceum (*monspessulanum* x *pseudoplatanus*, 1790) A handful are known. Westonbirt NA 14x58@1m (2002 OCJ); Pampisford, Cambs. 16x43 (1988 AFM).
A. crataegifolium Uri Maple Japan, 1879. Very rare; seldom a 'tree'. Windsor (Savill Garden) 8x25 (2000 OCJ).
A. davidii Père David's Maple China, 1879. Occasional; like other 'Snake-bark Maples' it appreciates summer warmth and a heavy soil. Ranelagh Gardens, London ('George Forrest') 10x59 on good bole (2001 OCJ); Lesnes Abbey, London ('Ernest Wilson') 10x60@0.8m under forks (2001 OCJ); Winkworth Arboretum, Surrey ('Madeline Spitta') 20x60@0.5m under branches (2000 OCJ); Birr Castle ('Ernest Wilson'?) 22x27 (2002 AF) – drawn up.
A. davidii x rufinerve 'Hatsuyuki'. Hillier Gardens 11x34 (2002 H M Brown).
A. diabolicum Horned Maple Japan, 1880. Very rare (most are f. *purpurascens*). Hergest Croft 11x63 (1995 VES).
A. x dieckii Dieck's Maple (*lobelii* x *platanoides*) A handful in collections. Kew RBG 12x54@0.6m under forks (sourced 1942), and 11x42 (2001 OCJ).
A. distylum Lime-Leafed Maple Japan, 1879. Very rare; seldom a 'tree'. Grayswood Hill, Surrey 9x26 (1998 OCJ) – dying back; ?
A. divergens SW Asia, 1923. A handful in collections. Kew RBG 10x27 (2001 OCJ) – original; Hillier Gardens 12x32@0m (2001 Ron Holley).
A. erianthum China, 1907. In a few collections. Borde Hill 8x30@0.9m under branches (1995 OCJ).
A. flabellatum – see *A. campbellii* ssp. *flabellatum*.
A. forrestii Forrest's Maple China, 1906. Very rare. Caerhays 14x71 (from Forrest 30631) and 15x62 (from Forrest 29395) (1991 AFM).
A. franchettii C China, 1901. In some collections. Windsor (Savill Garden) 10x31 (2000 OCJ).
A. fulvescens – see *A. longipes*.
A. ginnala – see *A. tataricum* ssp. *ginnala*.
A. giraldii Giraldi's Maple C China. In a few collections. Caerhays 15x35 (1984 AFM); Stanage Park,

Powys 18x53 (1995 Roger and Vicky Smith).

A. glabrum **Rock Maple**. W N America, 1884? No mature trees are known. (Kew RBG 12x28 (1967 AFM), from 1895 seed.)

A. grandidentatum **Canyon Maple** W N America, 1882. In some collections. Hillier Gardens 12x33 (2002 Harry James).

A. griseum **Paperbark Maple** C China, 1901. Rather occasional; likes a limey soil. Dyffryn Gardens, Glamorgan 11x68@1m on good short bole (1997 OCJ), p1911; Arley Arboretum, Worcs. (18)x41 (2003 John Bulmer).

A. grosseri Very rare. C China, 1923? Abbey Garden, Suffolk 9.5x62@1m (2001 DGA), p1949.

var. *hersii* Hers' Maple C China. Rather rare. Windsor (Valley Gardens) 9x54@0.2m under forks (2000 OCJ). (Wisley 17x49 (1992 AFM).)

A. heldreichii **Heldreich's Maple** Balkans, 1879. Very rare. Hergest Croft 24x90 (1995 VES).

ssp. *visianii* In a few collections. Hillier Gardens 14x37 (2002 H M Brown).

A. henryi **Henry's Maple** C China, 1903. Very rare. Caerhays 9x42@0.3m (1984 AFM); Powis Castle, Powys 7.5x75@0m (2002) – spread 21.5m.

A. hersii – see *A. grosseri* var. *hersii*.

A. x hillieri (*campestre* x *miyabei*) In a few collections to date. Hillier Gardens ('West Hill') 12.5x37 (2001 H M Brown), p1976.

A. x hybridum (*monspessulanum* x *opalus*) No mature trees known. (Bayfordbury, Herts. 18.5x69 (1973 AFM) – ?)

A. hyrcanum **Balkans Maple** By 1865. Very rare. Westonbirt NA 17x67 (2002 OCJ), p1876.

A. japonicum **Downy Japanese Maple** Japan, 1864 (and see *A. shirasawanum*). The type is scarcely grown: Wakehurst Place 12x43 on single bole (1997 OCJ).

'Aconitifolium' Rather rare. Wakehurst Place 8x28+27++ (1997 OCJ).

'Vitifolium' Full Moon Maple Rather rare. Cannizaro Park, London 14x53@0.3m (2001 OCJ).

A. laevigatum **Smoothbark Maple** Himalayas to China, 1907. In a few collections in mild areas. (Trewithen, Cornwall 20x31 (1971 AFM).)

A. laxiflorum W China, 1908. Genuine plants are in a few collections. Trewithen, Cornwall 21x50 (1987 AFM).

A. leucoderme – see *A. saccharum* ssp. *leucoderme*.

A. lobelii **Lobel's Maple** S Italy, by 1838. Now quite frequent as a street tree. Battersea Park, London 20x96@1.7m above graft (2001 OCJ); Westonbirt NA 25x82 (2002 OCJ), p1922. (Eastnor Castle, Herefords. (25)x120 (1989 AFM) – sprouts remain.)

A. longipes C China (*A. fulvescens*). In one or two collections. Borde Hill 13x50@0.7m (1995 OCJ), p1932.

ssp. *amplum* Broad Maple C China, 1901. In several collections. Borde Hill 13x43 (1995 OCJ), p1937.

A. macrophyllum **Oregon Maple** W N America, 1826. Rare; best in high humidity. Marlfield, Tipperary 19x123 (1968 AFM); Westonbirt NA 25x117 (2002 OCJ); Trinity College, Dublin 16x108 (1985 AFM).

'Aureum'. Glasnevin NBG x45 (2003 DGA) – 1922 original.

'Seattle Sentinel' In a few collections to date. Hillier

Gardens 14.5m (2000 H M Brown), p1966.

A. maximowiczianum **Nikko Maple** (*A. nikoense*) Japan and C China, 1881. Rare. Tortworth Court, Glos. 12x58 (1993), p1904; Westonbirt NA 17x45 (2002 OCJ).

A. maximowiczii **Maximowicz's Maple** C China, 1910. In some collections. Caerhays 15x32 (1984 AFM).

A. miyabei **Miyabe's Maple** Japan, 1892. Very rare. Headfort, Meath 15x46 (1980 AFM).

A. mono **Mono Maple** NE Asia and Japan, 1881. Rare. Tortworth Court, Glos. 23x94@? (1988 JW), p1868; Hergest Croft 18x93@0.5m (1995 VES).

'Marmoratum' Very rare. Glasnevin NBG 15x52 (2003 DGA).

var. *tricuspis* C China, 1901. In a few collections. Glasnevin NBG 16x84 (2003 DGA).

A. monspessulanum **Montpelier Maple** S Europe, W Asia, 1739. Now rare. Birr Castle 15x78 (1990 AFM); Bushy Park, London 16x65 (2001 OCJ).

ssp. *microphyllum* Collingwood Grange, Kent 12x30 (1995 OCJ) – wild-collected.

A. multiserratum China, 1907. In a few collections. Edinburgh RBG 12x31@1m (1985 AFM) – p1938 from Yu 8508.

A. negundo **Box Elder** N America, by 1688. Abundant. The one outstanding tree is at Gladstone Park, London, and has a straight 3m bole (slightly decayed by 2001): 14x100 (2001 OCJ). (Peckover House, Cambs. (18)x44 (1984 AFM).)

'Auratum' Golden Box Elder Rare. St Ronan's School, Kent 12x46@0.5m under forks (1995 OCJ); Gheluvelt Park, Worcs. 9x41@? (1989 JW).

'Variegatum' Variegated Box Elder Frequent, but the biggest (like those of other variegated clones) have all reverted completely: Gunnersbury Cemetery, London 13x78@1.3m and (spread 25m) 15x76@0.9m (2001 OCJ).

var. *violaceum* Rather rare. Wembley parish church, London 15x68 (2001 OCJ).

A. nigrum – see *A. saccharum* ssp. *nigrum*.

A. nikoense – see *A. maximowiczianum*.

A. nipponicum Japan. A handful in collections. Dawyck, Scottish Borders 12x38 (1997).

A. okamotoanum **Okamoto's Maple** NE Asia. A few young trees. Kew RBG 8x(25) (2001 OCJ), from 1989 seed.

A. oliverianum **Oliver Maple** C China, 1901. Very rare. Endsleigh, Devon 14x42 (1990 AFM).

A. opalus **Italian Maple** S Europe, 1752. Rather rare. Powerscourt, Wicklow 8.5x143@0.6m (2000 TROI) – cut back; Tortworth Court, Glos. 19x104@? (1992); Birr Castle 19.5x97@1m (2000 TROI); Grayswood Hill, Surrey 22x103@0.3m around 'waist' (1998 OCJ); St Roche's Arboretum, W Sussex 22x96@1m (1997 OCJ); Kew RBG (var. *obtusatum*) 16x105@0.9m around 'waist' (2001 OCJ).

A. palmatum **Japanese Maple** NE Asia, Japan, 1820. Frequent. Dislikes exposure and very dry soils but will make a good tree in most climates. Hendon Park, London 9x100@0.5m at 'waist' above huge root-plate (2001 OCJ); Escot, Devon 11x66@1.2m over one limb (2001 OCJ); Megginch Castle, Perth 14x62 (1993); Hergest Croft 16x33+26 (1995 VES).

'Albomarginatum' Very rare. Leonardslee, W Sussex

Maples are trees of many and varied charms. Box Elder (*Acer negundo* var. *violaceum*) in blossom.

9x30@1m (1996 OCJ).

f. *atropurpureum* Purple Japanese Maple Quite frequent. Hollycombe, W Sussex 9x57@1m on torn, splitting bole (1997 OCJ); South Lodge, W Sussex 11x43@0.9m under branching (1996 OCJ).

'Aureum' Very rare. Ashford Chace, Hants. 8x28+21 (2002 OCJ).

'Hagoromo' ('Sessilifolium') Very rare. Westonbirt NA 15x41 (2002 OCJ) – shapely tree, predominantly reverted.

'Higasayama' Rare. Batsford Arboretum, Glos. 12x34++ (2003 OCJ).

'Kagiri Nishiki' ('Roseomarginatum') Rare; tends to revert. Leonardslee, W Sussex 12x34 (1996 OCJ) – half-reverted.

'Linearilobum' Rare. Hever Castle, Kent 7x40@0m (1995 OCJ) – bush.

'Linearilobum Atropurpureum' Rare. Leonardslee, W Sussex 9x29 (1996 OCJ).

'Osakazuki' Almost as frequent as the type. Saltram House, Devon 13x54@0.5m (1984 AFM); Westonbirt School, Glos. 10x44@1.1m on decaying bole (2002 OCJ).

'Reticulatum' Rare. Leonardslee, W Sussex 10x28+26 (1996 OCJ).

'Sango-Kaku' Coral-barked Maple ('Senkaki') Quite frequent. Hillier Gardens 9.5x47@0.1m (2001 Ron Holley); Hergest Croft 11x26+24 (1995 VES).

'Shishigashira' ('Ribesifolium') Rather rare; semi-dwarf. Bute Park, Glamorgan 8x31@? (1988); Wayford Manor, Somerset 10m (2003 Robin Goffe).

A. pectinatum E Himalayas, Upper Burma. In a few collections. Hillier Gardens 10x40 (2001 Harry James).

***A. pensylvanicum* Moosewood** E N America, 1755. Rather rare. Westonbirt NA 12x42@1.2m and 14x34 (2002 OCJ).

'Aureubracifolia' ('Erythrocladum'). Of poor constitution and now very rare. (Birr Castle 13x33 (1990 AFM).)

***A. platanoides* Norway Maple** Abundant; a tree which narrowly missed being native to SE England but which has long been grown here and thrives everywhere except on light sands, sometimes naturalising. The biggest tend to be in humid areas. Kilfane House, Kilkenny 28x179@0.9m and 14x153@1m (2000 TROI) – both branchy; Hafodunos, Conwy 26x137@? (1990 AFM); Ballindean, Perth (30)x87 (1987 AFM).

'Aureum' Golden Norway Maple Few books mention this variant, but it seems to grow well into a neat dome: Hergest Croft 21x72 (1995 VES); Buckingham Palace, London (to be propagated as 'Golden Jubilee') 14x61 (2000 OCJ). (Strachur, Argyll 17x96 (1969 AFM).)

'Cleveland' Rare to date (cf. 'Olmsted'). Hillier Gardens 21x34 (2000 H M Brown).

'Columnare' Fastigiate Norway Maple An occasional street tree. Osterley Park, London 20x48 (2001 OCJ) – very erect but perhaps a sport.

'Cucullatum' Rare. Westonbirt NA 25x93 (2002 OCJ), p1876; Castle Ashby Gardens, Northants. 22x102 under narrow fork (2002 Steve Benamore).

'Dissectum' Rather rare (in various clones – 'Lorbergii', 'Palmitifidum') and slow-growing. Hillier Gardens 15x54

(2001 Harry James).

'Drummondii' Very frequent, but quickly reverts. The largest trees with only 10-20% reversion seen are at South Ealing Cemetery, London – 14x53 and 15x50@1.2m (2001 OCJ).

'Globosum' Rare; semi-dwarf. Kew RBG 8x62 (2001 OCJ), p1885; Westonbirt NA 9x55@0.5m (2002 OCJ). Both have lost their neat globular shape with age.

'Goldsworth Purple' Purple Norway Maple Abundant ('Crimson King' and 'Faassen's Black' are indistinguishable in the field). Knocklofty House, Tipperary 20x85@1.3m (2000 TROI) – much the largest yet seen.

'Laciniatum' Eagle-claw Maple Very rare. Belgrove, Cork 9.5x70@1m (2001 AF); Ryston Hall, Norfolk 21x57@? (1995 JW), p1908.

'Maculatum'. Kew RBG 10x55 (2001 OCJ), p1881.

'Olmsted' Rare to date? Foots Cray Lane, London 12x43 (2001 OCJ) – two the same size; Cannizaro Park, London 13x42 (2001 OCJ). (These may be unusually shapely examples of 'Columnare', or 'Cleveland'.)

'Pyramidale Nanum'. Kew RBG 7x33 (2001 OCJ), sourced 1900.

'Reitenbachii' Becoming rare; a clone of rather weak growth. Batsford Arboretum, Glos. 20x80 (2003 OCJ) - hollow.

'Rubrum'. Kew RBG 9x28 (2001 OCJ) – old, stunted tree.

'Schwedleri' Quite frequent; grows as big as the type. Knightshayes, Devon 25x111@1m? (2003); Westonbirt NA 26x78 (2002 OCJ).

'Stollii' Very rare. Birr Castle 17x97 (1990 AFM).

***A. platanoides* x *truncatum*.** Hillier Gardens 13x59@1m (2002 H M Brown).

A. x pseudoheldreichii (*heldreichii* x *pseudoplatanus*). Kew RBG 14x37 (2001 OCJ).

***A. pseudoplatanus* Sycamore** Abundantly naturalised. Posso House, Scottish Borders x275 (1992 JP) – long bole with huge root-platform; Abercairney, Perth 27x262@0.3m (1986 AFM); Tyninghame House, E Lothian 27.5x250 (1992 JP); Gormanstown College, Meath 25.5x249@0.6m (2000 TROI); Myshall, Carlow 24x235 (2000 TROI) – hollow; Charleville, Wicklow 23.5x232 (2000 TROI); Drymsynie, Argyll 26x232@1.2m around 'waist' (1989 AFM); Birnam, Perth (second of the 'Birnam Oaks') x230 around 'waist' (1990 AFM); Drumlanrig, Dumfries & Galloway 31.5x225 (2002 Donald Rodger); Thwaite Hall, Durham (25)x224 (1998 Den Gregson); Kilmore Cathedral, Cavan 20.5x223@0.9m (2000 TROI) – 'Bishop Bedell's Tree', p1631; Betteshanger, Kent 25x218@1m under limbs (1999 OCJ) – hollow; Plas Newydd, Anglesey 19x217 among branches (1987 AFM); Lennoxlove, E Lothian (40)x115 (1985 AFM); Cirencester Park, Glos. 38x60 (1989 JW).

'Brilliantissimum' Frequent; growing very slowly into a medium-sized tree. Ryston Hall, Norfolk 17x56@? (1995 JW).

'Corstorphinense' Corstorphine Plane Now rare. The 17th century original in Edinburgh blew down in 1999. Moncrieffe House, Perth 26x140 (1982 AFM).

'Erectum' Very rare? Jodrell Bank Arboretum, Cheshire

13x26 (1992 AFM).

'Nizetii' Occasional as a younger tree. Hillier Gardens 17.5x52 (2002 Harry James).

'Prinz Handjery' Locally occasional; growing as 'Brilliantissimum'. Fitzgerald Park, Cork 14.5x47 (2001 AF); Leonardslee, W Sussex 9x47@1m (1996 OCJ), p1930.

f. *purpureum* Purple Sycamore Frequent; a common wild sport which grows as well as the type. Henrietta Park, Somerset 25x140@1m around 'waist' (2002 OCJ); Woburn Park 29x114 (2003 DGA).

f. *variegatum* Variegated Sycamore Quite frequent; the only brightly-variegated tree which seems to grow as large as its type. Weston Park, Staffs. (29)x160 (2003 John Bulmer) – forks; Lismullen House, Meath 22x215@0.8m under forks (2000 TROI); Dalguise House, Perth (34)x142 (1986 AFM). Clones include 'Leopoldii' (Ellel Grange, Lancs. (?) 23x129@0.8m around 'waist' (2001)), and 'Simon-Louis Frères' (Burnham Park, Bucks. 14x47 (2002 OCJ) – p. after 1965?).

'Worleei' Golden Sycamore Rather occasional; slow-growing. Wakehurst Place 21x96 (1997 OCJ).

A. *pseudosiebolianum* Korean Maple NE Asia, 1903. Very rare; scarcely reaches 'tree' size here.

A. *pycnanthum* Japan; rare in the wild but in many collections as a young tree. Hillier Gardens 13.5x32 and 14x29+26 (2000 H M Brown), p1973.

A. x *rotundilobum* (*monspessulanum* x *opalus* var. *obtusatum*). Kew RBG 13x53 (2001 OCJ), sourced 1904.

A. *rubescens* China. Trewithen, Cornwall 21x59 (1987 AFM), p1912.

A. *rubrum* Red Maple E N America, by 1656. Occasional; needs summer warmth and seems to be the only Maple with a strong preference for light, sandy soils. Many recent plantings will be the autumn-colouring selections 'October Glory' or 'Schlesingeri'. The Bagshot trees are decayed veterans, the taller with much mistletoe. Bagshot Park, Surrey 19x129@0.8m under branches, and 16x110 (2000 OCJ); Hollycombe, W Sussex 26x97 (1997 OCJ) – bole 8m.

'Columnare' Rare but very vigorous. Hillier Gardens 19.5x36 (2001 Harry James).

'Scanlon' Rather rare to date. Hillier Gardens 16.5x47@1.3m (2001 Harry James); Old Kiln Museum, Surrey 17x33 (2000 OCJ). The similar clone 'Armstrong' was 19x31 at the Old Kiln Museum in 2000 (OCJ).

A. *rufinerve* Honshu Maple Japan, 1879. Rather rare. Kensington Gardens, London 13x56@1.1m (2001 OCJ).

'Hatsuyuki' (f. *albolimbatum*). Very rare and unstable. (Stourhead, Wilts. 13x38@1.2m (1977 AFM).)

A. *saccharinum* Silver Maple E N America, 1725. Abundant; likes a heavy soil but thrives everywhere. The outstanding tree is in woodland at Rowfant, W Sussex: 23x170 on 3m bole (2000 OCJ); Christ's Hospital, W Sussex 30x122 (1997 OCJ); Munches, Dumfries & Galloway 30x108 (1996); Westonbirt NA 30x(100) (2002 OCJ), p1876.

f. *laciniatum* Cut-leaved Silver Maple, is now the most planted selection (often as the rather slender 'Weiri'). Older, spreading trees are: St John's Gardens, London 18x109 (2002 OCJ); Borde Hill 26x99 (1995 OCJ).

Most of the giant broadleaves from the forests of the eastern United States, accustomed to long hot summers, make good ornamental plants on this side of the Atlantic but seldom grow very big or live very long. Silver Maple (*Acer saccharinum*), with its white-backed leaves, is something of an exception: there are grand specimens in Scotland, while this one near Rowfant in West Sussex rivals the best wild trees. Its crown is liberally hung with that most cosmopolitan of tree-parasites, Mistletoe.

A. *saccharum* Sugar Maple E N America, 1735. Rather rare, but growing well everywhere (a good tree in Stornoway). Hollycombe, W Sussex 22x102@0.5m around 'waist' (1997 OCJ); Belton House, Lincs. (22)x86 (1991 AFM) – shapely; Kew RBG 23x57 (2001 OCJ).

ssp. *leucoderme* Chalk Maple SE USA, by 1900. In a few collections. Westonbirt NA 22x54 (2002 OCJ).

'Newton Sentry'. Hillier Gardens 16x32@1m (2001 Harry James). ('Temple's Upright' has yet to reach 'tree' size.)

ssp. *nigrum* Black Maple 1812. Collections; only poor or young trees are now known: Borde Hill 13x41 (1995 OCJ), p1911; Edinburgh RBG 17x35 (1997). (Alexandra Park, E Sussex 22x96@1m around 'waist' (1993 OCJ), died 1995.)

A. *sempervirens* Cretan Maple E Mediterranean, 1752. Rare; often a bush. Tregothnan, Cornwall 12.5x58 (1995).

A. shirasawanum **Shirasawa's Maple** Japan. In some collections; scarcely a tree. High Beeches, W Sussex 7x49@0.1m (1997 OCJ); Hillier Gardens 8.4x30@0.25m (2001 Harry James).

'Aureum' Golden Moon Maple Occasional. Lancrigg Hotel, Cumbria 12x20+15++ (1995 DH).

A. sieboldianum **Siebold's Maple** Japan, by 1880. In a few collectons. Collingwood Grange, Kent 10x48@0.1m (1997 OCJ) – giant bush.

A. stachyophyllum **Birch-leaved Maple** (incorporating *A. tetramerum*) Himalayas to China, 1901. Rather rare; often bushy. Westonbirt NA 11x51@0.6m under forks (2002 OCJ); Glendoick, Perth 9x42 (1991 VES); Stanage Park, Powys 16.5m (1995 Roger and Vicky Smith) – bushy.

A. sterculiaceum (incorporating *A. villosum*) Himalayas, by 1850. Very rare, but makes a good tree. Ryston Hall, Norfolk 22x60@? (1995 JW).

ssp. *thomsonii* E Himalayas. Kew RBG 8x25 (2001 OCJ).

A. taronense China. In a few collections. Brodick Castle, Ayr 10x26+24 (1988 AFM).

A. tataricum **Tartar Maple** E Mediterranean, 1759. Very rare. Hillier Gardens 10x35 (2001).

ssp. *ginnala* **Amur Maple** N Asia, Japan, 1860. Occasional; usually a bush here (prefers a continental climate). Winkworth Arboretum, Surrey 9x58@0.1m under massive stems (2000 OCJ); Kippenross House, Stirling 11x37 (1986 AFM).

A. tetramerum – see *A. stachyophyllum*.

A. trautvetteri **Trautvetter's Maple** Caucasus, 1866. Very rare. Tortworth Court, Glos. 20.5x99@? (1988 JW); Arley Arboretum, Worcs. (23)x81 (2003 John Bulmer).

A. triflorum **Chosen Maple** NE Asia, 1923. Very rare; needs hot summers to grow well. Woburn Park, Beds. 7x34@1m (1994 DGA); Westonbirt NA 9x36@0.4m (2002 OCJ).

A. truncatum **Shandong Maple** China, 1881. Very rare. Kew RBG 13x55 (2001 OCJ), from 1935 seed.

A. turkestanicum Central Asia. Young trees in a few collections. Batsford Arboretum, Glos. 11x25 (2003 OCJ).

A. velutinum **Caucasian Maple** In some collections. Kew RBG 18x71 (2001 OCJ).

var. *vanvolxemii* **Van Volxem's Maple** 1873. Rare; thrives everywhere. National Stud, Kildare 16x109 (2002 AF); Westonbirt NA 26x98 (2002 OCJ) – long bole.

A. villosum – see *A. sterculiaceum*.

A. wilsonii **Wilson's Maple** SW China, 1907. In some collections. Birr Castle 9.5x27 (2000 TROI).

A. x zoeschense **Zoeschen Maple** (*campestre* x *lobelii*?) Rare. Abbeyleix, Laois 18.5x77 (2000 TROI); Syon Park, London 20x74 (2002 OCJ) – ?

Aesculus Horse Chestnuts

Aesculus assamica **Assam Horse Chestnut** In a few collections. Kew RBG 13x47 (2001 OCJ).

A. x bushii (*glabra* x *pavia*) SE USA. In one or two collections. Kew RBG 9x39 (2001 OCJ).

A. californica **Californian Horse Chestnut** By 1850. Rather rare; often a bush. Tortworth Court, Glos. 15.5x51 (1988 JW), p1908.

A. x carnea **Red Horse Chestnut** (*hippocastanum* x *pavia*, by 1820) Abundant; seldom a good tree. Fairlawne, Kent 18x120@1.1m under graft (1995 OCJ); Godinton Park, Kent 11x119 (1999 OCJ) – cut back. (Endsleigh, Devon 28x89 (1977 AFM).)

'Briotii' 1858. Now the most planted form; leafier, and tends to grow better. Busbridge Lakes, Surrey 17x104 (2000 OCJ); Westonbirt NA 25x94 (2002 OCJ) – slender.

'Plantierensis' Plantier's Chestnut (back-cross with Horse Chestnut). Locally occasional; showy but small-growing. Wisley 18x63@1m under burrs (2002 OCJ).

A. chinensis **Chinese Horse Chestnut** N China, 1912. In some collections. Kew RBG 12x39 (2001 OCJ) – original.

A. + dallimorii **Dallimore's Chestnut** A chimaera first noted in Kent in 1955; remains very rare in commerce. A branch-sport was first noticed on the grafted Yellow Buckeye at Bidborough by William Dallimore in 1955; the chimaera has since taken over the whole crown. The Farningham tree, with one branch-sport and the rest of the crown taken over by the Horse Chestnut stock, was found in 1999. Farningham, Kent 14x72@1m (1999 OCJ); Bidborough, Kent 15x66 (1999 OCJ).

A. flava **Yellow Buckeye** SE USA, 1764. Occasional in warm areas. Tandridge Court, Surrey 19x107 under graft (1997 Philip Webb); St Margaret's, London (23)x96 (1983 AFM) – long bole with no visible graft; Much Hadham Old Rectory, Herts. 22x74@1.7m above graft (2001 DGA) – carries mistletoe.

f. *virginica* **Virginian Buckeye** Very rare. Bishop's Palace, Chichester, W Sussex 17x112@0.4m/x73+63+52@1.7m (1997 OCJ) – spread 18m, flowers pink/cream; Kew RBG 21x80@1.2m (2001 OCJ) – flowers bright crimson.

A. glabra **Ohio Buckeye** SE USA, 1809. Very rare. Kew RBG 16x82 (2001 OCJ); Aldenham Park, Herts. 17x36 (2002 OCJ).

var. *leucodermis* **White-bark Buckeye**. Kew RBG 11x28 (2001 OCJ).

A. hippocastanum **Horse Chestnut** Mountains of Greece and Albania, 1616. Abundant. Hurstbourne Priors, Hants. 35x220 (1993) – superb symmetrical tree; Lough Key Forest Park, Roscommon 22.5x200@0.95m (2000 TROI); Screens Wood, W Sussex 39x144 (1997 OCJ) – slender; Busbridge Lakes, Surrey 38x125 (2000 OCJ), p1664? – slender.

'Baumannii' Double Horse Chestnut 1822. Quite frequent. As it puts no energy into conker-production it will probably outgrow the type. Green Park, Bath, Somerset 27x178@0.5m below forking, and 31x167@0.8m below branching (2002 OCJ); Hedgemead Park, Somerset 28x147 (2002 OCJ).

'Honiton Gold'. Honiton, Devon 17x85 (2001 OCJ) – original sport, growing better than the more popular 'Hampton Court Gold'.

'Incisa'. Kew RBG 13x39 (2001 OCJ).

f. *laciniata* **Cut-leaved Horse Chestnut** Very rare and slow. Bowood, Wilts. (?) 12.5x28 (1993).

'Memmingeri'. Kew RBG 16x77 (2001 OCJ).

'Pyramidalis' Fastigiate Horse Chestnut Very rare?

Thirty-nine metres of candles on the tallest known Horse Chestnut (*Aesculus hippocastanum*), in Screens Wood, West Sussex.

Many people imagine that Horse Chestnut is a native tree; in fact it is found wild only in the mountains of northern Greece and Albania. It can be long-lived here, and has become one of our very tallest broadleaves, though as it usually adds girth slower than most forest trees do, it cannot (as yet) boast any gigantic boles. Its timber is surprisingly soft, and limbs or whole trees may collapse abruptly under the weight of raindrops.

Kew RBG 15x71 (2001 OCJ); Regent's Park, London 16x62 (2001 OCJ) – ?

***A. x hybrida* Hybrid Buckeye** (*flava* x *pavia*) E USA. Very occasional in warm areas. Weybridge church, Surrey 15x104@1.2m under graft (2000 OCJ) – broad and ivy-clad, with crimson flowers; Singleton Park, Glamorgan (21)x64 (2000 Teifion Davies) – leans, with cream flowers; Hyde Park, London 21x61 (2001 OCJ) – slender graceful tree with crimson flowers.

***A. indica* Indian Horse Chestnut** NW Himalayas, 1851. Occasional; does well everywhere. Hidcote, Glos. 19x97 (1993); Westonbirt NA 22x83 (2002 OCJ). The original 'Sydney Pearce' at Kew RBG is 13x74 (2001 OCJ) – 1935 seedling.

A. x marylandica (*flava* x *glabra*). Kew RBG 8x26 (2001 OCJ).

A. x mutabilis (*discolor* var. *mollis* x *neglecta*) Very rare; normally a bush. Birr Castle ('Induta'; as recorded) 14x65@1m (2000 TROI).

***A. neglecta* 'Erythroblastos' Sunrise Horse Chestnut** Very rare; slow-growing. Westonbirt NA 11x34++@1.2m (2002 OCJ), p1935 – rather bushy.

***A. pavia* Red Buckeye** S USA, 1711. Rather rare; generally a bush. Esso Ireland HQ, Dublin ('*A. splendens*') 8.7x45@1m (2000 TROI); Innes House, Moray 16x38+28++ (1991 AFM).

A. sylvatica SE USA. In one or two collections. Kew RBG 17x43 (2001 OCJ), with yellow flowers.

***A. turbinata* Japanese Horse Chestnut** Japan, by 1880. Rare. Westonbirt NA 18x89 under graft, and 24x80 (2002 OCJ).

***A. wilsonii* Wilson's Horse Chestnut** China, 1908. In some collections. Caerhays (19)x85 (1991 AFM); Melbury House, Dorset (21)x54@0.1m (1989 AFM).

***Agathis australis* Kauri Pine** North Island, New Zealand, 1823. Survives to make a stunted tree in the mildest areas. Caragh Lodge, Kerry 11.5x29 (2001 AF). (Tresco Abbey, Cornwall 19.5x31 (1970 Major Darrien-Smith).)

***Ailanthus altissima* Tree of Heaven** N China, 1751 (incorporating *A. giraldii* and *A. sutchuenensis*). Abundant in warm areas; naturalising by suckers. Chichester, W Sussex 17x146 (1997 Nigel Muir) – clean flared bole, cut back; Escot, Devon 28x96 (2001 OCJ); Stoke Rochford, Lincs. 29x82 (1978 AFM).

'Pendulifolia'. In a few big gardens. Hillier Gardens 13.5x35 (2001 Harry James).

***A. vilmoriniana* Downy Tree of Heaven** China, 1897. In some collections; growing like the common species: Kew RBG 22x78 (2001 OCJ), from 1905 seed; Hergest Croft 24x63 (1995 VES).

***Albizia julibrissin* Pink Siris** Asia, 1745. Rare; yet to reach 'tree' size even in the hottest areas.

Alnus Alders

***Alnus cordata* Italian Alder** Corsica and S Italy, 1820. Very frequent in the south, though it does not need warmth to grow well. Derrymore House, Armagh 16x144 (2000 TROI); Westonbirt NA 28x102 (2002 OCJ) – slight lean; Marble Hill Park, London 28x77 (2001 OCJ) – leaning.

A. firma Japan, 1894. Very rare; often bushy. Hollycombe, W Sussex 13x46@1m (1997 OCJ).

***A. glutinosa* Alder** Native; abundant. Dundonnell, Highland x170 (1986 AFM) – ancient wild tree; Squerryes Park, Kent 21x166@1.2m (1995 OCJ) – pollard: three stems at 1.5m; Geltsdale, Cumbria 13x245@0.2m (2002

DH) – nine-stemmed stool with solid base; Reenadinna, Kerry 19.5x187@0.6m under forks (2000 TROI); Auchengavin Farm, Argyll 13.5x182@0.5m (1999 John Mitchell) – stool with solid, decayed base; Painswick Lodge, Glos. x150@? (1999); Tretower Court, Powys 14x145 (1995 VES); Cowden, Kent 18x139@1.8m on single trunk above aerial roots (2000 Philip Webb); Flitwick Manor, Beds. 21x139@1.1m on short trunk (1997 DGA); Old Roar Ghyll, E Sussex 28x50 (2001 OCJ) – drawn up and sinuous.

'Aurea' Golden Alder Rare. Jephson Gardens, Warwicks. (14)x49 (1989).

var. barbata Caucasus. Kew RBG 15x78 (2001 OCJ).

'Imperialis' Fern-leaved Alder Occasional; usually stunted but some plants grow well. Kington recreation ground, Herefords. 12x60 (1995 VES); Thorp Perrow, Yorks. 16.5x36 (1981 AFM), p1945. A big tree at Ryston Hall, Norfolk, grown as 'Imperialis', was 28x115@? (1995 JW).

'Laciniata' Cut-leaved Alder Rather rare; grows strongly. Painshill Park, Surrey 14x128 @1.2-1.5m (2000 OCJ) – leaning, slightly decayed trunk, cut at 4m, but regrowing vigorously; Syon Park, London 18x63 (2002 OCJ). (Cassiobury Park, Herts. 26x111 (1905 Elwes & Henry).)

'Pyramidalis' Fastigiate Alder Very rare indeed. Windsor (N of Savill Garden) 12x27 (2000 OCJ).

'Quercifolia'. Alexandra Park, E Sussex, 20x77@0.8m below forks (2001 OCJ).

A. hirsuta NE Asia, Japan, 1879. In some collections. Borde Hill 16x43 and 17x32 (1995 OCJ).

var. sibirica – see *A. sibirica*.

A. x hybrida (*glutinosa* x *incana*; *A.* x *pubescens*) Rare? Wisley 15x43 (2000 OCJ) – vigorous young plant.

A. incana Grey Alder Europe except Britain and Ireland, 1780. Locally abundant – shelterbelts and reclamation schemes. Seldom does well here. Uragh Woods, Kerry 14x129+111/x206@0.7m (2000 TROI) – as recorded; Ryston Hall, Norfolk ('var. *lobulata*') 12x78@? (1995 JW); Logie Lodge, Angus (25)x38 (1986 AFM), p1956.

'Aurea' Rare. Spalding Grammar School, Lincs. 9x26 (1991 AFM); Birr Castle 12x25 (1989 AFM). (Smeaton House, E Lothian 17x40 (1986 AFM).) 'Ramulis Coccineis' is doubtfully distinct: Hillier Gardens 12.5x30 (2001 Harry James).

'Laciniata' Very rare. Courteenhall, Northants. x65@1.1m (1999 DGA).

'Pendula' Weeping Grey Alder Rare. Jodrell Bank Arboretum, Cheshire 6x45 (1992 AFM); Talbot Manor, Norfolk 11x26 (1978 AFM), p1948.

A. inokumae Japan, 1965; in some collections. Westonbirt NA 14x26 (2002 OCJ); Wakehurst Place 10x25 (2001 OCJ) – growing faster.

A. japonica NE Asia, Japan, by 1880. Very rare. Ryston Hall, Norfolk 18x72@? (1995 JW); Stanage Park, Powys 21x41 (1995 Roger and Vicky Smith).

A. lanata W China. In one or two collections. Jodrell Bank Arboretum, Cheshire 9x27 (1992 AFM).

A. mairei W China. Young trees in a few collections are growing fast.

A. maritima var. formosana Taiwan. In one or two collections. Edinburgh RBG 17x98 (1997).

A. matsumurae Japan. Alice Holt, Hants. 16x45 (2001 OCJ) – dying back.

A. maximowiczii Japan, 1914. Some young trees, growing fast.

A. nitida Himalayan Alder 1882. Very rare. Whitfield, Herefords. 27x64 (1995 VES), p1934.

A. orientalis Oriental Alder Cyprus to Syria, 1924. Very rare. Woodcock Park, London 10x35 (2001 OCJ) – poor tree. (Edinburgh RBG 13x64 (1972 AFM).)

A. x pubescens – see *A.* x *hybrida*.

A. rubra Oregon Alder W N America, by 1880. Very occasional; vigorous but short-lived. Alice Holt, Hants. 17x52 (2001 OCJ); Thorp Perrow, Yorks. 23x49 (1991 AFM), p1940.

A. rugosa Speckled Alder E USA, 1769 (*A. serrulata*). In some collections. Hillier Gardens 16x48 (2002 Harry James).

A. sibirica NE Asia, Japan. In some collections. Holland Park, London (?) 11x46 (2001 OCJ); Talbot Manor, Norfolk 14x21 (1978 AFM), p1954.

A. x spaethii Spaeth's Alder (*japonica* x *subcordata*) A splendid tree, beginning to be more widely planted. Borde Hill 25x73 (1995 OCJ), p1938.

A. subcordata Caucasian Alder 1838. Rare. Very vigorous in warm areas, but short-lived. Cambridge UBG 17.5x89 (2002 DGA); Kew RBG 20x81 (2001 OCJ); seed 1928.

A. tenuifolia W N America, 1891. (Borde Hill 14.5x30 (1932) – blown.)

A. viridis Green Alder Europe, N Asia, 1820. In some collections; generally a bush, but 12x46@? recorded at Roath Park, Glamorgan (1991 JW).

ssp. sinuata Sitka Alder W N America, E Asia, 1903. In a few collections. Hillier Gardens 11x65 (2001 Harry James).

Amelanchier asiatica E Asia, Japan, 1865. In some collections; often bushy.

A. lamarckii Snowy Mespil (Origin uncertain; some garden plants may be *A. laevis*). Abundant; well naturalised on light sands in the south-east, where it grows largest. Brockwell Park, London 10x45@1.2m under scar (2001 OCJ); Ashburnham Place, E Sussex 13x28 (2003 OCJ).

A. ovalis S Europe; long grown here. Normally a bush. (Nymans, W Sussex 9x34 (1979 AFM).)

Aphananthe aspera NE Asia, Japan, 1895. In one or two collections. Kew RBG 6x33@1m (2001 OCJ), from 1968 seed.

Aralia elata Japanese Angelica Tree Japan, 1830? Very occasional; generally a bush. Woodbrooke, Wexford 8.5x25@1.2m (2001 AF) – recumbent; Marwood Hill, Devon 9x22 (1989 AFM); Powis Castle, Powys 10x18 (2002).

Araucaria araucana Monkey Puzzle S Andes, 1795.

Quite frequent. Lough Fea, Monaghan 23.5x135 (2000 TROI); Fair Oak, W Sussex 31x92 (1997 OCJ); Woodstock, Kilkenny 30x119 (1999 Michael Lear).

***A. bidwillii* Bunya-Bunya Pine** Queensland, 1843. Not reliably hardy. (Glendurgan, Cornwall 11x33 (1965 AFM).)

***A. heterophylla* Norfolk Island Pine** Norfolk Island, Australia. Not reliably hardy. (Tresco Abbey, Cornwall (30)x71 (1970 Major Darrien-Smith).)

Arbutus Strawberry Trees

***Arbutus andrachne* Grecian Strawberry Tree** SE Europe, 1724. Very rare; seldom a 'tree' even in hot areas. Jenkyn Place, Hants. 7x27+25+18 (1988 AFM). (Kew RBG 11.5x48++ 1m (1967 AFM).)

***A. x andrachnoides* Hybrid Strawberry Tree** (*andrachne* x *unedo*). Very occasional, but grows well everywhere. Battersea Park, London 15x88@0.4m on short single bole (2001 OCJ); Inzievar House, Fife 24x76 (2001 Donald Rodger) – dying from honey fungus.

***A. menziesii* Madrone** W N America, 1827. Rather rare. A huge tree in the wild, but generally short-lived in our apparently similar climate. Royden Park, Liverpool 16x134@0.5m/x85+65+57 (2000 Joe Walsh), p1868?; Hergest Croft (26)x67++ (1995 VES).

***A. unedo* Strawberry Tree** Native to SW Ireland; quite frequently planted everywhere. Dinis Cottage, Kerry 10.5x117@0.2m and 14x80@0.9m (2000 TROI) – wild trees; Chobham Place Wood, Surrey 15x78@0.3m (2000 OCJ) – drawn up under Scots pines, and self-sown?; Weybridge church, Surrey 9x55+ (2000 OCJ) – ancient tree strapped together.

***Atherospermum moschatum* Black Sassafras** SE Australia, Tasmania, 1824. A few young trees.

***Athrotaxis cupressoides* Smooth Tasmanian Cedar** 1857. 50-100 trees; hardy (one of the largest is in Dundee). Kilmacurragh, Wicklow 14x61+57+32 (1990) and 16x47 (1980 AFM).

***A. laxifolia* Summit Cedar** W Tasmania, 1857. Rare; hardy. Scorrier House, Cornwall 18x86 (1991 AFM), p1871; Duckyls Wood, W Sussex 20x64 (1996 OCJ).

***A. selaginoides* King William Pine** W Tasmania, 1857. Perhaps 100 trees, in milder areas. Kilmacurragh, Wicklow 14x63 (1990 AFM); Mount Usher, Wicklow 19x61 (1989 AFM).

***Austrocedrus chilensis* Chilean Incense Cedar** 1847. About 100 trees; needs high humidity to do well. Mount Usher, Wicklow 16.5x48 (1992 AFM).

***Azara microphylla* Small-leaved Azara** S Andes, 1861. Very occasional; reaching tree-size in mild areas. (Blandsfort, Laois 12.5x40+30 (1968 AFM); Annes Grove, Cork 13.5x26+ (1968 AFM).)

Betula Birches

***Betula albo-sinensis* var. *septentrionalis* Chinese**

Red Birch W China, 1908. Rather rare. Endsleigh, Devon 14x58 (1990 AFM); Westonbirt NA 20x45 (2002 OCJ) p1938; slender. The type, with a brighter orange bark, is rarer: Hergest Croft 25x40 (1995 VES).

***B. alleghaniensis* Yellow Birch** (*B. lutea*) E N America, 1767? Rather rare. Tilgate Park, W Sussex 20x82@0.6m under forks (2002 OCJ); Oriel Temple, Louth 17.5x71 (1980 AFM); Bodnant, Conwy (22)x56 (1990 AFM).

B. x aurata – see under *B. pendula*.

B. x caerulea (*coerulea-grandis* x *populifolia?*) E N America, 1905. Very rare. Aldenham church, Herts. (but perhaps an Asiatic hybrid) 14x56 (2001 OCJ); Bedgebury NP 17x45 (1995 OCJ), p1938.

B. celtiberica N Iberia. In a few collections. Windsor (Valley Gardens) 12x30 (2002 OCJ). (Collingwood Grange, Kent 22x67 (1990 VES).)

B. chinensis E Asia, 1920. A few young trees. Hillier Gardens 8x48@0m (2001 Ron Holley).

***B. coerulea-grandis* Blue Birch** E N America. A few young trees. (Hergest Croft, Herefords. 17x63 (1969 AFM).)

B. costata – see under *B. ermanii* 'Grayswood'.

B. davurica NE Asia, 1882. Collections; not currently known to tree size.

***B. ermanii* Erman's Birch** NE Asia, Japan, 1890. Occasional. A relatively long-lived tree which has already outgrown our wild birches; likes limestone. Westonbirt NA 22x124 (2002 OCJ) – short single bole; broad crown. Two more very big trees at Hollycombe, W Sussex, are probably hybrids with Downy Birch: 19x142@0.4m (branchy from the base) and 19x78@1m under branching (1997 OCJ). 'Grayswood', a selection of var. *japonica*, is now much planted (usually as *B. costata*, of which only young authenticated examples are known). The original at Grayswood Hill, Surrey, reached 19x111@0m (1968 AFM).

B. 'Fetisowii'. Rare; a poor grower, not currently known to tree size.

B. forrestii C China, 1918. In some collections. St Andrew's BG, Fife 15x36 (2003 Bob Mitchell).

***B. grossa* Japanese Cherry Birch** 1896. Collections. Hillier Gardens 15.5x49 (2001 Harry James).

B. 'Hergest'. Many young trees are growing well.

B. x intermedia (*nana* x *pubescens*). Hillier Gardens 9x34 (2001 Harry James).

B. jacquemontii – see *B. utilis* var. *jacquemontii*.

***B. kenaica* Alaskan Birch** (*B. papyrifera* var. *kenaica*) 1891. Collections. Westonbirt NA 17x37 (2002 OCJ), p1946?

B. x koehnei. Accidental hybrids of Paper-bark and Silver Birches are widespread and probably include: Greenwich Park, London 15x66@0.6m under fork (2001 OCJ); and Windsor (Valley Gardens) 21x57 (2000 OCJ). Others will be *papyrifera* x *pubescens*. The largest authentic *B. x koehnei* is at the Hillier Gardens: 20x50 (2001 Ron Holley).

***B. lenta* Cherry Birch** E N America, 1759. Rare. Mount Usher, Wicklow (18)x54 (1989 AFM).

B. luminifera W China, 1901. Very rare. Hergest Croft 19x35 (1995 VES), p1920.

B. lutea – see *B. alleghaniensis*.

***B. mandshurica* var. *japonica* Japanese Silver Birch** By 1887. Very rare. Alexandra Park, E Sussex 14x52

(2001 OCJ) – as planted, 1935); Hillier Gardens 17x23 (2001 Ron Holley).

B. maximowicziana Monarch Birch Japan, 1893. Rare, but making a fine sturdy tree: Frensham Hall estate, Surrey 17x66 (2000 OCJ); Wayford Manor, Somerset 22m (2003 Robin Goffe).

B. medwediewii Medwediew's Birch Transcaucasus, 1897. Rare; often a bush. Windsor (Valley Gardens) 4x31 on 2m bole (2000 OCJ), p1932; much died back; Thorp Perrow, Yorks. 11x26 (1987 AFM).

B. neoalaskana (*B. papyrifera* var. *humilis*) Alaska, 1905. Not currently known to 'tree' size.

B. nigra River Birch E USA, 1736. Rather rare; short-lived here. South Road, Horsell, Surrey 9x53 (2000 OCJ), cut back; Stanage Park, Powys 20x36 (1994 JW).

B. obscura E Europe. In a few collections. Kew RBG 15x40 (2001 OCJ).

B. occidentalis W N America (where often shrubby), 1897. Now confined to a few collections. Westonbirt NA 17x44 (2002 OCJ).

B. papyrifera Paper-bark Birch N America, 1750. Occasional. Many of the best are the large-leaved var. *commutata*. (Var. *subcordata*, in collections, is less vigorous.) See also *B.* x *koehnei*. Innes House, Moray 15x96@0.5m (1991 AFM); Rowallane, Down 21x76 (1991 AFM); Knightshayes, Devon (27)x52 (2003).

B. papyrifera x utilis var. jacquemontii. Coates Manor, W Sussex 12x41 (1997 OCJ) – original cross, donated c1972. A birch of exceptional beauty.

B. pendula Silver Birch Native. Abundant on light, sandy soils; the most planted birch. Specimens never live long enough to become impressively large or famous; they grow fastest in the south but live longest in the cold winters of Highland Scotland. Many wild trees are probably *B.* x *aurata*, the hybrid with Downy Birch. Penshurst, Kent (20)x127@0.2m under burr and fork (2001 Steve Young); Windsor (Savill Garden) 23x113@1m under fork (2000 OCJ); Kildrummy Castle Gardens, Aberdeen (28)x72 (1985 AFM).

'Fastigiata' Fastigiate Birch Rather rare. Alexandra Park, E Sussex 22x64 (2001 OCJ); Arley Arboretum, Worcs. (23)x56 (1991 AFM).

'Laciniata' Swedish Birch ('Dalecarlica') Very occasional; straight-stemmed and potentially the tallest birch (Taymouth Castle, Perth 30x52 (1970 AFM)). Knebworth House, Herts. 25x53 and 28x47 (1995 DGA).

'Purpurea' Purple Birch Quite frequent; scarcely attains 'tree' size.

Downy Birth, *Betula pubescens*, at Priory Park, Reigate.

'Tristis' Rare. Edinburgh RBG 14x78 (1997); Batsford Arboretum, Glos. 22x33 (2003 OCJ).

'Youngii' Young's Weeping Birch Abundant; grows very slowly into a small tree. Sheffield Park, E Sussex 12x48 (1994 OCJ), p1910.

B. platyphylla NE Asia. Very rare. Killerton, Devon (as label) 18x37 (2001 OCJ).

var. japonica – see *B. mandshurica* var. *japonica*.

var. szechuanica – see *B. szechuanica*.

B. populifolia Grey Birch E N America, 1750. Very rare. Westonbirt NA 17x45 and 20x37 (2002 OCJ).

B. pubescens Downy Birch Native. Abundant, replacing Silver Birch on wet or clay soils but much less often planted. Grows to almost identical sizes. Priory Park, Reigate, Surrey x129@1.2m under fork (2002 Steve

---

BIRCHES

With their gamut of glistening bark-colours, their autumnal golds and unique grace, birches are increasingly popular ornamentals. Producing a list of the biggest has some special headaches: forms from far corners of the world, introduced to one another in gardens, hybridise so promiscuously that identifying the next generation becomes impossible; plants from high mountains which characteristically hug the ground may grow tall and straight in a sheltered lowland arboretum. More air than tree even in the rudest of health, they also tend to die and vanish from one visit and the next.

Most are happiest on a light soil, and in 'continental' conditions with harsh winters.

Young); Tomies Wood, Kerry 12x143@0.6m under forks (2000 TROI); Westonbirt NA 28x52 (2002 OCJ) – slender shapely tree.

B. raddeana Caucasus, 1924. In one or two collections. Edinburgh RBG 12.5x33 (1997).

B. rockii China. In one or two collections. Batsford Arboretum, Glos. 19x47 (2003 OCJ) – x *pendula*?

B. schmidttii NE Asia, Japan, 1914. In some collections. Wisley 14x45 (2000 OCJ).

B. szechuanica Sichuan Birch W China, 1908. Rare. Hergest Croft (?) 20x76 and 21.5x56 (1995 VES).

B. x utahensis (*occidentalis* x *papyrifera*) In one or two collections. (Edinburgh RBG 10x31 (1985 AFM).)

B. utilis var. jacquemontii Jacquemont's Birch W Himalayas, by 1880. Now very frequent in various selections; will thrive on chalk. The largest (and oldest) may be hybrids with wild birches: Edinburgh RBG 16x87 (1991 AFM); Wakehurst Place 22x38 (1997 OCJ). 'Jermyns' is probably now the most popular and vigorous clone: Hillier Gardens 19.5x53 (2001 Harry James), p1961.

var. prattii C China; in some collections. Hergest Croft 23x43 (1995 VES).

var. utilis Himalayan Birch E Himalayas, 1849. Rather rare. Endsleigh, Devon (?) 20x57 and 23x46 (1995).

Broussonetia papyrifera Paper Mulberry E Asia; long grown here. Very rare; reaches tree-size in the warmest areas. Cambridge UBG 15x37+34 (1991 VES).

Butia capitata Pindo Palm Southern S America. Now planted in mild areas; a few old trees in Cornwall (Alverton, Penzance, at least 8m).

Buxus sempervirens Box Native. Very locally abundant on alkaline soils as a woodland shrub in S England; planted everywhere in hedges. Probably long lived but scarcely a 'tree'; to 11m. Bishop's Palace, Chichester, W Sussex 5x36@1m on short bole (1997 OCJ).

'Aureovariegata' Golden Box A rare, strong-growing clone. Faringdon church, Oxon. 5x26+ (1986 AFM).

Callitris rhomboidea Oyster Bay Pine Australia; in a few mild gardens. (Westlake, Devon (?) 14x39+32 (1984 AFM).)

Calocedrus decurrens Incense Cedar W USA, 1853. Increasingly frequent, growing more happily than most conifers in warm dry areas but longest-lived in the north and west. Doune Castle, Stirling 38x187 (1988 AFM) – four stems at 3m; much the tallest, but top damaged since; Castle Leslie, Monaghan 32x208@1.2m at forking (2000 TROI).

'Aureovariegata' Variegated Incense Cedar Rare. Bath BG, Somerset 20x64@0.6m under small limbs (2002 OCJ).

Calodendrum capense Cape Chestnut South Africa. A tree at Tresco Abbey, Cornwall, 14x97 (1984), froze in 1987.

Carpinus Hornbeams

Carpinus betulus Hornbeam Native to heavy clay soils in SE England; abundantly planted. Dunganstown Castle, Wicklow 18x181@1m on short bole (2000 TROI); Brocket Hall, Herts. 16x150@0.6-1m around 'waist' (2002 OCJ) – sparse; Lullingstone Park, Kent 19x148 (1999 OCJ) – hollow bole reduced to strips; Hurn Court, Dorset 20x146 around 'waist' (1985 AFM), p1740?; Brede, E Sussex 16x258@0.5m (1997 OCJ) – old hedge pleacher, the stems half-fused; Priory Park, Reigate, Surrey 31x68 (2000 OCJ); Knole Park, Kent 29x130 (1995 OCJ) – long bole; huge, broken limbs.

'Columnaris' Rare. Hillier Gardens 11.5x53@0.3m (2001 Harry James); City of Westminster Cemetery, London 12x29@0.8m (2001 OCJ) – leaning.

'Fastigiata' Fastigiate Hornbeam An abundant street tree. Kew RBG 20x94@1m (2001 OCJ), p1894; Colesbourne, Glos. (23)x51 (1984 AFM), p1902.

'Incisa' Cut-leaved Hornbeam Rather rare; often a giant bush. Beauport Park, E Sussex 12x111@0.6m under forks (1997 OCJ) – much broken; Quarry Park, Shropshire 15x103@1.1m (1998); Smeaton House, E Lothian 26x63 (1986 AFM) – reverting.

'Pendula' Weeping Hornbeam Very rare and not distinctive. Sezincote, Glos. 13x93@0.7m (2003 OCJ) – picturesque contorted tree, probably a sport; Kew RBG 16x53 (2001 OCJ). 'Pendula Dervaes' is an improvement: Hillier Gardens 9x33 (2001 Harry James).

'Purpurea' Purple Hornbeam Very rare; not at all distinctive. Kew RBG 19x51 (2001 OCJ).

'Quercifolia Aureus'. Glasnevin NBG 13x57 (1993).

'Variegata', also unmemorable, is not currently known to 'tree' size.

C. caroliniana American Hornbeam E N America, 1812. 10-20 in collections. Westonbirt NA 14x38 (2002 OCJ), p1929.

C. caucasica Caucasus. Kew RBG 8x26 (2001 OCJ), from 1967 seed.

C. fargesiana C China. Kew RBG 8x40@1m (2001 OCJ); ?

C. henryana C China, 1907. In one or two collections. Westonbirt NA 9x32 (2002 OCJ), p1923?; Kew RBG 11x25 (2001 OCJ), from Wilson 4443 (1912).

C. japonica Japanese Hornbeam Japan, 1895. In some collections. Oare House, Wilts. 8.5x29 (1994 VES).

C. laxiflora Japan, 1914. In a few collections. Borde Hill 9x32@0.4m under forks (1995 OCJ), from Wilson 7745.

var. macrostachya – see *C. viminea*.

C. orientalis Oriental Hornbeam SE Europe, Asia Minor, 1735. Now confined to a few big gardens. Kew RBG 19x53 (2001 OCJ), from 1908 seed.

C. tschonoskii Chonosuki's Hornbeam E Asia, Japan, 1901. 10-20 in collections. Kew RBG 14x63 (2001 OCJ), from 1907 seed; decaying; Wisley 12x76@0.4m under forks (2000 OCJ).

C. turczaninowii Turczaninow's Hornbeam NE Asia, 1914. A very rare but pretty hornbeam. Highdown, W Sussex 11x59 (1997 OCJ), p1914.

var. ovalifolia 1889. In a handful of collections. Burford Lodge, Surrey 11x45@1.2m (2000 OCJ).

The Hornbeam (*Carpinus betulus*) is easily taken for a slightly fragile, ailing Beech. It is native to heavy clay in south-east England, but grows at least as well when planted elsewhere in Britain and Ireland, or on lighter loams. The hard timber was used for chopping blocks, cog-wheels and as an exceptionally calorific firewood, and many trees were traditionally pollarded: that is, they were repeatedly cut above the height which browsing animals could reach, in order to provide a renewable supply of manageable poles. Pollarding has the side-effect of extending a tree's lifespan, as there is no longer a high crown to catch the wind. But through the twentieth century, pollarding was almost completely abandoned; hornbeams everywhere grew tall, their heavy but surprisingly weak timber rotted, and the old trees collapsed and died. (One at Easton Lodge, Essex, was x290cm in 1940; its remains were burnt down in 1956.) Pollarding has now been re-established by Sevenoaks District Council in Lullingstone Park, Kent, ensuring a future for hollow veterans like this tree.

C. viminea (*laxiflora* var. *macrostachya*) China, 1900. In a few collections. Wakehurst Place (?) 8x44@0.4m on lopped, sprouting bole (2002 OCJ); Kew RBG 11x29 (2001 OCJ).

***Carrierea calycina* Goat Horn Tree** W China, 1908. The only known mature tree, at Birr Castle (16x39 (2000 TROI), p1916) has flowered spectacularly since 1999.

***Carya cordiformis* Bitternut** E N America, 1766. Rather rare; the least heat-demanding hickory. Syston Park, Lincs. 23.5x85 (1983 AFM) – now dying back; Hollycombe, W Sussex 29x61 (1997 OCJ).
***C. glabra* Pignut** E N America, 1799. Rare. Trevorick, Cornwall (22)x62 (2003 Mrs Neale); Hollycombe, W Sussex 25x46 (1997 OCJ).
***C. illinoinensis* Pecan** E USA, 1760? A handful of trees; grows well only in the warmest areas. Cambridge UBG 19x47 (2002 DGA).
***C. laciniosa* Big Shellbark Hickory** E N America,
1804. Rare. Borde Hill 16x58 (1995 OCJ); Aldenham Park, Herts. 26x39 (2002 OCJ).
***C. ovalis* Red Hickory** E N America. Very rare. Kew RBG ('var. *odorata*') 23x70 (2001 OCJ).
***C. ovata* Shagbark Hickory** E N America, 1629. Rather rare. Reading University, Berks. (23)x82 (1993 Carol Hora); Hollycombe, W Sussex 27x40 (1997 OCJ).
***C. tomentosa* Mockernut Hickory** E N America, 1766. Very rare. Enys, Cornwall 21x54 (1996); Westonbirt NA 24x41 (2002 OCJ).

Castanea Sweet Chestnuts
***Castanea crenata* Japanese Sweet Chestnut** 1895. In a few collections. Bedgebury NP 9x38 (2002 OCJ), p1938.
***C. dentata* American Sweet Chestnut** By 1800. In some collections; not thriving here. Birr Castle 14x71 (2000 TROI); Hillier Gardens 16x36 (2001 Harry James).
C. henryi C China, 1900. In a few collections; seldom a

tree. Abbeyleix, Laois 10x48@0.9m (2000 TROI).

***C. mollissima* Chinese Sweet Chestnut**. A handful of trees. Buckingham Palace, London 7x40 (2000 OCJ) – ancient tree, with corkscrewed bole, long antedating the species' known 1903 introduction (unless misidentified); Kew RBG 11x35 (2001 OCJ).

C.* x *neglecta (*dentata* x *pumila*) North Carolina. Killerton, Devon 18x83 (2001 OCJ), p1935.

***C. pumila* Chinquapin** E N America, 1699. In one or two collections; nominally a bush. Hillier Gardens 12.5x29 (2001 Harry James).

***C. sativa* Sweet Chestnut** Abundant and thoroughly naturalised in S England. Canford School, Dorset 17x(433) (1992 AFM) – sprouty and forking; Three Sisters, Denbigh 10x(403)@0.55m under burrs (1984 Rex Wheeler) – short, hollow bole; Cowdray Park, W Sussex 25x364@0.5-2m under one huge limb but over buttresses (1997 OCJ) – huge healthy crown; Tortworth church, Glos. ('The Tortworth Chestnut') 17.5x350@1m-1.5m (1988 AFM); Milton Malsor, Northants. 19x349 (1987 AFM) – single sprouty trunk; Rossanagh, Wicklow 21x334@1.2m under burrs (1989 AFM), p1718; Rydal Hall, Cumbria ('The Rydale Chestnut') 23x333+36 (1995 DH); Kateshill House, Worcs. x326 (2002); Howletts Park, Kent ('The Howletts Chestnut') 23x337@0.3-1m under huge, wide limbs (2000 OCJ); Willesley Park, Leics. 15x323@1-1.2m (2001 DGA); Thenford House, Northants. 22x310@1m (1986 AFM); Keir House, Stirling 14x287@1m (1970 AFM) – burry; Petworth Park, W Sussex 35x226 (1997 OCJ) – long slanting bole.

'Albomarginata' Variegated Sweet Chestnut Rare. The largest have mostly reverted: Osterley Park, London 17x103 (2001 OCJ); Alderbrook Park, Surrey 21x86 (2000 OCJ).

'Aspleniifolia' Cut-leaved Sweet Chestnut. Rare. Bushy Park, London 14x118 (2001 OCJ) – much reverted; Westonbirt NA 25x94 (2002 OCJ).

'Aureomarginata' Very rare. Swiss Garden, Beds. 9.5x37 (2003 DGA) – propped.

'Gros-Merle'. Kew RBG 17x75 (2001 OCJ).

'Laciniata' ('Crispa') Very rare. Westonbirt NA 16x69 (2002 OCJ).

'Marron de Lyon' Very rare. Kew RBG 15x68, p1872, and ('Macrocarpa') 16x50 (2001 OCJ).

'Monstrosa'. Kew RBG 9x34 (2001 OCJ), p1873.

'Purpurea'. Not currently known to 'tree' size.

'Pyramidalis'. Kew RBG 13x50 (2001 OCJ), p1907.

C. seguinii China, 1853. In one or two collections; a bush in the wild. Borde Hill 18x67 (1995 OCJ), p1930.

Castanopsis concolor SW China. Caerhays 14x35 and 15x30 (1984 AFM), from Forrest 26848?

C. cuspidata Japan, Korea, 1830. In a few big gardens in milder areas. Muncaster Castle, Cumbria 10x36 (2000 DH).

Catalpa Bean Trees

***Catalpa bignonioides* Indian Bean Tree** SE USA, 1726. Confined to warm areas, where frequent. Inner Temple Garden, London 16x139@0.5m under burrs and wide fork (2001 OCJ); Palace Yard, London 11x129@1m under burrs, and 12x126 on good bole (2001 OCJ); Abington Park, Northants. 19.5x102 (2003 Steve Benamore) – fine bole.

'Aurea' Golden Bean Tree Locally occasional where summers are hottest. Hammersmith Cemetery, North Sheen, London 9x78 (2001 OCJ) – hung with chimes; Orleans House Gallery, London 14x70 (2001 OCJ).

'Nana' Very rare. A miniature tree if top-grafted: Lordship Recreation Ground, London 4x52 (2001 OCJ).

C. bungei N China, 1905. In some collections. Kew RBG 14x45 (2001 OCJ), from 1973 seed.

***C.* x *erubescens* 'J C Teas' Hybrid Bean** (*bignonioides* x *ovata*, 1891). Occasional in warm areas. Chilham Castle, Kent 17x123 (1995 OCJ); Fanhams Hall, Herts. 18x81 (2002 OCJ).

Champion Hybrid Bean (*Catalpa* x *erubescens* 'Purpurea') at Cambridge University Botanic Garden.

'Purpurea' Very rare. Cambridge UBG 11x93@0.7m/x75+46 (2002 DGA); Parliament Square, London 12x59 (2001 OCJ).

C. fargesii **Farges' Catalpa** China, by 1901. Rare, in warm areas. Kew RBG 18x73 (2001 OCJ), from 1907 seed; Eton College, Berks. 18x56 (1997 OCJ).

C. ovata **Yellow Catalpa** China, 1849. Rather rare; in warm areas. Sydney Gardens, Somerset 19x78 (2002 OCJ); Leatherhead, Surrey 12x78 (2000 OCJ).

C. speciosa **Western Catalpa** C USA, 1880. Very occasional; not exclusive to areas with hot summers. Radnor Gardens, London 18x121 (2001 OCJ) – hollow; grafted on Indian Bean at 1.4m.

Cedrela sinensis – see *Toona sinensis*.

Cedrus Cedars

Cedrus atlantica **Atlas Cedar** Atlas Mountains, by 1840. Occasional. Dryburgh Abbey, Scottish Borders 24x187 (1992 AFM); Whitfield, Herefords. (38)x114 (1995 VES).

'Aurea' **Golden Atlas Cedar** Very rare. Cirencester Abbey, Glos. 19x107@? (1989 JW).

f. *fastigiata* **Fastigiate Atlas Cedar** Rare. Kingsway Gardens, Hants. 19x64 (1983 AFM); Bedgebury NP 21x59 (1995 OCJ), p1926. (Mount Usher, Wicklow 22x86 (1975 AFM).)

f. *glauca* **Blue Atlas Cedar** Abundant. Eastnor Castle, Herefords. 32x181 (1984 AFM); Brockhampton Park, Herefords. 38.5x136 (1978 AFM) – much the tallest, but top lost since.

'Glauca Pendula' **Weeping Blue Atlas Cedar** Rare and tricky to grow. Glasnevin NBG 6.5x49 (2003 DGA) – planted around 1875; not the usual clone?

C. brevifolia **Cyprus Cedar** Mt Paphos, Cyprus, 1879. Rare. Windsor (Valley Gardens) 22x71 (2000 OCJ); Wakehurst Place 23x54 (1997 OCJ).

C. deodara **Deodar** W Himalayas, 1831. Abundant; tending to prefer warm but humid areas. Several rather indistinct foliage variants are grown; Ballykealy House, Carlow 23x208 over scar (2000 TROI); K Club, Kildare 29x200 (2000 TROI); Eastnor Castle, Herefords. 38x169 (1984 AFM).

'Aurea' **Golden Deodar** Rare. Stratford Park, Glos. (?) 24x108@? (1991 JW); Endsleigh, Devon 27x95 (1995).

'Pendula' **Weeping Deodar** Rare. Hillier Gardens 15x27 (2002 Harry James).

C. libani **Cedar of Lebanon** E Mediterranean; long grown here. Quite frequent as an older tree. All the largest trunks are variously inflated by low forks; the Goodwood tree is probably the most impressive. Gray House, Angus 28x346@0.5m (1986 AFM); Eden Hall, Cumbria 33x331@1m (1995 DH), p1617?; Painshill Park, Surrey 29x326@0.2-0.6m (2000 OCJ); Goodwood, W Sussex 23x289@1m around 'waist' (1997 OCJ), p1761; Hampden House, Bucks. (39)x304@1m (1999 Tim Oliver).

'Aurea' **Golden Cedar of Lebanon** Very rare. Larchfield, Down 16x68 (2000 TROI).

'Comte de Dijon' Very rare; semi-dwarf. Sheffield Park, E Sussex 6x37 over low branches (1994 OCJ); Hergest Croft 11x33+32 (1995 VES).

ssp. *stenocoma* Anatolia, 1938? A few young trees. Hillier Gardens 13x38 (2002 Harry James).

Celtis australis **Nettle Tree** Mediterranean, 1796. Now very rare. Needs summer heat to grow well. Shirley, Hants. 14x97@1m under fork (1993); Lacock Abbey, Wilts. 15x76 (1987 AFM) – three stems, splitting.

C. biondii C China, 1902. (Kew RBG 11x34 (1967 AFM).)

C. bungeana N China, 1882. Young plants in some big gardens. (Kew RBG 14x43 1991 AFM).)

C. caucasica **Caucasian Nettle Tree** Bulgaria, W Asia, 1885. Kew RBG 12x60 (2001 OCJ) – original.

C. glabrata W Asia, 1870. In one or two collections. (Borde Hill 9x29 (1984 AFM), p1934.)

C. jessoensis Japan, Korea, 1892. In a few collections. Cambridge UBG 15.5x48 (2002 DGA).

C. labilis China, 1907. Borde Hill (?) 8x37 (1995 OCJ), p1934.

C. laevigata **Sugarberry** SE USA, 1811. Kew RBG (var. *smallii*) 13x64 (2001 OCJ), from 1912 seed.

C. occidentalis **Hackberry** N America, 1656. Rare; needs summer warmth. Most big trees here are var. *crassifolia*. Charlton Park, London 16x66 (2001 OCJ).

C. sinensis NE Asia, Japan, 1910. In some collections. Kew RBG 11x27@1m (2001 OCJ), from 1976 seed.

C. tenuifolia **Georgia Hackberry** SE USA. In one or two collections. Kew RBG 9x32 (2001 OCJ), from 1900 seed.

Cephalotaxus fortunei **Fortune's Plum Yew** C China, 1848. Rare; best in warm but humid areas. Knocklofty House, Tipperary 7.5x77@0.1m/x48++ (2000 TROI); Belvedere, Westmeath 11x28+ (2000 TROI).

C. harringtonia **Plum Yew** NE Asia, Japan, 1844. Very rare ('Fastigiata' is an occasional bush). Cheslyn Gardens, Herts. 8x25 (2001 OCJ) – slender and straight.

Cercidiphyllum japonicum **Katsura** China, Japan, 1881. Occasional; likes a moist soil and shelter. (Single-stemmed trees are more likely to be the Chinese var. *sinense*.) Wisley 15x73 on good bole (2000 OCJ); Endsleigh, Devon 25x48++ (1995).

C. magnificum Japan. Very rare and scarcely to 'tree' size yet.

Cercis chinensis **Chinese Redbud** A small tree in some big gardens. (Nymans, W Sussex 13x31 (1983 AFM).)

C. occidentalis **Western Redbud** California. Oxford BG, Oxon. 7x31 (1996 VES).

C. racemosa China, 1907. In some collections. Highdown, W Sussex 8x35 (1997 OCJ); Hillier Gardens 12x30 (2001 Harry James).

C. siliquastrum **Judas Tree** E Mediterranean; long grown here. Quite frequent in warm areas. Worthing Crematorium, W Sussex 12x188@0.1m (1996 OCJ); Vernon Grange, Kent 11x64 (1995 OCJ), p1927 and remarkable upstanding; Cheltenham College, Glos. 16x60@? (1989 JW).

A Cedar of Lebanon (*Cedrus libani*) has long been the essential accessory to a stately home. Cedars are long-lived, but by no means immortal, and have become a classic demonstration of how unfortunate can be the misconception that many trees grow very slowly over a very long period. Few landowners have recently thought it apropos to plant young ones – which do in fact grow up with great and gratifying vigour. Today's biggest and oldest have forks and low branches which make comparisons odious. Perhaps the most imposing was planted in 1811 at Higham House, East Sussex, and blew down in 1987. It had about 30 trunks radiating from a base which, according to Alexander Howard in 1947, was 5 metres thick. The tallest (at Leaton Knolls, Shropshire, and 42 × 113 in 1981) was unusual in being spire-shaped, with a long bole; it was blown down in 1993. Cedars are also notoriously difficult to height, because of the distractions posed by high flat branches spreading towards the observer. Today's champion grows at Eden Hall, Cumbria.

Chamaecyparis False Cypresses

Chamaecyparis formosensis Taiwan Cypress 1910. About 100 trees. Fota, Cork 23x81@0.8m on short bole (1999 TROI), p1916; Hergest Croft 18x77 (1995 VES), p1919.

C. lawsoniana Lawson Cypress Oregon, California, 1854. Abundant; self-seeding in humid areas, where it continues to grow for longest. Coollattin, Wicklow 27.5x159 on single bole (2001 AF); Gregynog, Powys 29x194 (1993 VES) – 3 stems from 2m; Westonbirt NA 28x219@0.4m under narrow forks (2002 OCJ), p1878 – with additional wide low limbs; Ardkinglas, Argyll 41x81 (1989 AFM), p1875; slender.

'Albomaculata' Rather rare. The name is used here for a vigorous creamy-yellow-splashed clone distributed by Veitch in 1886: Escot, Devon 20x63 (2001 OCJ); Monteviot, Scottish Borders 22x57 (1983 AFM).

'Albovariegata' Rare; used here for trees with bright silver splashes. Stonefield House, Argyll 17.5x61 (1981 AFM); Gareloch House, Dunbartons. 23x55 (1979 AFM) – slender. Several very occasional clones, more finely variegated in white or yellow, tend not to grow large.

'Allumii' Abundant in small gardens, but becomes big: Brahan, Highland (12)x100 (1989 AFM), p1901; Glamis Castle, Angus 30x78 (1981 AFM).

'Blue Jacket' Rare? Bedgebury NP 16x43 (1995 OCJ), p1925; Westonbirt NA 18x36 (2002 OCJ) – slender.

'Columnaris' Abundant; can be very vigorous: Bedgebury NP 20x72 (1999 OCJ), p1955; Glebe House, Godstone, Surrey 20x71 (2000 OCJ) – moved when 8m tall.

'Depkenii' Very rare. Glasnevin NBG 22x47 (1992).

'Ellwoodii' Abundant; scarcely to tree-size. Guildford Cemetery, Surrey 11x24+21 (2000 OCJ).

'Erecta Viridis' Very frequent as an older tree; the most vigorous cultivar. Gliffaes, Powys 28x180@1m under forks (1995 VES); Snaigow House, Perth 28.5x180@0.5m under forks (1999 Donald Rodger) – layered; Bodnant, Conwy (33)x140 (1990 AFM), p1876?

'Filifera' Very rare. Dyffryn Gardens, Glamorgan 12x36 (1997 OCJ); Bedgebury NP 14x32@1.3m (1995 OCJ), p1925.

'Filiformis' Very rare. Sheffield Park, E Sussex 19x59 (1994 OCJ), p1924.

'Fletcheri' Abundant; and no dwarf: Wisley 15x67@0.1m (2000 OCJ); Bedgebury NP 13x40@1m (1995 OCJ), p1955.

'Fraseri' Rare. Stourhead, Wilts. 25x85 (1987 AFM).

'Glauca Pendula' Very rare. Cawdor Castle, Highland 32x95 (1980 AFM).

'Golden King' Rare. Bedgebury NP 16x48 (1995 OCJ), p1943.

'Gracilis Pendula' Very rare. Derreen, Kerry 24x96 (1966 AFM); Gosford Castle, Armagh 28x79 (1976 AFM).

'Grayswood Pillar' Abundant? Grayswood Hill, Surrey 18m (1998 OCJ) – original.

'Green Pillar' Rare? Bedgebury NP 16x46 (1995 OCJ), p1943.

'Hillieri' Rather rare. Grayswood Hill, Surrey 12x(38) (1998 OCJ); Kew RBG 16x22 (2001 OCJ), sourced 1923.

'Intertexta' Rather rare. St Roche's Arboretum, W Sussex 30x81 (1997 OCJ).

'Kilmacurragh' Rare. Mount Usher, Wicklow 20x99 (1992 AFM).

'Lanei Aurea' ('Lane') Abundant as a semi-dwarf, but does much better in a woodland soil: Crarae, Argyll 16x64 (1987 AFM); Wisley 19x(50) (2000 OCJ).

'Lutea' Abundant as an older tree. Brahan, Highland 22x74 (1989 AFM), p1901 as 'Aurea Nova'; Murthly Castle, Perth 26x43 (1983 AFM).

'Lycopodioides' Very rare. Kew RBG 11x26 (2001 OCJ).

'Naberi' Rare but very striking. Grayswood Hill, Surrey 16x36 (1998 OCJ).

'New Silver' Very rare. Abbeyleix, Laois 18x66 (1985 AFM).

'Pembury Blue' Abundant; often semi-dwarf. Hillier Gardens 13x34+29++ (2001 Harry James).

'Pendula Vera' Very rare. Ballathie House, Perth 23x86 (1984 AFM); Glencormac, Wicklow 26x86 (1991 AFM); Glamis Castle, Angus 29x47 (1981 AFM).

'Pottenii' Abundant as a semi-dwarf, but can grow fast: Nymans, W Sussex 18x66 (1996 OCJ), p1940; leans.

'Rosenthalii' Very rare. St Clere Pinetum, Kent 17x(75) (1999 OCJ); Priestwood, Bucks. 20x36 (1984 AFM).

'Silver Queen' Occasional. Fairburn, Highland 28x90 (1987 AFM).

'Smithii' Occasional? Westonbirt NA 17x40 (2002 OCJ).

'Stewartii' Quite frequent. Dochfour, Highland 16x71 and 22x66 (1992 AFM).

'Triomf van Boskoop' Quite frequent. Caledon Castle, Tyrone 28x116 (1983 AFM); Fairburn, Highland 30x90 (1987 AFM).

'Westermannii' Occasional. Fairburn, Highland 29x92 (1987 AFM).

'Winston Churchill' Abundant. Grayswood Hill, Surrey 16x(40)@2m over one limb (1998 OCJ).

'Wisselii' Frequent. Avondale, Wicklow 24x135 (1991 AFM); Frensham Hall estate, Surrey 26x(70) (2000 OCJ).

'Youngii' Rare. Ardross Castle, Highland 21x100 (1989 AFM).

C. nootkatensis – see *Xanthocyparis nootkatensis*.

C. obtusa Hinoki Cypress S Japan, 1861. Occasional. Ardkinglas, Argyll (26)x84 (1991 AFM).

'Albospica' Very rare. Bicton Park, Devon 21x75@1m under narrow fork (2001 OCJ) – reverted?

'Aurea' Now rare. Cowdray Park, W Sussex 17x82@1.2m under narrow fork (1997 OCJ); Bicton Park, Devon 18x69 and 23x56 (2001 OCJ).

'Crippsii' Very frequent. Kilmacurragh, Wicklow 17x63+54 (1980 AFM); Tilgate Park, W Sussex 19x62 (2002 OCJ), p1905; Lancrigg Hotel, Cumbria 22x48+44 (1995 DH).

'Erecta' Very rare. Bedgebury NP 11x51@0m under forks (1995 OCJ), p1929.

'Filicoides' Fern-spray Cypress Rare. Endsleigh, Devon x87@0.3m? (1991 AFM); Annamoe, Wicklow 15x45+32 (2000 TROI).

var. formosana Taiwan, 1910. Scarcely to 'tree' size in a few collections.

Judas Trees (*Cercis siliquastrum*) are grown for their cerise, sweet-pea flowers, an extraordinary and endearing sight in May as they bud from the gnarled bark of the bole itself.
The grounds of Muntham House in West Sussex were long neglected before their development as Worthing Crematorium, and the vast Judas Tree near the site of the house is a perfect example of how most trees revel in total neglect. Six moss- and fern-encrusted trunks snake outwards from a hollow base, rooting along their lengths and covering 25m.

'Lycopodioides' Rare. Stonefield House, Argyll (18)x87 (1991 AFM); Tregrehan, Cornwall 19.5x57 (2002 Tom Hudson).

'Magnifica' Rare. Bedgebury NP 14x64@0.3m under forks (p1929), and 13x43 (1995 OCJ).

'Nana Gracilis' Abundant; grows very slowly into a small tree. The Watergardens, London 11x52@0.6m under branches (2001 OCJ).

'Tetragona Aurea' Abundant; grows slowly into a small tree. Tregrehan, Cornwall 18x41 (2002 Tom Hudson); Wisley 12x88@0.1-0.5m under narrow forks (2000 OCJ).

***C. pisifera* Sawara Cypress** S Japan, 1861. Occasional. Leckmelm, Highland 15x93 (1991 AFM); Borden Wood, W Sussex 25x59 (1997 OCJ).

'Aurea' Rare. K Club, Kildare 17.5x76 (2000 TROI); Wakehurst Place 23x56 (1997 OCJ).

'Boulevard' Abundant; usually a dwarf. Hillier Gardens 10x45@1.2m (2001 Harry James).

'Filifera' Thread Cypress Occasional; tends to revert. Endsleigh, Devon 18x84 (1991 AFM); Castle Leslie, Monaghan 21x79 (2000 TROI); Minterne, Dorset 21x78@0.3m under fork (1996).

'Filifera Aurea' Golden Thread Cypress Frequent. Tregrehan, Cornwall 15x49 (2002 Tom Hudson).

'Gold Spangle' Very rare. Hillier Gardens 8.4x26 (2002 Ron Holley).

'Plumosa' Abundant. Golden Grove, Carmarthen 22x102 under narrow fork (1993), p1863; Aldershot Cemetery, Hants. 23x95 (2002 OCJ) – good 4m bole; Cowdray Park, W Sussex 25x90@1m under fork (1997 OCJ) – reverting at top; Balloch CP, Dunbartons. (27)x42 (1985 AFM).

'Plumosa Argentea' Rare. Powerscourt, Wicklow (?) 17x87 (2000 TROI); Fota, Cork 21x63 (1994 DGA).

'Plumosa Aurea' Frequent; tends to revert to 'Plumosa'. Heckfield Place, Hants. 23x91@1m (1982 AFM); Powerscourt, Wicklow 21x82 (2000 TROI); Ardkinglas, Argyll 25x64 (1991 AFM). Semi-dwarf variants are commoner.

'Plumosa Flavescens' Rare? Bedgebury NP 9x36 (1997 OCJ), p1931.

'Pygmaea' Frequent? Bedgebury NP 12x33 (2002 OCJ), p1935.

'Squarrosa' Frequent. Lower Coombe Royal, Devon (20)x94 (1988 AFM) – top lost since; Borden Wood, W Sussex 26x86@0.8m under fork (1997 OCJ).

'Squarrosa Intermedia' Very rare? Bedgebury NP 11m (1995 OCJ).

'Squarrosa Sulphurea' Abundant; scarcely to 'tree' size.
C. thyoides White Cypress E USA, 1680? Rare.
Probably prefers a continental climate. Brookwood
Cemetery, Surrey 18x40 (2000 OCJ) – narrow column;
Bedgebury NP ('Glauca') 12x51 (1995 OCJ), p1928.

Chionanthus retusus Chinese Fringe Tree 1845.
Very rare. Has grown into a shapely tree at Kew RBG:
10x39 (2001 OCJ), from 1922 seed.

Chrysolepis chrysophylla Golden Chestnut W
USA, 1844. Very rare. Mount Usher, Wicklow (14)x59
(1989 AFM). (Wexham Place, Bucks. 18x31 (1978 AFM).)

Cinnamomum camphora Camphor Tree Malaya
to Japan, 1727. Survives in the mildest, warmest regions.
Overbecks, Devon 8x48@1m+40 (1988 AFM) – bigger
tree frozen; Westlake, Devon 14x39+32 (1984 AFM).
C. glanduliferum E Asia. A smaller plant in the mildest
areas.

Citronella gongonha Naranjillo (*Villaresia mucronata*)
S Andes, c1840. Very rare. (Glasnevin NBG 7x27 (1993) –
felled.)

Cladrastis kentukea Yellow-wood (*C. lutea*) SE USA,
1812. Rare; likes hot summers. Tilgate Park, W Sussex
12x61@0.5m on short bole (2002 OCJ); Woolborough Hill,
Devon 10.5x53 (2002 Graham Joyce); Kew RBG
11x48@1.2m on short bole (2001 OCJ), from 1923 seed.
C. platycarpa Japan. An imposing tree in a few
collections. Kew RBG 24x109 (2001 OCJ), from 1873 seed.
C. sinensis Chinese Yellow-wood China, 1901. Very
rare. Kew RBG 9x48@1.1m (2001 OCJ); Newcastle
House, Glamorgan 13x28 (1990 AFM).
C. wilsonii W China, 1910. Wisley 9x36 (2000 OCJ).

Clethra arborea Madeira, 1784. Reaches tree-size only
in the mildest areas; naturalised in Kerry. Glan Leam,
Kerry 15x63 and 17x50 (2001 AF).

Cordyline australis Cabbage Palm New Zealand,
1823. Abundant away from cold parts; growing fast but
surviving long enough to make a big tree only in the mildest
areas. Glendalough House, Kerry 10x104@1.2m (2001
AF); Cappoquin House, Waterford 11x82 (2000 TROI);
Glan Leam, Kerry 15x43 (2001 AF).

Cornus Dogwoods
Cornus capitata Bentham's Cornel Himalayas, 1825.
Tender; to tree-size in the mildest areas. Glengarriff church,
Cork 11x57@1.4m (2001 AF); Mount Usher, Wicklow (?)
(18)x51@0.3m (1989 AFM).
C. controversa Table Dogwood China, Japan, by 1880.
Rather rare, but grows well everywhere. Forde Abbey,
Dorset 14x52+37+32, and 19x46+42 (1993).
'Variegata' Wedding-cake Tree Occasional, and more
vigorous than is often assumed. Errol House, Perth 12x34
(1986 AFM).
C. florida Flowering Dogwood E USA, by 1730.

Rather rare and scarcely to 'tree' size: needs summer heat.
Most here are f. *rubra*.
C. kousa NE Asia, Japan, 1875. Very occasional. The
largest are var. *chinensis*: Tilgate Park, W Sussex 8x40@1.1m
(2002 OCJ); Leonardslee, W Sussex 10x27 (1996 OCJ).
C. macrophylla Big-leaved Cornel Himalayas to
Japan, 1827. Very rare. Grayswood Hill, Surrey 12x59
(1998 OCJ) – hollow.
C. mas Cornelian Cherry S Europe; long grown here.
Quite frequent; reaching tree-size when summers are
warm. Peckover House, Cambs. (9)x51@0.9m under fork
(1997); Kew RBG 13x29+ (2001 OCJ).
C. 'Norman Hadden' (*capitata* x *kousa*?) In a few big
gardens. Knightshayes, Devon 9x36 near base (2003).
C. nuttallii Pacific Dogwood W N America, 1835.
Rare; short-lived here. Hanchurch Yews, Staffs. 8x36
(1995); Hillier Gardens 13m (2002) – bushy.
C. officinalis Japan, Korea, 1877. In a few collections;
often a bush. Kew RBG 9x34 (2001 OCJ).
C. sanguinea Dogwood Native; frequent on richer soils
in England, Wales and Ireland. A 'tree' sized example has
yet to be measured.
C. walteri China, 1907. In a few big gardens. Wakehurst
Place 10x43 and 15x27 (1997 OCJ).

Corylus Hazels
Corylus avellana Hazel Native. Abundant.
Coldharbour, Surrey 10x45@0.6-1m+40+33++ (2000
OCJ) – first stem leans; second rotting; others younger;
Quinloch Wood, Stirling 5x44 below branching at 1.4m
(1985); Rookery Wood, Penshurst, Kent 10x95@0.3m
around 'waist' (2001 Steve Young); The Warren, Clanna,
Glos. 15x23 (+?) (1992 JW).
'Aurea' Golden Hazel Rather rare but vigorous: York
House, London 11x50@0.8m on short single bole (2001
OCJ).
'Pendula' Weeping Hazel Rare but vigorous. Fanhams
Hall, Herts. 5x52 under graft on *C. maxima* (?) (2002 OCJ)
– very knobbly bole.
C. chinensis Chinese Hazel 1900. In a few big gardens.
Blairquhan, Ayr 8x39 (1993 VES), p1940. (Mount Usher,
Wicklow 17x43 (1966 AFM).)
C. colurna Turkish Hazel SE Europe, W Asia, 1582.
Quite frequent. Syon Park, London 18x100 (2002 OCJ) –
9m bole; Abbey Gardens, Bury St Edmunds, Suffolk
x126@0.8m-1m/x90@1.3m+60cm@1.7m (2001 DGA)
– cut back; Brocklesby Park, Lincs. (26)x72 (1993).
C. x colurnoides (*avellana* x *colurna*) Very rare. Kew RBG
9x39 (2001 OCJ).
C. jacquemontii Jacquemont's Hazel Himalayas,
1898. Edinburgh RBG 23x71 (1997).
C. maxima Filbert Balkans, 1759. Very occasional in
old gardens and a few commercial nutteries; usually a bush
but more vigorous than Hazel. Charleston Manor, E Sussex
7x43@0.9m on short bole (1994 OCJ) – rather weeping;
Chilham Castle, Kent 12x30++ (1995 OCJ).
C. x vilmorinii (*avellana* x *chinensis*). Hergest Croft 20x59
(1995 VES).

Cotinus obovatus Chittam Wood SE USA, 1882. Very

Cornus includes some of our most charming trees. Cornelian Cherry (*Cornus mas*) flowering in February in a Bedfordshire garden.

rare. Reaches tree-size in hot areas. Kew RBG (hybrid?) 9x58@0.3m/x30+29+23 (2001 OCJ).

***Cotoneaster frigidus* Himalayan Tree Cotoneaster** 1824. Frequent; preferring warm but humid areas. Lisnavagh Gardens, Carlow 15x60 (2000 TROI) – x111@0.3m.

'Cornubia' Occasional? Herstmonceux Castle, E Sussex 11x48@1.2m under graft (2001 OCJ).

C. glaucophyllus* f. *serotinus W China, 1907. Rare. Bath BG, Somerset 7x32@1m++ (2002 OCJ) – bushy.

C. multiflorus NW China, 1837. Scarcely a tree: Westonbirt NA 6x35 on a stem of *C. frigidus* (2002 OCJ).

***C. x watereri* Waterer's Cotoneaster** (*frigidus* x *henryanus*, 1928) Abundant in various forms. Coleton Fishacre, Devon 6x57 (1984 AFM).

+ *Crataegomespilus dardarii* Bronvaux Medlar (*Crataegus monogyna* + *Mespilus germanica*). Very rare; scarcely reaching 'tree' size.

Crataegus Thorns

***Crataegus altaica* Altai Mountain Thorn** C Asia. Scarcely surviving to make a tree – probably needs a continental climate. Cambridge UBG 8x26 (1991 VES).

C. arkansana Arkansas, 1902. Dyffryn Gardens, Glamorgan 5x26 (1997 OCJ).

C. arnoldiana NE USA, 1901. Very rare. (Oxford BG, Oxon. 8x31 (1986 AFM).)

***C. azarolus* Azarole** Mediterranean. Long grown here but now very rare and not known to 'tree' size. Some may be hybrids.

C. champlainensis N America, 1901. In a few collections. Birr Castle 9.5x32 (2000 TROI).

C. chrysocarpa E N America. Probably one of the less rare and strongest-growing 'Scarlet Thorns': Hawkinge Cemetery, Kent 8x45 (1999 OCJ).

var. *phoenicea* In a few collections. Birr Castle 9x25 (2000 TROI).

C. coccinioides E USA, 1883. Now very rare. (Cobham Hall, Kent 14x50 (1982 AFM).)

***C. crus-galli* Cockspur Thorn** E N America, 1691. Now rare. Wells House, Wexford (?) 7.5x45 (2000 TROI). (Golders Hill Park, London x58 (1920 A D Webster).)

C. x dippeliana (*punctata* x *tanacetifolia*?) Very rare. Southgate Cemetery, London 6x39 (2001 OCJ); Hillier Gardens 8.2m (2001 Harry James).

C. douglasii N America. In a few collections. (Cambridge UBG 7x31 (1991) p1953, died 2002.)

C. durobrivensis E N America, 1901. In a few collections. (Alexandra Park, E Sussex 11x28++ (1983 AFM), p1935, blown 1987.)

C. ellwangeriana N America, 1900. Probably one of the less rare 'Scarlet Thorns'. Goodmayes Park, London 8x30 (2001 OCJ) – ?

C. flabellata E N America, 1830. Pembroke Lodge Gardens, London 7x32+ (2001 OCJ) – leans.

***C. x grignonensis* Grignon's Thorn** (*stipulacea* x ?) 1873? A rather rare but handsome thorn. Alexandra Park, E Sussex 8x30@1.2m (2001 OCJ), p1935.

C. heldreichii Greece, the Crimea. Very rare. (Wisley 7x27@0.9m (2000 OCJ) – died 2001.)

C. henryi C China, 1909. In one or two collections. Borde Hill (?) 5x35@0.4m (1995 OCJ) – p.1941 from Forrest 30713; hung up.

C. heterophylla Armenia. Now very rare. (Mill Hill School, London 11x53@1m (1920 A D Webster).)

C. jonesiae NE N America. Dyffryn Gardens, Glamorgan 6x25 (1997 OCJ).

***C. laciniata* Oriental Thorn** Asia Minor, 1810. Very occasional. Faversham Recreation Ground, Kent 5x42 (1999 OCJ).

***C. laevigata* Midland Thorn** Native. Abundant on heavy clays in ancient woods and old hedges in S England. Regent's Park, London 9x61@0.6m on short single bole (2001 OCJ) – cut back; Mortlake Green, London 8x52@1.1m (2001 OCJ); Museum Gardens, Yorks. 12x39 (1989 AFM).

'Gireoudii' Very rare. Haberdashers' Aske's School, Herts. 4x30@1m (2002 OCJ).

'Masekii' Rare. Waterlow Park, London 7x32 (2002 OCJ).

'Paul's Scarlet' Red May Abundant and big-growing. Kensington Palace, London 6x51@1.2m (2001 OCJ) – largest of series clipped into domes; Faversham Recreation Ground, Kent 12x50 (1999 OCJ).

'Plena' Rather rare. Watling Park, London 8x50 (2002

HAWTHORNS

Hawthorns are perhaps the commonest trees in the wild: indispensably prickly in hedgerows, tolerant of deep shade, quick to colonise abandoned fields, and shunning only the lightest sands. It is easy to think of them as shrubs; in fact, they can be immensely long-lived and feature more than any other species as landmark trees in Dark Age charters. They never build enormous boles: veteran trees crumble away as fast as they grow, and the Hethel Old Thorn (Hethel, Norfolk), ×108cm in 1841 (Grigor), is now quite healthy but only ×78cm (Ted Palmer). The ancient hollow tree in St Mary's Quad (St Andrews University, Fife), 5×77 in 1992 (VES), is a survivor of a clone called 'Regina' – all scions of one in the Regent Murray's garden near Edinburgh under which Mary Queen of Scots spent much time.

Common Hawthorn's elusive cousin, the Midland Thorn, is confined as a native to ancient woods and hedge-lines on heavy clay in southern England. Wild trees of much stature have never been found, and the few imposing planted examples may be reversions from popular flowering forms. Many of these are likely to be hybrids with Common Hawthorn.

Tolerant of heavy clay and hard weather, and almost vandal-proof, many exotic thorns should make ideal urban trees. None grow large; all have showy flowers and fruit. But many are represented today only by old trees in the odd public park. Trees of the American Red Haw group are particularly hard to distinguish, and some of the identifications here may not be right.

OCJ); Hillier Gardens 11x27 (2001 Harry James).

'Punicea' Rare. Waterlow Park, London 5x42@1.1m (2002 OCJ) – trunk decaying; Holborn, London (St Andrew's church) 7x(40) around lumps and masonry (2001 OCJ).

'Punicea Flore Pleno' Occasional. Winchelsea church, E Sussex 8x51 (1994 OCJ); Gladstone Park, London 9x45 (2001 OCJ) – half a torn bole remains.

C. x lavallei Hybrid Cockspur Thorn (*crus-galli* x *stipulacea*, about 1870.) Frequent. Luton Hoo, Beds. 9x53 (1992 DGA); Bath BG, Somerset x53 (2002 OCJ) – nearly dead; Valentines Park, London 11x46 (2001 OCJ).

C. macracantha N America, 1819. Very rare. Birr Castle x26 (1988 AFM).

C. mollis Red Haw C N America; long grown here; almost extinct? Knighton Park, Leics. 8x39 (1985 AFM).

C. monogyna Hawthorn Native; abundant. Ducklington, Oxon. x88@? (1988 Allen Meredith); Springfield House, Carlow 12x84 (1999 TROI) – poor condition; Avenue House, London 15x31 (2001 OCJ) – drawn up.

'Biflora' Glastonbury Thorn Very rare. Kew RBG 5x33 under graft (2001 OCJ) – died back.

'Multiplex' Rare. Stanmer Park, E Sussex 7x30 (2002 OCJ), p1964; Mallet Court, Somerset ('Flore Plena') 8x25 (1989 AFM).

'Nordica Splendens'. Cambridge UBG 9.5x29+20+ (1994 VES).

'Pendula' Weeping Thorn Very rare. Buckingham Palace, London 9x43 (2000 OCJ) – sparse.

'Pink May' Very rare. Crittenden, Kent 6x29 (1997 OCJ).

'Stricta' Fastigiate Thorn Frequent. Bute Park, Glamorgan 12x41@0.5m (1990 JW); Dyffryn Gardens, Glamorgan 11x32 (1997 OCJ).

C. nigra Hungarian Thorn 1819. A few trees known. Greenwich Park, London 6x45 (2001 OCJ).

C. oliveriana SE Europe. City of Westminster Cemetery, London 6x27 (2001 OCJ).

C. oxyacantha – see *C. laevigata*.

C. pedicellata Scarlet Haw NE N America, 1683. One of the less rare 'Scarlet Thorns'. Golders Hill Park, London (?) 9x35 (2001 OCJ).

C. pentagyna E Europe. A few trees known. Kew RBG 7x39@1.2m (2001 OCJ).

C. persimilis N America. Kew RBG 5x35@1.2m (2001 OCJ), from 1949 seed.

'Prunifolia' Broad-leaved Cockspur Thorn By 1797; very frequent. Cirencester College, Glos. 7.5x49@? (1989 JW).

C. pinnatifida Big-leaved Thorn NE Asia, 1860. Increasingly rare. Clissold Park, London 8x45@1.7m above graft (2001 OCJ) – dying back; Pymmes Park, London 9x43 (2001 OCJ); Maryon Park, London (var. *major*) 8x42@1.3m (2001 OCJ) – broken.

C. prunifolia – see *C. persimilis* 'Prunifolia'.

C. punctata Spotted Thorn E N America, 1746. Locally very occasional; a particularly vigorous, handsome species. Hampstead Heath, London 5x66 (2001 OCJ) – spread 12m; Dyffryn Gardens, Glamorgan 12x42 (1997 OCJ).

f. aurea. Hillier Gardens 8x26 (2001 Harry James).

C. schraderiana Greece, the Crimea. In one or two collections. Westonbirt NA 5x27 (2002 OCJ).

C. spathulata SE USA, 1806. Westonbirt NA 5x28@1.2m under graft (2002 OCJ).

C. straminea An American 'Scarlet Thorn' – probably now almost extinct here.

C. submollis NE N America. One of the less rare 'Scarlet Thorns'. Singleton Park, Glamorgan 7x30 (2000 OCJ).

C. succulenta An American 'Scarlet Thorn' – probably now very rare here.

C. tanacetifolia Tansy-leaved Thorn Asia Minor, 1789. Rare, but potentially large-growing. Warnham

Court, W Sussex 8x48 (1997 OCJ); Lindridge Park, Devon 10x40 (2001 OCJ). (Brocklesby Park, Lincs. 9x81 (1977 AFM) – half a torn bole.)
C. wattiana C Asia. In a few collections. (Thorp Perrow, Yorks. 9x31 (1975 AFM).)

X Crataemespilus grandiflora Medlar-thorn (*Crataegus laevigata?* x *Mespilus germanica*, by 1800) Rather rare. Brynmill Park, Glamorgan 10x49 (2000 OCJ).

Crinodendron patagua Patagua Chile, 1901. Very rare; to tree size in mild areas. Glencormac, Wicklow 14x77@0.2m (2000 TROI).

Cryptomeria fortunei – see *C. japonica var. sinensis*
C. japonica Japanese Red Cedar Japan, 1861 (as 'Lobbii'). Occasional. Needs humidity but tends to do best when summers are warm. Caher House, Clare x186 above two large limbs (2002 AF); Boconnoc, Cornwall ('Lobbii') 29x(181) on fine bole (1991 AFM); Endsleigh, Devon ('Lobbii') 39x98 (1995).
'Aurea' and other golden clones have yet to reach 'tree' size.
'Compacta' Rather rare; slow-growing. Dangstein, W Sussex 15x53 under fork (1997 OCJ).
'Cristata' Rare. (Borde Hill 29x67 (1989 AFM), p1927.)
'Elegans' Abundant; often a sprawling bush. Woodstock, Kilkenny 21x134 among branches (1999 Michael Lear); Portmeirion, Gwynedd (24)x110 (1990 AFM).
'Gracilis'. Bedgebury NP 16x43 (1997 OCJ).
'Kusari-Sugi'. Kew RBG 10x32 (2001 OCJ).
'Pygmaea' Very rare; an ultimately enormous bush. Kitlands, Surrey 9x164@0.1-0.5m/x52++ (2000 OCJ).
var. sinensis Chinese Red Cedar C China, 1842. Now

scarcer than the Japanese variety, and perhaps better adapted to cool regions. Kilmory Castle, Argyll 27x186 (1986 AFM) – four boles diverge well above 1.5m; Monk Coniston, Cumbria (var. *japonica?*) 33x175 (1994 DH).
'Spiralis' Grannies' Ringlets Rare; sometimes dwarf. Muncaster Castle, Cumbria 29x79 (2000 DH).
'Viminalis' Rare (including 'Araucarioides', 'Dacrydioides' and 'Lycopodioides'). Tregrehan, Cornwall 17x70+43 (2002 Tom Hudson; 'Selaginoides').
'Yoshino'. Very rare to date. Hillier Gardens 12x33 (2002 Harry James).

Cunninghamia konishii Taiwan, 1918. Very rare. Borde Hill 12x31 (1995 OCJ).
C. lanceolata Chinese Fir C China, 1804. Rare; likes high humidity but summer warmth. Pencarrow, Cornwall 27x(93) (1995), p1850; Mount Usher, Wicklow 20x93 (1989), p1880?; Tregrehan, Cornwall 24x93 (2002 Tom Hudson).

X Cupressocyparis leylandii (*Cupressus macrocarpa* x *Xanthocyparis nootkatensis*). Abundant in various clones:
'Castlewellan Gold' Golden Leylandii 1962. Abundant; growing very fast everywhere. Bicton Park, Devon 14x68 (2001 OCJ); Epsom Cemetery, Surrey 17x52 (2000 OCJ).
'Golconda' 1977. Very occasional to date (along with 'Gold Rider'); vigorous.
'Haggerston Grey' Leylandii 1888. Abundant. Kyloe Wood, Northumberland 35x105 (2000) – first cutting, p1897.
'Leighton Green' Now rather rare. Leighton Hall, Powys 31x172@0m (2002 DH) – 1911 original.
'Naylors Blue' Rather rare. Wisley 20x62 (2000 OCJ), p1972; Alice Holt, Hants. 26x60 (1997) – first cutting, p1954.
'Robinson's Gold' 1962. Rare. Bedgebury NP 13x(48) (2002 OCJ), p1983; Windsor (Valley Gardens) 15x(43) (2000 OCJ), p1978.
'Rostrevor' The earliest clone (around 1870); always rare. Castlewellan NA 19x55 and 19.5x46 (1982 AFM), p1949.
'Silver Dust' 1960. Rare. Windsor (Valley Gardens) 11x45 (2000 OCJ); Kew RBG 12x33 (2001 OCJ) – both original introductions from 1977. 'Harlequin' has reached similar sizes.
'Skinner's Green' ('Stapehill 21'). Rare. Stapehill Nursery, Dorset 16x62 (1984 AFM) – 1940 original; Alice Holt, Hants. 17x(60) (2001 OCJ), p1967.
'Stapehill' ('Stapehill 20') 1940. Rather rare. Stowe, Bucks. 20x66 (1986 AFM); Stanmer Park, E Sussex 24x60 (2002 OCJ), p1965.
'Variegata' Rare. Withersdane Hall, Kent 12x53@0.5m (1999 OCJ) – some reversion; Bedgebury NP 12x(45) (2002 OCJ), p1980.
X C. notabilis (*Cupressus arizonica* var. *glabra* x *Xanthocyparis nootkatensis*) Rare. Alice Holt, Hants. 18x80@0.8m under fork (2001 OCJ) – 1958 original; Westonbirt NA 22x51 (2002 OCJ).
X C. ovensii (*Cupressus lindleyi* x *Xanthocyparis nootkatensis*) In some collections. Alice Holt, Hants. 15x43 (2001 OCJ); Westonbirt NA 17x37 (2002 OCJ) – 1962 original.

Japanese Red Cedar (*Cryptomeria japonica*) at Caher House, Clare – one of Ireland's westernmost champions.

The Monterey Cypress (*Cupressus macrocarpa*) grows much faster and larger in Ireland that on its native Californian cliff-tops. It is an example of a tree confined by climate and geology to a habitat much hotter and drier than the montane conditions to which it is adapted. No true cypress is very hardy; many other kinds are at home in semi-desert conditions, but all seem to do better here in the wetter west.

The easternmost really big Monterey Cypress, at Beauport Park, East Sussex, was planted, from the first importation of seed, on the freely draining soil covering a Roman road; its huge branches have taken root at wide distances all around the shattered remains of the single central trunk.

Cupressus True Cypresses

Cupressus abramsiana – see *C. goveniana* var. *abramsiana*.

C. arizonica var. arizonica Arizona Cypress SW N America, 1880. Now rare. Avondale, Wicklow 25x77 (1980 AFM); Westonbirt School, Glos. 24x60 (2002 OCJ) – very narrow.

var. bonita In one or two collections. Bodnant, Conwy 23x41 (1990 AFM), p1927.

var. glabra Smooth Arizona Cypress Frequent, in various selections (most commonly 'Pyramidalis'). Powerscourt, Wicklow 25x86@1m (2000 TROI).

var. glabra 'Aurea' Rare. Hillier Gardens 11x51@0.7m (2001 Harry James), p1966.

var. nevadensis Piute Cypress SW USA. In some collections. Bedgebury NP 9x27++ (1999 OCJ).

var. stephensonii Cuyamaca Cypress California, c1950. In one or two collections. Hillier Gardens 13.5x44 (2001 Harry James).

C. bakeri Modoc Cypress California, 1930. In some collections. Hillier Gardens 14x56@0.9m (2001 Harry James); Avondale, Wicklow 15x38 (1991 AFM).

ssp. matthewsii Siskiyou Cypress California, Oregon, 1917. In a few collections. Batsford Arboretum, Glos. 13x30 (2003 OCJ).

C. cashmeriana Kashmir Cypress 1862. Very rare; tender but needs warm summers. Ashbourne House, Cork 22x95 (1987 AFM).

C. corneyana Himalayas, 1847? Almost extinct here. Batsford Arboretum, Glos. 22x58 (2003 OCJ).

C. duclouxiana Grey Cypress China, c1910. Now very rare. Rowallane, Down 18.5x36 (1991 AFM).

C. forbesii – see *C. guadalupensis* var. *forbesii*.

C. funebris Mourning Cypress C China, 1849. Now very rare. Kilmacurragh, Wicklow 15.5x32+29 (1990 AFM). (Penjerrick, Cornwall 9x74 (1928).)

C. gigantea S Tibet. Spectacularly slender trees in one or two collections: Kew RBG 12x29 (2001 OCJ) – 1957 original.

C. glabra – see *C. arizonica* var. *glabra*.

C. goveniana Gowen Cypress Monterey, California, 1846. Very rare. Bicton Park, Devon 22x66 (2001 OCJ).

var. abramsiana Santa Cruz Cypress California, c1950. In some collections. Hillier Gardens 25.5x67 (2000 H M Brown), p1967.

C. guadalupensis Tecate Cypress Guadalupe Island, Mexico, 1880. In some collections. Castlewellan NA 22x39

Peeling bark of the champion Quince (*Cydonia oblonga*) at Pertenhall, Bedfordshire – a handsome fruit tree which is seldom now planted.

(1994 VES).

var. *forbesii* SW California, after 1927. In some collections. Castlewellan NA 8x28 (1994 VES).

C. lindleyi **Mexican Cypress** Long grown here (usually as *C. lusitanica*, the Cedar of Goa); occasional. Woodstock, Kilkenny (25)x157@1m among branches (1989 AFM); Borde Hill 28x77 (1995 OCJ) – slender column.

var. *benthamii* 1838? Very rare. Woodstock, Kilkenny 29x121 (1999 Michael Lear) – type tree?; Tregrehan, Cornwall 32x80 (2002 Tom Hudson).

'Flagellifera' In a few collections. (Castle Leod, Highland 19x62 (1966 AFM).)

'Glauca Pendula' Very occasional. Kilmacurragh, Wicklow 18x112 (1990 AFM); Annamoe, Wicklow 25.5x87 (2000 TROI).

***C. lindleyi* x *macrocarpa*.** Hillier Gardens 27x70 (2002), p1968.

C. lusitanica – see *C. lindleyi*.

C. macnabiana **MacNab Cypress** N California, 1854. In a few collections. Glasnevin NBG 14x55 (2003 DGA); Bayfordbury, Herts. 20x39 (1985 AFM).

C. macrocarpa **Monterey Cypress** California, 1838? Abundant near S and W coasts. Ringdufferin House, Down 32x385@0.2m (2000 TROI); Innishannon, Cork 27.5x384@0.3m (2000 TROI); Ards Priory, Donegal 29.5x369@0.5m (2000 TROI); Strete Ralegh House, Devon 30x332@0.5m around 'waist' (2001 OCJ); Beauport Park, E Sussex 17x325@0.7-0.2m under huge limbs (1997 OCJ), p1843?; Gyles Quay, Wicklow 31x299@1.4m (2002 AF); Powerscourt, Wicklow 42x178 (2000 TROI), p1867.

'Coneybearii' Very rare. Bicton Park, Devon 11x44++ (2001 OCJ) – huge broad bush.

'Donard Gold' Rare? Wakehurst Place 17x69@1.2m (2002 OCJ).

f. *fastigiata* Rare. A particularly tight tree at Clandeboye, Down, is 35x193@0.3m (2000 DGA).

'Goldcrest' The first of several brilliant gold clones which are now abundant. Grayswood Hill, Surrey 20x56 (1998 OCJ). 'Golden Pillar' has reached 14x60 in the Hillier Gardens (2002).

'Lutea' Golden Monterey Cypress Frequent; particularly good in maritime exposure. Ballyconnell House, Donegal 19x190@0.5m (2000 TROI); Castlewellan NA 35x171@1m? (1994 VES), p1894; Johnstown Castle, Wexford 24x160 (1989 AFM).

'Pendula' Glencormac Cypress Very rare. Glencormac, Wicklow 11x129@1.2m (2000 TROI) – 1874 original; Hillier Gardens 19x59@0.75m (2002).

C. nootkatensis – see *Xanthocyparis nootkatensis*.

C. sargentii **Sargent Cypress** California, 1908. In a few collections. Wakehurst Place 13x40 (2002 OCJ); Kew RBG 13x27 (2001 OCJ).

C. sempervirens **Italian Cypress** E Mediterranean; long grown here. Occasional; the hardiest true cypress but growing best in the mildest, warmest areas. Birdham church, W Sussex (var. *horizontalis*) 11x137 (1997 OCJ) – ancient tree, gnarled and died back (a larger is now a stump). (Fota, Cork 24x93 (1994 DGA), p1841.)

C. stephensonii – see *C. arizonica* var. *stephensonii*.

C. torulosa **West Himalayan Cypress** 1824. Rare. Abbeyleix, Laois 20.5x102@0.5m (2000 TROI). (Nettlecombe Court, Somerset 31x144 (1984 AFM).)

var. *corneyana* – see *C. corneyana*.

Cydonia oblonga **Quince** SW Asia; long grown here; now very occasional in older gardens. Pertenhall Old Rectory, Beds. 6x40@0.6m+30 (2000 DGA) – supported by customised swing and seat; spread 15m.

Dacrydium franklinii – see *Lagarostrobus franklinii*.

Daphniphyllum macropodum China, Japan, 1879. Rare; usually a bush. Hollycombe, W Sussex 6x27@0.9m (1997 OCJ).

Davidia involucrata **Dove Tree** C China, 1897. Very occasional; drought-sensitive so doing best in woodland in humid areas. 80% here are var. *vilmoriniana*. Tregrehan, Cornwall (var. *vilmoriniana*) 16x100 among branches (2002 Tom Hudson); Heligan, Cornwall (var. *involucrata*) 12x95@0.6m among branches (AFM); Hergest Croft (var. *involucrata*) 16x70 (1995 VES), p1903, and (var. *vilmoriniana*) 21x95@0.2m under fork (2002 Lawrence Banks);

Frensham Hall estate, Surrey (var. *vilmoriniana*) 21x60 (2000 OCJ); Fosbury Manor, Wilts. (var. *involucrata*) (21)x47 (1984 AFM) – shapely.

***Dicksonia antarctica* Hardy Tree Fern** E Australia, Tasmania. Now popular; old examples are confined to the mildest, wettest areas, where naturalised. Trebah, Cornwall 4.5x63 (2003 DGA), p1890; Trelissick, Cornwall 7x49 (1991 AFM).

***D. fibrosa* Golden Tree Fern** E Australia, Tasmania. In a few mild gardens. Fota, Cork 4x42 (1999 TROI).

***Diospyros kaki* Kaki** China, 1796. Very rare; a bush except where summers are hottest. Kew RBG 6x25 and (var. *lycopersicon*) 6x27 (2001 OCJ).

***D. lotus* Date Plum** E Asia, 1597. Rather rare; needs warm summers. Westonbirt NA 16x56 (2002 OCJ), p1926.

***D. virginiana* Persimmon** E N America, 1629. Very rare; likes warm summers. Glasnevin NBG 11x41+38 (2003 DGA); Kew RBG 14x40 (2001 OCJ).

***Dipteronia sinensis* **China, c1900. Very rare, and very seldom a 'tree'. (Crathes Castle, Aberdeen 10x27 (1981 AFM).)

***Drimys winteri* Winter's Bark** The Andes, 1827. Occasional in milder areas; probably needs high humidity to grow well. Kilmacurragh, Wicklow 16x98@1.1m under fork (2001 AF); Powerscourt, Wicklow (22x80) (1989 AFM); Monksgrange, Wexford 19.5x78@1.2m (2001 AF).

***Ehretia acuminata* var. *obovata* **(*E. ovalifolia*; *E. thyrsiflora*) E Asia, Japan, Taiwan, 1900. In a few collections. Kew RBG 8x36 (2001 OCJ), from Yu 10334; Bath BG, Somerset (?) 12x29+25 (2002 OCJ). (Spetchley Park, Worcs. 12x50 (1981 AFM).)

***E. dicksonii* Ehret Tree** (*E. macrophylla*) China, Taiwan, 1897. In some collections. Kew RBG 9x42+32 (2001 OCJ), p1928 from Wilson 10242; Birr Castle 17x40 (2000 TROI), p1934.

***Elaeagnus angustifolia* Oleaster** C Asia; long grown here. Occasional. Needs a continental climate with hot summers to grow large. Woodcock Park, London 8x61@0.3m under branching (2001 OCJ) – spread 14.5m; Roath Park, Glamorgan 9x36@1m (1990 AFM).

***Embothrium coccineum* Chilean Fire-bush** S Andes, 1846. A vigorous but short-lived tree in mild, humid areas. Most are 'Norquinco Valley'. Clandeboye, Down 14x64@1.1m+43 (2000 DGA); Brodick Castle, Ayr 20x42@? (1988 JW), p1962.

***Emmenopterys henryi* **China, 1907. Very rare; needs summer heat to grow large. Roath Park, Glamorgan 14x38@1.3m (2001 Roger and Vicky Smith); Caerhays 17x37 (1991 AFM), from Forrest 26619?

***Eriobotrya japonica* Loquat** China, Japan, 1787. Occasional; rather tender, but remains a bush except where

summers are hot. Antony House, Cornwall (8)x32 (1991 AFM); Paignton Zoo, Devon 9m (1984 AFM).

Eucalyptus Gum Trees

***Eucalyptus acaciaformis*. **Bickham House, Devon 12x27+26 (2001 OCJ), p1991.

***E. aggregata* Black Gum** Very rare. Herstmonceux Castle, E Sussex 19x108@0.5m under fork, and 18x85 (2001 OCJ); Rowallane, Down 20.5x42 (1991 AFM).

***E. alpina*. **Young trees only.

***E. amygdalina*. **No old trees are now known.

***E. approximans*. **Young trees only.

***E. archeri* Alpine Cider Gum** Very rare. A tree at Cobham Hall, Kent, is much the oldest, having been planted by Australian troups in the First World War: 14x75@1.2m under burrs (1999 OCJ); Edinburgh RBG 20x67 (1991 AFM).

***E. archeri* x *delegatensis*. **Kilmun, Argyll 26x48 (1994 VES).

***E. bicostata* Eurabbie** Very rare. Mount Usher, Wicklow 18x39 (1989 AFM).

***E. bridgesiana* **Very rare. Mount Usher, Wicklow (35)x124 and (38)x110 (1989 AFM), p1910.

***E. brookeriana* Brooker's Gum**. Glencormac, Wicklow 14x74 (1991 AFM).

***E. caesia* Grey Gum**. Architectural Plants, W Sussex 12x34 (1996 OCJ), p1987?

***E. camphora* Broad-leafed Sally** Very rare. Grey Timbers, Devon 18x43 (1979 AFM).

***E. chapmaniana* **In a few collections. Kew RBG 14x41 (2001 OCJ); Wakehurst Place 19x24+21 (2001 OCJ) – both

The biggest known Chilean Fire-bush (*Embothrium coccineum*), in the garden of Clandeboye, Down.

from 1988 seed.

E. cinerea Argyle Apple Very rare. John F. Kennedy Arboretum, Wexford 14x32 (1989 AFM).

E. coccifera Mount Wellington Peppermint Rare. Kilmacurragh, Wicklow 27x122 (1990 AFM); Avondale, Wicklow 31.5x66 (1974 AFM). (Powderham Castle, Devon 26x198 (1963 AFM); 1840 original, died 1964.)

E. cordata Heart-leaved Silver Gum Very rare. Menabilly, Cornwall 23x66 (1984 AFM); Inverewe, Highland 30x61 (1991 AFM), p1901.

E. coriacea. Dundonnell House, Highland 11x49 (1991 AFM).

E. crenulata. Young trees only.

E. dalrympleana Mountain Gum Frequent in milder areas. Mount Usher, Wicklow (33)x94 (1992 AFM), p1945.

E. delegatensis Alpine Ash Rare. Ashbourne House, Cork (ssp. *tasmaniensis*) 27x123 (1999 TROI); Mount Usher, Wicklow (42)x87 (1989 AFM).

E. delegatensis x gunnii. Kilmun, Argyll 23.5x73 (1994 VES).

E. glaucescens Tingiringi Gum Very rare. Wisley 15x52 and 20x50+42 (2000 OCJ).

E. globulus Blue Gum Tasmania, 1829. Survives to make a big tree only in Ireland and on Man; very occasional as a younger plant elsewhere. St MacNissi's College, Antrim (30)x259 under narrow fork at 2m (1999 TROI), p1857; Eccles Hotel, Cork 31.5x222 and 36x177 (1999 TROI) – cut back; Glencormac, Wicklow 40x122 (2000 TROI).

E. gregsoniana Wolgan Snow Gum. Newcastle House, Glamorgan 4.5x28 (1990 AFM).

E. gunnii Cider Gum Abundant in milder areas; hardy. Sidbury Manor, Devon x163 (1994), p1885; Staplefield Place, W Sussex 25x153 (1996 OCJ) – forks at 3m; Sheffield Park, E Sussex 22x148 (1994 OCJ), p1912; Castle Kennedy, Dumfries & Galloway (30)x125 (1993 VES); Selehurst, W Sussex (33)x113 (1993 VES), p1914.

var. divaricata. Rare, as a young plant. Batsford Arboretum, Glos. 18x31 (2003 OCJ), p1992.

'Whittingehamensis' Whittingehame Gum. Whittingehame Tower, E Lothian x123 (1996 Alistair Scott) – unconfirmed as a descendant of the 1854 original (which was 29x184 in 1957); Kinloch Hourn, Highland 30x71 (1978 AFM).

E. kitsoniana Very rare. Newcastle House, Glamorgan 6x28 (1990 AFM).

E. linearis Young trees only. (Mount Usher, Wicklow 15.5x30 (1966 AFM).)

E. mannifera Young trees only.

E. mitchelliana Weeping Sally Very rare. Kilmun, Argyll 17.5x50 (1994 VES); John F. Kennedy Arboretum, Wexford 21x38 (1989 AFM).

E. mooreana. Bicton College, Devon 19x33 (2001 OCJ).

E. muelleriana Yellow Stringybark. A tree recorded at Fota, Cork: 36x107 (1999 TROI), p1951.

E. neglecta Very rare. Kew RBG 7x29 (2001 OCJ).

E. nicholii Narrow-leaved Black Peppermint Rare. Whitcombe, Devon 13x48 (2001 OCJ) – young tree.

E. niphophila – see *E. pauciflora* ssp. *niphophila*.

E. nitens Silver Top Rather rare; a particularly handsome species. Ashbourne House, Cork (ssp. *denticulata*) 29x104 (1999 TROI).

E. nitida Smithton Peppermint Very rare. John F. Kennedy Arboretum, Wexford 14x47 (1989 AFM).

E. obliqua Messmate Stringybark Very rare. John F. Kennedy Arboretum, Wexford 10x32 (1989 AFM).

E. ovata Swamp Gum In a few collections. John F. Kennedy Arboretum, Wexford 15x43 and 21x38 (1989 AFM), p1970.

E. parvifolia Small-leaved Gum Rather rare. Hillier Gardens 20x70 (2001 Harry James); Fota, Cork 22x55 (1999 TROI), p1975.

E. pauciflora ssp. debeuzevillei Jounama Snow Gum Rare. Wisley x67@1m (2000 OCJ), pollarded; Westonbirt NA 13x27+ (2002 OCJ), p1980.

ssp. niphophila Snow Gum Frequent in milder areas. Dundonnell House, Highland 14x56 (1991 AFM); Ashbourne House, Cork 25x47 (1987 AFM).

ssp. pauciflora Cabbage Gum Rare, and generally a bush. 25x106 recorded at Mount Usher, Wicklow (1989 AFM).

E. perriniana Spinning Gum Occasional. Batsford Arboretum, Glos. 18x61 (2003 OCJ); Kilmun, Argyll 24x22 (1978 AFM), p1949.

E. pulverulenta Silver-leafed Mountain Gum Rare. Kilmacurragh, Wicklow (35)x97 (1990 AFM).

E. regnans Mountain Ash In a few mild collections. Mount Stewart, Down (37)x52 (1991 AFM).

E. rodwayi. Kew RBG 14x59 (2001 OCJ), from 1972 seed; Westonbirt NA 19x32 (2002 OCJ).

E. rubida. Young trees only.

E. simmondsii Very rare. Kilmun, Argyll 22x82 and 28x68 (1994 VES).

E. stellulata Black Sally Very rare. John F. Kennedy Arboretum, Wexford 15x40 (1989 AFM), p1970; Mount

---

EUCALYPTUS

Milder winters are encouraging British and Irish gardeners to experiment with more and more of the huge variety of Australian and Tasmanian eucalypts. No other trees can make tall spreading crowns on stout boles within two decades; none have such varied barks or richer aromas, and none are harder to identify. The oldest and biggest examples of most forms tend to be found along the mild western coasts, though growth is probably best where summers are hottest. Most are prone to fungal infections and windblow here, and all this makes it particularly hard to maintain an up-to-date list of the largest examples.

Usher, Wicklow 18x31 (1989 AFM), p1951.
E. subcrenulata. Young trees only.
E. tenuiramis. Young trees only.
E. urnigera Urn Gum Rare. Castlewellan NA 26x126 (1994 VES); Stonefield House, Argyll 26x123 (1986 AFM); Mount Usher, Wicklow (39)x106 (1989 AFM).
E. vernicosa Varnished Gum Very rare; often a bush. 31x57 recorded from Kilmun, Argyll (1994 VES).
ssp. *johnstonii* Tasmanian Yellow Gum Rare. Mount Usher, Wicklow (38)x96 (1989 AFM); Castlewellan NA (39)x56 (1994 VES).
E. viminalis Ribbon Gum Rare. Mount Usher, Wicklow (36)x131 (1989 AFM) and (39)x114 (1992 AFM).

Eucommia ulmoides Hardy Rubber Tree China, 1896? Rare. Kew RBG 11x56 (2001 OCJ), from 1930 seed; Hergest Croft (20)x44+34 (1995 VES).

Eucryphia cordifolia Ulmo S Andes, 1851. Rare; needs humidity. Magnolia Cottage, Jersey 17x66@? (1992) – since damaged; Castle Kennedy, Dumfries & Galloway 21x61+30 (1993 VES); Castlewellan NA 22x36 (1994 VES).
E. glutinosa S Andes, 1859. Rare; the hardiest Eucryphia, but often a bush. Arduaine, Argyll 13x27+25+ (1991 VES).
E. x intermedia Rostrevor Eucryphia (*glutinosa* x *lucida*). Rare; the usual clone is 'Rostrevor'. Glenarn, Dunbartons. 13x28 (1986 AFM); Borde Hill 15x26+ (1995 OCJ), p1937.
E. lucida Tasmanian Leatherwood. Tender and very rare. Castlewellan NA 14x38 (1994 VES).
E. moorei Australia, 1915. Tender and very rare. Muncaster Castle, Cumbria 16x40+31 (2000 DH); Trewithen, Cornwall 18x36 (1987 AFM); Mount Usher, Wicklow 20x35+21 (1989 AFM).
E. x nymansensis Nymans' Eucryphia (*cordifolia* x *glutinosa*, 1915). Occasional; largest in high humidity. The common clone is 'Nymansay'. Tregrehan, Cornwall 21x62+35 and 23x51+47 (2002 Tom Hudson).

Euodia hupehensis – see *Tetradium daniellii*.

Euonymus bungeanus N China, 1883. A very rare but handsome tree. Edinburgh RBG 10.4x60@? (1997); Joyce Green, Kent 9x45@1.1m (1997 OCJ).
E. europaeus Spindle Native. Frequent on clay or limestone, in woods hedges and scrub; now much planted. Nearly always a bush; to 10m. Lake House, Westmeath 6.3x32+16+14 (2000 TROI).
E. fimbriatus Himalayas. In a few mild gardens. Tregothnan, Cornwall 12x51 (1995).
E. hamiltonianus NE Asia, Japan. Very rare. Wisley (ssp. *sieboldianus*) 7x50@1m (2000 OCJ).
E. hupehensis C China. Edinburgh RBG 9x35 (1985 AFM), from Forrest 8496.
E. lucidus Himalayas, 1850. In a few mild gardens. Powerscourt, Wicklow 12x51 (1989 AFM); Tregothnan, Cornwall 18x47+31 (1989 AFM).
E. tingens Himalayas to China. In a few big gardens. Brodick Castle, Ayr 12x39+ (1988 AFM).

Euptelea polyandra Japan, 1877. Just reaching 'tree' size in a few collections.

Fagus Beeches
Fagus crenata Japan, 1892. 10-20 trees? Dawyck, Scottish Borders 24.5x74 (1997).
F. engleriana Engler's Beech C China, 1907. A rare but beautiful tree which does not grow large. Westonbirt NA 18x59@0.3m under narrow fork (2002 OCJ); Borde Hill 15x52 (1995 OCJ) – both p1928.
F. grandifolia American Beech E N America, 1766. In some collections; would need summer heat to thrive. Kew RBG 13x55 (2001 OCJ). (Eastnor Castle, Herefords. 19x69@1m and 16x62 (1989 AFM).)
F. japonica Japanese Beech 1905. A few young trees. (Borde Hill x42 (1960), p1932.)
F. lucida W China, 1905. In a few collections. Birr Castle 16x35 (1990 AFM).
F. orientalis Oriental Beech SE Europe, Asia Minor, 1904. Rare, but can outgrow common Beech. Wakehurst Place 28x150 (1998 OCJ), from about 1915; Birr Castle 29x73 (2000 TROI), p1927.
F. sylvatica Beech Native to S England and Wales; abundant on lighter soils. Broadstone Warren, E Sussex 27x253@1.5-2m above burr (2002 OCJ) – ancient pollard; Frant, E Sussex 29x275@0.8-1.1m under forkings (2002 OCJ); Stradbally Hall, Laois (36)x247 (1990 AFM); Buckland Hall, Powys x242@1.2m? (1988 JW); Shurdington, Glos. x240@1.2m (1998); The Knowles, New Forest, Hants. x239 (1999 Chris Read) – fine old pollard; Gort na mona, Galway 26.5x235 (2000 TROI); Beaufront Castle, Northumberland (44)x172 (2000).
'Albovariegata' (and 'Albomarginata') Very rare. Rossdhu, Argyll 21x115 (1985 AFM); Castle Leslie, Monaghan 27x112 (2000 TROI).
'Asplenifolia' Fern-leafed Beech Rather occasional. Kyre Park, Worcs. 22x179@1m under fork (1995) – spread 33m; Storrsthwaite, Cumbria (20)x165 (1995 DH) – spread 26m; Rydal Mount, Cumbria 30x101 (1996 DH).
'Aurea Pendula' Rare to date. Birr Castle 7x24+22 (1996 DGA).
'Birr Zebra'. Birr Castle 12.5x25 (2000 TROI) – original.
'Bornyensis'. Kew RBG 6x31 (2001 OCJ).
'Cockleshell' Very rare. Hillier Gardens 13x35 (2002 Harry James).
'Cristata' Cock's Comb Beech Rare. Wray Castle, Cumbria 28x106 (1997 DH); The Yair, Scottish Borders 18x103 (1984 AFM); Brathay Hall, Cumbria 30x81 (2000 DH).
'Dawyck' Dawyck Beech Quite frequent as a young planting. Dawyck, Scottish Borders 29x86@0.3m (1992 AFM) – original sport, transplanted around 1860; Tortworth Court, Glos. 28x82 (1992), p1908.
'Dawyck Gold' Golden Dawyck Beech 1969; rare to date. Hillier Gardens 14x38@? (2000 H M Brown), p1975.
'Dawyck Purple' Purple Dawyck Beech 1969; rare to date. Hillier Gardens 16x27 (2000 H M Brown), p1975.
'Grandidentata' In a few collections. Kew RBG 18x77 (2001 OCJ), sourced 1872.
f. *latifolia* Very rare (often as 'Prince George of Crete').

Broadstone Warren champion Beech (*Fagus sylvatica*). With their iron-hard timber, oaks and sweet chestnuts can retrench and grow hollow but still look forward to hundreds of years of happy life. But a Beech that sheds a limb or sprouts a crop of toadstools will be firewood in the twinkling of any eye. The soft timber and shallow roots mean that Beeches that were pollarded and never developed huge, sail-like crowns tend to be longest lived: areas where pollarding was traditional, such as the New Forest and the forests of the High Weald, still have huge old trees, but the end of traditional management has made these top-heavy and prone to collapse. The very beautiful old tree near Frant, East Sussex, which was the largest known at 26x284@1.1m in 1994 (OCJ), fell to bits on Christmas Day 1999. Until about 1950, the 'King Beech' at Knole in Kent was even larger (32x310 in 1945).

Beeches can rear up to great heights from the poorest of soils. It is easier to group them mentally with the giant conifers we can grow than with other native trees: clean-boled and dark-leaved, they tend to dominate the landscape rather than settling into it, and are acutely vulnerable to air pollution, sudden droughts and wind-throw. The dense foliage makes heighting the tallest difficult; some have certainly reached 40m.

Alexandra Park, E Sussex 15x85 (1993 OCJ) – much broken; Hillier Gardens 22x65 (2002 Harry James).
'Luteovariegata' Very rare. Highnam Court, Glos. 22x116 (1992); Hever Castle, Kent 27x84 (1995 OCJ).
'Miltonensis' Rare and local. Dane John Gardens, Kent 25x155@0.3m under graft on short bole (1995 OCJ); Wincheap Playground, Kent 19x121 (1999 OCJ).
'Pendula' Weeping Beech Rather occasional. Pantglas Hall, Carmarthen x170@1m (1993); Endsleigh, Devon 29x167@0.5m? under fork (1995); Wokingham Road Cemetery, Reading, Berks. 23x162 (1994 Carol Hora) –

forking at 2.5m; Belton House, Lincs. 29x89 (1978 AFM).
f. *purpurea* Copper Beech Abundant in various clones; grows as well as the type, though its lifespan has hardly ever been extended by pollarding. Syston Park, Lincs. (19)x231@1.2m over branch scar (2003 Shirley Clegg) – decaying; Kilkenny Castle, Kilkenny 27x196 on good bole (2000 TROI); Northampton, Northants. x189 (2001 DGA) – x227@0.5m just above graft; spread 30m; Dalguise House, Perth (38)x103 (1986 AFM).
'Purpurea Pendula' Weeping Purple Beech Rather rare; reaches no height. Ascott House, Bucks. 4x43@1.1m

(2000 DGA).

'Purpurea Tricolor' Rare. Syon Park, London 24x79 (2002 OCJ); Stourhead, Wilts. (24)x74 (1992 AFM).

'Quercifolia' Oak-leaved Beech Very rare. Charlton Park, Kent 22x118 (1995 OCJ); Capenoch, Dumfries & Galloway 25x100 (1979 AFM).

'Remilyensis'. Kew RBG 9x46@1.3m under graft (2001 OCJ), sourced 1873.

'Rohan Gold' 1970; very rare to date. Hillier Gardens 13x35 (2002 Ron Holley).

'Rohan Pyramid'. Hillier Gardens 12x26 (2002 Ron Holley).

'Rohanii' Rather rare; slow-growing. Winkworth Arboretum, Surrey 15x68@0.2m under branches (2000 OCJ).

'Rotundifolia' Very rare. Highdown, W Sussex 12x65 (1997 OCJ); Woburn Park, Beds. 23x64@0.75m (2000 DGA) – leans.

f. *tortuosa* Very rare. Parkanaur, Armagh 4x59 (1982 AFM) – an original sport, transplanted around 1820; Hillier Gardens 5.5x32 (2002 Harry James).

'Zlatia' Golden Beech Rare; very vigorous. Westonbirt NA 22x93 (2002 OCJ), p1934; Edinburgh RBG 24x90 (1991 AFM).

***Ficus carica* Fig** W Asia; long grown here. Locally frequent. Needs maximum warmth to reach tree-size; all the largest, with long clean boles, are in inner London: Clifford's Inn 13x(43+40+32) (2001 OCJ); Westminster College Garden 11x42 (2001 OCJ); Victoria Park, Hackney 6x42 (2001 OCJ).

***Firmiana simplex* Parasol Tree** China, 1757. Needs summer heat to ripen its wood, and has only reached tree-size at Fota, Cork (8x26 (1984 AFM), p1909).

***Fitzroya cupressoides* Patagonian Cypress** Rare; best in cool moist areas. Kilmacurragh, Wicklow 18x86 (1990 AFM); Ardkinglas, Argyll 21x71 (1991 AFM).

Fraxinus Ashes

***Fraxinus americana* White Ash** E N America, 1724. Occasional; likes summer warmth. Eton College, Berks. 21x87 (1997 OCJ); Batsford Arboretum, Glos. 24x69 (2003 OCJ).

***F. angustifolia* Narrow-leaved Ash** Mediterranean, by 1800 (incorporating *F. elonza*). Rather occasional (often as 'Lentiscifolia'). Grafts always bizarrely outgrow their Common Ash stock. Kew RBG 26x145 on graft-swellings (2001 OCJ); Victoria Park, Hackney, London 24x122 (2001 OCJ) – no visible graft, Tortworth Court, Glos. 29x87@? (1988 JW).

ssp. *oxycarpa* Caucasian Ash S Europe to Iran, 1815. Rare. Clissold Park, London 21x96 (2001 OCJ) – most leaves trifoliate; Myddelton House, London 24x89 (2001 OCJ) – a tree of extraordinary beauty.

'Pendula' Weeping Narrow-leaved Ash Very rare. Horniman Gardens, London 15x99@1.6m above graft-swelling (2001 OCJ) – cut back.

'Raywood' Raywood Ash Abundant. Syon Park,

London 18x61 (2002 OCJ); Woodbridge, Suffolk 26m (1994 Daniel Sanford), p1930.

ssp. *syriaca* C and W Asia, by 1880. Very rare. Kew RBG 14x33 (2001 OCJ), p1947.

'Veltheimii' About 30 trees. Kensington Gardens, London 21x108@2m above graft swellings, and 22x75 (2001 OCJ).

***F. anomala* Utah Ash** SW USA, 1893. Glasnevin NBG 22x40@1.1m under graft (2003 DGA).

F. berlandieriana Mexico and Texas. Only young trees currently known.

F. bungeana N China, 1881. (Edinburgh RBG 8x30 (1967 AFM), p1903.)

***F. chinensis* ssp. *rhyncophylla* Chinese Ash** NE Asia, 1892. Very rare. Stanmer Park, E Sussex 16x33 (2002 OCJ) – as planted, 1964.

***F. excelsior* Ash** Abundant on richer soils. Ardfort House, Tipperary 29x336@1.4m (2000 TROI) – all one tree?; Clapton Court, Somerset 12x283 (1995) – singularly pot-bellied; Talley Abbey, Carmarthen x(250@2m/x350@1m) (1985 Allen Meredith) – hedge tree, almost unmeasurable; Coalraine, Offaly 20.5x244 (2000 TROI); Haremere Hall, E Sussex 24x240@1m (1996 OCJ) – low pollard on bank; Penny Bridge, Cumbria 6x236 (1995 DH) – pollard, splitting; Castlepollard, Westmeath 28x234 (2000 TROI); Chelsworth, Suffolk 25x229 (2002 JP) – good tree; Brignall, Durham 21x226 (2001 Den Gregson) – shapely pollard; Cirencester Park, Glos. 38x95 (1989 JW); Rossie Priory, Perth (38)x91 (1985 AFM) – superb 20m bole.

'Aurea Pendula' Golden Weeping Ash Rare and stunted. Southall Park, London 6x27 (2002 OCJ).

'Concavifolia'. Kew RBG 22x70 (2001 OCJ); sourced 1902.

'Diversifolia' Single-leafed Ash Occasional; grows as the type. Cullen House, Moray x130 (1980 JP); Culcreuch Castle Hotel, Stirling (32)x128 (1984 AFM).

'Diversifolia Pendula' Weeping Single-leaved Ash Very rare. Ryston Hall, Norfolk 12x51 (1995 JW), p1911; Kew RBG 14x48 (2001 OCJ).

'Erosa'. Hillier Gardens 16x43 (2001).

'Jaspidea' Golden Ash Quite frequent as a younger tree. (Stunted examples are probably the clone 'Aurea'.) Highnam Court, Glos. 21x108 (1992 JW); Moncrieffe House, Perth 23.5x71 (1982 AFM).

'Pendula' Weeping Ash Frequent. Bedgebury School, Kent 12x136 (1995 OCJ); Money House, Wicklow 19x73 (2000 TROI); Yealand Manor, Lancs. 19x72 (1997). In 1848, a graft at Elvaston Castle, Derbyshire, was made at 27m on a stem of Common Ash.

'Pendula Wentworthii' Wentworth Weeping Ash Very rare; a tall-growing tree. Hampstead Heath, London 22x84 (2001 OCJ) – may be a sport as no graft is visible; Lindridge Park, Devon 25x74 (2001 OCJ).

'Scolopendrifolia'. Kew RBG 20x53 (2001 OCJ), sourced 1900.

'Stricta'. Kew RBG 24x62 (2001 OCJ).

f. *variegata* Variegated Ash Some very rare clones. A sport (?) with yellow splashes in Virginia Water, Surrey is 18x(40) (2000 OCJ).

'Verrucosa' Very rare. St James' Park, London 13x61

Ashes

All ashes prefer a fertile, alkaline soil. The native species is a tree of modest proportions, light-limbed and short-lived, except on the very richest sites, where it can grow monstrous: the largest have nearly always been found in the well-watered limestones of the Irish lowlands, though the stump of an ancient pollard in Kilmalie churchyard, Argyll, burnt down by soldiers in 1746, was x560cm when examined 18 years later by Dr Walker.

Many trees, especially in exposure or on intensively farmed land, are currently suffering from Ash Dieback – probably the product of cocktail of environmental stresses. This has affected the heights to which Ash can grow: until the mid twentieth century, it rivalled Common Lime and London Plane as our tallest broadleaf (45x102 at Duncombe Park, Yorkshire, in 1956; 44x116 at Cobham Hall, Kent, in 1907); today, you are lucky to see trees of 30m.

(2002 OCJ); Kew RBG 18x54 (2001 OCJ), sourced 1902.

F. holotricha Balkans, by 1870. In a few collections. Kew RBG 23x59 (2001 OCJ); sourced 1909.

F. latifolia **Oregon Ash** W N America, by 1870. Rare. Regent's Park, London 18x86 (2001 OCJ); Aldenham Park, Herts. 24x54 (2002 OCJ).

F. mandshurica **Manchurian Ash** NE Asia, 1882. A few young trees. (Borde Hill 14x38 (1968 AFM).)

F. mariesii **Maries' Ash** C China, 1878. Very rare and small-growing here. Ryston Hall, Norfolk (?) 10x40@? (1995 JW).

F. nigra **Black Ash** E N America, 1800. Borde Hill 17x33 (1995 OCJ).

F. ornus **Manna Ash** Mediterranean; long grown here. Abundant; often small-growing. Horton, Surrey 15x110 (1995 PJB); Birr Castle (recorded as the usually dwarf var. *rotundifolia*) 28x73 (2000 TROI); Trentham Gardens, Staffs. 27x96 (1994).

F. oxycarpa – see *F. angustifolia* ssp. *oxycarpa*.

F. pallisiae **Pallis' Ash** Balkans area. In a few collections. Kew RBG 15x52 (2001 OCJ) – 1933 original.

F. paxiana China, 1901. In some collections. Tortworth Court, Glos. 22.5x54 (1988 JW).

F. pennsylvanica **Red Ash** E N America, 1783 (incorporating var. *lanceolata*, Green Ash). Occasional in warm areas. Highnam Court, Glos. 22x107 (1988 AFM); Ryston Hall, Norfolk (?) 21x75 and 25x51 (1995 JW), p1911.

'**Aucubifolia**' Very rare. Birr Castle 14x38 (2000 TROI). (Dyrham Park, Glos. 22x53 (1976 AFM).)

'**Variegata**' Very rare; tends to revert. Ryston Hall, Norfolk 16x49 (1995 JW); Kensington Gardens, London 18x43 (2001 OCJ) – reverting at top.

F. platypoda China, 1909. In one or two collections. Abbeyleix, Laois 17x35 (2000 TROI).

F. quadrangulata **Blue Ash** E USA, 1823. In a few collections. Kew RBG 14x42 (2001 OCJ).

F. sieboldiana Japan, Korea, 1894. In a few collections. Birr Castle 10x33+31 (2000 TROI).

F. sogdiana Turkestan, by 1890. A few young trees. Surrey University Campus 12x36@0.5m under fork (2002 OCJ). (Ryston Hall, Norfolk 15x57 (1969 AFM, p1910).)

F. spaethiana **Spaeth's Ash** Japan, 1873. Very rare; not thriving here. Borde Hill 6x32@1.2m (1996 OCJ); Deene Park, Northants. 12x24@0.5m (1990 AFM) – grown well since.

F. syriaca – see *F. angustifolia* ssp. *syriaca*.

F. texensis Texas. In a few collections. Glasnevin NBG 19x48 (2003 DGA) – graft at 1m.

F. tomentosa **Pumpkin Ash** E USA, 1912. In one or two collections. Westonbirt NA 15x38 (2002 OCJ).

F. velutina **Arizona Ash** SW N America, 1891. Very rare. Birr Castle 19x38 (2000 TROI); Kew RBG (var. *toumeyi*) 15x55 (2001 OCJ) – aerial roots swathing bole.

F. xanthoxyloides **Afghan Ash** W Himalayas, by 1870. Very rare; often bushy. Syon Park, London 10x63 (2002 OCJ) – several stems diverge above graft; Kew RBG 13x46 under graft (2001 OCJ).

Fuschia excorticata New Zealand, c1820. Can reach 'tree' size in the mildest parts.

Genista aetnensis **Mount Etna Broom** Sardinia, Sicily. Rather occasional, reaching tree-size in warm summers. Worthing, W Sussex 8x(40)@1m (1996 OCJ); Southsea Castle Gardens, Hants. 12x37@? (1989 JW).

Gevuina avellana **Chilean Hazel** S Andes, 1826. Confined as a tree to the mildest wettest areas. Crarae, Argyll x34 (1986 AFM) – since topped; Inverewe, Highland 17m (1986 AFM) – died back since?

Ginkgo biloba **Maidenhair Tree** China, 1758. Frequent. Whitfield, Herefords. 20.5x140 (1995 VES), p1778; good bole; Maesllwch Castle, Powys 23x144 (1989 AFM), p1780; three stems; Merrie Cottage, Hants. (17)x137@0.8m under fork (2003 DGA); Tregrehan, Cornwall 28x77 (2002 Tom Hudson).

'**Fastigiata**' **Sentry Ginkgo** Tightly erect trees are sometimes seen, but may be sports. Cumberland House, W Sussex 19x78@0.5m under fork, and 17x46 (1997 OCJ); Ryston Hall, Norfolk 22x40 (1995 JW).

'**Pendula**' **Weeping Ginkgo** In a few collections. Roath Park, Glamorgan 4x33 (1990 AFM).

Gleditsia aquatica **Water Locust** SE USA, 1723. A few young trees. (Kew RGB 14x56 (1968 AFM).)

G. caspica **Caspian Locust** N Iran, 1822. In one or two collections. Kew RBG 8x63 (very burred and much died back) and 11x32 (2001 OCJ).

G. japonica **Japanese Honey Locust** 1894. In some

The slender leaflets of Narrow-Leaved Ash (*Fraxinus angustifolia*) create a uniquely airy, glistening texture. The champion stands in Victoria Park, London.

collections. Kew RBG 8x37 and 11x36 (2001 OCJ).

G. macracantha C China, by 1800. In a few collections. Kew RBG 16x32 (2001 OCJ), from 1946 seed.

G. sinensis Chinese Honey Locust 1774. Rare. Cambridge UBG 15.5x106@0.3m/x77(fused stems?)+43 (2002 DGA).

G. triacanthos Honey Locust E USA, 1700. Quite frequent where summers are hot; thrives in very poor soils. (Most are the thornless f. *inermis*.) Broom's Down, Kent 25x86 (1995 OCJ); The Hall, Wilts. (29)x53 (1984 AFM) – much decayed by 2003.

'Nana'. A very rare locust of ambiguous origin. Victoria Park, Hackney, London 19x79@0.8m under forking (2001 OCJ); Holland Park, London 14x62 (2001 OCJ).

'Sunburst' Golden Honey Locust 1954. Occasional in warm areas. Wisley 11x43 (2000 OCJ); Notcutt's Nursery, Suffolk 13x42 (1994 Daniel Sanford); Kew RBG 14x39 (2001 OCJ), sourced 1961.

Glyptostrobus pensilis Chinese Swamp Cypress S China. Very rare; tender, but likes hot summers; seems to demand a wet soil. Dunloe Castle, Kerry 10m (1993 HPG).

Grevillea robusta Silk Oak SE Australia. Very rare and tender (a few recent street plantings in London), but shows the potential to grow quickly to 'tree' size.

Griselinia littoralis Papauma New Zealand, c1850. Frequent in mild areas; to tree size near W coasts. Ballyconnell House, Donegal 11x218@0.2m under forks (2000 TROI); Castle Kennedy, Dumfries & Galloway (14)x108@1m under branching (1984 AFM); Kilmacurragh, Wicklow 20x121@0.3m under forks (1980 AFM).

Gymnocladus dioica Kentucky Coffee Tree E USA, by 1748. Rather rare; needs hot summers. Royal Victoria Park, Somerset 16x57 (2002 OCJ); Ashford Chace, Hants. 17x41 (2002 OCJ) – fine tree.

Halesia carolina Carolina Snowdrop Tree SE USA, 1756. Rather rare; generally a bush. Hergest Croft 12x46@0.5m (1995 VES); Norney Grange, Surrey 9x44+ (2002 OCJ); Hillier Gardens 13x27 (2001 Ron Holley).
H. monticola Mountain Snowdrop Tree SE USA, 1897? Rare. Winkworth Arboretum, Surrey (var. *vestita*) 12x67 (2000 OCJ); Llangoed Hall, Powys 10x65 (1993 VES); Endsleigh, Devon (19)x35+33+32 (1990 AFM).

Hemiptelea davidii NE Asia, 1908. Now represented only by young, bushy plants (susceptible to DED?). (Kew RBG 12x29 (1989 AFM).)

Hesperopeuce mertensiana Mountain Hemlock (*Tsuga mertensiana*) W N America, 1854. Rather rare; grows large only in coldest areas. Murthly Castle, Perth 26x116 (1988 AFM); Fairburn, Highland 36x78 (1987 AFM).
var. jeffreyi Jeffrey's Hemlock (*T.* x *jeffreyi*) 10-20 trees? Blair Castle, Perth 22x54 (1989 AFM), p1927.

Hippophae rhamnoides Sea Buckthorn Native to E coasts of England and S Scotland; frequently planted. Usually a bush. Falloden Hall, Northumberland 6x39 (1992) – leans; Kew RBG 11m (2001 OCJ) – columnar.
ssp. yunnanense W China (*H. sinense*). Wisley 8x49 (2000 OCJ).
H. salicifolia Himalayan Sea Buckthorn 1822. Very rare. Windsor (Valley Gardens) 12x46 (2000 OCJ).

Hoheria angustifolia New Zealand. Very rare. Meadow Wood, Kent 9x24 (1995 OCJ) – good straight tree.
H. lyallii Mountain Ribbonwood South Island, New Zealand. Rare; to tree-size in the mildest areas. Arduaine, Argyll 10x32+22 (1998); Brodick Castle, Ayr 12x24@? (1988 JW).
H. populnea Lacebark North Island, New Zealand. In a few mild gardens. Fota, Cork 17x109@0.6m under forks (1999 TROI), p1948.
H. sexstylosa Houhere New Zealand. Rather rare; to tree size in the mildest areas. Ringdufferin House, Down 14.5x45 (2000 TROI).

Hovenia dulcis Japanese Raisin Tree China, 1812. Very rare; usually a bush here. Singleton Park, Glamorgan 11x42 (2000 OCJ).

Idesia polycarpa Idesia China, Japan, 1864? Very rare. Bute Park, Glamorgan 15x50 (1990 AFM); Stourhead, Wilts. (21)x37 (1990 AFM).

Ilex Hollies

Ilex x altaclarensis Highclere Holly (*aquifolium* x *perado*) Occasional, most often as 'Hodginsii': Merlewood, Kent 16.5x63@0.55m under lumps (2002 DGA); Calderstones Park, Liverpool 14x58 (1988 AFM);

The wild Holly *(Ilex aquifolium)* can be caught out by intense cold in the Scottish Highlands, but is otherwise a surprisingly tough tree, thriving on shingle-banks and high mountain-sides. Indeed, the largest examples tend to be on poor soil and extreme habitats.

The one European species has some claim to the prettiest of all its huge genus. Only the more distinguishable of its myriad cultivars are listed here; some, like the Hedgehog Holly whose leaves have spines over the tip as well as around the edge, have been grown in gardens in Stuart times. Others, like the Weeping Golden Holly *(I. a.* 'Aurea Pendula') (seen here at the Swiss Garden, Bedfordshire) remain strangely rare.

Easthampstead Park, Berks. 21x46@? (1992 JW). Other distinctive clones include:

'Belgica Aurea' Now very rare. Central Park, East Ham, London 10x38 (2001 OCJ) – largely reverted.

'Camelliifolia' Rather occasional. Sutton Place, Surrey 12x51 (1996); Windsor (Savill Garden) 19x40 (2000 OCJ).

'Golden King' Frequent; small-growing. Godinton Park, Kent 9x32 (1999 OCJ).

'Hendersonii' Rather rare. Park Hotel, Forres, Moray 15x45 (1989 AFM) – two the same size; Muncaster Castle, Cumbria (22)x35 (1991 AFM).

'Lawsoniana' Frequent; small-growing. Castleward, Down 8x28 (1982 AFM).

***I. aquifolium* Holly** Native; abundant. Greencombe, Somerset x162 near base (2000 Joan Loraine) – larger of two huge low pollards; Cloghfune, Kerry 12x174@0.4m (2000 TROI) – multi-stemmed; Dundonnell House, Highland 14x125@1.3m (1991 AFM), p1685?; Staverton Thicks, Suffolk 22.5x75 (1967 A Kerr) – 7m bole; one of many tall old Hollies here.

'Argenteomarginata' Silver Holly Abundant (in various clones). Ballydarton House, Carlow 13.5x90@0.5m under forks and 15x68 (2000 TROI) – both in poor condition; Dalvey, Highland 18x53+45 (1989 AFM). 'Silver Queen' is one of the brightest forms: Clermount Park, Louth 15.5x69@1m (2000 TROI).

'Aurea Marginata' Golden Holly Abundant (in various clones). Buxted Park, E Sussex 11x55 (1994 OCJ) – narrow leaves; Gatton Hall, Surrey 16x(40) (2000 OCJ) – male. 'Golden Queen' is one of the more distinctive forms: Gartmore House, Stirling 11x50 (1984 AFM); Monreith, Dumfries & Galloway 18x40 (1979 AFM).

'Aurea Pendula' Weeping Golden Holly Very rare; not yet measured to 'tree' size.

f. *bacciflava* Yellow-berried Holly Rare. Gliffaes, Powys 11x47 (1995); Staunton CP, Hants. 16x22 (1985 AFM).

'Ciliata Major' Very rare. Handcross Park, W Sussex 9x41@0.8m (1998 OCJ).

'Contorta' Very rare. Kew RBG 9x(40) (2001 OCJ).

'Crassifolia' Leather-leaf Holly Very rare. Kew RBG 6x28@1.2m (2001 OCJ).

'Crispa' Rare. Glasnevin NBG 11x49 (2003 DGA) – sparse; Sedgwick House, Cumbria 17x48 (1995 DH).

'Ferox' Hedgehog Holly Rather rare; small-growing. Ickham church, Kent 6x(40) (1999 OCJ); Swiss Garden, Beds. 13x19 (1994 DGA).

'Ferox Argentea' Silver Hedgehog Holly Rather rare. Kinfauns Castle, Perth 13x38 (1985 AFM).

'Flavescens' Moonlight Holly Rare; small-growing. Kew RBG 7x34@1m (2001 OCJ).

'Golden Milkmaid' Rare; usually reverts. Alnwick Castle, Northumberland 23x43 (1977 AFM). The other 'Milkboy' and 'Milkmaid' Hollies seldom reach tree size.

'Latispina' Very rare. Kew RBG 13x36 (2001 OCJ).

'Myrtifolia' Myrtle-leaved Holly Rather rare. Myddelton House, London 13x26+25+25 (2001 OCJ) – sprawling with age. 'Myrtifolia Aurea' is usually bushy.

f. *pendula* Weeping Holly Occasional. Endsleigh, Devon x54 (1990 AFM).

'Perry's Weeping' Occasional. West Dean House, W Sussex 3x33@1m (1997 OCJ).

'Pyramidalis' Much planted, but seldom identifiable as an old tree. Putteridge Bury, Herts. 15x49@1.3m under bumps (2002 DGA) – grafted at base.

'Recurva' Very rare. Kew RBG 8x38 (2001 OCJ).

I.* x *beanii (*aquifolium* x *dipyrena*). Bagshot Park, Surrey 9x59 (2000 OCJ).

I. cyrtura C China. In one or two collections. Trewithen, Cornwall 19x38@2m (1985 AFM).

I. dipyrena **Himalayan Holly** 1840. Rare. Leonardslee, W Sussex 14x51 (1996 OCJ).

I. fargesii C China, 1908. Very rare. Abbotsbury, Dorset 14.5x37+26 (1980 AFM).

I. kingiana E Himalayas. In a few mild gardens. Caerhays 12x50 and 17x42 (1984 AFM).

I. latifolia **Tarajo** Japan, 1840. Very rare. Holker Hall, Cumbria 13x95@0.8m/x84+48 (2002 DH).

I. macrocarpa C China, 1907. In a few big gardens. Kingston Bagpuize House, Oxon. 8x45@? (1996); Westonbirt NA 13x21 (2002 OCJ) – crowded.

I. opaca **American Holly** E USA, 1744. Now very rare. Kew RBG 11x36 (2001 OCJ).

I. pedunculosa Japan, 1893. Very rare; often bushy. Borde Hill 11x28 (1995 OCJ).

I. perado var. *platyphylla* Canaries, Azores, by 1760. Confined to the mildest areas. Caerhays 14x29 (1984 AFM).

Jubaea chilensis **Chilean Wine Palm** Considered tender, but a large tree grew out of doors at Kew RBG in the 19th century. (Torquay, Devon 7x96 (1972).)

Juglans Walnuts

Juglans ailanthifolia **Japanese Walnut** 1860. Rare. Belgrove, Cork 15x162@1m (2001 AF) – four stems by 1.4m; Edinburgh RBG (20)x77 (1991 AFM), p1906; Canford School, Dorset 20x52@0.5m (1995 VES).

J. cathayensis **Chinese Walnut** 1903. Very rare. Hergest Croft 17x59 (1995 VES), p1912.

J. cinerea **Butternut** E N America, 1633. Rare. Lower Coombe Royal, Devon 9x104 (1988 AFM) – now an ancient hollow shell; Cliveden, Bucks. 24x83 (2002 OCJ).

J. elaeopyren SW USA, 1894? In some collections. Cambridge UBG 17.5x69 (2002 DGA), p1923.

J. hindsii C California, 1878. In a few collections. Windsor (Valley Gardens) 12x40@1m (2000 OCJ), p1958.

J. x intermedia (*nigra* x *regia*) In some collections. Hergest Croft (var. *vilmoriniana*) 31x134@0.5m (1995 VES).

J. mandshurica **Manchurian Walnut** NE Asia, 1859. Very rare. Firle Park, E Sussex 11x69 (1994 OCJ); Syon Park, London 17x62 (2002 OCJ).

J. microcarpa **Texan Walnut** SW USA, 1868. Very rare. Kew RBG 16x59 (2001), from 1906 seed; Canford School, Dorset 19x49@0.5m (1995 VES).

var. **major** – see *J. elaeopyren*.

J. nigra **Black Walnut** E USA, by 1686. Frequent in warm areas, where it grows largest. Much Hadham Old Rectory, Herts. 20x217 (2001 DGA), p1820; cut back; Mote Park, Kent 27x190 (1995 OCJ), p1805?; much died back; Marble Hill Park, London 27x184 (2001 OCJ); Hatfield Forest, Essex 31x156 (2002 OCJ); Battersea Park, London 31x110 (2001 OCJ).

var. *alburyensis* **Albury Walnut** In a few collections. Albury Park, Surrey 20x128 (2000 OCJ) – original tree, with mistletoe.

J. regia **Walnut** SE Europe to China; long grown here. Frequent. Gayhurst, Bucks. 20x197 (2002 DGA); Boxted

One of Britain's champion Common Walnuts (*Juglans regia*) at Gayhurst, Bucks.

Hall, Suffolk 23x196 on 4m bole and 27x123 (2002 JP); Ballinlough Castle, Westmeath 21x196@0.75m on short bole (2000 TROI); Garth House, Perth (30)x119 (1988).

'Laciniata' **Cut-leaved Walnut** Rare. Hergest Croft 15x66 (1995 VES), p1912; Hopefield House, Cumbria 18x53 (1998 DH).

J. rupestris – see *J. microcarpa* and *J. elaeopyren*.

J. stenocarpa NE Asia. A few young trees. (Nymans, W Sussex 22x49 (1970 AFM).)

Juniperus Junipers

Juniperus bermudiana **Bermuda Juniper** By 1684. In a few collections; hardy, but seldom a tree here. (Fota, Cork 17x39 (1987 AFM), p1916.)

J. cedrus **Canary Island Juniper** In some collections; tender? (7x38+38 at Highdown, W. Sussex in 1983 (AFM).)

J. chinensis **Chinese Juniper** China, Japan, 1804. Occasional. Bedgebury School, Kent 21x87@0.4m (1995 OCJ) – dense spire; Hengrave Hall, Suffolk (13)x79@1m (1999 DGA) – leans; Colquhalzie, Perth 12x75 (1997).

'Albospica' Rare. Crowsley Park, Oxon. 10x41 (1978 AFM); Trawsgoed, Ceredigion 13x37@0.6m+35 (1982 AFM).

'Aurea' **Young's Golden Juniper** Rather occasional. Witney Cemetery, Oxon. 13x51@? (1988 JW); Golden Grove, Carmarthen 16x49 (1993 VES).

'Kaizuka' Very rare. Bedgebury NP 10x26 (1995 OCJ), p1927. A spreading tree with the typically spiky habit at Staplefield church, W Sussex, 9x65@1m (1996 OCJ), may

Champion Himalayan Weeping Juniper (*Juniperus recurva*) at Birr Castle, Offaly.
Junipers grow slowly, but will do so almost anywhere and can keep going almost indefinitely; even forms from Bermuda, the Canaries and tropical east Africa have been successfully grown in British and Irish collections, though many species remain sulky bushes here. The wild Juniper is the only tree native both to Europe and northern North America; it is becoming rarer as taller trees shade it out on downs and heaths and as mild winters allow fungal infections to take hold.
Much the biggest Juniper in Britain, an American Pencil Cedar, is a relic of the 18th century landscape garden at Painshill, Surrey. Most of its branches have been blown out over the years, while a 15-metre Rowan grows from the main fork at 2 metres.

be a sport.

'Keteleeri' Rare. Etal, Northumberland 12x44 (1991 AFM); Bedgebury NP 12x32 (1995 OCJ), p1926.

'Leeana' Very rare. Bedgebury NP 9x42@1m (1995 OCJ), p1937.

'Pendula'. Kew RBG 12x29 (2001 OCJ), p1927; a handsome weeping tree.

J. communis **Common Juniper** Native. Locally abundant: chalk downs, moorlands. Seldom a 'tree'; to 9m. Armadale Castle, Highland 6.5x29 (1978 AFM).

'Hibernica' Irish Juniper An occasional planted clone. Hafodunos, Conwy 8x46@0.8m (1984 AFM).

J. drupacea **Syrian Juniper** Greece to Syria, 1820? Very rare. Brickendon Grange, Herts. 19x52 (2001 OCJ), p1850?; Batsford Arboretum, Glos. 17x82@0.2m (2003 OCJ).

J. excelsa **Grecian Juniper** Balkans to Iran, 1806. Very rare. High Canons, Herts. 14x50 (2002 OCJ).

J. flaccida **Mexican Juniper** Mexico, Texas, 1838. In some collections as a small plant. (Bicton Park, Devon 12x41 (1959 AFM), blown 1967).

J. monosperma **Cherrystone Juniper** SE N America, c1900. A few bushes. (Wisley 10x36 (1996), died 2000.)

J. oxycedrus **Prickly Juniper** Mediterranean to Iran, 1739. A few bushes. (Leonardslee, W Sussex 20x27 (1985 AFM), blown 1987.)

J. phoenicea **Phoenician Juniper** Mediterranean, 1683. Almost extinct here. Tortworth Court, Glos. 16x45+26 (1980 AFM).

J. procera **East African Juniper** Kenya, Ethiopia, 1914. In one or two mild gardens. (Fota, Cork (14)x105@1.3m (1994 DGA), p1918.)

J. recurva **Himalayan Weeping Juniper** E Himalayas to China, 1830. Rather rare; thriving only in high humidity. Birr Castle 15.5x135@0.3m/x69+57+ (2002 AF); Hafodunos, Conwy (20)x67+49 (1990 AFM); Castlewellan NA 21m (1994 VES) – forking.

var. *coxii* Cox's Juniper Upper Burma, 1930. Now the commoner form. Mount Usher, Wicklow x71 under fork (1989 AFM); Hergest Croft 16x39+17 (1995 VES), p1925; Drenagh, Derry (18)x36 (1983 AFM).

J. rigida **Temple Juniper** NE Asia, Japan, 1861. Rare. Bedgebury NP 11x41 (1995 OCJ), p1926; Westonbirt NA 15x31 (2002 OCJ), p1937.

***J. scopulorum* Rocky Mountain Juniper** W N America, 1839. In some collections; scarcely to 'tree' size.
'Skyrocket' Skyrocket Juniper Frequent. Grayswood Hill, Surrey 9x25 (1998 OCJ).
***J. squamata* Flaky Juniper** Afghanistan to Taiwan, 1824? A few bushes. (Headfort, Meath 11x33 (1980 AFM) when dead; p1925.)
'Meyeri' Meyer's Juniper Abundant. Westonbirt NA 9x30 (2002 OCJ), p1941; fine symmetrical tree with single bole.
***J. thurifera* Spanish Juniper** France to Morocco, 1752. In a few collections. Borde Hill 14x30 (1995 OCJ) – as label.
***J. virginiana* Pencil Cedar** E N America, c1660. Occasional. Painshill Park, Surrey 16x149@1m (2000 OCJ); Holkham Hall, Norfolk 21x63 (1973 AFM).
'Burkii' Very rare. Hillier Gardens 11x39@0m (2001 Ron Holley); Bedgebury NP 9x28 (1995 OCJ), p1943.
'Canaertii' Rare. Bedgebury NP 11x31 and 12x26 (1995 OCJ), both p1926.
'Glauca' Blue Pencil Cedar Rare. Tulliallan Castle, Fife 11x35+ (1990 AFM); Borde Hill 13x30 (1995 OCJ), p1936.
***J. wallichiana* Black Juniper** Himalayas, 1849. Rare. Birr Castle 11x31 (2000 TROI), p1942; Bodnant, Conwy (15)x29 (1991 AFM).

***Kalopanax septemlobus* Castor Aralia** (*K. pictus*) Japan, 1874. Rare; grows well everywhere. Greenwich Park, London 14x(60) (2001 OCJ); Lythe Hill Park, Surrey 18x54 (2000 OCJ).
var. *maximowiczii* The less rare form. Endsleigh Devon 20x103 under fork (1995); Durris, Aberdeen 17x72 (1987 AFM) – long bole.

***Keteleeria davidiana* David's Keteleeria** China, Taiwan, 1888. About ten small trees; probably needs hot summers to thrive. Headfort, Meath 9x49 (1980 AFM), p1921; Wakehurst Place 11x26 (1997 OCJ), p1918.

***Koelreuteria paniculata* Golden Rain Tree** China, 1763 (including var. *apiculata*). Occasional in the warmest areas. Syon Park, London 14x63 (2002 OCJ).
'Fastigiata' Fastigiate Rain Tree Very rare. Woodford, London 13x27@1m (2001 OCJ).

+ *Laburnocytisus adamii* Adam's Laburnum (*Cytisus purpureus* + *Laburnum anagyroides*, 1825) Now very rare. Westonbirt NA 8x35 (2002 OCJ).

***Laburnum alpinum* Scotch Laburnum** C and S Europe; long grown here. Rather rare; happiest in cool humid areas. Megginch Castle, Perth 8x115@0.5m (1993) – ancient leaning tree; Brooklands, Somerset 15.5x31 (1982 AFM).
***L. anagyroides* Common Laburnum** C and S Europe; long grown here. Abundant as an older tree; likes a rich soil. Usually short-lived, but some 'veterans' have been recorded (Abercynrig, Powys 5x140@base? (1988 JW), p1749). Barra Hall Park, London 9x69 (1996 PJB).

'Aureum' Golden-leafed Laburnum Very rare. (Arley Arboretum, Worcs. 6x35 (1991 AFM).) Several other cultivars scarcely attain 'tree' size.
***L. x watereri* Hybrid Laburnum** (*alpinum* x *anagyroides*) Now the most planted laburnum (as 'Vossii'). Homes Garden, Bristol (12)x64@0.6m (1991 AFM).

***Lagarostrobus franklinii* Huon Pine** (*Dacrydium franklinii*) Tasmania, c1840. About 20 plants; a tree in the mildest parts. (Fota, Cork 12x41 (1987 AFM), p1854.)

Larix Larches

Larix* x *czekanowski (*gmelinii* x *sibirica*) Windsor (Valley Gardens) 14x35 (2000 OCJ) – ?
***L. decidua* European Larch** Mountains of C Europe; by 1629. Abundant. Monzie Castle, Perth 35x192 (1991 AFM), p1737; bole 6m long; Dunkeld Cathedral, Perth 33.5x179 (1999 Donald Rodger), p1737; Glenlee Park, Dumfries & Galloway 45x95 (1979 AFM).
'Pendula' Very rare. Craighall, Perth 15x97 (1986 AFM).
var. *polonica* Polish Larch 1912. Very rare. Bedgebury NP 27x56 (1999 OCJ), p1925. (Ashburnham Place, E Sussex (30)x86 (1983 AFM), blown 1987.)
***L. x eurolepis* Dunkeld Larch** (*decidua* x *kaempferi*, 1897) Abundant: now the preferred larch in forestry. Blair Castle, Perth 24x100 (1983 AFM), p1905; Ardkinglas, Argyll 40x80 (1985 AFM); Dunkeld House, Perth 40x67 (1983 AFM).
***L. gmelinii* Dahurian Larch** E Siberia, 1827. About 50 trees; not thriving. Achamore, Argyll 17x67 (1986 AFM); Hergest Croft 23x39 (1995 VES).
var. *japonica* Kuriles, 1888. In some collections; not thriving. Dawyck, Scottish Borders 9.5x49 (1992 AFM), p1909; Borde Hill 16x25 (1995 OCJ).
var. *principis-rupprechtii* Prince Rupert's Larch NE Asia, 1903. In a few collections. Borde Hill 19x51 (1995 OCJ), p1927; Bridge Gardens, Berks. 21x51 (1995) – as supplied, 1960; Batsford Arboretum, Glos. 22x45 (2003 OCJ).
***L. griffithiana* Himalayan Larch** 1848. Poor plants in a few collections. (Flowerdale, Highland 22x50 (1991 AFM), died by 2001.)
***L. kaempferi* Japanese Larch** 1861. Occasional; sometimes in forestry. Dunkeld House, Perth 29x105 (1990 AFM), p1887; Blair Castle, Perth 40x95 (1989 AFM), p1886.
'Pendula' Very rare. Hillier Gardens 18x50 (2002 Harry James).
***L. laricina* Tamarack** Alaska to E USA, 1737? Rare; not thriving. Kew RBG 18x54 (2001 OCJ).
***L. occidentalis* Western Larch** NW N America, 1881. Very rare. One of the few W North American conifers which seldom does well here. Powerscourt, Wicklow 23.5x78 (2000 TROI); Kyloe Wood, Northumberland 33x40 (2000), p1925; very slender.
***L. x pendula* Weeping Larch** (*decidua* x *laricina*?) Long grown here; a handful remain. Spa Hotel, Kent 24x88 (1995 OCJ); Bedgebury NP 26x48 (1995 OCJ).
'Repens'. Henham Hall, Suffolk 3x95@1m (2000 DGA).
***L. potaninii* Chinese Larch** SW China, 1904. In one

or two collections; not thriving. Headfort, Meath 16x30 (1980 AFM), p1915.

L. sibirica Siberian Larch W Siberia, 1806. Needs long hard winters to thrive; the few grown here may not be authentic. Windsor (Valley Gardens) 17x43 (2000 OCJ).

***Laurelia sempervirens* Peruvian Nutmeg** (incorporating *L. serrata*) S Andes, by 1868. Rare; a handsome large tree in the mildest, warmest areas. Kilmacurragh, Wicklow 17x90 (1990 AFM), p1868; Trebah, Cornwall 21.5x51 (2000).

***Laurus azorica* Canary Laurel** Canaries, Azores. A tree in the mildest areas. Caerhays 15x53 (1971 AFM).
L. nobilis Bay Mediterranean; long grown here. Abundant but not very hardy; a tree in warmer parts. Knocklofty House, Tipperary 12x77@0.9m on single bole (2000 TROI); Notting Hill, London 11x63@0.7m on single bole under fork at 1m (2002 OCJ); Margam Park, Glamorgan (21)x29+ (1985 AFM).
'Angustifolia' Willow-leaved Bay Very rare. Beechwood House, W Sussex 10x32 (1997 OCJ).
'Aurea' Golden Bay Rather rare; tends to remain bushy.

***Leptospermum scoparium* Manuka** New Zealand, 1772. A tree only in the mildest, warmest areas. Garinish Island, Kerry 5.3x28 (2001 AF).

***Libocedrus bidwillii* Pahautea** New Zealand. In a few collections. Headfort, Meath 8.5x34@1m (1980 AFM), p1929.
L. chilensis – see *Austrocedrus chilensis*.

Ligustrum compactum Himalayas, SW China, 1877. In one or two collections. Kew RBG 12x34 (2002 OCJ) – fine tree.
L. confusum Himalayas, 1919. In one or two collections. Caerhays 12x79@0.5m (1984 AFM).
L. lucidum Chinese Tree Privet China, 1794. Occasional; a tree if summers are warm. Battersea Park, London 14x103@0.4m (2001 OCJ) – huge bush; Kingsmere, Hants. 15x79 (1977 AFM); Thorn House, Devon 18x67 (1977 AFM); York House, London 18x66@0.7m under forks (2001 OCJ). A gold form in the Central Gardens, Bournemouth, Dorset was 11x36+31+ (1985 AFM).
'Aureovariegatum' Very rare. Goodmayes Park, London 8x56@0.2m/x33+++ (2001 OCJ).
'Excelsum Superbum' Rather rare. Kensington Gardens, London 12x77@0.1m (2001 OCJ).
'Tricolor' Rather rare. (West Hill, Hants. 11m (pre-1970).)
L. sinense China, 1852? Westonbirt NA 12x36@0.3m (2002 OCJ).

Lindera megaphylla C China, 1900. In a few big gardens. Borde Hill 13x52 (1995 OCJ), p1914; Caerhays 16x29 (1984 AFM).

***Liquidambar formosana* Chinese Sweet-gum** China, Taiwan, 1884. Rare (as 'var. *monticola*'). Killerton, Devon 22x56 (2001 OCJ), p1916.

L. orientalis Oriental Sweet-gum Asia Minor; long grown here but very rare. St Patrick's College, Kildare 12x61 (2000 TROI) – the only respectable 'tree' recorded.
L. styraciflua Sweet Gum E USA; long grown here. Frequent in warm areas; needs hot summers to grow well. Many recent plantings are autumn-colouring clones such as 'Lane Roberts' and 'Worplesdon' (which is of rather bushy habit). Stratfield Saye, Hants. (28)x99 (1996 VES); Syon Park, London 27x96 (2002 OCJ) – long bole.
'Variegata' ('Aurea') Very rare to date. Hillier Gardens 13x25 (2001 Harry James). Other foliage forms have yet to reach 'tree' size here.

***Liriodendron chinense* Chinese Tulip Tree** China, 1901. Rare; less vigorous than the American species. Ashford Chace, Hants. 25x94@1.2m under scar (2002 OCJ); Borde Hill 19x87 (1995 OCJ), p1913.
L. tulipifera Tulip Tree E N America. Frequent. Esher Place, Surrey 21x288@0.9m under wide fork (2000 OCJ) – 1685 original?; cut back; Golden Grove, Carmarthen 25x281 under fork (2003) – ivy-clad; The Hirsel, Scottish Borders x231 (1993 JP), p1742; Taplow House, Bucks. 35x221 (2002 OCJ) – 4m bole; magnificent; Waterlooville, Hants. 20x220@0.7m (1998) – low pollard; Staunton CP, Hants. (34)x214 (1998); Bloomsbury House, Meath 21.5x214@1.1m on short bole (2000 TROI); Leith Hill, Surrey 30x209 on good bole (2000 OCJ); Kitlands, Surrey 34x202 (2000 OCJ), p1860?; very fine; Killerton, Devon 36x120+105 (2001 OCJ), p1808; massive base.
'Aureomarginatum' Variegated Tulip Tree Rather rare. Gunnersbury Park, London 22x75 (2001 OCJ).
'Cortortum' Very rare. Bicton Park, Devon 14x69@0.5m (2001 OCJ).
'Fastigiatum' Fastigiate Tulip Tree Rare. Windsor (Valley Gardens) 19x58 (2000 OCJ); Arduaine, Argyll 26x50 (1998).
'Integrifolium' Very rare. Kew RBG 19x92 (2001 OCJ) – hollow and broken.

Lithocarpus cleistocarpus C China, 1901. Caerhays 21.5x96@0.4m and 22x67 (1984 AFM).
L. densiflorus Tanbark Oak California, Oregon, 1874. In a few big gardens everywhere. Edinburgh RBG 10x48 (1997); Kew RBG 17x45 (2001 OCJ), from 1923 seed.
L. edulis Japanese Stone Oak In a few big gardens. Wakehurst Place 14x26 (1997 OCJ) – slender.
L. henryi Henry's Stone Oak C China, 1901. In a few big gardens. (Caerhays 16x32 (1975 AFM).)
L. pachyphyllus E Himalayas. Caerhays 18x50+ (1984 AFM).

Lomatia ferruginea S Andes, 1846? Confined to the mildest areas. Mount Usher, Wicklow 13x40 on double stem (1989 AFM); Bantry House, Cork 7x27 (2001 AF); Castlewellan NA 16.5m (1994 VES) – five-stemmed bush.
L. hirsuta Andes, 1902. In a few collections. (Nymans, W Sussex 11x31+31 (1985 AFM).)

Lonicera maackii NE Asia, 1880. Rare; a honeysuckle which can grow as a small tree. Cambridge UBG (f. *podocarpa*) 6.5x61@0.3m/x38++ (2002 DGA).

***Luma apiculata* Chilean Myrtle** (*Myrtus luma*) S Andes, 1843. Rather rare; a beautiful tree in the mildest areas. Castlefreke, Cork 17.5x77@0.5m/x43++ (2000 TROI); Ardnagashel, Cork 11x62 (2001 AF); Tresco Abbey, Cornwall (20)x27+27 (1987 AFM).

***Lyonothamnus floribundus* Catalina Ironwood** Santa Catalina Island, California, 1900. Rare (usually as var. *aspleniifolius*); growing into a small tree in warm areas.

Maackia amurensis NE Asia, Japan, 1864. Rare; needs hot summers and scarcely reaches 'tree' size here.
M. chinensis China, 1908. Rare; very seldom reaching tree-size here. (9x34@1m at Wakehurst Place (1969 AFM).)

***Maclura pomifera* Osage Orange** S USA, 1818. Very rare; likes hot summers. Haberdashers' Aske's School, Herts. 14x70 under fork (2002 OCJ); Roath Park, Glamorgan 18x63 (1990 AFM).

Magnolia Magnolias

***Magnolia acuminata* Cucumber Tree** E USA, 1736. Rather rare. Likes hot summers. Eastnor Castle, Herefords. 16x110 (2002); Albury Park, Surrey 22x72 (2000 OCJ).
var. ***subcordata* Southern Cucumber Tree** (*M. cordata*) 1801. Nominally bushy. Dyffryn Gardens, Glamorgan 16x78@0.7m and 19x63 (1997 OCJ).
M. 'Buzzard' (*campbellii* x *sargentiana* var. *robusta*) Very rare. Chyverton, Cornwall 15x29+20 (1991 AFM) – 1953 original.
***M. campbellii* Campbell's Magnolia** Himalayas, c1870. Rather rare. Belgrove, Cork 19.5x155@1m under fork (2001 AF); Trengwainton, Cornwall x172 under multiple stems (2003 Ian Wright) – spread 43m; Wakehurst

---

Tulip Tree (*Liriodendron tulipifera*) has proved itself one of the biggest and longest-lived of introduced broadleaves. It is less reliant on summer heat than most of the trees of the eastern United States: there is even a fine example in Stornoway Woods on Lewis. Its wood is brittle, and it never grows here the long clean boles which are such a feature of the American forests. The 'veteran' at Esher Place, Surrey, is believed to have been planted by Bishop Compton in 1685; it remains in the best of health. This champion of the rare form 'Contortum' at Bicton Botanical Gardens, Devon, has strangely twisted leaves which, like the type's, turn yellow in autumn.

Place 18x91 on good bole (1997 OCJ); Leonardslee, W Sussex 23x72 (1996 OCJ).

'Alba' White Campbell's Magnolia Rare. Borde Hill 20x53 (1995 OCJ), p1925; Clyne Gardens, Glamorgan 22x50 (2000 OCJ) – long straight bole.

'Charles Raffill' 1946?; the most widespread clone of the hybrid with ssp. *mollicomata*. Trengwainton, Cornwall 16x68 (1995); Antony House, Cornwall 19x67 (1991 AFM), p1948.

'Lanarth' (Forrest 25655) Rare. Killerton, Devon 18x64 (2001 OCJ).

ssp. *mollicomata* E Himalayas, 1920. Now more planted than the type. Trewithen, Cornwall (17)x107@0.6m (1995), p1912; Lanhydrock, Cornwall 17x66 (1987 AFM); Borde Hill 20x39 (1995 OCJ), p1940.

M. campbellii x sprengeri. Westonbirt NA 18x35 (2002 OCJ).

M. cordata – see *M. acuminata* var. *subcordata*.

M. dawsoniana Dawson's Magnolia W China, 1908. Very rare. Birr Castle 18.5x71 (2000 TROI), p1946; Chyverton, Cornwall 17x64 (1993) – 1944 original of 'Chyverton'.

M. delavayi Chinese Evergreen Magnolia SW China, 1899. Locally occasional in mild, warm areas. Borde Hill 10x57 (1995 OCJ), p1911; Caerhays 18x55+ (1993).

M. denudata Yulan China, 1789. Now rare; grows slowly into a small tree. Lower Coombe Royal, Devon x57 (1988 AFM) – now almost supine; Endsleigh, Devon 16x31 (1995).

M. fraseri Fishtail Magnolia SE USA, 1786. Very rare; likes warm summers. Muncaster Castle, Cumbria 14x44 (2000 DH); Leonardslee, W Sussex 16x41 (1996 OCJ).

M. grandiflora Bull Bay SE USA, 1734. Frequent; needs year-round warmth to reach tree-size. Most of the largest are the clone 'Exmouth'. Fota, Cork 11.5x86 (1999 TROI); Gaunts, Dorset 14x(58)@0.3m (1973 AFM) – against wall.

M. hypoleuca – see *M. obovata*.

M. 'Kewensis' (*kobus* x *salicifolia*) Rare. Winkworth Arboretum, Surrey 15x53 (2000 OCJ); Kew RBG 9x68@0.5m (2001 OCJ).

M. kobus Kobushi N Japan, 1865. Very occasional (the largest are 'var. *borealis*'). Kew RBG 13x70 (2001 OCJ), p1915; Coverwood House, Surrey 15x58@1m (1986 AFM).

M. x loebneri (*kobus* x *stellata*) Occasional in various clones; 'Merrill' tends to be the most tree-like. Bristol Zoo, Bristol 10x30 (1990 AFM).

M. macrophylla Big-leaved Magnolia SE USA, 1800. Rare. Need shelter but warm summers. Mount Congreve, Waterford 17x35@1.3m (2002 AF).

M. 'Micheal Rosse' (*campbellii* 'Alba' x *sargentiana* var. *robusta*). Nymans, W Sussex 12x30+26 (1996 OCJ) – original.

M. nitida SW China to Tibet. In a few mild gardens. Caerhays 9x37 (top lost), and 12x35 (1984 AFM).

M. obovata Japanese Big-leaved Magnolia (*M. hypoleuca*) Japan, 1865. Rare. Trewidden, Cornwall (16)x93@1.4m (2003 Alison Clough), p1897?; Weasenham Woods, Norfolk (20)x28 (1990 AFM).

M. officinalis Chinese Big-leaved Magnolia C China (extinct in the wild), 1900. Very rare. Windsor (Valley Gardens; 'Biloba') 20x45 (2000 OCJ).

M. 'Princess Margaret' (*campbellii* 'Alba' x *sargentiana* var. *robusta*) Very rare. Windsor (Valley Gardens) 16x58@1.2m (2002 OCJ) – original.

M. robusta – see *M. sargentiana* var. *robusta*.

M. rostrata SW China. No large examples remain. (Sidbury Manor, Devon 20x44 (1990 AFM), p1935.)

M. salicifolia Willow-leaved Magnolia Japan, 1892. Very occasional. Inner Temple Garden, London 13x71@1.2m (2001 OCJ); Caerhays 15x66 (1991 AFM), p1921; Wakehurst Place 18x32 (2001 OCJ) – very slender.

M. sargentiana Sargent's Magnolia W China, 1908. Very rare. Nymans, W Sussex 15x53 (1996 OCJ); Trewithen, Cornwall 16x51 (1987 AFM); Caerhays 16.5x35 (1984 AFM), p1948.

var. *robusta* Rare. Windsor (Savill Garden) 11x61 (2000 OCJ), p1948; cut back; Caerhays 18x60 (1984 AFM); Borde Hill 18x39@0.8m (1995 OCJ), from 1940 seed.

M. x soulangiana Saucer Magnolia (*denudata* x *liliiflora*) Abundant in many clones; grows slowly into a small tree. Riverhill House, Kent 11x45+42 (1995 OCJ); Camberley, Surrey 13x40+36+31 (1996).

M. x soulangiana x campbellii. Windsor (Savill Garden) 15x37 (2000 OCJ).

M. 'Spectrum' (*lilliflora* 'Nigra' x *sprengeri* var. *diva*) Very rare to date. Windsor (Valley Gardens) 8x25 (2002 OCJ).

M. sprengeri var. diva Sprenger's Magnolia C China, 1901. Rare. Trewithen, Cornwall 18.5x87@1m? (1995); Caerhays x74 (1984 AFM), p1912; Borde Hill 22x54 (1995 OCJ).

var. *elongata* W China, 1904. Very rare; of poor growth. Birr Castle 14x31 (2000 TROI); Bodnant, Conwy 16x27 (1984 AFM).

M. stellata Star Magnolia Japan, 1862. Abundant; grows very slowly into a small tree. Kew RBG 5x27+21 (2001 OCJ). 'Norman Gould', the cream of a series of colchicene-induced mutants, is larger: Windsor (Valley Gardens) 9x27 (2000 OCJ).

M. 'Thomas Messel' Very rare. Nymans, W Sussex 9x38@1.2m (1996 OCJ).

M. 'Treve Holman' (*campbellii* ssp. *mollicomata* x *sargentiana* var. *robusta*) Very rare. Chyverton, Cornwall 17x33 (1991 AFM) – 1966 original.

M. tripetala Umbrella Tree E USA, 1752. Now rare; often a bush. Collingwood Grange, Kent 10x30@1.2m (1995 OCJ); Richmond Park, London 14x22 (2001 OCJ).

M. x veitchii Veitch's Magnolia (*campbellii* x *denudata*, 1907). Very occasional. The most vigorous magnolia here: Chapel Knap Gardens, Somerset 15x116 (1993), p1931; Caerhays (29)x67 (1984 AFM), p1920. The usual clone is 'Peter Veitch'; rarer are 'Alba' (Kew RBG 16x118@0.3m (2001 OCJ), rather bushy), and 'Isca' (Muncaster Castle, Cumbria 21x76 (2000 DH)).

M. virginiana Sweet Bay E USA, long grown here. Now very rare. Weston Park, Staffs. 7.5x31@? (1992 John Bulmer); Tilgate Park, W Sussex 9x27+26 (1996 OCJ) – cut back.

M. x wieseneri (*M.* x *watsonii*; *obovata* x *sieboldii*, by 1889).

Rare; generally bushy. Nymans, W Sussex 8x32@1.2m++ (1996 OCJ).

M. wilsonii Wilson's Magnolia W China, 1908. Rather rare; generally a bush. Howick Hall, Northumberland 8x29 (1991 VES).

Malus Crabs

Malus x adstringans (*baccata* etc. x *niedwetzkyana*). Includes the 'Rosybloom' Crabs – rarely planted and seldom thriving here. 'Simcoe' has reached 8x32@1.2m at the Chelsea Physic Garden, London (2001 OCJ).

M. angustifolia E USA, 1750. One or two poor trees. (Birr Castle 8x32 (1990 AFM).)

M. baccata Siberian Crab Across Asia, 1784. Frequent as var. *mandshurica*: Collingwood Grange, Kent 15x78@0.4m on short bole (1995 OCJ), p1920; Ashwicke, Glos. (recorded as the type – ?) 19x60@? (1995); Borde Hill ('Jackii') 15x65@0.3m under forks (1995 OCJ), p1932.

var. himalaica Himalayas. Kew RBG 8x36 (2001 OCJ), p1937.

'Lady Northcliffe' (a hybrid? by 1929) Rare. Kew RBG 8x37 (2001 OCJ).

M. bhutanica W China, 1904 (*M. toringoides*). Rather rare. Oxford BG, Oxon. 9x31 (1996 VES), p1946; Birr Castle (recorded as the bushy *M. sargentii* – ?) 11x23 (2000 TROI).

M. coronaria Garland Crab E N America, 1724. A handful of poor trees. (Westonbirt NA 12x30 under graft (1977 AFM).)

M. 'Crittenden' Very rare. Crittenden, Kent 6x36 (1997 OCJ) – graft at 1.8m of the Japanese original.

M. domestica Orchard Apple Abundant in innumerable clones. The largest trees are wild-growing and probably have hybridised with Wild Crabs ('*M. pumila*'): Kentchurch Court, Herefords. 13x83 (1975 AFM); Wychwood, Oxon. 18x66 (1984 AFM).

'Elise Rathke' A weeping ornamental clone, 1886. Rare. Batsford Arboretum, Glos (?) 5x31 (2003 OCJ).

M. 'Echtermeyer' – see *M.* x *gloriosa*.

M. florentina Italian Crab S Europe, 1877. Very rare. Warnham Court, W Sussex 10x39 (1997 OCJ), p1956; Hillier Gardens 10x39 (2001 Harry James).

M. floribunda Japanese Crab 1862. Abundant. Cator Park, London 8x70 (2001 OCJ) – straight bole tapers suddenly at 2.2m; Woburn Park, Beds. 14.5x50 (1995 DGA).

M. 'Frettingham Victoria'. Windsor (Savill Garden) 11x30 (2000 OCJ).

M. fusca Oregon Crab W N America, 1836. A few poor trees. Thorp Perrow, Yorks. 12x39 (1991 AFM).

M. x gloriosa 'Oekonomierat Echtermeyer' Weeping Purple Crab Occasional; a poor grower. Westonbirt School, Glos. 8x62@0.1m around forkings (2002 OCJ); West Ham Cemetery, London 4.5x31 (2002 OCJ) – spread 8m.

M. 'Golden Gem' Rare? Hillier Gardens 11x41@1.2m (2001 Harry James).

M. 'Golden Hornet' – see *M.* x *zumi*.

M. halliana Hall's Crab China, 1863. Rare. Cowdray Park, W Sussex 9x30 (1997 OCJ).

M. x hartwigii (*baccata* x *halliana*) Rare (usually as 'Katherine'). Tilgate Park, W Sussex (?) 12x80@0m (2002 OCJ) – huge bush.

M. 'Hillieri' – see *M.* x *scheideckeri*.

M. hupehensis Hubei Crab China, Japan, 1900. Quite frequent; luxuriates everywhere. Bodnant, Conwy (13)x73@1m? (1989 AFM); Hannah Peschar Sculpture Garden, Surrey 16x45 (2000 OCJ).

M. 'John Downie' 1875. Occasional. High Beeches, W Sussex 9x42 (1994 VES).

M. kansuensis W China, 1904. In a few collections. (Priestfield Pinetum, Bucks. 11x26@1m (1984 AFM).)

M. lancifolia USA, 1912. Hillier Gardens 8.5x25 (2001).

M. 'Laxton's Red' 1939. Kew RBG 8x40@1.2m (2001 OCJ).

M. x moerlandsii 'Profusion' and 'Liset' (by 1938) are occasional, but seldom recorded.

M. orthocarpa China. Hillier Gardens 9.5x32 (2001 Harry James).

M. prattii China, 1904. In a few big gardens. Borde Hill 10x49@0.4m (1995 OCJ), p1926.

M. prunifolia NE Asia; long grown here. Occasional. Bushy Ruff Wild Park, Kent 13x64@0.6m under forks (1999 OCJ).

var. rinki Rare. Hillier Gardens 10x30 (2001).

M. pumila – see *M. domestica*.

M. x purpurea Purple Crab (x *atrosanguinea* x *niedzwetzkyana*, by 1900) Abundant in various clones; 'Lemoinei' is probably the commonest and most vigorous. Croydon Cemetery, London 8x49 (2001 OCJ) – dying?; King George's Park, London 8x48 (2001 OCJ); Henrietta Park, Somerset 11x47 (2002 OCJ). The largest recorded trees of some distinctive clones include: Kew RBG ('Aldenhamensis') 11x27 (2001 OCJ), p1928; Welwyn Garden City, Herts. ('Eleyi') 9x40 (2002 OCJ).

M. x robusta Cherry-Crab (*baccata* x *prunifolia*) By 1815. Abundant; often of poor growth. Luxuriant trees are: Clyne Gardens, Glamorgan 9x58@1m (2000 OCJ); Orchards, W Sussex 11x49@0.6m under forks (1999 OCJ).

M. rockii China, 1922. In one or two collections. Kew RBG (?) 8x39@0.7m (2001 OCJ).

M. 'Royalty' 1958. Occasional as a young plant. Kew RBG 9x41@0.5m on short bole (2001 OCJ).

M. x schiedeckeri 'Hillieri' (*floribunda* x *prunifolia*) Rare? Oxford BG, Oxon. 6x28 (1996 VES), p1946.

M. 'Red Jade' 1935. Occasional as a small weeping plant. Crittenden, Kent 5x36@0.4m (1997 OCJ).

M. sieboldii – see *M. toringo*.

M. sikkimensis Sikkim Crab Himalayas, 1849. In a few big gardens. Benmore, Argyll 10x64 (1991 AFM); Westonbirt NA 12x45@1m (2002 OCJ), p1930.

M. x soulardii (*domestica* x *ioensis*, 1868) Very rare. Clarence Park, Herts. 8x61@0.2m under forks (2002 OCJ); Talbot Manor, Norfolk 10x28 (1978 AFM), p1960.

M. spectabilis Chinese Crab China, by 1750. Now very occasional. Finsbury Park, London 10x47 (2001 OCJ); Osterley Park, London 14x37 (2001 OCJ).

M. x sublobata (*prunifolia* x *toringo*, 1892?) Very rare. Hillier Gardens 9.5x34 (2001).

M. sylvestris Wild Crab Native. Frequent in ancient woodlands on rich or clay soils. Many wild trees (in scrub

No trees offer a greater contrast than do the ornamental crabs between the delicate glory of the plant in blossom and the gawky, unobtrusive thing which lives through the other 50 weeks of the year. As recorders may not be lucky enough to encounter them in their hour of glory, these trees are under-recorded, and, of the huge range which are now available to gardeners, cultivars are only featured here when the measured example seems reasonably likely to be the largest.

The Wild Crab (*Malus sylvestris*) is an unobtrusive as any: a thorny presence in ancient woodlands and old hedgerows on rich or clay soils, outnumbered by the 'wilding' descendants of orchard apples. Very occasionally, it finds room to grow into an imposing specimen, like this gnarled champion in a field near Durham. The hollows in its trunk are filled with aerial roots.

---

etc) will be hybrids with Orchard Apple (qv). Croxdale Hall, Durham 6x113@1.3m (2001 Den Gregson); Naas, Kildare 11x89@1.35m (2000 TROI); Savernake Forest, Wilts. x87 (1999 Jack Oliver) – very burred; Quakers Field, Laois 13x84 (2002 AF); Bedford Purlieus, Cambs. 17x57@? (1990 JW); Eridge Park, E Sussex 17x54@0.4m under narrow forks (2002 OCJ); The Mens, W Sussex 17x29+27 (1993 OCJ) – with a taller tree fallen.

M. toringo Siebold's Crab (*M. sieboldii*) Japan, 1856. Rather rare; often a bush. Edinburgh RBG 11x32@0.7m (1997).

M. toringoides – see *M. bhutanica*.

M. transitoria Cut-leaved Crab NW China, 1911. In a few big gardens. Hillier Gardens 8x31 (2001 Harry James).

M. trilobata Turkish Apple E Mediterranean, 1877. A rare but fine tree: Mill House, Shoreham, Kent 12x53 (1999 OCJ); Winkworth Arboretum, Surrey 15x50 (2000 OCJ), p1938.

M. tschonoskii Pillar Apple Japan, 1892. Very frequent; usually short-lived. Alderbrook Park, Surrey 15x62@0.5m under forks, and 16x57 (2000 OCJ); Westonbirt NA 19x28@1.7m above graft (2002 OCJ).

M. 'Wisley' Rare. Withersdane Hall, Kent 8x30 (1999 OCJ).

M. yunnanensis Yunnan Crab W China, 1901. Rare. Stanage Park, Powys 10x61 and 13x57 (1995 Roger and Vicky Smith).

M. x zumi (*baccata* x *toringo*, 1892) Very rare. Edinburgh RBG 9x37 (1997); Westonbirt NA 10x29 (2002 OCJ).

'Golden Hornet' 1949. Abundant. Hall Place, Kent 9x52 (1999 OCJ) – much the largest found.

Manglietia hookeri Upper Burma. Caerhays 19x51 (1984 AFM) – bole 4m.

M. insignis Himalayas to W China, 1912? In a few mild gardens. Caerhays 20x99 (1984 AFM).

Maytenus boaria **Maiten** S Andes, 1822. Rare; reaches tree size in mild humid areas. Glasnevin NBG 14x130@0.1m (2003 DGA) – splitting; Fota, Cork 14.5x 80@0.6m on short bole (1999 TROI); Portmeirion, Gwynedd (18)x38 (1991 AFM).

Melia azedarach **Bead Tree** India to China. Long grown here but very rare: needs summer heat. Les Vaux, Jersey 5x25+25 (1989).

Meliosma beaniana C China, 1907. In a few collections. Caerhays 12x32 (1984 AFM); Edinburgh RBG 13x25 (1985 AFM) – original (from Wilson 258).

M. dilleniifolia **ssp.** *cuneifolia* W China, 1901. In some big gardens; often a bush. Birr Castle 12x18@1m (2000 TROI), p1916?

M. pinnata **var.** *oldhamii* NE Asia, 1900. In a few big gardens. Kildangan, Kildare 12x47@1m (1988 AFM); Windsor (Savill Garden) 13x41 (2000 OCJ).

M. pungens Himalayas. Caerhays 11x25 (1984 AFM).

M. veitchiorum **Veitch's Meliosma** W China, 1901. Very rare. Kildangan, Kildare 12x57 (1990 AFM); Nymans, W Sussex 14x47 (1996 OCJ) – shapely dome.

Mespilus germanica **Medlar** SE Europe, Asia Minor; long grown here. Occasional; rarely, well naturalised in SE England. Tunbridge Wells, Kent 5x59 (1999 OCJ); Knocklofty House, Tipperary 11x39 (2000 TROI).

Metasequoia glyptostroboides **Dawn Redwood** W China, 1948. Frequent. Woking Park, Surrey 20x129 (2000 OCJ) – about 40 years old; Leonardslee, W Sussex 31x71 (1996 OCJ) – 1950 original.

Metrosideros excelsa **New Zealand Christmas Tree** 1840. Has survived to make big trees at Tresco Abbey, Cornwall: 16x242, 20x225 and 21x173 (1987 AFM).

Michelia doltsopa Himalayas to China. Rare; to tree-size in mild areas. Caerhays (21)x81+ (1991 AFM) – original, p1918?

Morus alba **White Mulberry** China; long grown here. Very occasional; likes warm summers. Oxford BG, Oxon. 9x70 (1996 VES) – supine; Bayfordbury, Herts. 12.5x50@0.7m under fork (2002 DGA).

'Laciniata' Very rare. Tilgates, Surrey 8x27@1m under fork (2000 OCJ) – young tree.

'Pendula' Weeping Mulberry Rare, but one of the finest weeping trees. Kew RBG 3x38 (2001 OCJ).

'Venosa' In a few collections. Haberdashers' Aske's School, Herts. 8x27 (2002 OCJ) – old tree.

M. cathayana China, 1907. In a few collections. Kew RBG 13x40 (2001 OCJ), from 1907 seed.

M. mongolica NE Asia, 1907. Cambridge UBG 13.5x38@1.3m (2002 DGA).

M. nigra **Black Mulberry** W Asia; long grown here. Frequent. Shillington, Beds. 7x138@0m (1994 DGA); Withersdane Hall, Kent 9x102@0.3m on short single bole (1999 OCJ); Little Addington, Northants. 8x92@? (1994) – hollow; Evesham Hotel, Worcs. 5x92 (1993 AFM); Mill House, Dedham, Essex (12)x85@1.4m (1993).

Myrtus luma – see *Luma apiculata*.

Neolitsea sericea NE Asia, Japan. In a few mild collections. Caerhays 6x38++ (1984 AFM).

Nothofagus Southern Beeches

Nothofagus **x** *alpina* (*nervosa* x *obliqua*) S Andes. Very rare. Alice Holt, Hants. 19x64 (2001 OCJ); Westonbirt NA 24x63 (2002 OCJ), p1963.

N. antarctica **Antarctic Beech** S Andes, 1830. Occasional; generally small-growing. Arduaine, Argyll (?) 26x76 (1998); Abbeyleix, Laois 11.5x82@0.5m (2000 TROI).

N. betuloides **Guindo** S Andes, 1830. Now very rare. Kitlands, Surrey 15x98@1m under scar (2000 OCJ); Benmore, Argyll 20x52 (1991 AFM).

N. **x** *blairii* (*fusca* x *solanderi* var. *cliffortioides*) New Zealand. In a few milder gardens. Ardanaiseig, Argyll 20x47 and 21x34 (1994 VES).

N. cliffortioides – see *N. solanderi* var. *cliffortioides*.

N. cunninghamii **Myrtle Beech** Tasmania, by 1860. Rare; tender. Rowallane, Down (21)x66 (1991 AFM); Stonefield House, Argyll (24)x61+51 (1991 AFM).

N. dombeyi **Coigue** S Andes, 1916. Occasional; best in cool humid areas. Muncaster Castle, Cumbria 33x136 and 35x104 (2000 DH); Mount Usher, Wicklow (35)x135 (1992), p1928.

N. fusca **Red Beech** New Zealand, c1875. Rare; rather tender. Castlewellan NA (21)x102 (1994 VES); Tregrehan, Cornwall (30)x88@0.5m? (2002 Tom Hudson).

N. glauca **Hualo** S Andes. Tender; young trees growing fast in a few collections.

N. menziesii **Silver Beech** New Zealand, c1850? Rare. Caerhays (27)x103@0.3m/x72+? (1984 AFM); Nymans, W Sussex 14x78 (1996 OCJ) – cut back.

N. menziesii **x** *obliqua*. In one or two collections. Kew

MULBERRIES

A few Black Mulberries are probably sprouts of sprouts of 16th century plantings, but this is a tree whose reputation for longevity and excruciatingly slow growth is quite undeserved. New ones are seldom planted, but will make a broad leafy dome and fruit profusely after little more than a decade. Even the biggest - confined to areas with warm summers - continue to grow (and to disappear) quite rapidly.

Nyssa sinensis is a small tree now being more widely planted for its brilliant autumn colours.

RBG 15x27 (2001 OCJ), p1976.

N. moorei Australian Beech New South Wales, 1892. In a few mild gardens. Mount Usher, Wicklow 16x47+38 (1989 AFM).

N. nervosa Rauli (*N. procera*) S Andes, 1913. Occasional; best in high humidity. Brodick Castle, Ayr 30x131 (1988 AFM); Mount Usher, Wicklow (32)x106 (1989 AFM).

N. nitida S Andes. Young trees in a few collections. Royal Holloway College, Surrey 18x48 (2000 OCJ), p1979.

N. obliqua Roblé Beech S Andes, 1902? Rather occasional; the toughest southern beech. Ashbourne House, Cork (30)x100 (1987 AFM); Muncaster Castle, Cumbria 35x61 (2000 DH).

N. procera – see *N. nervosa*.

N. pumilio Lenga S Andes. Very rare to datc. Kew RBG 22x55 (2001 OCJ) – 1950 original.

N. solanderi Black Beech New Zealand, by 1917. Very rare. Benmore, Argyll 20x82 (1991 AFM); Tregrehan, Cornwall (29)x61 (2002 Tom Hudson).

var. cliffortioides Mountain Beech c1890. Rare. Ashbourne House, Cork (26)x66@0.6m (1987 AFM); Muncaster Castle, Cumbria 18x62 (2000 DH).

Notelaea excelsa – see *Picconia excelsa*.

Nyssa aquatica Water Tupelo SE USA, 1735. Poor plants in some collections.

N. sinensis Very occasional as a young planting; scarcely reaching 'tree' size.

N. sylvatica Tupelo E N America, 1750. Rather rare; appreciates warm summers. Coedarhyddglyn, Glamorgan 14x72@? (1991 JW); Bicton Park, Devon 14x72 (2001 OCJ) – good bole; Sheffield Park, E Sussex 20x48 (1994 OCJ), p1909 – the tallest of about 90.

***Olea europaea* Olive** Mediterranean, long grown here. Very seldom a tree, as it needs mild winters but hot summers. Chelsea Physic Garden, London 7x29+26+17 (2001 OCJ).

***Olearia argophylla* Muskwood** SE Australia, Tasmania, 1804. In a few mild gardens. (Rossdohan, Kerry 12x44++ (1966 AFM) – seeding widely.)
***O. paniculata* Akiraho** New Zealand, 1816. Rare; a tree in mild areas. Glencormac, Wicklow (?) 14x84@0.2m (2000 TROI); Sausmarez Park, Guernsey 11x57@? (1995 JW).
O. traversii Chatham Islands, 1887. In a few mild gardens. Logan House, Dumfries & Galloway 12x48+37 (1993 VES).

***Osmanthus yunnanensis* Giant Osmanthus** W China, 1923. Rare. Caerhays 16x40 (1984 AFM).

***Ostrya carpinifolia* Hop Hornbeam** S Europe, Asia Minor, 1724. Rather rare; almost confined to the south, though growing well near Aberdeen. Petworth Park, W Sussex 14x81 (1997 OCJ); Killerton, Devon 24x59+59+52+++ (2001 OCJ).
***O. japonica* Japanese Hop Hornbeam** NE China, Japan, 1888. In some big gardens. Albury Park, Surrey 17x74 (2000 OCJ) – as label.
***O. virginiana* Ironwood** E N America, 1692. Rare. Kew RBG 12x61@1.2m (2001 OCJ), from 1973 seed; Westonbirt NA 15x36 (2002 OCJ).

***Oxydendrum arboreum* Sorrel Tree** E USA, 1752. Rare; needs an acid soil and summer heat. St Fagans Castle Gardens (?), Glamorgan 11.5x54 (1993); Bransgore House, Hants. 20x38 (2002 John Hearne).

***Parrotia persica* Persian Ironwood** The Caucasus, by 1840. Occasional; likes warm summers. Abbeyleix, Laois 8x72@0.15m (2000 TROI); Briggens, Herts. 8x54@1.2m on fine short bole (2002 OCJ); Nuneham Park, Oxon., 9x53 (1993); Westonbirt NA 15x53@0.3m (2002 OCJ).

Paulownia fargesii W China, 1896? In a few big gardens to date, but grows well. Churchill Hall, Bristol 12x74@1m (1991 AFM), p1961.
P. fortunei SE China, by 1934. In a few big gardens to date. Hampton Court, London 17x66 and 17x60 (2001 OCJ).
P. kawakamii S China, Taiwan. Vigorous young plants in one or two collections.
P. taiwaniana Taiwan. Kew RBG 12x41+33 (2001 OCJ), from 1979 seed.
***P. tomentosa* Foxglove Tree** China, 1834. Occasional; likes long warm summers; short-lived. Kettering Crematorium, Northants. 22x111@0.2m (2002 Steve Benamore) – forking near base; Bute Park, Glamorgan 19x89 (1990 AFM). (Westonbirt NA 26x75 (1990) – died in 1990.)
'Lilacina' (*P. lilacina*). In a few big gardens. Rowallane, Down 17.5x44 (1991 AFM).

***Phellodendron amurense* Amur Cork Tree** NE Asia, Japan, 1885. Rare; likes warm summers. Most labelled trees are probably *P. lavallei*. Kew RBG 12x65 (2001 OCJ).
var. *sachalinense* Sakhalin Cork Tree Japan. Very rare. Tortworth Court, Glos. 19x78 (1992), p1880; Hergest Croft 21x56 (1995 VES).
P. chinense C China, 1907. In some big gardens in warmer areas. Borde Hill 14x53@0.8m (1995 OCJ), p1932 as 'var. *glabriusculum*'; Dawyck, Scottish Borders 17x52 (1997).
P. japonicum Japan, 1863. Very rare, but not confined to the south. Auchincruive, Dunbartons. 13x82@0.5m (1979 AFM); Edinburgh RBG 14x57 (1991 AFM), p1898; Wakehurst Place 17x38 (1997 OCJ).
***P. lavallei* Japanese Cork Tree** Japan, by 1899. Rather rare but not confined to the south; often recorded under *P. amurense*. Nymans, W Sussex 15x83 (1996 OCJ) – very broad; Borde Hill 17x53 (1995 OCJ), from Wilson 11283.

***Phillyrea latifolia* Phillyrea** (incorporating *P. media*) Mediterranean; long grown here but now rather rare. Likes warm summers but relatively mild winters; to 11m. Luddesdown church, Kent 8x80@0.7m under fork (1999 OCJ); Stable Cottage, Binsted, W Sussex 8x51 (1997 OCJ).

***Phoenix canariensis* Canary Palm** Now much planted; old trees are confined to the mildest areas. Candie Gardens, Guernsey 11x65 (1995 JW).

Spring catkins and characteristically scaly bark of a fine Hop Hornbeam (*Ostrya carpinifolia*) in a Bedfordshire garden.

Photinia beauverdiana W China, 1900. Very rare. Singleton Park, Glamorgan (var. *notabilis*) 10x37 (2000 OCJ).

P. glabra Japan, 1903? Mount Congreve, Waterford 15x31 (2002 AF).

P. nussia Himalayas to the Phillipines. Abbotsbury, Dorset 13x51@1m (1980 AFM).

P. serratifolia (*P. serrulata*) China, 1804. Rather rare; best in mild areas. Bath BG, Somerset 12x80@0.5m (2002 OCJ) – huge bush; Killerton, Devon 14x33++ (2001 OCJ); Magheramore, Wicklow 14x25 (2001 AF).

***Phyllocladus trichomanoides* Tanekaha** New Zealand. A broad-leaved conifer in one or two mild gardens. Fota, Cork 11.5x38@0.9m (1999 TROI), p1941.

Picconia excelsa (*Notelaea excelsa*) Madeira, the Canaries, 1784. A few trees in mild areas. Abbotsbury, Dorset 13x87 (1993 VES).

Picea Spruces

***Picea abies* Norway Spruce** Mountains of Europe; long grown here. Abundant; seldom a big tree. Lingholm, Cumbria 40x146 (1995 DH); Reelig Glen Wood, Highland (52)x80 (1986 AFM).

'Argentea'. Hillier Gardens 16x43 (2002 Harry James).

'Aurea' Golden Norway Spruce Rare. Castlewellan NA 30.5x78 (1994); Westonbirt NA 32x66 (2002 OCJ).

'Cincinnata' In a few big gardens. Hillier Gardens 14x38 (2002 Harry James).

'Clanbrassiliana' A dwarf which ultimately reaches tree-size: Abbeyleix, Laois 10x38 (2000 TROI); Bicton Park, Devon 12x28+++ (2001 OCJ).

'Cranstonii'. Hillier Gardens 15x25 (2001 Ron Holley).

'Cupressina'. Hillier Gardens 13x27 (2002 Harry James).

'Finedonensis'. Glasnevin NBG 20x44 (1980 AFM).

'Inversa' Very rare. Dunira, Perth 18x41 (2002 DH).

f. *monstrosa*. Endsleigh, Devon (?) x94 including ivy (1995).

'Pyramidata' Very rare. Bedgebury NP 12x26 (1995 OCJ), p1975.

'Virgata' Snake-bark Spruce Very rare. Magheramore, Wicklow x70 (1994 John Anderson).

***P. abies* x *asperata*.** Westonbirt NA 23x57 and 25x56 (2002 OCJ).

***P. alcoquiana* Alcock's Spruce** (*P. bicolor*) Japan, 1861. About 100 trees; grows well in drier areas. Scone Palace, Perth 17x76 (1992 AFM); Dunkeld Cathedral, Perth 24.5x58 (1999 Donald Rodger).

***P. asperata* Dragon Spruce** W China, 1910. Rare. Eastnor Castle, Herefords. 27x55 (2002); Hergest Croft 20x55 (1995 VES), p1916.

var. *retroflexa* Very rare. Fenagh House, Carlow x34 (1995 John Anderson), p1921; Windsor (Valley Gardens) 19x34 (2000 OCJ).

***P. asperata* x *koyamae*.** Westonbirt NA 24x49 (2002 OCJ).

P. bicolor – see *P. alcoquiana*.

***P. brachytyla* Sargent Spruce** W China, 1901. About

Tresco Abbey on Scilly is noted for large examples of tender trees, such as the Canary Palm (*Phoenix canariensis*) which is now popular in south coast gardens.

100 trees. Tregrehan, Cornwall 24x95 (2002 Tom Hudson); Stourhead, Wilts. 32x71 (1992 AFM).

***P. breweriana* Brewer Spruce** California, Oregon, 1891. Occasional; seldom thrives here for long. Cortachy Castle, Angus 12x70 (1992 AFM); Hergest Croft 20x56 (1995 VES), p1916.

***P. engelmannii* Engelmann Spruce** W N America, 1862. 50-100 trees. Dawyck, Scottish Borders 31x83 (1992 AFM) p1904.

f. *glauca* Blue Engelmann Spruce Very rare. Invermay Castle, Perth 24x76 (1988 AFM); Fairburn, Highland 31x47 (1982 AFM).

P. farreri Upper Burma. A few young trees. The original at Exbury Gardens, Hants., 18x56 (1987 AFM), died in 1995.

***P. glauca* White Spruce** NE USA, 1700. Very few trees of stature remain. Blair Drummond, Stirling 23x73 (1974 AFM). (Eridge Park, E Sussex ('Caerulea') 22x91 (1957 AFM); Rhinefield Drive, Hants. 31x57 (1976 AFM).)

***P. glehnii* Sakhalin Spruce** 1877. Perhaps 30 trees. Blairquhan, Ayr 17x52 (1993 VES), p1937; Murthly Castle, Perth 24x51 (1989 AFM), p1897.

P. x hurstii (*engelmannii* x *pungens*). 10-20 trees. Westonbirt NA 20x50 (2002 OCJ).

P. jezoensis ssp. *jezoensis* **Hokkaido Spruce** Siberia to N Japan, 1861. Very rare; does not thrive. Darnaway, Moray 11x28 (1989 AFM).

ssp. *hondoensis* **Hondo Spruce** Japan, 1861. Rather rare. Benmore, Argyll 28x110 (1991 AFM), p1880; Tal-y-Garn, Glamorgan 31x95 (1986 AFM); Gnaton Hall, Devon 31x78 (1978 AFM).

P. jezoensis ssp. *hondoensis* x *sitchensis*. Vivod, Denbigh 19x56 (1988 JW), p1954.

P. koyamae **Koyama's Spruce** Mt Yatsuga, Japan, 1914. About 100 trees. Blairquhan, Ayr 13x57 (1993 VES), p1918; Stanage Park, Powys 22x53 (1995 Roger and Vicky Smith).

P. likiangensis **Likiang Spruce** W China, 1910. Rather rare. Powerscourt, Wicklow 30.5x82 (2000 TROI).

var. *montigena* W China, 1908. In a few collections. Thorp Perrow, Yorks. 23x57 (1991 AFM).

var. *purpurea* – see *P. purpurea*.

var. *rubescens* Balfour's Spruce (var. *balfouriana*) W China, 1910. Perhaps 20 trees. Dawyck, Scottish Borders 18x51 and 21x48 (1997), p1921.

P. x lutzii (*glauca* x *sitchensis*) Alaska, 1962. In one or two collections. Vivod, Denbigh 14x33 (1988 JW).

P. mariana **Black Spruce** NW N America, by 1700. Very rare. Abbeyleix, Laois 26x60 (2000 TROI).

P. x mariorika (*mariana* x *omorika*). Hillier Gardens 10.2m (2001 Ron Holley).

P. maximowiczii **Maximowicz's Spruce**. Japan, 1865. Perhaps 20 trees. Dawyck, Scottish Borders 18x69 (1995), p1913; Westonbirt NA 24x60 (2002 OCJ), p1935.

P. meyeri W China, 1910. In a few collections. Glen Tanar House, Aberdeen 19.5x49 (1980 AFM); Bedgebury NP 13x44 (1999 OCJ).

P. montigena – see *P. likiangensis*.

P. morrisonicola **Taiwan Spruce** A handful of trees. Birr Castle 18x46 (2000 TROI) – 1928 original.

P. obovata **Siberian Spruce** 1908. Perhaps 20 genuine examples. Glen Tanar House, Aberdeen 11x43 (1980 AFM), p1922; Batsford Arboretum, Glos. 20x41 (2003 OCJ). A tree at High Close, Grasmere, 37x87 (2002 DH), identified as *P. obovata*, must be considered doubtful.

P. omorika **Serbian Spruce** Drina Valley, Serbia, 1889. Occasional; grows well in dry areas but always short-lived. Endsleigh Devon 24x69 (1990 AFM) – three stems from 2m; Murthly Castle, Perth 28x68 and 33x66 (1990 AFM), p1897.

P. omorika x *sitchensis*. Murthly Castle, Perth 36x90 (1989 AFM).

P. orientalis **Oriental Spruce** Asia Minor, 1839? Occasional. Cortachy Castle, Angus 28x125 (1981 AFM); Camperdown Park, Angus 40x98 (1985 AFM).

'Aurea' Very rare. Achnacarry, Highland 17.5x53 (1982 AFM); Vernon Holme, Kent 19x53 (1995 OCJ), p1906.

'Gracilis' Very rare. Bedgebury NP 12x39 (1995 OCJ), p1929.

P. polita – see *P. torano*.

P. pungens **Colorado Spruce** SW USA, 1862? Rare. Likes a continental climate; the largest are evenly spread. Kinnettles House, Angus 16x58 (1986 AFM); Kew RBG 21x45 (2001 OCJ).

f. *glauca* **Blue Colorado Spruce** Abundant in various selections such as 'Moerheimii', 'Koster' and 'Hoopsii', but seldom thriving for long. Beaufront Castle, Northumberland 21x65 (1982 AFM); Highnam Court, Glos. (25)x45 (1989 AFM).

P. purpurea (*P. likiangensis* var. *purpurea*) W China, 1910. Rare. Hergest Croft 16x53 (1995 VES), p1928; Westonbirt NA 24x52 (2002 OCJ), p1931.

P. rubens **Red Spruce** NE N America, by 1755. Perhaps 50 trees. Rhinefield Drive, Hants. 28x68 (1992 AFM).

P. schrenkiana **Schrenk's Spruce** C Asia, 1877. Perhaps 20 trees. Borde Hill 20x45 (1995 OCJ).

P. sitchensis **Sitka Spruce** W N America, 1831. Abundant in high-rainfall areas. Castle Hill, Devon 46x258 (1989 AFM) – layered; Fairburn, Highland 44.5x249 (2002 Donald Rodger); Kilravock Castle, Highland 47x244 (2002 Donald Rodger), p1856; The Doune of Rothiemurchus, Highland (59)x137 (2002 DGA) p1870; Randolphs Leap, Moray 58x184 (2002 DGA); Caledon Castle, Tyrone 57m (2001 AF).

P. smithiana **Morinda Spruce** W Himalayas, 1818. Occasional; does well in dry areas and on chalk but longer-lived in the north. Taymouth Castle, Perth 35x145 (1990 AFM); Fairburn, Highland 26.5x145 (2002 Donald Rodger); Cuffnells, Hants. 39x110 (1992). (Bicton, Devon 24x178 (1957 AFM) when dead; p1842.)

P. spinulosa **Sikkim Spruce** E Himalayas, 1878? 50-100 trees. Sidbury Manor, Devon 22x78 (1994), p1918; Fota, Cork 27.5x60 (1999 TROI), p1914.

P. torano **Tiger-tail Spruce** (*P. polita*) Japan, 1861. Rare. Pencarrow, Cornwall (26)x105 (1995); Stourhead, Wilts. 29x77 (1987 AFM).

P. wilsonii **Wilson's Spruce** W China, 1901. 50-100 trees. Birr Castle 21x56 (2000 TROI), p1916.

Pilgerodendron uviferum **Alerce** S Andes, 1849. A handful of bushes. Kilmacurragh, Wicklow 6x28 (1980 AFM).

Pinus Pines

Pinus aristata **Bristlecone Pine** SW USA, 1863. Rare. Adapted to very harsh dry conditions; thrives nowhere here. Bayfordbury, Herts. 12x28 (1985 AFM); Beaufront Castle, Northumberland 13x24 (2000) – very poor.

P. armandii **Armand's Pine** E Asia, 1895. Perhaps 100 trees; likes humidity. Fota, Cork 29x101 (1999 TROI).

P. attenuata **Knobcone Pine** SW USA, 1847? In some big gardens. Bedgebury NP 16x51 (1999 OCJ), p1926; Wakehurst Place 18x43 (1997 OCJ).

P. ayacahuite **Mexican White Pine** 1840. Rare. Likes mild winters and high humidity. Bodnant, Conwy 25x(110) (1989 AFM), p1902; Parkfield, Worcs. 29x55 (1993 VES).

var. *veitchii* seems currently to be represented only by younger trees: Hillier Gardens 14.5x68 (2001 Harry James); Kew RBG 16x49 (2001 OCJ), p1933.

P. ayacahuite x *peuce*. Bedgebury NP 11x38 and 12x34 (1999 OCJ), p1975.

P. balfouriana **Foxtail Pine** California, 1852. About 10 trees; adapted to very harsh conditions. Newby Hall, Yorks. 15x42 (1989 AFM), p1900; Painshawfield Park,

Northumberland (ssp. *austrina*) 15x41 (2000).

P. banksiana Jack Pine N North America, 1783. Rare. Blairquhan, Ayr 16x58 (1993 VES), p1916. (Fairburn, Highland 25x37 (1982 AFM).)

P. bhutanica Himalayas. A few young trees are growing fast.

P. brutia Calabrian Pine E Mediterranean; long grown here. In a few collections. Kew RBG 13x121@0m at forking, and 11x65 (2001 OCJ); Glasnevin NBG 18x46 (1980 AFM).

P. bungeana Lace-bark Pine China, 1846. Very rare. Kew RBG 11x63@0.2m/x46@1.2m++ (2001 OCJ); Wisley 14x31 (2000 OCJ) – narrow spire.

P. canariensis Canary Island Pine By 1890. In a few mild gardens. Mount Usher, Wicklow (25)x49 (1989 AFM).

P. cembra Arolla Pine Mountains of C Europe, 1746. Becoming rare; lives longest in cool, humid areas. Airthrey Castle, Stirling 22x95 (1984 AFM); near Welshpool, Powys (19)x94 (1989 AFM); Castle Leslie, Monaghan 18x201@0.3m (2000 TROI) – 15 stems at 0.5m; Achnacarry, Highland 27x90 (1986 AFM).

'Aurea'. Hergest Croft 14x44+34 (1995 VES).

P. cembroides Mexican Nut Pine Very rare. Kew RBG (ssp. *orizabensis*) 10x45 (2001 OCJ), p1910.

var. edulis – see *P. edulis*.

var. monophylla – see *P. monophylla*.

P. contorta var. bolanderi Bolander Pine California, 1959. Bedgebury NP 17x38 (2002 OCJ), p1980.

var. contorta Shore Pine W N America, 1831. Occasional; in some plantations. Tannadyce Estate, Angus 28x112 (1990 AFM); Kyloe Wood, Northumberland 32x57 (1991 AFM).

var. latifolia Lodgepole Pine W N America, 1853? Abundant in upland plantations. Westonbirt NA 26x84 (2002 OCJ), p1875; graft – on Scots Pine?; Culcreuch Castle Hotel, Stirling 29.5x69 (1984 AFM).

var. murrayana Oregon, California, 1853. Very rare. Thorp Perrow, Yorks. 16.5x33 (1981 AFM).

P. cooperi Mexico, 1962. In a few mild gardens. Westonbirt NA (?) 13x35 and 15x29 (2002 OCJ).

P. coulteri Big-Cone Pine SW N America, 1832. Rare; likes warm summers. Wisley 20x99 (2000 OCJ), p1956; Edinburgh RBG (26)x60 (1991 AFM).

P. densiflora Japanese Red Pine 1852. Rare. Wisley 21x81 (2000 OCJ); Cirencester Park, Glos. 26x55 (1989 JW).

'Umbraculifera' Rare; semi-dwarf. Syon Park, London 9x29@1.3m+++ (2002 OCJ).

P. durangensis Durango Pine Mexico, 1962. In some mild gardens. Bedgebury NP 14x60@1.8m above branches (1999 OCJ), p1967; Bicton Park, Devon 16x49 (2001 OCJ).

P. echinata Short-leaf Pine E USA, 1739. About 10 trees. Bicton Park, Devon 14x29 (2001 OCJ).

P. echinata x rigida. Bedgebury NP 15x73 (p1938) and 16x60 (p1931) (1999 OCJ).

P. edulis Two-leafed Nut Pine SW N America, 1848. In one or two collections. Bedgebury NP 11x41 (1999 OCJ), p1979.

P. eldarica Afghan Pine. Kew RBG 11x35 (2001 OCJ), p1978.

P. elliottii Slash Pine SE USA. In a few collections. Hillier Gardens 10.5x31 (2002 Ron Holley).

P. engelmannii Apache Pine Mexico, 1962. In a few mild gardens to date.

P. flexilis Limber Pine W N America, 1851. Perhaps 50 trees. Windsor (Great Park) 22x77 (1990 AFM), p1933; Kew RBG 18x59 (2001 OCJ).

P. gerardiana Chilgoza Pine W Himalayas, 1839. In one or two collections. Cambridge UBG 14x42 (2002 DGA), p1875.

P. greggii Gregg Pine Mexico, c1905. 10-20 trees? Kew RBG 15x50 (2001 OCJ).

P. halepensis Aleppo Pine W Mediterranean; long grown here. Rare; needs warm summers. Kew RBG 12x80@1m and 20x72 (2001 OCJ).

P. hartwegii – see *P. montezumae* var. *hartwegii*.

P. heldreichii Bosnian Pine (incorporating *P. leucodermis*) 1864. Occasional; now more planted. Bicton Park, Devon 26x118@0.5m under forks (2001 OCJ) – very spreading; Chatsworth House, Derbyshire 28x101 (2001 DGA).

P. x holfordiana Holford's Pine (*ayacahuite* x *wallichiana*) Rare. Wisley 22x116 (2000 OCJ) – branchy; Westonbirt NA 32x75 (2002 OCJ) – 1906 original.

P. jeffreyi Jeffrey Pine SW USA, by 1852. Rather rare. The largest are well distributed. Scone Palace, Perth (36)x136 (1990 AFM), p1860.

P. kochiana Caucasus. Bedgebury NP 12x34 (1999 OCJ).

P. koraiensis Korean Pine E Asia, 1861. 50-100 trees; likes high humidity. Crarae, Argyll 22x55 (1994 VES).

P. lambertiana Sugar Pine Oregon, California, 1851. Very susceptible to Blister-rust; a handful survive. Hawkstone Park, Shropshire 23x97 (1992 AFM).

P. leucodermis – see *P. heldreichii*.

P. massoniana Masson Pine SE China, 1829. In a few collections. Kew RBG 13x44 (2001 OCJ), p1957.

P. monophylla Single-leaved Nut Pine SW N America, 1848. In a few collections. Cambridge UBG 11x49 (2002 DGA), recumbent.

P. montezumae Montezuma Pine Mexico. The type as now understood (with lax, bright green leaves) is scarcely grown here (cf. var. *rudis*).

var. hartwegii Hartweg's Pine Mexico, 1839. Perhaps 20 trees. Kilmacurragh, Wicklow 22x86 (1990 AFM); Woodstock, Kilkenny 27x70 (1999 Michael Lear).

var. lindleyi Mexico. Almost extinct here. (Tregothnan, Cornwall 15.5x96 (1928).)

var. rudis Endlicher Pine Mexico, 1839. Rather rare, in warmer areas; usually grown as 'Montezuma Pine'. Sidbury Manor, Devon 19x137 (1994), p1902; Mount Usher, Wicklow 27x111 (1989 AFM), p1909; Woodstock, Kilkenny (27)x93 (1999 Michael Lear).

P. monticola Western White Pine W N America, 1831. Very rare. Vulnerable to Blister-rust; likes high humidity. Lude House, Perth 35x94 (1991 AFM).

P. mugo Mountain Pine Mountains of C Europe, 1779. Occasional, usually in dwarf selections. Wisley 11x43+36++ (2000 OCJ); Bedgebury NP 14x21 (1995 OCJ).

ssp. uncinata grows larger: Patterdale church, Cumbria 17x99 and 20x82 (1995 DH); Cambridge UBG 20x56

An unexpected champion in Patterdale churchyard, Cumbria, is the biggest known Mountain Pine (*Pinus mugo* ssp. *uncinata*).

(1995).

P. muricata Bishop Pine California, 1848. Rather rare; likes warm summers. Grayswood Hill, Surrey 24x117 (1998 OCJ); Birr Castle 26x89 (2000 TROI).

P. nelsonii NE Mexico. Not currently known to 'tree' size.

P. nigra ssp. laricio Corsican Pine (var. *maritima*) 1759. Abundant; thrives everywhere. Powerscourt, Wicklow 39.5x155 (2000 TROI); Stanage Park, Powys 43x119 (1995 Roger and Vicky Smith), p1828.

ssp. nigra Austrian Pine 1835. Very frequent; particularly tough and will grow on chalk. Tetton House, Somerset 33x187@? (1995) – triple trunk; Ashtead church, Surrey 20x163 (2000 OCJ) – knobbly 5m bole; Powerscourt, Wicklow 43x134 (2000 TROI).

ssp. pallasiana Crimean Pine (var. *caramanica*) 1798. Rather rare. Beaufort Castle, Highland (37)x162 (1983 AFM) and (41)x137 (1985 AFM); Arley Arboretum, Worcs. (38)x162 (2003 John Bulmer).

ssp. salzmannii Pyrenean Pine (var. *cebennensis*) 1834. Rare. Nonsuch Park, Surrey 22x113 (2000 OCJ); Buscot Park, Oxon. 32x82 (1981 AFM).

P. palustris Southern Pitch Pine SE USA, 1730. Survives in one or two mild gardens. Glencormac, Wicklow 20x67 (2000 TROI).

P. parviflora Japanese White Pine 1861. Rather rare, often in semi-dwarf selections. Boconnoc, Cornwall 14x89 (1991 AFM); Stourhead, Wilts. 25x68 (1984 AFM); Endsleigh, Devon 25m (1995) – multi-stemmed.

P. patula Jelecote Pine Mexico, by 1837. Very occasional as a younger tree in mild areas. Tregrehan, Cornwall (20)x65 (2002 Tom Hudson). (Bicton Park, Devon 19.5x126@0.6m (1928).)

P. peuce Macedonian Pine Balkans, 1864. Occasional; very tough but prefers high humidity. Stourhead, Wilts. 34x134 (1992); Chatsworth House, Derbyshire 41x92 (2001 DGA).

P. pinaster Maritime Pine Mediterranean; long grown here. Occasional; thrives everywhere. Carey House, Dorset 25x133 under fork (1986 AFM); Caerhays 28x124 (1984 AFM); Ashburnham Place, E Sussex 30x108 (2003 OCJ); Sheffield Park, E Sussex 30x93 (1994 OCJ), p1797?

P. pinea Stone Pine Mediterranean; long grown here. Occasional in warm areas. Woodley, Berks. 14x140@0.5m (1994 Carol Hora); Portmarr, Powys 18x111 (1988 JW), p1820?; Wayford Manor, Somerset 26m (2003 Robin Goffe).

P. ponderosa Western Yellow Pine W N America, 1826. Occasional; the largest are evenly spread. Near Welshpool, Powys 34x150 and 40x137 (1989 AFM); Bayfordbury, Herts. x140 (1999), p1837.

ssp. scopulorum Perhaps 20 trees. Wisley 15x47 (2000 OCJ); Arley Arboretum, Worcs. 25x46 (2003 John Bulmer).

P. pseudostrobus Smooth-barked Mexican Pine 1839. Young trees in one or two collections. (20x68 at Pencarrow, Cornwall, in 1937 when dying.)

P. pungens Hickory Pine E N America, 1804. A handful of small trees. (Leonardslee, W Sussex 26x40 (1984 AFM), blown 1987.)

P. radiata Monterey Pine California, 1833. Abundant in mild coastal areas; grows much less well inland. Much bigger here than on its native Californian cliffs. Lisalene Gardens, Cork 33.5x244@0.8m on short bole (2000 TROI); Tregothnan, Cornwall 34x226 among branches (1995), p1855; Queens Drive, Kerry 45x156 (1999 TROI).

P. resinosa Red Pine NE N America, 1736. Perhaps 50 trees; not thriving here. Bedgebury NP 19x51 (1999 OCJ), p1931.

P. rigida Northern Pitch Pine E N America, 1759. 50-100 trees. Inveraray Castle, Argyll 17x86 (1982 AFM); Batsford Arboretum, Glos. 19x76 (2003 OCJ).

P. rudis – see *P. montezumae* var. *rudis*.

P. sabiniana Digger Pine California, 1832. Perhaps 20 trees. Glasnevin NBG x68 (1992 AFM).

P. x schwerinii (*strobus* x *wallichiana*, 1905) In a few collections. Alice Holt, Hants. 24x76 (2001 OCJ), p1957.

P. serotina Pond Pine SE USA, 1713. Perhaps 10 trees. Kew RBG 14x48 (2001 OCJ).

P. sibirica Siberian Stone Pine In one or two collections. Coedarhyddglyn, Glamorgan 14.5x25 (1991 JW).

P. strobiformis South-western White Pine New Mexico. Vigorous young trees in a few collections.

P. strobus Weymouth Pine E N America; long grown here. Occasional; longest-lived in humid areas. Rhinefield

The tallest Maritime Pine (*Pinus pinaster*) at Sheffield Park, E. Sussex, probably dates from the late 18th century.

Drive, Hants. (33)x141 on fine bole (2002 Ted Palmer); Cannop, Glos. 42x113 (1988 JW), p1787; Hazelwood Lodge, Lancs. 41x102 (1998 DH).
'Aurea'. Littlehall Pinetum, Kent 15x36 (1995 OCJ), p1912.
'Contorta' Very rare. Hillier Gardens 15x48@1m (2002).
'Fastigiata' Very rare as a young tree. (Ardross Castle, Highland 16x63@0.3m (1980 AFM), blown 1985.)
'Nivea'. Windsor (Valley Gardens) 13x28 (2000 OCJ).
'Pendula' In a few collections. Windsor (Valley Gardens)

7x27 (2000 OCJ).
***P. sylvestris* Scots Pine** Native to Scottish Highlands; abundantly naturalised everywhere on light sandy soils. Usually best in drier areas but longest-lived in cool parts (at least 650 years in natural forests; moribund at 150 years in SE England). Mar Lodge, Aberdeen (20x200) – domed tree with fluted bole; Coolmore House, Kilkenny 27x287@0.5m under forks (2000 TROI); Scone, Perth 34x185 (1993 JP) – 'The King of the Forest'; multiple stems part at 6m; Abbeyleix, Laois 34x177@0.8m on short bole

(2000 TROI); Comrie, Perth 21x173 (1990 JP) – good bole; Ballogie, Aberdeen (39)x144 (1994 JP), p1792; 12m bole.
'Alba'. Bedgebury NP 16x54 (1995 OCJ) – 1926 original.
'Argentea' Very rare. Anglesey Abbey, Cambs. 13x35@1.2m (2001 DGA).
'Aurea' Golden Scots Pine Rare. Castlewellan NA 16.5x93 (1994 VES).
'Fastigiata' Fastigiate Scots Pine Rare. Dryburgh Abbey, Scottish Borders 15x43 (1992 AFM).
'Watereri' Rare; semi-dwarf. Sutton Place, Surrey 14x59 (1996).
P. tabuliformis Chinese Red Pine 1862. Perhaps 50 trees. Wisley 15x46 (2000 OCJ); Powerscourt, Wicklow 18.5x39 (2000 TROI).
var. yunnanensis – see *P. yunnanensis*.
P. taeda Loblolly Pine SE USA, 1741. 25-50 trees, in warm areas. Bicton Park, Devon 17x81 (2001 OCJ) – leaning; Bedgebury NP 18x73 (1999 OCJ).
P. taiwanensis Taiwan Pine c1930; extinct here? (Ilnacullin, Cork 11.5x29 1966 AFM.)
P. teocote Teocote Pine Mexico, by 1826. Almost extinct here. (Bicton Park, Devon 17x67 (1898 Elwes & Henry).)
P. thunbergii Japanese Black Pine Japan, Korea, 1852. Rare; a very tough tree. Heligan, Cornwall 21x81 (1975 AFM); Borde Hill 27x75 (1995 OCJ), p1890.
P. torreyana Torrey Pine California, 1853. Now confined to one or two collections. Powerscourt, Wicklow 22x53 (2000 TROI).
P. uncinata – see *P. mugo*.
P. virginiana Scrub Pine E USA, 1739. In a few collections. Bicton Park, Devon 8x43 (2001 OCJ); Alice Holt, Hants. 11x29 (2002 OCJ), p1953.
P. wallichiana Bhutan Pine Himalayas, 1823? Frequent; short-lived. Killruddery, Wicklow 29x139+79 (1989 AFM); Haldon Grange, Devon 30x181@0.5m under forks (2001 OCJ); Coed Coch, Conwy (36)x130@0.5m under forks (1984 AFM).
P. yunnanensis Yunnan Pine W China, 1909. 10-20 trees. Kew RBG 14x61 (p1910, from Wilson 1369), and 16x55 (p1945) (2001 OCJ).

Pistachia chinensis Chinese Pistachio 1897. Collections in warm areas. Kew RBG 5x28+@1m (2001 OCJ).
P. terebinthus Turpentine Tree Mediterranean; long grown here. Not currently known to 'tree' size.

Pittosporum crassifolium Karo North Island, New Zealand. A tree in mild areas. Abbotsbury, Dorset 9x29 (1993 VES).
P. dallii South Island, New Zealand. Very rare; bushy. Wakehurst Place 6x27++ (1997 OCJ).
P. eugenioides Tarata New Zealand. A tree in the mildest areas. Bosahan, Cornwall 14x46@1m (1985 AFM); Cockington Court, Devon 14x45@0.3m (1984 AFM); Kilmacurragh, Wicklow 8.5x41 (2001 AF).
'Variegatum' In a few mild gardens; hardier. Bosahan, Cornwall 12x62@0.1m and 13x52@0.3m (1985 AFM).
P. tenuifolium Kohuhu New Zealand. Frequent in warmer areas; to tree size near W coasts. Castlewellan NA

13x74@1m (1994 VES); Culzean Castle, Ayr 17x21++ (1989 AFM).
'Silver Queen' Frequent. Mount Usher, Wicklow 9x42@1m (1989 AFM); Fota, Cork 16x20 (1987 AFM). The other popular cultivars have failed to reach 'tree' size.

Plagianthus regius Ribbonwood (*P. betulinus*) New Zealand, c1870. A few trees in milder areas. Islay House, Argyll (16)x97 under narrow fork (2001 Peter McGowan).

Planera aquatica Water Elm SE USA, 1816. Probably extinct here – vulnerable to DED? (Windsor (Home Park), Berks. 22x80 (1972 AFM).)

Platanus Planes
(and see p. 119)
Platanus x hispanica London Plane (*occidentalis* x *orientalis*?; *P. x acerifolia*) Abundant in areas with warm summers. Bishop's Palace, Cambs. 33.5x293@1.2m under branch swell (1997), p1680; Lydney Park, Glos. 33x270 (1983 AFM) – bole a 4.5m column; Barnes, London 35x262 (2001 OCJ), p1680?; bole 5m; Mottisfont Abbey, Hants. 34x367 (1996 VES) – two trunks fused for 2m; West Hall, Surrey 28x298@0.8m over small limbs and under forkings (2000 OCJ); Westbrook House, Devon 29x283 under forkings at 1.3m (1986); Tourin, Waterford 21.5x241 (2000 TROI) – fine tree; Westgate Gardens, Kent 16x255 round massed burrs (1999 OCJ); Bryanston, Dorset 43x187 (1998 Geoff Rouse), p1749; long columnar bole.
'Augustine Henry' A rather rare but beautiful clone. Tortworth Court, Glos. 15x169 (1973 AFM); Kew RBG 30x115 (2001 OCJ).
'Pyramidalis' Occasional. Green Park, Bath, Somerset 23x182@1m under burrs (2002 OCJ).
'Suttneri' Variegated Plane Very rare. Glasnevin NBG 20x49 (2003 DGA). (Heath Cottage, Puttenham, Surrey 22x68 (1963 AFM); blown 1987.)
P. occidentalis Buttonwood Plane E N America, 1636. Scarcely survives here: needs long hot summers. Royal Holloway College, Surrey 14x29 (2000 OCJ), p1968. A possible tree at Lyndon Hall, Rutland, was 15x104 in 1984 (AFM).
P. orientalis Oriental Plane SE Europe; long grown here. A lower more spreading tree than London Plane, less exclusive to warm areas. Chilton Foliat, Wilts. 23x290 (1993); Rycote Park, Oxon. 21x280 (1993); Trowbridge, Wilts. 24x272 (1993); Hawstead Place Farm, Suffolk 25x249 (2002 JP), p1578; Duntish Court, Dorset 28x245@0.3m (1986 AFM); Corsham Court, Wilts. 25x228 (1989 JW), p1757; layered – average spread 64m; Petersham Lodge woodlands, London (30)x191 (2002 OCJ) – long clean slanting bole.

Platycarya strobilacea NE Asia and Japan, 1845. Vigorous young trees in a few big gardens.

Platycladus orientalis Oriental Thuja (*Thuja orientalis*) NE Asia, 1752. Frequent; best in hot dry areas on alkaline soils. Kew RBG 16x74@0.4m on short bole (2001 OCJ), p1898. (24x90 at Lamorran House, Cornwall, in 1928

Old photographs of Mottisfont Abbey, Hampshire, showed two London Planes (*Platanus* x *hispanica*) on the lawn. These have now fused to make one gigantic bole.

seems incredible.)

'Elegantissima' Abundant; grows slowly to tree size. Stonham Aspal church, Suffolk 10x74@0.1m round three stems (2002 DGA); Tempsford church, Beds. 10x74@0m/x36+35+++ (2000 DGA); Mereworth church, Kent 10.5x49@0.5m under forks (1999 OCJ).

Podocarpus acutifolius South Island, New Zealand. Bushes in a handful of mild gardens. Castlewellan NA 7.5x40 (1991 AFM).

P. andinus – see *Prumnopitys andina*.

P. nubigenus Chilean Totara S Andes, 1847. Very rare; to tree-size in the mildest areas. Kilmacurragh, Wicklow 16x85 (1990 AFM).

P. salignus Willow Podocarp S Andes, 1849? Rare; a beautiful tree best in high humidity. Ardnagashel, Cork 21x109@1.2m on short bole (2001 AF); Powerscourt, Wicklow 24x94@1m (1992 AFM).

P. totara Totara New Zealand. Rare; to tree-size in warm, mild, humid areas. Heligan, Cornwall 19x99 (1975 AFM); Trebah, Cornwall 18x96 (1990 AFM); Enys, Cornwall 21.5x69 (1996); Tregrehan, Cornwall 22x52 (2002 Tom Hudson).

var. hallii In a few collections. Fota, Cork 13x49 (1999 TROI); Tregrehan, Cornwall 14x36 (2002 Tom Hudson).

Poliothyrsis sinensis China, by 1908. In a few collections. Glasnevin NBG 9x29 (1992). (Caerhays 15x36 (1971 AFM).)

Populus Poplars

Populus x acuminata (*angustifolia* x *sargentii*) W N America, 1898. In some collections. Cambridge UBG 21x56 (1989 AFM), p1957.

P. adenopoda China, 1906. In one or two collections. Kew RBG 15x39 (2001 OCJ).

P. alba White Poplar Abundant. Possibly native; well naturalised. Likes warm summers; river valleys in Hertfordshire seem to suit it particularly. St Albans, Herts. 27x95 (2002 OCJ); Rockbeare Park, Devon 23x95 (2001 OCJ) – good tree. (Bayfordbury, Herts. 24x166@1.2m under fork (1962 AFM).)

'Pyramidalis' Bolle's Poplar Outgrows the type in hot summers; big trees are almost exclusive to London. Sydenham Wells Park, London 21x113 (2001 OCJ); Marble Hill Park, London 26x95 (2001 OCJ).

'Raket' Still very rare. Vigorous, shapely young trees are: Ravenor Park, London 18x45 (2001 OCJ); Rectory Park, London 19x43 (2002 OCJ).

'Richardii' Rare; often stunted. Preston Park, London 16x67 (2001 OCJ).

P. 'Andover' (*nigra* ssp. *betulifolia* x *trichocarpa*) 1934. Collections only? Thorp Perrow, Yorks. 32x66 (1991 AFM).

P. 'Androscoggin' (*maximowiczii* x *trichocarpa*) 1934. A few vigorous young trees. Edinburgh RBG (24)x54 (1985 AFM), p1958.

P. 'Balsam Spire' (*balsamifera* x *trichocarpa*) Abundant; very vigorous everywhere. Peper Harow, Surrey 30x93 (2000 OCJ); Bushy Park, London 34x71 (2001 OCJ).

P. balsamifera Eastern Balsam Poplar (*P. tacamahaca*) Now rare. Colesbourne, Glos. (41)x100 (1984 AFM).

P. x berolinensis Berlin Poplar (*laurifolia* x *nigra* 'Italica') Now very occasional. Aldenham Park, Herts. 19x113 under fork (2002 OCJ); Ryston Hall, Norfolk 30x89 (1995 JW), p1914.

P. x canadensis Hybrid Black Poplar (*deltoides* x *nigra*) Abundant in a variety of clones. Growth is usually best where summers are warm.

'Carriereana'. Thorp Perrow, Yorks. 34x77 (1991 AFM).

'Casale 78' ('I-78') In a few southern plantations. Alice Holt, Hants. 29x75 (2001 OCJ), p1954.

'Eugenei' Eugene's Poplar Rather rare. Colesbourne, Glos. (43)x135 (1984 AFM); Ryston Hall, Norfolk 42x127 (1995 JW), p1916; Hutton-in-the-Forest, Cumbria 42x56 (1996 DH), p1950.

'Florence Biondi' ('OP226') In a few southern plantations. Alice Holt, Hants. 32x85 (2001 OCJ), p1956.

'Gelrica' Rare. Alice Holt, Hants. 29x90 (2001 OCJ), p1952; Thorp Perrow, Yorks. 34x71 (1991 AFM), p1950.

'Ghoy' Rare to date. Alice Holt, Hants. 21x40 (2001 OCJ), p1965.

'Heidemij' Very rare. Alice Holt, Hants. 25x67 (2001 OCJ).

'Lloydii' Very rare. Alice Holt, Hants. 29x78 (2001 OCJ); Thorp Perrow, Yorks. 34x57 (1991 AFM).

'Pacheri'. Alice Holt, Hants. 26x69 (2002 OCJ), p1954.

'Regenerata' Railway Poplar Abundant in various clones (includes trees recorded as the original clone 'Marilandica'). Copes well in exposure. Peper Harow, Surrey 34x198 (2000 OCJ); Boultham Park, Lincs. (40)x152 (1993).

'Robusta' Abundant. Aldenham Park, Herts. 27x144 (2002 OCJ); Hutton-in-the-Forest, Cumbria 36x53 (1996 DH), p1950.

'Serotina' Black Italian Poplar Occasional as an older tree. Chelsworth, Suffolk 39x237 (2002 JP) – bole 9m; Bowood, Wilts. ('Robusta'?) 41x156 (1993).

'Serotina Aurea' Golden Poplar Occasional. The largest golden tree: Hampton Court, London 30x149 (2001 OCJ) – with mistletoe; tip reverted; Munden, Herts. 30x124 (2001 OCJ).

'Serotina de Selys' Spectacular but very rare. The only old tree noted is at Bicton College, Devon, 37x93 (2001 OCJ).

P. x candicans – see *P.* x *jackii*.

P. canescens Grey Poplar C Europe. Frequent; naturalised by suckers. Grows well throughout. Birr Castle 42x191 (1999 TROI) – magnificent; Ardross Castle, Highland (44)x120 (1989 AFM).

'Macrophylla' Picart's Poplar In a few collections. Hillier Gardens 31x85 (2001 Ron Holley).

P. cathayana Chinese Balsam Poplar NE Asia, 1908? A few small trees – likely to be hybrids.

P. ciliata Bangikat Poplar Himalayas, 1982? Vigorous trees in some collections. Sandling Park, Kent 15x26 (1995 OCJ).

P. deltoides Eastern Cottonwood E N America. Now confined to a few collections. Alice Holt, Hants. 27x(85) (2001 OCJ), p1955.

P. x euramericana – see *P.* x *canadensis*.

P. fremontii Western Cottonwood W USA. In one or two collections. Thorp Perrow, Yorks. 31x77 (1991 AFM).

P. 'Frye' (*laurifolia* x *nigra*) 1934. Collections only? Alice Holt, Hants. 25x80 (2001 OCJ), p1954.

P. x generosa (*deltoides* x *trichocarpa*) 1912. Occasional. Boughton Place, Kent 27x119@1m under fork (1995 OCJ); Wisley 28x110 (2000 OCJ); Rozelle Park, Ayr 32x84 (1989 AFM). (Albury Park, Surrey (42)x104 (1986 AFM), p1928.) The selections 'Beaupré' and Boelare' are growing fast as young trees.

P. 'Geneva' (x *berolinensis* x x *jackii*) 1934. Collections only? Alice Holt, Hants. 20x53 (2001 OCJ), p1954.

P. grandidentata Big-tooth Aspen E N America, 1772. In some collections. Highnam Court, Glos. 21x80 (1996) – half-bole remains.

P. x jackii Balm of Gilead (*balsamifera* x *deltoides*; *P.* x *candicans*) 1773. The occasional vigorous tree is probably a reversion from 'Aurora'. Stanborough Park, Herts. 21x69 (2002 OCJ).

'Aurora' Frequent. Little Bookham, Surrey 13x64@1.2m (2000 OCJ); Duncton Mill House, W Sussex 20x49 (1999 OCJ).

P. koreana Korea, 1918. Threave Garden, Dumfries & Galloway 13x25 (1984 AFM).

P. lasiocarpa Chinese Necklace Poplar 1900. Rare; seldom thrives. Bath BG, Somerset 24x89 (2002 OCJ) – very fine; Combe House, Devon x105@1m (2001 OCJ) – tall sprouting stump.

var. tibetica (*P. szechuanica*) W China, 1904. Very rare; short-lived. Batsford Arboretum, Glos. 21x52 (2003 OCJ).

P. lasiocarpa x wilsonii. Hillier Gardens 14x30 (2001 Harry James).

P. laurifolia C Asia, c1830. No big examples are currently known.

P. laurifolia x nigra Alice Holt, Hants. 28x90 (2001 OCJ), p1956.

P. 'Maine' (x *berolinensis* x x *jackii*) 1934. Collections only? Thorp Perrow, Yorks. 34x81 (1991 AFM) – top lost by 1981.

P. maximowiczii Japanese Balsam Poplar NE Asia, Japan, c1890. Rare; likes mild humid areas. Belvedere, Westmeath 27.5x76 (2000 TROI).

P. nigra European Black Poplar The continental type, with hairless shoots, may not be grown here.

'Afghanica' ('Thevestina') C Asia. Poor trees in one or two collections. Ryston Hall, Norfolk 34x107 (1995 JW).

ssp. betulifolia Wild Black Poplar Native to England and Wales; very locally abundant as an old tree on river plains. Crickhowell, Powys 24x226@? (1988 JW); Kilve Priory, Somerset 11x215 (1970 AFM); Longnor Hall, Shropshire 38x201 (1984 AFM); Christ's College, Powys 33.5x209 (1982 AFM) – superb; Old Malling Deanery, E Sussex 10x201 (1994 OCJ) – cut back; Cannington, Somerset 27x184 (1990? AFM); Killaloan Lodge, Tipperary (recorded under the type) 27x169 (2000 TROI); Leighton Hall, Powys (38)x163 (1984 AFM).

'Charkowiensis' Poor trees in a few collections. Alice Holt, Hants. 22x35 (2001 OCJ), p1960.

'Criollo' Alice Holt, Hants. 26x43 (2001 OCJ), p1950; moved 1955.

Given a rich, wet soil, poplars can outgrow almost any tree. Shouldering up above their fellows, they often rival the dominance of church towers in the landscape. They have attracted much interest from foresters, but the numerous hybrids and clones that have been bred are here-today, gone-tomorrow trees and can be difficult to tell apart. The list of champions for these forms is consequently dominated by the National Collection at Alice Holt, Hampshire – where the poor soils are in fact far from ideal.
The biggest Black Italian Poplar (*Populus* x *canadensis* 'Serotina') grows in a field near Chelsworth, Suffolk.

'Italica' Lombardy Poplar 1758. Abundant. Does best in warm dry areas (cf. 'Plantierensis' – with downy young shoots – which some of these trees may be). Haresfield, Glos. 30x169 (1993); Killinane, Carlow 30.5x163 (2002 AF); Morden Cemetery, London 30x179@0.8m under wide branches (2001 OCJ); Ryston Hall, Norfolk 36x111 (1995 JW), p1909; The Fen, Cambs. 36x110 (1991 JW).

'Italica Foemina' Female Lombardy Poplar ('Gigantea') Quite frequent. Fawley Court, Bucks. 32x117 (1985 AFM); Stanway House, Glos. 33x60 (1982 AFM).

'Lombardy Gold' Very rare to date; of poor growth. Kew RBG 11x27 (2001 OCJ).

'Plantierensis' Plantier's Lombardy Poplar Under-recorded; probably locally frequent and outgrowing 'Italica' in wetter areas. Brockley Cemetery, London 31x145 (2001 OCJ). (Leighton Hall, Powys 31x162@1.2m and 34x152 (1964 AFM).)

'Vereecken' A fine vigorous tree, rare to date. Alice Holt, Hants. 30x74 (2001 OCJ), p1954.

'Vert de Garonne'. Thorp Perrow, Yorks. 29x46 (1991 AFM).

var. *viadri* C Europe. In a few collections. Thorp Perrow, Yorks. 31x77 (1991 AFM).

P. nigra* x *trichocarpa. Alice Holt, Hants. 25x78 (2001 OCJ), p1954.

P. **'OP265'**. Alice Holt, Hants. 25x52 (2001 OCJ), p1957.

P. **'OP42'** In a few collections. Thorp Perrow, Yorks. 34x73 (1991 AFM).

P. **'OP66'**. Alice Holt, Hants. 25x59 (2001 OCJ), p1954.

P. **'Oxford'** (x *berolinensis* x *maximowiczii*) 1934. Collections only? Wisley 21x83 (2000 OCJ) – two the same size.

P. **'Petrowskyana'** (*laurifolia* x *nigra* 'Italica'?) In a few collections. Ryston Hall, Norfolk 30x97 (1995 JW).

P. **'Rasumowskyana'** (*laurifolia* x *nigra* 'Italica'?). Kew RBG 13x41 (2001 OCJ).

P. **'Rochester'** (*maximowiczii* x *nigra* 'Plantierensis') 1934. Rare. Terrace Gardens, London 29x99 (2001 OCJ).

P. **'Roxbury'** (*nigra* x *trichocarpa*) 1934. Collections only? Thorp Perrow, Yorks. 34x93 (1991 AFM).

P. **'Rumford'** (*deltoides* x *nigra* 'Plantierensis'?) 1934. Collections only? Wisley 19x53 (2000 OCJ) – as planted, 1979.

***P. sargentii* Great Plains Cottonwood** C N America, 1919. Alice Holt, Hants. 18x48 (2001 OCJ), p1956.

***P. simonii* Chinese Weeping Poplar** 1862. Rather rare; very susceptible to canker in the south. Acton Park, London 18x65 (2001 OCJ) – fine weeping tree; Cambridge UBG ('Fastigiata') 21x44 (1989 JW), p1964.

P. **'Strathglass'** (*laurifolia* x *nigra*) 1934. Collections only? Thorp Perrow, Yorks. 36x67 (1991 AFM).

P. suaveolens E Siberia, 1834. A tree at Alice Holt, Hants., 28x87 (2001 OCJ), p1960, is probably *P. balsamifera*.

P. szechuanica – see *P. lasiocarpa* var. *tibetica*.

P. tacamahaca – see *P. balsamifera*.

P. tomentosa China, 1897. Alice Holt, Hants. 19x65 (2001 OCJ), p1959.

P. tremula **Aspen** Native; very short-lived. The few known sizeable trees are evenly distributed: Wester Downie, Highland 20x89 (1993); Ballinlough Castle, Westmeath 26x88 and 27x84 (2000 TROI); Kearsney Manor, Kent 22x85 (1999 OCJ); Cerney House Gardens, Glos. 31x68 (1995).

'Erecta' Very rare. Dogflud Way, Farnham, Surrey 14x27 (2000 OCJ).

'Gigas' In a few collections. Threave Garden, Dumfries & Galloway 22.5x33 (1984 AFM).

'Pendula' Weeping Aspen Rare. Wisley 7x26 (2000 OCJ).

P. tremuloides **American Aspen** N America, 1812. In a few collections. Stanage Park, Powys 22x66 (1994 JW).

'Pendula' Parasol de St Julien Very rare. Talbot Manor, Norfolk 17x27 (1978 AFM) – as planted, 1957.

P. trichocarpa **Western Balsam Poplar** W N America, 1892. Frequent; best in cool, humid areas. Brobury House, Herefords. (26)x118 (2002 DGA); Wester Elchies, Highland (41)x83 (1989 AFM).

P. 'TT37' (*balsamifera* x *trichocarpa*) Rare. Alice Holt, Hants. 22x72 (2001 OCJ), p1954; Forde Abbey, Dorset 28x57 (1988 AFM), p1968.

P. wilsonii **Wilson's Poplar** W China, 1907. In a few collections. Batsford Arboretum, Glos. 15x62@1.2m (2003 OCJ) - decaying.

P. yunnanensis **Yunnan Poplar** SW China, by 1905. In some collections. Mount Usher, Wicklow 28x75 and 29x67 (1989 AFM).

Prumnopitys andina **Chilean Plum Yew** (*Podocarpus andinus*) S Andes, 1860. Occasional; best in mild, humid areas. Ashbourne House, Cork 18.5x61+35+30 (1987 AFM); Birr Castle 18x44 (2000 TROI); Huntington Castle, Wexford 18x38+37 (1991 AFM).

Prunus Cherries

Prunus **'Accolade'** (*sargentii* x x *subhirtella*, c1935). Abundant. East Wickham Community Centre, London 8x70 under graft (2001 OCJ).

P. alabamensis **Alabama Cherry**. Kew RBG 9x26@1m (2001 OCJ), p1965.

P. **'Amanogawa' Flagpole Cherry** Abundant. Bodnant, Conwy 10x45@1m? (1981 AFM).

P. x *amygdalo-persica* (*dulcis* x *persica*). Several clones, scarcely to 'tree' size and now very rare. Hillier Gardens ('Pollardii') 8x27 (2001 Harry James).

P. **'Asagi'** Very rare. (x42 at Hillier Gardens in 1991 (AFM).)

P. **'Asano'** – see *P.* 'Geraldinae'.

P. **'Ariake'** Very rare. Kew RBG 5x36 (2001 OCJ).

P. armeniaca **Apricot** E Asia; long grown here, but a free-standing 'tree' only where summers are warmest. Aldon Old Rectory, Kent (var. *ansu*) 5x29 (1999 OCJ).

P. avium **Wild Cherry** Native; abundant and planted everywhere. Large trees are rarely seen. Studley Royal, Yorks. 17x182 (1994); Ardmullchan, Meath 15x132@1m (2001 AF); Leigh Woods, Somerset 29x64 (1988 JW).

'Adiana'. Kew RBG 8x40 among branches (2001 OCJ), p1946.

'Decumana'. Hillier Gardens 12.5m (2002 Harry James).

'Pendula' Weeping Gean Very rare. Sedgewick Park, W Sussex 11x33 (1997 OCJ).

'Plena' Double Gean Abundant; grows as large as the type. The Murray Home, Edinburgh 16x107@0.5m (1999 Donald Rodger); South Park, Ilford, London 18x91@1.3m (2001 OCJ); Windsor (Savill Garden) 21x66 (2000 OCJ).

P. **'Benden'** Very rare, but vigorous. Westonbirt NA 10x32@1.1m (2002 OCJ); Batsford Arboretum, Glos. 13x30 (2003 OCJ) – both young trees.

P. x *blireana* **Double Cherry Plum** 1895. Frequent (as 'Moseri'). Hastings, E Sussex 6x(35) (2001 OCJ).

P. canescens **Grey Cherry** China, 1898. Authentic examples are confined to a few collections. (Talbot Manor, Norfolk 10x39@1m (1973 AFM), p1946.)

P. canescens x *serrula*. Hillier Gardens 11x40 (2001).

P. cerasifera **Myrobalan Plum** W Asia; long grown here. Abundantly naturalised; the largest-growing plum. Lordship Recreation Ground, London 8x71@1m among burrs (1995 PJB); Finnstown, Dublin 13x63@0.9m (2001 AF).

'Hessei' Rare; slow-growing. Briggens, Herts. 9x40 (2002 OCJ).

'Lindsayae' Very rare. Windsor (Valley Gardens) 15x56@0.8m (2000 OCJ).

'Pissardii' Pissard's Plum ('Atropurpurea') Abundant. Cirencester College, Glos. 8.5x65@? (1989 JW); Creech St Michael church, Somerset 12x31 (1986 AFM). The pink-flowered 'Nigra' is now more popular: Hafodunos, Conwy 9x54@1m (1984 AFM); Spalding Cemetery, Lincs. 12x35 (1991 AFM).

P. cerasus **Sour Cherry** Long grown here. Occasionally well naturalised; typically a bush. Godalming, Surrey 9x43 (2000 OCJ) – ?

'Rhexii' Now very occasional. Cuckfield church, W Sussex 5x51 under graft (1996 OCJ) – cut back; Sherston church, Wilts. 8x44 (2002 OCJ).

'Semperflorens' All Saints' Cherry Almost extinct. Waterer's Nursery, Surrey 5x33 (2000 OCJ).

P. **'Choshu-hizakura'** Rare. Central Park, East Ham, London 8x40 under graft (2002 OCJ).

P. cocomilia **Naples Plum** Sicily to S Balkans. Kew RBG 5x28 among branches (2001 OCJ), from 1950 seed.

P. conradinae – see *P. hirtipes*.

P. cornuta **Himalayan Bird Cherry** 1860. In some big gardens. Westonbirt NA 15x52 (2002 OCJ); Edinburgh RBG 19.5x40 (1997), p1904.

P. cuthbertii Georgia (USA), 1901. Hillier Gardens 16x39@0m (2001 Ron Holley).

P. cyclamina China, 1907. In a few collections as a small tree.

P. **'Daikoku'** Very rare. (Birr Castle 8x68 under graft (1988 AFM).)

P. x dasycarpa Black Apricot (*armeniaca* x *cerasifera*). Almost extinct? (Cambridge UBG 7.5x32 (1989 JW).)

P. x dawyckensis Dawyck Cherry (*canescens* x *dielsiana*?) In a few big gardens. Windsor (Savill Garden) 6x29@1.2m (2002 OCJ).

P. dielsiana C China, 1907. In one or two collections. Dunloe Castle, Kerry 12m (1993 HPG).

P. domestica Plum Long grown here. Abundant. Most orchards are in warm but relatively humid areas; the Lydd tree grows over raw shingle. Lydd church, Kent 10x60 (1999 OCJ) – small purple fruit.

var. insititia – see *P. insititia*.

P. dulcis Almond Mediterranean; long grown here. Very frequent; to tree-size only when summers are warm. Updown House, Kent 6x61@1.2m (1999 OCJ); Hammersmith Cemetery, Fulham, London 11x48 (2001 OCJ) – spread 12m.

'Alba' White Almond Rare. Eastbourne, E Sussex 8x(38)@0.8m (2003 OCJ). Various other ornamental forms scarcely reach 'tree' size and are now very rare.

P. x fontanesiana (*avium* x *mahaleb*). Very rare. Hillier Gardens 12x31 (2001 Ron Holley).

P. 'Fudanzakura' Very rare. (Wisley 7.5x52 under graft (1975 AFM).)

P. 'Fugenzo' Occasional. Havelock Cemetery, London 7x73@1.3m under graft (2002 OCJ).

P. 'Geraldinae' ('Asano') Rare. Cathays Park, Glamorgan 5x37 (1985 AFM).

P. 'Gyoiko' Very rare. Westonbirt NA 8x34 under graft (2002 OCJ). (Bosahan, Cornwall 9x48 under graft (1985 AFM).)

P. 'Hatazakura' Flag Cherry Very rare. Kew RBG 7x26 (2001 OCJ), p1979.

P. 'Hillieri' Hillier's Cherry (*incisa* x *sargentii*, c1930) Very rare. Church House Gardens, London 9x45@1m under graft (2001 OCJ).

P. 'Hilling's Weeping' Very rare. Wisley 4x32 (2000 OCJ).

P. hirtipes (*P. conradinae*) China, 1907. Rare. Westonbirt NA 8x60@0.4m under graft (2002 OCJ); Kew RBG ('Semiplena' – the commonest form) 12x45 (2001 OCJ).

P. 'Hokusai' Becoming rare. Leicester UBG, Leics. 5.5x57 under graft (1985 AFM); Cathays Park, Glamorgan 11x47 under graft (1985 AFM).

P. 'Ichiyo' Rather occasional; a vigorous cherry, usually grown on its own stem. Twydall, Kent 8x70 (1999 OCJ); Dartington Hall, Devon 12x45 (1995 VES).

P. incisa Fuji Cherry Japan, 1910. Rather rare; often bushy. Westonbirt NA 5x52@0.8m under graft (2002 OCJ); Birr Castle 8.5x50@1.2m (2000 TROI).

'February Pink' Very rare. Hillier Gardens 7x29 (2001 Harry James).

P. insititia Bullace Long grown here. Abundantly naturalised; generally a suckering bush. Painswick, Glos. 12x41@? (1992).

P. 'Itokukuri' Very rare. Hurst Mill, W Sussex ('Yae-murasaki'?) 11x36 (1997 OCJ).

P. jamasakura Hill Cherry (*P. serrulata* var. *spontanea*) Japan, 1914? Undeservedly rare; a large tree of great beauty. Collingwood Grange, Kent 9x66@0.4m (1996 OCJ); Worthing Crematorium, W Sussex 8x59 (1996 OCJ) – spread 18m; Duckyls Wood, W Sussex 19x28+ (1996 OCJ) – drawn up.

P. 'Jo-nioi' Rather rare. Birr Castle 6x59 under graft (2002 DGA).

P. x juddii Judd's Cherry (*sargentii* x x *yedoensis*) 1914. Rare. Wisley 10x82@0.4m under branching (2000 OCJ).

P. 'Kanzan' Abundant; the most vigorous 'Japanese Cherry'. Acton Park, London 10x92 among burrs under graft (2001 OCJ); Pashley Manor, E Sussex 14x56@0.9m over cut limbs (1994 OCJ).

P. 'Kiku-shidare-zakura' Cheal's Weeping Cherry Abundant; always stunted by fungal infections. St Nicholas at Wade, Kent 3x(28) under graft (1999 OCJ).

P. 'Kursar' (*campanulata* x *kurilensis*) Rare. West Ham Park, London 8x47 under graft (2002 OCJ), p1955.

P. laurocerasus Cherry Laurel E Europe, Asia Minor; long grown here. An abundantly naturalised layering bush on clay; to tree size in warm humid areas. Cahemahallia, Tipperary 9x59@1.25m (2000 TROI); Borden Wood, W Sussex 18x40@1m+36+ (1997 OCJ) – six stems.

'Latifolia' Rare. Hollycombe, W Sussex 8x50@1m (1997 OCJ) – layered over 29m.

P. litigiosa C China, 1907. (Borde Hill 10x31 (1971 AFM).)

P. lusitanica Portugal Laurel Iberia, 1648. Abundantly naturalised on heavy soils. Byeways, Northants. (?) 18.5x100@? (1994); Castle Lough, Tipperary 12.5x72 (2001 AF).

'Myrtifolia' Rare. Dyffryn Gardens, Glamorgan 10x54 (1997 OCJ) – layering.

P. maackii Manchurian Cherry NE Asia, 1910. Rather rare; vigorous but short-lived. Great Comp, Kent 11x42 (1995 OCJ), p1970?; shapely tree. (Wakehurst Place 11.5x90 (1981 AFM).)

P. mahaleb St Lucie Cherry C and S Europe, 1714. Very occasional; rarely well naturalised as a suckering bush. Archbishop Park, London 6x34 (2001 OCJ) – spread 11m.

P. maximowiczii NE Asia, Japan, 1892. In a few collections. Edinburgh RBG 8.5x40 (1997).

Not all champion trees grow beside stately homes or in big arboreta: the street tree outside your window may be one too. The biggest recorded example of the Japanese Cherry 'Ichiyo' (*Prunus* 'Ichiyo') is one of a wealth of imaginative street plantings in Twydall, Kent. This cherry remains curiously scarce: its flowers are long-lasting, with the neat, tiered design of a ballerina's tutu and with green or red 'eyes' that stare at you from all over the tree.

Flowering cherries grow best when springs are dry and fewer fungal pathogens can attack them; they also enjoy a rich or limey soil. Most seem happiest in the warmth of London and northern Kent, but this concentration of champions must partly be considered an artefact of the recording process: cherries are an ubiquitous constituent of today's suburban scene which is all too often ignored completely because of the difficulty of distinguishing these trees out of flower.

All are short-lived, and some have failed to grow big enough to merit inclusion on this list. It is customary to graft 'Japanese Cherries' on a Wild Cherry stock, and it is generally these whose thickness is measured. (They seldom attain much height, so in general only champions for trunk thickness are featured here.) It is interesting to discover, however, how greatly apparently similar clones can differ in vigour. *Prunus* 'Shirotae' (Redstone Cemetery, Surrey).

P. **'Mikuruma-gaeshi'** Rare. Malt House, W Sussex 6x35 under graft (1997 OCJ).

P. **'Ojochin'** Rare. Preston Hall Hospital, Kent 6x69@1m under graft (1999 OCJ).

P. **'Okame'** (*campanulata* x *incisa*) Frequent; always stunted by fungal infections. Newcastle House, Glamorgan 5x29 (1990 AFM).

P. **'Okumiyako'** Very rare. Oare House, Wilts. 6.5x42 (1994 VES), p1950.

P. padus **Bird Cherry** Native to N Britain and Ireland; a small tree. Only odd examples in gardens (some of them the more vigorous 'Watereri'?) have been recorded to date. Glenleigh, Tipperary 15x56@1.3m (2002 AF); Achnacarry, Highland 11x55 (1986 AFM); Winderwath, Cumbria 15x40 (1996 DH).

'Albertii' Occasional as a younger municipal tree. Sydenham Wells Park, London 12x37 (2001 OCJ).

'Colorata' Purple Bird Cherry Occasional as a younger planting. Windsor (Savill Garden) 11x29 and 14x22 (2000 OCJ).

var. *commutata* Manchuria. Rare. Hillier Gardens 13m (2001 Harry James).

'Watereri' Frequent. Stratford Park, Glos. (?) 21x80@? (1991 JW); Westonbirt NA 20x62 (2002 OCJ).

P. **'Pandora'** (x *subhirtella* x x *yedoensis*) Frequent; vigorous. Richmond Cemetery, London 8x68 under graft (2001 OCJ).

P. pendula Japan, 1884? 'Wild' forms are in a few big gardens. Kilmory Castle, Argyll 12x29 (1986 AFM). (And see *P.* x *subhirtella*.)

var. *ascendens* 'Flore Pleno'. Hillier Gardens 8x28 (2001 Harry James).

'Rosea' Rose-bud Cherry Rare. Mote Park, Kent 8x73 under graft (1999 OCJ).

'Pendula Plena Rosea' Rare; scarcely reaches 'tree' size.

'Pendula Rosea' Occasional. Nymans, W Sussex 5x59 under graft (1996 OCJ).

'Pendula Rubra' Very occasional. Hall Place, London 3x44 under graft (2001 OCJ) – spread 11m.

'Stellata' Rare; scarcely to 'tree' size.

P. pensylvanica **Pin Cherry** N America, 1773. In one or two collections. City of Westminster Cemetery, London 8x27 (2001 OCJ).

P. pilosiuscula W China, 1907. Westonbirt NA 10x30 (2002 OCJ).

P. **'Pink Perfection'** Very frequent. Beech Court, Kent 9x53 under graft (1999 OCJ).

P. pseudocerasus China? 1819. Very rare as a small tree.

P. rufa Himalayas, 1897. Vigorous young trees in some big gardens.

P. salicifolia Mexico to Ecuador. (Kew RBG x85 (1981 AFM).)

P. sargentii **Sargent's Cherry** Japan, Korea, 1890. Very frequent. Leonardslee, W Sussex 13x90 (1996 OCJ); Lynford Arboretum, Norfolk 16x47 (1990 AFM).

'Fastigiata' Occasional. Dorking, Surrey 9x(30) (2000 OCJ); Mamhead, Devon 16x22 (2001 OCJ).

'Rancho' Rare? Kildangan, Kildare 10x30 (1989 AFM).

P. x schmittii **Schmitt's Cherry** (*avium* x *canescens*) A locally frequent street tree. Southall, London 10x57 (2002 OCJ) – cut back; Borde Hill 20x56@0.8m (1995 OCJ) – planted as *P. canescens*.

P. scopulorum China. In a few big gardens; scarcely reaches 'tree' size.

P. serotina **Black Cherry** E N America, 1629. Occasional; sometimes well naturalised. Newick Park, E Sussex 19x104@0.15m (1994 OCJ) – huge bush; Kew RBG 19x72 (1991 AFM); Arley Arboretum, Worcs. (21)x61 (1992 AFM).

P. serrula **Tibetan Cherry** W China, 1908. Rather occasional. Best in cool, humid areas. Bodnant, Conwy 9x66 (1989 AFM); Edinburgh RBG 15x42 (1991 AFM), p1938 from Yu 7728.

P. serrulata 'Albi-plena' 1822. Occasional. Funtington Church, W Sussex 5x77@0.2m (1997 OCJ) – spread 13m; Richmond Cemetery, London 5x70 under graft (2001 OCJ).

var. *hupehensis* **Hubei Hill Cherry** China, 1900. In a few big gardens. Hillier Gardens 10x37 (2001 Harry James).

var. *pubescens* – see *P.* x *verecunda*.

var. *spontanea* – see *P. jamasakura*.

P. **'Shibayama'** Very rare. Alexandra Park, E Sussex 8x34@1.2m under graft (2001 OCJ).

P. **'Shimidsu-zakura'** – see *P.* 'Shogetsu'.

P. **'Shirofugen'** Very frequent. Bulstrode Park, Bucks. 6x58 under graft (2001 OCJ). (Farnham, Surrey 7x82 under graft (1973 AFM).)

P. **'Shirotae'** Frequent. Abbey School, Faversham, Kent 5x62 under graft (1999 OCJ); Rowallane, Down 9x48 (1991 AFM).

P. **'Shogetsu'** ('Shimidsu-zakura') Frequent; of poor growth. Woburn Park, Beds. 4.5x63@0.8m (1995 DGA).

P. **Shosar'** Rare as a small young tree.

P. x *sieboldii* **Naden** Japan, by 1864. Rather rare; often stunted. Beech Hurst Gardens, W Sussex 7x45@1.2m under graft (1996 OCJ).

P. **'Snow Goose'** (*incisa* x *speciosa*). Very rare as a small tree.

P. speciosa **Oshima Cherry** Japan, 1909. In a few collections. Windsor (Valley Gardens; ?) 8x30+ (2002 OCJ).

P. **'Spire'** (*incisa* x *sargentii*) Frequent. Hale, Surrey 8x56 under graft (2000 OCJ); Dormer's Wells, London 8x56 under graft (2002 OCJ); Capel Manor, London 12x31 under graft (2001 OCJ).

P. x *subhirtella* **'Autumnalis' Winter Cherry** 1900. Abundant (including 'Autumnalis Rosea'). St Leonards, E Sussex 7x69@1m under graft (1994 OCJ); Doddington Place, Kent 9x62 under graft (1995 OCJ). (And see *P. pendula*.)

P. **'Tai Haku' Great White Cherry** Frequent. Godinton Park, Kent 6x73 under graft (1999 OCJ).

P. **'Takasago'** – see *P.* x *sieboldii*.

P. **'Taoyame'** Rather rare. Crawley, W Sussex 8x48 under graft (2002 OCJ).

P. **'Ukon'** Frequent. Leonardslee, W Sussex 5x55 under graft (1996 OCJ) – cut back.

P. **'Umineko'** (*incisa* x *speciosa*) Frequent; vigorous. Kew RBG 9x76 under graft (2001 OCJ).

P. x *verecunda* **Korean Hill Cherry** 1907 (*P. serrulata* var. *pubescens*). In some big gardens. Collingwood Grange, Kent 9x76@0.5m (1996 OCJ); Syon Park, London 9x51 under graft (2002 OCJ).

P. virginiana **Choke Cherry** E N America, 1724. In one or two collections; 'Schubert', the Canada Red Plum, is rare as a small young tree.

P. **'Washino-o'** Rare. (Birr Castle 6x38 (1985 AFM).)

P. **'Yae-beni-oshima'**. Kew RBG 8x26@1.2m (2001 OCJ).

P. **'Yae-murasaki'**. Very rare.

P. **'Yedo Zakura'** Very rare. The Hyde, W Sussex 6x37 under graft (1996 OCJ) – as label.

P. x *yedoensis* **Yoshino Cherry** (*speciosa* x *pendula*?) Japan, 1902. Frequent; the most vigorous flowering cherry here. Mote Park, Kent 9x112 under graft (1999 OCJ); Windsor (Valley Gardens) 15x52 (2002 OCJ).

'Ivensii' Rare. Ipswich, Suffolk 2.7x41 under graft (1995 Daniel Sanford).

'Perpendens' Weeping Yoshino Cherry ('Shidare Yoshino') Occasional. Westonbirt NA 4.5x51 (2002 OCJ), p1937 on a 4m stem of Wild Cherry.

'Tsubame' Rare. Pyrford church, Surrey 3x32 under graft (2000 OCJ).

Pseudocydonia sinensis **Chinese Quince** Very rare; often a bush. Clock House, Lindfield, W Sussex 6x42 (1987 AFM); Coverwood House, Surrey 10x25 (1986 AFM).

Pseudolarix amabilis **Golden Larch** E China, 1853. Perhaps 100 trees. Grows well only where summers are warm. Carclew, Cornwall 23x86 (1989 AFM).

Pseudopanax arboreus New Zealand, 1820. In a few mild gardens. (Ashbourne House Hotel, Cork 7x27+17 (1966 AFM).)

Pseudotsuga Douglas Firs

Pseudotsuga japonica **Japanese Douglas Fir** 1898. Poor plants survive in a few collections. (Powerscourt, Wicklow 18x56 (1966 AFM).)

P. macrocarpa **Big-cone Douglas Fir** California,

1910. About 10 trees. Bedgebury NP 24x83 (1999 OCJ), p1925.

P. macrolepis Mexican Douglas Fir 1962. In a few collections. Bicton Park, Devon 15x33 (2001 OCJ).

P. menziesii Douglas Fir W N America, 1827. Abundant. The huge tree at Eggesford has a huge branch from ground level which has now fused with another at 1.2m, making it impossible to tape meaningfully. Dunkeld Cathedral, Perth 33x225 (1999 Donald Rodger), p1846; some small low branches on single bole; Eggesford, Devon x234@1m/x195@1.8m (1970 AFM) – original; much died back (39m in 1908); Hyslop Arboretum, Argyll 62x175 (2002 DGA); Reelig Glen Wood, Highland 62x108 (2002 DGA), p1882 – several similar; Lake Vyrnwy, Powys 61.5x147 (2002 DH), p1887; Benmore, Argyll 60x(120) (2002 Stephen Verge); The Hermitage, Perth 59x(135) (2002 DGA).

'Brevifolia'. Hillier Gardens 12x33 (2000 H M Brown).

var. _flahaultii_ Arizona Douglas Fir 1962. Bedgebury NP 18x40 (1999 OCJ), p1967.

'Fretsii' Very rare. Avondale, Wicklow 23x58 (1991 AFM), p1921.

var. _glauca_ Blue Douglas Fir Montana to Mexico, 1885? Occasional; does better than the type in the driest areas. Sotterley Hall, Suffolk 26x100 (1985 AFM), p1880; White Crags, Cumbria 30x57 (1993 DH).

'Moerheimii' Very rare. Hillier Gardens 14x25 (2001 Ron Holley).

'Stairii' Very rare. Munches, Dumfries & Galloway 22x57 (1985 AFM); Cortachy Castle, Angus x57 (1992 AFM).

Pterocarya fraxinifolia Caucasian Wingnut 1782. Occasional; now more planted in warm areas. Melbury House, Dorset (36)x186 (1989 AFM) – good bole; Abbotsbury, Dorset 27.5x182 (1991 AFM), and 33x136 (1993 VES); Lacock Abbey, Wilts. 26x193 (1987 AFM) – forking and burred.

P. x rehderiana Hybrid Wingnut (_fraxinifolia_ x _stenoptera_) 1879. Rather rare. Frensham Manor, Kent 21x148 (1995 OCJ) – from 1928 seed of _P. fraxinifolia_; Westonbirt NA 25x138@1.8m over huge limbs (2002 OCJ); Kew RBG 25x132@1.2m under branches (2001 OCJ), p1908.

P. rhoifolia Japanese Wingnut 1888. Very rare to date. Singleton Park, Glamorgan 17x70 (2000 OCJ) – shapely.

P. stenoptera Chinese Wingnut 1860. Rather rare. Kew RBG 24x143@0.7m under forks (2001 OCJ); Dyffryn Gardens, Glamorgan 15x93 (1997 OCJ), p1902; 25m before 1990.

Pterostyrax hispida Epaulette Tree China, Japan, 1875. Rather rare; sometimes a bush. Magnolia Cottage, Jersey 12x60@? (1989); Borden Wood, W Sussex 21x43 (1997 OCJ).

Pyrus Pears

Pyrus amygdaliformis Almond-leaved Pear Mediterranean, 1810. Rare. Holland Park, London 10x63 (2001 OCJ); Dyffryn Gardens, Glamorgan 13x36 (1997 OCJ).

var. _persica_ A garden hybrid? Edinburgh RBG 12x40 (1991 AFM).

P. balansae W Asia. In one or two collections. Edinburgh RBG 13x57 (1997), p1898.

P. betulifolia N China, 1882. In a few collections. (Cambridge UBG 8x44 (1984 AFM).)

P. bretschneideri N China. Kew RBG 17x74@1.2m under scar (2001 OCJ), from 1925 seed.

P. calleryana Callery Pear China, 1908. Rare. Glasnevin NBG 12x61 (1993); Borde Hill 14x45 (1995 OCJ).

'Bradford' Very rare. Hadlow College, Kent (?) 12x37 (1999 OCJ).

'Chanticleer' Chanticleer Pear Abundant as a young municipal tree. Parsloes Park, London 12x34 (2001 OCJ); Windsor (Savill Garden) 14x27 (2000 OCJ), p1978.

P. x canescens (_nivalis_ x _salicifolia_?) In a few collections. Hillier Gardens 11x30@1m (2001 Ron Holley).

P. caucasia Caucasus. Hillier Gardens 10.5x48@1m (2002), p1977.

P. communis Pear Long grown here and widely naturalised (cf. _P. pyraster_). Abundant; can be big. Haresfield, Glos. 12x133 (1993); Chargrove House, Glos. 21x72 (1988 JW). (And see _P. pyraster_.)

'Beech Hill' Very occasional. Kew RBG 10x43 (2001 OCJ), p1966; Holland Park, London 13x35 (2001 OCJ); Clancarthy Road, London 13x27 (2001 OCJ).

P. cordata Plymouth Pear A very rare native bush (Cornwall, Devon); young trees in some collections. Kew RBG 11x40 (2001 OCJ).

P. cossonii Algeria, 1875. Very rare. Collingwood Grange, Kent (?) 20x57 (1995 OCJ); long leaning spire.

P. elaeagrifolia SE Europe, 1800. Rare. Museum Gardens, York 9x61 (1989 AFM); Abbotsbury, Dorset 14x53 (1980 AFM).

P. glabra Iran. In one or two collections. (Birr Castle 12x50 (1987 AFM).)

P. x lecontei (_communis_ x _pyrifolia_) Rare. Aldenham Park, Herts. 16x39 (2002 OCJ).

P. lindleyi NE Asia. (Kew RBG 11x41 (1972 AFM).)

P. x michauxii (_amygdaliformis_ x _nivalis_) Rare. City of Westminster Cemetery, London 9x33 (2001 OCJ); Holland Park, London 12x32 (2001 OCJ).

P. nivalis Snow Pear S Europe, 1800. Occasional as a younger tree. Kew RBG 10x50 (2001 OCJ).

P. pashia Himalayas to China, 1908. Rare. Wisley 13x87@0.5m (2000 OCJ); Haberdashers' Aske's School, Herts. 17x72 (2002 OCJ) – ?; Aldenham Park, Herts. 21x65 (2002 OCJ) – ?

P. pyraster Wild Pear A very rare tree, probably native to S England. (Most 'wild' pears are _P. communis_.) Broome, Shropshire 12x108 (1993); Alexandra Park, E Sussex 16x84 (2001 OCJ) – regular dome.

P. pyrifolia Sand Pear China, 1909. Rare. Aldenham Park, Herts. 7x58@1m (2002 OCJ) – leans; Eton College, Berks. 7x49 (1997 OCJ); Borde Hill ('Chojura') 15x47@0.5m under forks (1995 OCJ).

P. salicifolia Willow-leafed Pear Caucasus, 1780. Frequent; often as a miniature weeping dome ('Pendula'). Hall Place, Kent 9x70 under graft (1999 OCJ); Holland Park, London 12x40 (2001 OCJ). (Kelvingrove Park, Glasgow 14.5x45 (1974 J Lister).)

Willow-leafed Pear (*Pyrus salicifolia*) is popular as a miniature, silvery weeping dome in suburban gardens. Given the chance, it grows into a substantial tree, but the champion at Hall Place, Kent, remains exceptional.

P. serrulata China. Thorp Perrow, Yorks. 11x36 (1991 AFM).

P. syriaca Cyprus to Iran, by 1874. In a few collections. Westonbirt NA 12x35@0.9m (2002 OCJ).

P. ussuriensis Ussurian Pear NE Asia, 1855. In some big gardens. Borde Hill (var. *hondoensis*) 9x75@1.1m (1995 OCJ), p1911 from Wilson 9683, and now recumbent; Kew RBG 12x57 (2001 OCJ), from 1923 seed; very fine; Hillier Gardens 13.5x36@1m (2001).

Quercus Oaks

Quercus acuta Japanese Evergreen Oak 1878? Rare; a bush except where winters are mild and summers warm. Caerhays 14x68 (1991 AFM).

Q. acutissima Japanese Chestnut Oak E Asia, 1862. Rare. Highnam Court, Glos. 23x75 (1988 AFM).

ssp. chenii In a few collections. Hillier Gardens 17x30 (2001 Ron Holley).

Q. afares Atlas Mountains, 1869. In one or two collections. Kew RBG 19x65 (2001 OCJ).

Q. agrifolia Encina SW N America, 1843. Rare; likes hot summers. Kew RBG 16x77 (2001 OCJ); Sunbury Park,

Surrey 17x67@1.2m (2000 OCJ).

Q. alba White Oak E N America, 1724. Stunted trees in some collections. Royal Holloway College, Surrey 15x56 (2000 OCJ), p1964.

Q. aliena Japan. In a few big gardens. Kew RBG 17x52 (2001 OCJ) – 1908 original.

var. acuteserrata C China. In a few collections. Kew RBG 21x78 (2001 OCJ) – 1908 original.

Q. alnifolia Golden Oak of Cyprus 1815. A bush in a few big gardens. East Bergholt Place, Suffolk 9x28 (1992 AFM).

Q. arkansana Arkansas, Alabama. In one or two collections. Kew RBG 14x40 (2001 OCJ) – 1912 original.

Q. x audleyensis Audley End Oak (*ilex* x *petraea*) The original at Audley End, Essex, is (23)x147 (2000 Henry Girling), with a spread of 35m; a few grafts are known.

Q. baronii W China, 1914. Bushy plants in one or two collections. Glasnevin NBG x38@1.2m (1992).

Q. x bebbiana (*alba* x *macrocarpa*). Hillier Gardens 11x27 (2001 Harry James).

Q. x benderi (*coccinea* x *rubra*). Hillier Gardens 16x33 (2001 H M Brown).

SESSILE OAKS

Two halves remain of the Marton Oak in Cheshire – the Sessile Oak (*Quercus petraea*) which a hundred years ago must have been the biggest and most spectacular in Britain. A miniature half-timber garden house, built inside the tree, once gave it an Alice-in-Wonderland sense of scale.

The Sessile Oak is one of the most unjustly neglected of our wild forest trees. With its larger leaves and often straighter growth it is at least as handsome a plant as the English Oak, and seems if anything to have the edge when it comes to growth and stature. Its leaves play host to as many insects. But it is more exclusive to light sandy soils, often in the wetter west, and does not seed itself into gardens, scrub and neglected fields in the same way. Even in areas where the Cinderella Sessile Oak is the characteristic wild species, people wanting to plant a tree to benefit wildlife opt for English Oak 99 times out of 100.

Q. bicolor **Swamp White Oak** E N America, 1800. Now very rare; does well if summers are hot. Kensington Gardens, London 21x79 (2001 OCJ); Kew RBG 22x72 (2001 OCJ), from 1873 seed; Pampisford, Cambs. 25x47 (1988 AFM).

Q. boissieri Cyprus to Iran, 1870. Kew RBG 9x28 (2001 OCJ) (and 18x61 (1967 AFM)).

Q. x bushii (*marilandica* x *velutina*). Hillier Gardens ('Seattle Trident') 10x25 (2002 H M Brown).

Q. canariensis **Algerian Oak** Iberia, N Africa, 1845? Rather rare, but growing well everywhere. Many – including all the largest? – are hybrids with English Oak (*Q. x carrissoana*). Royal Holloway College, Surrey 28x175@1m under branch-spring (2002 OCJ) – fine tree on steep bank; Melbury House, Dorset (30)x126 (1989 AFM); Tregrehan, Cornwall 30x112 (2002 Tom Hudson).

Q. canariensis x faginea. Hillier Gardens 11x25 (2001 H M Brown).

Q. x capesii (*nigra* x *phellos*). Hillier Gardens 15x62 (2001 Harry James).

Q. castaneifolia **Chestnut-leaved Oak** Caucasus. Rare, but very vigorous: Kew RBG 31x228 (2001 DGA) – 1846 original.

'Green Spire' Rare to date. Hillier Gardens 14.5x32 (2001 H M Brown).

Q. castaneifolia x cerris Several plantings seem to be this cross. Albury Park, Surrey 31x87 (2000 OCJ).

Q. castaneifolia x libani. Hillier Gardens 13x26 (2001 Ron Holley).

Q. cerris **Turkey Oak** S Europe, Asia Minor, 1735. Abundant (including the variant 'Laciniata'). Shute Barton, Devon 31x274 (2002 Simon Major); Knightshayes, Devon (40)x262 (2003); Beckenham Place Park, London 25x228 (2002 OCJ) – veteran tree, cut back, its trunk reduced to strips; Threecastles House, Kilkenny 23.5x227@1.2m around 'waist' (2000 TROI); Ballyrahan, Wexford 26.5x225@1.2m around 'waist' (2000 TROI); Bulstrode Park, Bucks. 37x224 (2001 OCJ) – impressive long bole. (And see p. 122-3)

'Argenteovariegata' Variegated Turkey Oak Rare. Wisley 10x45 (2000 OCJ). Largely reverted trees are: Beningbrough Hall, Yorks. 25x143 (1994); Combe House, Devon 27x112 (2001 OCJ).

'Marmorata' Very rare. Torry Hill, Kent 15x74 (1999 OCJ) – very bright, and probably a sport.

Q. chrysolepis **Californian Live Oak** SW N America, 1877. In a few collections. Kew RBG 13x57 (2001 OCJ), from 1904 seed.

Q. coccifera **Kermes Oak** W Mediterranean; long grown here. Very rare. Borde Hill 8x51@0.5m under forks, and 12x27 (1995 OCJ).

Q. coccinea **Scarlet Oak** E N America, 1691. Frequent in areas with warm summers, on light soils. Petham, Kent 24x118 (1995 OCJ); Tortworth Court, Glos. 24x115@? (1987 JW), p1880; Borden Wood, W Sussex 28x89 (1997 OCJ).

Q. crassifolia Mexico. In one or two collections. Kew RBG 13x48 (2001 OCJ); Caerhays 17x35 (1984 AFM) – 1939 original).

Q. crassipes Mexico, 1839. Extinct here? (Carclew, Cornwall 19x51 (1908 Elwes and Henry).)

Q. dalechampii Italy. In one or two collections. Glasnevin NBG 19x59@1.1m under graft (2003 DGA).

Q. dentata **Daimyo Oak** NE Asia, Japan, 1830. Rare; usually fails to grow well. Gunnersbury Park, London 14x68 (2001 OCJ) – fine dome. (Kensington Gardens, London 22x68 (1988) – blown.)

Q. ellipsoidalis **Northern Pin Oak** E N America, 1902. Very rare to date. Borde Hill 17x34 (1995 OCJ), from 1935 seed.

Q. emoryi x hypoleucoides. Hillier Gardens 11x36 (2001 H M Brown).

Q. faginea **Portuguese Oak** (incorporating *Q. lusitanica*) Iberia, 1835. Very rare. Tortworth Court, Glos. 20x66 (1973 AFM).

ssp. *tlemcenensis* Moroccan Oak In a few collections. Collingwood Grange, Kent 17x66 (1995 OCJ) – original.

Q. falcata **Spanish Oak** SE USA, 1763. Very rare. Kew RBG (?) 21x81 (2001 OCJ), from 1921 seed.

var. *pagodifolia* – see *Q. pagoda*.

Q. floribunda **Tilong Oak** Himalayas. Borde Hill (?) 16x28 (1995 OCJ), p1932.

Q. frainetto **Hungarian Oak** SE Europe, 1838. Occasional and becoming more popular; thrives everywhere. Some plantings are hybrids with English Oak. Buxted Park, E Sussex 26x181 (2002 OCJ); Camperdown Park, Angus (38)x106 (1985 AFM).

Q. garryana **Oregon Oak** W N America, 1873. Small plants in a few collections. Bicton Park, Devon 22x99 (2001 OCJ) – as label.

Q. georgiana **Georgia Oak** SE USA. Hillier Gardens 11x30 (2001 H M Brown).

Q. glabrescens Mexico, 1839. In one or two collections. Kew RBG 8x32 (2001 OCJ).

Q. glandulifera – see *Q. serrata*.

Q. glauca **Bamboo Oak** Himalayas to Japan, 1804. Rare; warm areas. South Lodge, Horsham, W Sussex 8x53@0.6m+29 (1996 OCJ); Syon Park, London 13x44 above one branch on good bole (2002 OCJ); Borde Hill 15x39@0.3m (1995 OCJ); Caerhays 11x41 (1984 AFM). All except the last are the narrow-leaved form sometimes distinguised as *Q. myrsinifolia*.

Q. gravesii **Chisos Red Oak** Southern N America. Kew RBG 8x25 (2001 OCJ), from 1972 seed.

Q. haas Anatolia. (Borde Hill 14x44 (1962).)

Q. hartwissiana Bulgaria to Iran. In a few collections. Kew RBG 13x50 (2001 OCJ), from 1956 seed; Hillier Gardens 15x37 over vine (2000 H M Brown).

Q. x heterophylla (*phellos* x *rubra*) SE USA, 1822. In a few collections. Kew RBG 20x50 (2001 OCJ), sourced 1926.

Q. x hickelii (*pontica* x *robur*) 1922. One or two trees. Edinburgh RBG 12x77 (1997).

Q. x hispanica **'Lucombeana' Lucombe Oak** (*cerris* x *suber*) Quite frequent in various clones. The largest probably all derive from the 1762 'William Lucombe'. Phear Park, Devon 26x252 and 24x252 (2001 OCJ); Red Oaks, W Sussex 22x230@0.8m under forks (1997 OCJ) – cut back after 1987; Trinity Manor, Jersey 20x219@1m (1989 AFM) – very spreading; Pollacton, Carlow

If the oak is the king of trees, then the king of oaks must be the Hungarian Oak (*Quercus frainetto*). The leaves are large, rich-green and have the most elaborate of lobes; the crown, at its best, is a great cartwheel of clean limbs. The largest of all Hungarian Oaks, at Buxted Park, East Sussex, is appropriately perhaps the most shapely.

25.5x216@1m (1999 TROI); Carclew, Cornwall (35)x187 (1989 AFM) – original.

Q. iberica Transcaucasus. (Kew RBG 19x57 (1978 AFM).)

Q. ilex Holm Oak Mediterranean; long grown here. Abundant and naturalising in milder areas; thrives in coastal exposure; likes warm summers. Westbury Court, Glos. 14x257@1m around burrs and under fork (1993); Chilham Castle, Kent 20x243@0.5m under the spring of 7 trunks (1995 OCJ); Kilfane Glebe, Kilkenny 22x208@0.8m (2000 TROI); Courtown, Wexford 21x429@0m (2002 AF), p1648; multi-stemmed; Bicton Park, Devon 27x170@0.8m on short knobbly bole (2001 OCJ). Various narrow- and broad-leaved clones have been distributed, but are often mis-identified.

var. ballota Round-leaved Oak (*Q. rotundifolia*) Iberia, N Africa. Very rare. Records may include broad-leaved Holm Oaks (ie 'Rotundifolia').

Q. ilicifolia Bear Oak E USA, c1800. Caerhays 11.5x28 (1971 AFM).

Q. imbricaria Shingle Oak E USA, 1786. Rather rare; likes warm summers and an acid soil. Sedgewick Park, W Sussex 22x88 (1997 OCJ) – unusually spreading; Syon Park, London 27x72 (2002 OCJ).

Q. infectoria SW Asia to Greece, 1850. In some collections; bushy in the wild. Syon Park, London (?) 20x94 (2002 OCJ).

ssp. veneris. In a few collections. Hillier Gardens 11x29+28 (2001 H M Brown).

Q. ithaburensis SW Asia. In a few collections. Hillier Gardens 21x51 (2001 H M Brown).

ssp. macrolepis Valonia Oak Italy to SW Asia. Very rare. Lyndon Hall, Rutland 13x76 (1984 AFM); Batsford Arboretum, Glos. 22x56 (2003 OCJ).

Q. kelloggii Californian Black Oak 1878. In some collections. Tortworth Court, Glos. 25x99 (1988 AFM).

THE LARGEST OAKS

Marton, Cheshire 9×426 (1992) - two pieces remain; *petraea*.

Pontfadog, Wrexham ×409 (1999 Jeroen Pater) – burred and splitting; *petraea*.

Bowthorpe, Lincs. 12×407 (1999 Jeroen Pater) (×386@1.8m in 1986 (AFM)) – burred, with a gap in the hollow bole; *robur*.

Cowdray Park, W Sussex 8×399 (1999 Jeroen Pater) (×389@1.8-2m) 'The Queen Elizabeth Oak' – 2m gap in hollow bole; *petraea*.

Lydham Manor, Shropshire ×399 (1999 Jeroen Pater) – burred and growing fast; *robur*.

Fredville Park, Kent ×385 (1999 Jeroen Pater) 'Majesty' – 6m bole; full crown; *robur*.

Chaceley, Glos. 13×385@0.5m under torn limb (1995 JW) – low pollard; *robur*.

Hampton Court, London 6×390@1-1.5m (2001 OCJ) 'The Medieval Oak' - two pieces remain; *robur*.

Melbury House, Dorset ×378 over scar and burrs (2002 Andrew Major). 'Billy Wilkins'; *robur*.

Near Welshpool, Powys ×374@1.2-1.6m between burrs (1997 HPG); *robur*.

Barrington Hall, Essex (16)×402 (1995) 'The Great Oak' - halves sag outwards (×344@1.2m in 1983); *robur*.

Eastwood Park, Glos. ×359 (1999 Jeroen Pater); *robur*.

Croft Castle, Herefords. 11×357@1.8m above large branch (1992 AFM); *petraea*.

New Bells Farm, Suffolk ×357@1.2m (2002 JP) 'The Haughley Oak', largely collapsed; *robur*.

Penshurst, Kent 20×356@1m (1996 Philip Webb) – very gnarled; *robur*.

Windsor (Cranbourne) ×356@1m (1998 DGA) – fragment of an even larger tree; *robur*.

Savernake Forest, Wilts. ×355 (1999 Jack Oliver) 'The Pot-Belly Oak'; × *rosacea*.

Bitterley, Shropshire ×352 (1999 Jeroen Pater) 'The Crowleasowes Oak'; *robur*.

Near Welshpool, Powys ×350@1.3m (1999) 'The Giant'; two limbs from 4m; *petraea*.

Hazlegrove, Somerset ×342 (1999 Jeroen Pater) 'The King's Oak' - full crown; *robur*.

Spye Park, Wilts. 17.5×342 (1999 JW) 'The Great Oak' – pollard; *robur*.

Mottisfont Abbey, Hants. ×341@0.9m (1999 Jeroen Pater) 'The Oakleigh Oak' – 4m bole; *robur*.

Sherwood Forest, Notts. 16×337 (1990 AFM) 'The Major Oak'; *robur*.

Cowarne Court, Herefords. ×327@2.1m (1976 AFM) – large gap in bole (12×378 in 1955); *robur*?

Kings Walden, Herts. ×325@1m (2000 University of Hertfordshire) 'The Great Oak' – pollard; *robur*.

Easthampton Farm, Herefords. ×324 (1999 Jeroen Pater) 'The Shobdon Oak' – fine tree, growing fast; *petraea*.

Lullingstone Park, Kent 15×321 (1999 OCJ) – pollard; *petraea*.

Teigngrace, Devon ×(320) (Andrew Morton) 'The Prince of Orange's Oak'; *robur*.

Croft Castle, Herefords. 25×319 (1992) 'The Waggoners' Oak'; *robur*.

Garthmyl House, Powys 18×318@1.2m under wide limbs (1984 AFM); *robur*?

Cowdray Park, W Sussex 9×318@0.5m under burrs (1997 OCJ); *petraea*.

Kentchurch Court, Herefords. ×315 (1998 William Linnard) 'Jack Kemp's Oak' - ×356 in 1975; *robur*.

Silton, Dorset 9×314@1.2m (1982 AFM) 'Wyndham's Oak' - relic boundary marker from Marlborough Forest?; *robur*.

Penrhos Farm, Monmouth 18.5×312 (1998) – pollard; *robur*.

Darnaway, Moray ×310 (1998 JP); *petraea*.

Brenchley Old Parsonage, Kent 14×310 (1999 OCJ) - very hollow; *robur*.

Easton Lodge, Essex 18×310 (1987 AFM) - burr adds 140cm; *robur*.

Edge, Glos. 25×307@1.3m (1999 DGA) - hollow pollard; *robur*.

Ickworth, Suffolk ×305 (2002 DGA) 'The Tea Party Oak' - huge burred pedestal; *robur*.

Penshurst Place, Kent 8×300 (1995 OCJ) 'Sir Philip Sidney's Oak' - one branch left; *robur*.

Stradbally, Laois 20×315@1m under fork (2000 TROI); *robur*.

The Bowthorpe Oak (*Quercus robur*).

Q. x kewensis (*cerris* x *wislizenii*) Very rare. Kew RBG 9x66@0.6m under limbs (2001 OCJ) – 1914 original.

Q. lamellosa Himalayas to China, 1924. Caerhays 13x47 and 20x29 (1984 AFM).

Q. laurifolia Laurel Oak E USA, 1786. Very rare. Stanage Park, Powys 15x67 (1994 JW); Winkworth Arboretum, Surrey 15x61@0.8m (2000 OCJ).

Q. x leana Lea's Oak (*imbricaria* x *velutina*) E USA, 1850. Very rare. Hollycombe, W Sussex 21x83 (1997 OCJ); Tregrehan, Cornwall 24x65 (2002 Tom Hudson), p1892.

Q. leucotrichophora Himalayas, 1815; in a few mild gardens. Trewithen, Cornwall 18x37 (1993).

Q. x libanerris (*cerris* x *libani*). Young trees in a few collections.

Q. libani Lebanon Oak Syria, Asia Minor, 1855? Rare. Grayswood Hill, Surrey 11x67 (1998 OCJ) – supine; Dyffryn Gardens, Glamorgan 12x64 (1997 OCJ); Bedgebury NP 19x55 (1999 OCJ) p1934; Borde Hill ('var *angustifolia*') 19x45 (1995 OCJ).

Q. lobata Valley Oak California, 1874. In a few collections. Kew RBG 20x71 (2001 OCJ), from 1929 seed.

Q. x ludoviciana Ludwig's Oak (*pagoda* x *phellos*) SE USA, 1880. A very rare but beautiful oak. Kew RBG 21x100 under fork (2001 OCJ), sourced 1935; Borde Hill 22x47 (1995 OCJ) – fine straight tree.

Q. lusitanica – see *Q. faginea*.

Q. lyrata Overcup Oak SE USA, 1786. Edinburgh RBG 17.5x37 (1997).

Q. macranthera Caucasian Oak 1873. Rather rare. Some are hybrids with English Oak. Melbury House, Dorset (20)x101 (1989 AFM); Westonbirt NA 27x89 (2002 OCJ), p1875.

Q. macranthera x petraea. Hillier Gardens 14x32 (2001 H M Brown).

Q. macrocarpa Burr Oak E N America, 1811. Very rare, but doing well in hot areas. Syon Park, London 24x86 (2002 OCJ); Holland Park, London 25x84 (2001 OCJ) – very fine.

Q. macrolepis – see *Q. ithaburensis* ssp. *macrolepis*.

Q. marilandica Black Jack Oak E USA, 1739. Now very rare. Tortworth Court, Glos. 12x40 (1973 AFM).

Q. michauxii Swamp Chestnut Oak E USA, 1737. In a few collections. Merthyr Mawr, Glamorgan 17.5x41 (1980 AFM).

Q. mongolica ssp. crispula var. grosseserrata Japan, 1873. In some collections. Kew RBG 18x80 (2001 OCJ), from 1930 seed.

Q. x moreha (*kelloggii* x *wislizenii*) In one or two collections. Borde Hill 13x30 (1995 OCJ).

Q. muehlenbergii Chinquapin Oak E N America, 1822. The only old tree seems to be a supine one at Syon Park, London, 10m in 2002 (OCJ). (Kensington Gardens, London 20x92 (1981 AFM), blown 1987.)

Q. myrsinifolia – see *Q. glauca*.

Q. nigra **Water Oak** SE USA, 1723. Rare. Kew RBG 16x76@1.7m above lumps (2001 OCJ); Windsor (Empire Oaks) 19x68 (2000 OCJ), p1937.

Q. nuttallii SE USA. Hillier Gardens 13x30 (2001 H M Brown).

Q. oxyodon E Himalayas to China, 1900. Small plants in a few big gardens. Caerhays 8x25 (1984 AFM), p1920.

Q. pagoda **Cherrybark Oak** (*falcata* var. *pagodifolia*) SE USA. In one or two collections. Syon Park, London (?) 22x86 (2002 OCJ).

Q. palustris **Pin Oak** E N America, 1800. Very frequent but confined to areas with warm summers. Corsham Court, Wilts. 17x108 (1989 JW) – grown well since; Hyde Park, London 26x110 and 28x91 (2001 OCJ); Mill Hill School, London 15x110 (2002 OCJ) – cut back after 1987; Hall Place, Kent 25x108 (1994 OCJ); Godinton Park, Kent 21x108 (1999 OCJ).

Q. petraea **Sessile Oak** Native; locally abundant. See 'the largest oaks'. Knole Park, Kent 40x188 (1995 OCJ) – 10m bole. (Whitfield, Herefords., 12x146 (1973 AFM a superb slender tree, broken at 17m by 1995.)

'Acutifolia' Very rare. Borde Hill (?) 19x63 (1995 OCJ); Hillier Gardens 13.5x40 (2000 H M Brown), p1982.

'Cochleata'. Kew RBG 19x61 (2001 OCJ), p1871 and mostly reverted. Similar sports are widespread in SE London, including 25x154 at Franks Park (1996 PJB).

'Columna' Fastigiate Sessile Oak Very rare. Hillier Gardens 15x28 (2001 H M Brown).

'Mespilifolia' Medlar-leaved Oak Rare. Brocket Hall, Herts. 28x107 (2002 OCJ); Hergest Croft 29x58 (1995 VES).

'Muscoviensis' Moscow Oak Very rare. Windsor (Empire Oaks) 22x74 (2000 OCJ), p1937.

Q. phellos **Willow Oak** Rare; likes hot summers. Kew RBG 24x93 (2001 OCJ), from 1901 seed. (Knaphill Nursery, Surrey 20x128 (1985 AFM).)

Q. phillyreoides **Ubame Oak** China, Japan. Very rare; generally a bush. Kew RBG 9x46@0.4m++ (2001 OCJ) – 1861 original; Caerhays 11x43 (1984 AFM).

Q. **'Pondaim'** (*dentata* x *pontica*). Hillier Gardens 6x20 (1986 AFM) – original, since grown well.

Q. pontica **Armenian Oak** Rare; generally a bush. Hidcote, Glos. 10x58@0.15m (1983 AFM); Kew RBG 8x47@0.8m (2001 OCJ), from 1904 seed.

Q. prinus **Chestnut Oak** E N America, 1688. Very rare; would need hotter summers to thrive. Hergest Croft 19x86@0.5m (1995 VES).

Q. pubescens **Downy Oak** S Europe; long grown here but now rare. Ickworth, Suffolk 25x126 (2002 JP) – perhaps a hybrid; Melbury House, Dorset 27x102 (1980 AFM).

Q. **'Pyrami'** Cilicia? Very rare. Albury Park, Surrey 13x39 (2000 OCJ) – as label; Edinburgh RBG 16x38 (1985 AFM).

Q. pyrenaica **Pyrenean Oak** SW Europe, 1822. Rare. Clonmannon, Wicklow 21x134 (1991 AFM) – felled?; Bicton Park, Devon 25x83 (2001 OCJ) – ?; Westonbirt NA ('Pendula') 24x81 (2002 OCJ).

Q. rhysophylla Mexico. Very rare to date. Hillier Gardens 13x30 (2000 H M Brown) – 1978 original.

Q. robur **English Oak** Native. Abundant and abundantly planted. See 'the largest oaks'. Tall examples

are: Belvoir Castle, Leics. (42)x99 (1987 AFM), and Studley Royal (40)x119 (1984 AFM). Historic oaks have included: 'The Newland Oak', Coleford, Glos, 13x434 (1954) – collapsed during a snowstorm in May 1955, and burnt out 1970; 'The Cowthorpe Oak', Cowthorpe, Yorks. 14x436@1m (1829 Strutt); Salcey Forest, Northants. x455 towards base (1825 Strutt); 'The Doodle Oak', Hatfield Forest, Essex x407 (1907 Elwes & Henry); and 'the Queen Elizabeth Oak', Huntingfield Hall Farm, Suffolk x384 (1906 Elwes & Henry) – one third remaining by 1997.

'Atropurpurea' Rare; often stunted. Fenagh House, Carlow 13x37 (1975 AFM).

var. **brutia** S Italy; in a few collections. Kew RBG 12x43 (2001 OCJ), from 1962 seed.

'Concordia' Golden Oak Very rare. Luton Hoo, Beds. 19x92@1.2m (1992 AFM).

'Cristata' Savernake Oak Very rare. Winkworth Arboretum, Surrey 11x31 (2000 OCJ); Savernake Forest Arboretum, Wilts. 12x26 (1994), p1956.

f. *fastigiata* **Cypress Oak** Occasional; variably narrow and neat. Knole Park, Kent 21x131@0.8m under branches (2000 OCJ); St Roche's Arboretum, W Sussex 29x78 (1997 OCJ). The largest shapely tree is at Bagshot Park, Surrey: 27x100@1.2m (2000 OCJ), p1908.

'Fennessii' Very rare. Birr Castle 21.5x87 (1999 TROI). (Smeaton House, E Lothian 23x102 (1966 AFM).)

'Filicifolia' – see *Q.* x *rosacea* 'Filicifolia'.

f. *pendula* **Weeping Oak** Very rare. Whitfield, Herefords. 29.5x152 (1995 VES), p1785.

f. *purpurascens* Rare; includes wild trees which flush red. Seaforde, Down 27.5x87 (1976 AFM).

'Thomasii' S Italy. Kew RBG 20x95 (2001 OCJ), p1904.

f. *variegata* **Variegated Oak** Some very rare clones, none showy. Horton Court, Glos. 25x116 (1989 JW). (Dupplin Castle, Perth 30x146 (1983 AFM) – lost or reverted.)

Q. x *rosacea* **Hybrid English Oak** Frequent when the parents grow together. See 'the largest oaks'.

'Filicifolia' Cut-leaved Oak Rare. Smeaton House, E Lothian 16x70 (1986 AFM).

Q. rotundifolia – see *Q. ilex* var. *ballota*.

Q. rubra **Red Oak** E N America, 1724. Abundant. Grows as well as in the wild; slight preference for warm summers and likes light sands. Oatlands Hotel, Surrey 25x211@1.1m at 'waist' (2000 OCJ) – huge spread; Stockwood CP, Beds. 21x197@1m under large limb (1996 DGA) – dying back; Hall Place, Leigh, Kent 24x192 (1999 OCJ); Cowdray Park, W Sussex 30x145 (1997 OCJ) – leans; Crowsley Park, Oxon. 32x129 (1978 AFM) – superb.

'Aurea' Golden Red Oak Rare. Watson House, Stirling 22x100 (1988 AFM).

'Variegata' Very rare. Abercairney, Perth 28x107 (1986 AFM).

Q. salicina Japan. In one or two collections. (Tortworth Court, Glos. 12x41@? (1993).)

Q. x *sargentii* (*bicolor* x *robur*). In one or two collections. Bedgebury NP 12x47@1.2m under limbs (1999 OCJ), p1937.

Q. x *schochiana* (*palustris* x *phellos*) E N America, 1894. Very rare. Winkworth Arboretum, Surrey 17x51 (2000

> ### RHODODENDRONS
> Rhododendrons have the misfortune to be generally considered bushes, even when they are 20m high. Most are long-lived, growing with slow persistence, and a number of Himalayan species are already aspiring to be trees here – they tend to thrive best in the mild, rain-soaked gardens of the far north and west. The list presented below is a far from complete one of recent measurements.

OCJ).

Q. semecarpifolia Afghanistan to E China, 1900. In a few collections. Tregrehan, Cornwall (20)x83 (2002 Tom Hudson).

Q. serrata (*Q. glandulifera*) NE Asia, Japan, 1877. Very rare. Kew RBG 18x68 (2001 OCJ), from 1893 seed; sickly.

Q. shumardii **Shumard Oak** E USA, 1897. Very rare. Kew RBG 20x70 (2001 OCJ), from 1901 seed. (Tortworth Court, Glos. 26x82 (1976 AFM).)

Q. spathulata W China. Borde Hill 12x(25) (1995 OCJ) – as label.

Q. suber **Cork Oak** Mediterranean, 1699. Occasional; the best growth is in areas with warm summers but mild, humid winters. Standish Hospital, Glos. 21x178@1.2m under branches (1992 AFM); Mount Edgcumbe, Cornwall 20x168 (1991 AFM) – graft on Turkey Oak; Coldrennick, Cornwall 12x165@? (1992); Dillington House, Somerset 18x164@? (1988 JW); Antony House, Cornwall 22x150 (1988 AFM) – shapely; Osborne House, Isle of Wight 15x149 (1992 AFM); Tregrehan, Cornwall 22x104 (2002 Tom Hudson).

Q. texana S USA. In one or two collections. Glasnevin NBG (*Q. shumardii?*) x33 (1992).

Q. trojana **Macedonian Oak** E Mediterranean, c1890. Rare. Kew RBG 19x73 (2001 OCJ), from 1904 seed; Hergest Croft 20x51 (1995 VES). (Tortworth Court, Glos. 24x74 (1975 AFM).)

Q. x *turneri* **Turner's Oak** (*ilex* x *robur*) Occasional. Kew RBG 16x185@0.3-0.6m under many limbs (2001 OCJ); Golden Grove, Carmarthen 27x173 (1994); Gourdie, Perth 27x115 (1991 AFM). These are assumed to be 'Pseudoturneri'; the original clone, 'Spencer Turner', is almost extinct: Sawbridgeworth, Herts. 17x122@1m under scars (2002 OCJ).

Q. variabilis **Chinese Cork Oak** (NE Asia, Japan, 1861) Very rare. Hollycombe, W Sussex 19x55 (1997 OCJ); Windsor (Valley Gardens; hybrid?) 22x37 (2000 OCJ) – spire-shaped.

Q. velutina **Black Oak** E USA, 1800. Rather rare. Grayswood Hill, Surrey 18x97 (1998 OCJ) – very broad; Albury Park, Surrey 25x87 (2000 OCJ). (Knaphill Nursery, Surrey 25x122 (1987 AFM).)

Q. x *viveri* (*canariensis* x *petraea*). Probably a few accidental plantings. Hillier Gardens 18x65 (2001 Harry James).

Q. 'Warburgii' **Cambridge Oak** (*robur* x *rugosa?*) Very rare. Petworth Park, W Sussex 20x85 (1997 OCJ); Cambridge UBG 17.5x84 (2002 DGA).

Q. wislizenii SW N America, 1874. Very rare. High Beeches, W Sussex 13x48 (1994 VES); Hillier Gardens 17m (2001 Harry James).

Reevesia pubescens E Himalayas, W China, 1910. Extinct here? (Trewithen, Cornwall 12x46+36 (1971 AFM).)

Rehderodendron macrocarpum **Rehder Tree** W China, 1934. In a few mild gardens. Trewithen, Cornwall 12x38 (1987 AFM) – original.

Rhamnus cathartica **Buckthorn** Native to England, Wales and Ireland; frequent on limestone in scrub and woodland; very seldom to tree size. Wicken Fen, Cambs. 9x51@? (1989 JW); Horton Court, Glos. 14.5x30@? (1989 JW).

R. purshiana **Cascara Sagrada** W N America, 1870. Very rare. Speech House, Glos. 12.5x46@? (1988 JW), p1934.

Rhododendron arboreum **Gurass** India, Sri Lanka, c1810. Frequent in big, mild gardens. Stonefield House, Argyll 8x67 (1991 AFM); Castle Kennedy, Dumfries & Galloway 16x50 (1993 VES).

'Album'. Kilmory Castle, Argyll 9x47+36+30 (1998).

R. auriculatum W China, 1900. Rare. Wisley 8x27 (2000 OCJ).

R. campanulatum Himalayas, by 1825. (To 9x45@? at Benmore, Argyll.)

R. decorum W China, 1904. Occasional. Logan House, Dumfries & Galloway 12x37+28 (1993 VES).

ssp. *diaprepes* 1913. Clyne Gardens, Glamorgan 10x28+22 (2000 OCJ).

R. falconeri **Korlinga** Himalayas, 1850. Occasional in mild gardens. Stonefield House, Argyll 9x47 (1991 AFM); Muncaster Castle, Cumbria 11x32+21 (2000 DH).

R. fortunei ssp. *discolor* W China, 1900. Occasional in mild gardens. Logan House, Dumfries & Galloway 14x45 (1993 VES).

R. x *geraldii* (*R. sutchuenense* var. *geraldii*) W China, 1900? Wakehurst Place 7x28 (2002 OCJ).

R. grande E Himalayas, 1849. Logan House, Dumfries & Galloway 11x30 (1993 VES).

R. 'Polar Bear' (*auriculatum* x *decorum* ssp. *diaprepes*) 1926. Occasional. Windsor (Savill Garden) 10x48@0.3m (2000 OCJ).

R. ponticum Caucasus, 1763. Abundantly naturalised; almost always a sprawling bush. Windsor (Rhododendron Ride) 6x58@0.7m where the single bole branches out (2000 OCJ).

R. vernicosum W China, 1904. Ardanaiseig, Argyll 8x25+25++ (1994 VES).

R. zeylanicum Sri Lanka. by 1840. Arduaine, Argyll 8x26 + ten stems (1991 VES) – seed 1898.

Rhus chinensis E Asia, 1737. Small trees in a few collections.

R. potaninii Chinese Varnish Tree W China, 1902. Rare. Stanage Park, Powys 19x110@1m (1994 JW).

R. punjabensis W Himalayas. In a few collections. Chelsea Physic Garden, London (?) 8x36 (2001 OCJ).

R. sylvestris NE Asia, Japan, 1881. In some collections. Westonbirt NA 14x39 (2002 OCJ).

R. trichocarpa NE Asia, Japan, 1894. In a few collections. (Hidcote, Glos. 15x33 (1983 AFM).)

R. typhina Stag's-horn Sumach E N America, 1629. Abundant, but seldom to tree-size. Shefford, Beds. 6x30 (1995 Bob Morwood).

R. verniciflua Varnish Tree Himalayas to Japan, by 1862. Rather rare. Witham Hall School, Lincs. 13x82@1m under fork (1983 AFM) – since cut back; Cambridge UBG (19)x72 (2002 DGA).

Robinia x ambigua Pink Robinia (*pseudoacacia* x *viscosa*) Rather rare. Kew RBG 17x95 (2001 OCJ), p1869; Borde Hill 21x79 (1995 OCJ). Both are the vigorous clone 'Decaisneana'.

R. hartwegii SE USA, 1904. A bush in the wild; to 'tree' size in a few big gardens. Borde Hill 16x41@0.1m (1995 OCJ).

R. x holdtii (*luxurians* x *pseudoacacia*) In a few big gardens. Glasnevin NBG ('Britzensis') 18x51 (1992).

R. kelseyi SE USA, 1901. Very rare; a bush in the wild. Holker Hall, Cumbria 12.5x32 (2002 DH).

R. luxurians SE N America, 1887. Kew RBG 16x60 (2001 OCJ), from 1918 seed.

R. pseudoacacia False Acacia E USA; long grown here. Abundant in areas with hot summers; naturalising by suckers. Long lived, but easily broken by storms. Oaklands House, E Sussex 17x174@0.9m on the short burred bole (1993 OCJ); p1850 or later, and much died back; Sudborough Old Rectory, Northants. 17x172 (1987 AFM) – single bole with low branches; Kew RBG 27x112 (2001 OCJ) – slender.

'Aurea' Now very rare. Moreton-in-Marsh, Glos. 15x97 (2003 OCJ).

'Bessoniana'. An occasional street tree. Acton Park, London 13x92 (2001 OCJ); Glasnevin NBG 18x61 (1987 AFM).

'Frisia' Golden Robinia 1935. Abundant, but seems short-lived. Templemere, Surrey 15x48 (2000 OCJ), p1984?; Emmanuel College, Cambs. 18x35 (1990 AFM); Lincoln's Inn, London 18x35 (2001 OCJ).

'Monophylla Fastigiata'. Kew RBG 13x77 (died back), and 14x27 (2001 OCJ).

'Pyramidalis' Fastigiate Robinia Rare. Kew RBG 15x71@0.3m (2001 OCJ); Reigate Town Hall, Surrey 14x65@1m (2000 OCJ), p1901; much cut back; Maryon Park, London 20x36 (2001 OCJ) – leans.

'Rehderi' Very rare. Kew RBG 10x64@0.8m around fused stems? (2001 OCJ).

'Rozynskyana' Rare. Nymans, W Sussex 21x64+ (1996 OCJ); Community of the Resurrection, Mirfield, Yorks. 24x46 (1995).

'Semperflorens' Very rare? Nymans, W Sussex 21x40+31 (1996 OCJ).

'Tortuosa' Rare. Kew RBG 10x92 (2001 OCJ); Edinburgh RBG 19x57 (1985 AFM), p1903.

'Umbraculifera' Mop-head Acacia Quite frequent. Teddington Cemetery, London 9x74 (2001 OCJ); Sandford Park, Glos. 11x62 (1989 JW).

'Unifoliola' Single-leaved Robinia Rare. St Cuthman's School, W Sussex 22x70 (1997 OCJ).

R. x slavinii (*kelseyi* x *pseudoacacia*) Occasional as a younger tree (generally as 'Hillieri'); small-growing. Borde Hill 18x44 (1995 OCJ) – ? (catalogued as the American bush *R. kelseyi*).

R. viscosa Clammy Locust SE USA, 1791. In a few big gardens. Hever Castle, Kent 11x46 (1995 OCJ).

Salix Willows

Salix aegyptiaca Musk Willow SW Asia, 1820. Very rare. Clarence Park, Somerset 7x46 (1995 Geoff Rouse) – weeping; Boughton House, Northants. 14x29 (1987 AFM), p1970.

S. alba White Willow Native to wet, lowland sites; can grow very large if its life is prolonged by pollarding. Amberley Wild Brooks, W Sussex 10x238@1.2-1.8m (1997 OCJ) – veteran pollard; Moreton-on-Lugg, Herefords. 23x235@? (1989 JW); Holywell-cum-Needingworth, Cambs. 15x210@? (1994 JW); Tempsford, Beds. 27x197 (1994 DGA); Mount Juilliet, Kilkenny 22.5x190@0.7m (2000 TROI). (Woodbrook College, West Midlands 33x70 (1975 AFM).)

'Aurea'. Very rare; weak-growing.

'Britzensis' Coral-bark Willow ('Chermesina') Very frequent. Croydon Cemetery, London 22x134@1.1m on short straight bole (2001 OCJ); Birr Castle 29x110 (2000 TROI); Pinkney Park, Wilts. (the female form, 'Cardinalis'?) 29x99+99 (2002 OCJ) – two trees very close together?

var. caerulea Cricket-bat Willow Very frequent; plantations on rich wet soils, mainly in Essex. It quickly makes an impressive tree, but is short-lived. Batford Springs Nature Reserve, Herts. 14x141 (2002 OCJ) – good, decaying bole, cut at 7m; Hutton-in-the-Forest, Cumbria 33x77 (1996 DH). (Robertsbridge, E Sussex x(200) when felled in 1902.)

var. sericea Silver Willow Rather occasional; usually small-growing. Brocket Hall, Herts. 15x134 around scar (2002 OCJ); Belton House, Lincs. 25x104 (1978 AFM).

'Tristis' Weeping White Willow Very rare; has been confused with the common Golden Weeping Willow. Windsor (Savill Garden) 18x83 (2000 OCJ), p1933; as label.

var. vitellina Golden Willow Now rare. Cambridge UBG 17x85 (2002 DGA).

S. babylonica Chinese Weeping Willow c1730. The true species is very rare and has hardly even grown well here. A vigorous young tree (from Rushforth 305) at Wakehurst Place was 9x32 in 2001 (OCJ).

'Crispa' Rare and usually bushy. (Kew RBG 12x44 (1987 AFM), blown 1987).

var. pekinensis 'Tortuosa' Corkscrew Willow (*S. matsudana* 'Tortuosa') Abundant but very short-lived; needs hot summers. Oxford BG, Oxon. 17x91@0.8m (1996 VES), p1950.

Coyote Willow (*Salix exigua*), growing here at Castle Howard, Yorkshire, is a tree whose ornamental qualities have yet to be widely appreciated.

S. x calodendron (*caprea* x *dasyclados*?). Kew RBG 14x32 among branches (2001 OCJ), sourced 1973.

S. caprea Goat Willow Native; abundant everywhere except on the lightest soils. Sometimes a bush. Highland trees (including the largest measured examples) are likely to be var. *sphacelata*. Rie Crathie, Aberdeen x114@1.1m on buttressed trunk (2000); Ardross Castle, Highland (21)x66 (1989 AFM); Reelig Glen Wood, Highland (21)x49 (1987 AFM). And see *S.* x *reichardtii*.

'Kilmarnock' and 'Pendula' are abundant, but scarcely live to reach 'tree' size.

S. cinerea ssp. oleifolia Grey Sallow Native. Abundant everywhere except on dry soils. Generally a bush. Cloghfune, Kerry 10x92 (2000 TROI) – recorded under the type; Horse Pasture Wood, Pembury, Kent 15x18 (1999 OCJ) – drawn up among Sitka Spruce.

S. daphnoides Violet Willow Europe to the Himalayas, 1829. Rare. Gladstone Park, London 4x98 (2001 OCJ) – decayed bole, cut at 1.5m; Danson Park, London 15x65 (2001 OCJ).

'Aglaia' Rare. Hillier Gardens 14x38 (2001 Harry James).

S. x dasyclados (*caprea* x *cinerea* x *viminalis*?) Rare in the wild. Westonbirt NA 8x28@0.8m (2002 OCJ).

S. x ehrhartiana (*alba* x *pentrandra*) A wild hybrid; rare? A veteran pollard at Bushy Park, London, believed to be this cross, was 6x188@1.2m in 2001 (OCJ).

S. exigua Coyote Willow W N America, 1921. Westonbirt NA 9x31@1m (2002 OCJ).

S. fragilis Crack Willow Native; abundant in wet sites in warmer areas. The largest trees are likely to be hybrids (ie. 'Decipiens', 'Russelliana' or *S.* x *rubens*; qv. for the clone 'Britzensis'). Terling Place, Essex 12x203 (1977 AFM) – veteran pollard; Shoreham, Kent 8x151@1m (1999 OCJ) – ancient pollard, much decayed; Much Hadham Old Rectory, Herts. 29.5x131 (2001 DGA).

S. kinuyanagi Japanese Osier. Wisley 4x35@0.5m under fork (2000 OCJ).

S. lucida Shining Willow NE N America, 1830. In one

or two collections. (Wisley 15x100@1.2m (1985 AFM).)

S. matsudana – see *S. babylonica* var. *pekinensis*.

S. x meyeriana (*fragilis* x *pentandra*) A wild hybrid; rare? Hunton, Kent 20x70 (1995 OCJ).

S. x mollissima (*triandra* x *viminalis*) Rarely naturalised or wild. Not yet recorded to 'tree' size.

S. myrsinifolia (*S. nigricans*) Native to high ground in N England, Scotland and Ireland (usually in the north). Mount Leader, Cork 9.5x74@0.6m (2000 TROI).

S. x pendulina **'Blanda' Wisconsin Weeping Willow** (*babylonica* x *fragilis*?) Rare. Regent's Park, London (?) 10x73 (2001 OCJ) – hollow.

'Elegantissima' Thurlow Weeping Willow Rather rare. Richmond Cemetery, London 13x110 (2001 OCJ); Pitville Park, Glos. 25.5x108@? (1995 JW).

S. pentandra **Bay Willow** Native to N Britain and Ireland; rather rarely planted elsewhere. Generally small-growing. Wicken Fen, Cambs. 20x84@? (1989 JW); Tatton Park, Cheshire 22x40 (1983).

S. purpurea **Purple Osier** Occasional in the wild, but not yet recorded to 'tree' size. The weak-growing 'Pendula' is a popular garden plant.

S. x reichardtii **Hybrid Sallow** (*caprea* x *cinerea*) Probably abundant in the wild. Ardross Castle, Highland 16.5x108@? (1995).

S. x rubens **'Basfordiana' Basford Willow** Rather rare (some trees may be the female clone 'Sanguinea'). Roath Park, Glamorgan 23x112@? (1991 JW).

S. x rubra (*purpurea* x *viminalis*) Rare in the wild; not yet recorded to 'tree' size.

S. scouleriana **Scouler Willow** NW N America. Westonbirt NA 10x30@0.8m on short bole (2002 OCJ).

S. x sepulcralis **'Chrysocoma' Golden Weeping Willow** (*alba* var. *vitellina* x *babylonica*?) 1888. Abundant in areas with warm summers. West Kingsclere Farm, Hants. 18x172 (1987 AFM); Fassnidge Park, London 23x110 (2002 OCJ).

'Salamonii' Salamon's Weeping Willow (*alba* x *babylonica*?) 1869. Locally occasional as an older tree in areas with hot summers. Ewell Court Park, Surrey ('Chrysocoma'?) 15x141 (2000 OCJ); Regent's Park, London 20x136@0.6m (2001 OCJ) – cut back; St Mark's church, Wandsworth, London 21x121 (2001 OCJ).

S. x sericans (*S. x smithiana*; *caprea* x *viminalis*) A wild hybrid; planted for basketry and in some gardens. Young planted trees are surprisingly vigorous: Surrey University Campus, Surrey 9x61 (2002 OCJ), p1973; Dundee UBG, Angus 13x27 (1998), p1972.

S. triandra **Almond Willow** Native to wet places in the south. Usually a bush, but some big examples have been recorded: St Neots, Cambs. 18x108@? and 23x87@? (1990 JW).

S. viminalis **Osier** Native to wet places; nearly always a bush. To 11m. Banks Farm, E Sussex 7x32@1m on rugged bole (1995 OCJ).

Sambucus nigra **Elder** Native; abundant except on light soils. Generally a bush. Ruskin Park, London 7x(70) (1995 PJB) – veteran tree, its hollow, gnarled bole (inside a wire mesh guard) perhaps a series of long-fused stems; Cahemahallia, Tipperary 8x56@0.8m under fork (2000 TROI); Court Lodge Farm, Aldington, Kent 6x56@1m under fork (1999 OCJ); White Moss Common, Cumbria 11x24+20 (1996 DH). Its garden forms ('Aurea', f. *laciniata*, etc.) have not yet been recorded to 'tree' size.

Sassafras albidum **Sassafras** E USA, 1633. Now very rare; seldom grows well here. Cannizaro Park, London 18x50 (2001 OCJ).

Saxegothaea conspicua **Prince Albert's Yew** S Andes, 1847. 20-30 trees; best in high humidity. Castlewellan NA 13.5x58@1m (1982 AFM); Woodhouse, Devon 18x55 (1985 AFM).

Schima wallichii **ssp. *noronhae* var. *superba*** (*S. argentea*) S China, 1898. In a few mild gardens; no large examples remain. (Trewithen, Cornwall 11x26+ (1971 AFM).)

ssp. *wallichii* var. *khasiana* Himalayas to S China, 1924. In a few mild gardens. Trewithen, Cornwall 16x47 (1971 AFM); Castlewellan NA 16x36 (1994 VES).

Sciadopitys verticillata **Umbrella Pine** Japan, 1853. Rather rare; best in high humidity. Avondale, Wicklow 12x62 (1991 AFM), p1906; Headfort, Meath (13)x60 (1990), p1916; Benenden School, Kent 20x54 (1995 OCJ) – leans.

Sequoia sempervirens **Coast Redwood** California, 1843. Quite frequent; luxuriates in warm summers but proving longer-lived in the cooler but wetter west and north. The tallest are confined to deep shelter. Woodstock, Kilkenny 41x255 (1999 Michael Lear); Taymouth Castle, Perth 38x240 (1990 AFM); Bodnant, Conwy (47)x159 (1984 AFM), p1887.

'Adpressa' Rather rare; generally small-growing. Highnam Court, Glos. 25x116 and 28x102 (1984 AFM).

'Cantab' Rare to date; sometimes prostrate. Hillier Gardens 17x70 (2001 Harry James).

WILLOWS

The Bat Willow is one of our fastest-growing wild trees, and huge knobbly old White Willow pollards include some of our largest. Several other species and hybrids are among our rarest and least-understood – willows hybridise with wild abandon and most recorders fight shy of them. Few make upstanding specimens – they are always inclined to split, collapse and sprawl on the ground, throwing up new sprouts and making a list of the biggest examples an unreliable one.

Whenever the soil is not too heavy and the climate not too dry, the crowns of Giant Sequoias
(*Sequoiadendron giganteum*) tower above roofs and the heads of other trees, like bar-charts of Victorian
prosperity. In its native Californian Sierras this is the biggest tree in the world, and it caused a sensation when
its seed was brought here in 1853 and it quickly showed willing to grow away with the same reckless vigour.
Few conditions defeat it – it dislikes raw chalk, and urban pollution, and is very sensitive to salt spray, while
height-growth usually ceases when the tree collects its first lightning-strike: tall, spire-shaped examples are
almost confined to the glens of Scotland and the Irish mountains. But it seems likely to prove long-lived here,
so that the Victorians' legacy to us will grow only the more pronounced.
1876 planting at Tilgate Park, W Sussex.

Sequoiadendron giganteum **Giant Sequoia**
California, 1853. Frequent. Cluny Castle Garden, Perth
39x352 (1998) – very flared bole; Fasque House, Aberdeen
28x350 (1990 AFM) – rough layered tree; Llangattock,
Powys ('The Courting Tree') 39.5x336 (1999 DGA);
Princeland, Perth 32x329 (1985 AFM); near Welshpool,
Powys 42x312 (1989 AFM); Balmacaan, Highland 52x231
(1993); Castle Leod, Highland 51x283 (2002 DGA) –
original; Achnacarry, Highland 51x(240) (2002 DGA) –
fine spire.
'Aureum' Golden Giant Sequoia Very rare. Cerne
Abbey, Dorset 26x109 (1996).
'Glaucum' Very rare. Hillier Gardens 21.5x52 (2002 Ron
Holley).
'Pendulum' Weeping Giant Sequoia Rare. Bodnant,
Conwy 29x83 (1989 AFM), p1890; Inveraray Castle, Argyll
30.5x77 (1982 AFM).

Sophora affinis Texas, Arkansas, 1890. In one or two
collections. Kew RBG 11x36 (2001 OCJ).
S. japonica **Pagoda Tree** China, 1753. Occasional in
warm areas, where it occasionally makes an impressive
specimen: Abbey Gate House, Herts. 26.5x159 (1999
DGA).
'Pendula' Weeping Pagoda Tree Very rare. Knaphill
Nursery, Surrey 8x83@0.5m under fork (2000 OCJ).
var. *pubescens*. Kew RBG 11x35 (2001 OCJ) – leans.
'Variegata' Variegated Pagoda Tree Very rare.
Haberdashers' Aske's School, Herts. 10x51 (2002 OCJ);
Kew RBG 14x50 (2001 OCJ), p1877.
S. microphylla New Zealand, 1772. In a few milder
gardens. Mount Usher, Wicklow 9x38@0.5m? (1992
AFM).
S. pachycarpa Iran to W China. Kew RBG 18x78 (2001
OCJ).
S. tetraptera **Kowhai** North Island, New Zealand, 1772.
Rare; best in mild humid areas. Ballywalter Park, Down
12.5x82@0.5m (1985 AFM).

X *Sorbaronia alpina* (*Aronia arbutifolia* x *Sorbus aria*, by
1809) Very rare; generally a bush. Hillier Gardens 10m
(2001 Harry James). (Kew RBG 9x34 (1971 AFM).)

X *Sorbopyrus auricularis* **Bollwyller Pear** (*Pyrus
communis* x *Sorbus aria*, by 1619) Very rare, in various clones.
Edinburgh RBG 11x53 (1997); Bedgebury NP
12x48@0.4m under branches (1999 OCJ); Oxford BG,
Oxon. 12x43 (1996 VES).

Sorbus Whitebeams, Rowans

Sorbus alnifolia **Alder-leaved Whitebeam** Japan,
1892. A rare but pretty tree. Dawyck, Scottish Borders
16x52 (1997).
S. alnifolia **x** *aria*. Kew RBG 11x46@0.5m (2001 OCJ).
S. americana **American Rowan** E N America, 1782.
Rare. Kensington Gardens, London 11x38 (2002 OCJ).
S. anglica SW England, Wales and Kerry; a scarce bush
in the wild; growing larger in collections.
S. aria **Whitebeam** Native; Locally abundant in the wild
on limestone and light sands in S England and Ireland;

abundantly planted everywhere. Very tough, but seeming
short-lived: no veterans are known. St Clere Pinetum, Kent
12x163@0.1m/x65+59+43 (1997 Philip Webb) – stool or
'bundle planting'; Sevenoaks, Kent 17x76@1.1m on short
clean bole (2002 DGA) – under fungal attack; Earlham
Cemetery, Norfolk 18x73 (1990 AFM) – bole 2m; Chesham
Bois, Bucks. 23x55@1m under fork (2001 DGA).
(Nunnington Hall, Yorks. 10x129@1m (1955 Maynard
Greville).)
'Chrysophylla' Golden Whitebeam Rare. Hillier
Gardens 14x30 (2002 Harry James).
'Lutescens' Abundantly planted. Windsor (Great Park)
14x60 (2000 OCJ); Hergest Croft 16x38 (1995 VES),
p1954.
'Majestica' Frequent. Woburn Park, Beds. 18x91@1m
(1993 DGA) – shattered by 2002; Lythe Hill Park, Surrey
21x65 (2000 OCJ).
'Pendula' Weeping Whitebeam Very rare. Ramsey
Abbey, Cambs. 8x86@0.4m under forks (1993); two
remaining branches propped.
S. arranensis N Arran, Ayrshire. Typically a bush; young
trees in a few collections.
S. aucuparia **Rowan** Native; abundant on light sands
particularly in the north (though one of the biggest, and
the tallest, are on chalk); very tough. Planted everywhere
but short-lived except in harsh conditions. Bolderwood
Holms, Hants. 9x156@0.6m (2002 Chris Read) – broad
windswept tree hollow at the base; four trunks from 1m;
Brook Vessons, Shropshire 13.5x101@0.7m+ (2001
Andrew Morton) – single decayed bole spreads into many
branches from 1.5m; Mount Leader, Cork 8.8x99@1.1m
on short bole (2000 TROI); Gatton Hall, Surrey 14x76
(2000 OCJ) – clean bole; Bellingdon Wood, Bucks. 28x56
(1995) – drawn up in Beech plantation; long bole.
'Asplenifolia' Cut-leaved Rowan Rather rare. Mayow
Park, London 10x41 (2001 OCJ); Borde Hill 16x31 (1995
OCJ) – leans.
'Beissneri' Frequently planted. Marsworth House,
London (?) 10x38 (2001 OCJ); Scotney Castle, Kent 15x28
(1999 OCJ).
'Dirkenii' Golden Rowan Rare. Arniston House,
Midlothian 14x36+29 (1987 AFM).
'Edulis' and 'Rossica Major', with edible fruit, are rare
and under-recorded.
'Fructu Luteo' Yellow-berried Rowan Occasional;
under-recorded. East Durham and Houghall College,
Durham 7x30 (1987 AFM), p1960.
'Sheerwater Seedling' Frequent: the best of several
fastigiate clones. Hillier Gardens 15x30 (2002 Harry
James); Windsor (Valley Gardens) 15x25 (2000 OCJ).
S. bristoliensis **Bristol Service** Avon Gorge, Bristol;
young trees in some collections have out-grown the wild
plants: Westonbirt NA 13x44@0.9m and 12x42 (2002
OCJ), p1945.
S. caloneura C China, 1904. In a few collections.
Winkworth Arboretum, Surrey 8x42@0.6m (2000 OCJ)
– dying back.
S. commixta **Japanese Rowan** (including trees grown
as *S. discolor*, *S. matsumurana*, *S. randaiensis* and *S. reflexipetala*).
c1880. Abundantly planted. Westonbirt NA ('Serotina')

13x59@0.4m under graft (2002 OCJ); Oare House, Wilts. ('Marchant's Form') 17.5x50@0.5m (1994 VES), p1935; Huntswood, Surrey 10x46 (2000 OCJ).

'Embley' is about as common as the type. Thorp Perrow, Yorks. 13x41 (1981 AFM); Stratford Park, Glos. 17x31 (1984 AFM) – crowded.

var. *rufoferruginea* Rare. Kew RBG 11x45 under graft (2001 OCJ), from 1933 seed; Hergest Croft 14x38 (1995 VES), p1968.

***S. croceocarpa* Orange-berried Service** (*S.* 'Theophrasta') Rare; naturalised on Anglesey. Aldenham Park, Herts. 23x53 (2002 OCJ) – slender.

S. cuspidata – see *S. vestita*.

S. decipiens (continental form of *aria* x *torminalis*; or a microspecies). Grows well in a few town parks. Hastings Cemetery, E Sussex 18x71 (1993 OCJ) – bole 4m.

S. decora E N America. In a few big gardens. Westonbirt NA 16x40@1.2m (2002 OCJ) – as label.

***S. devoniensis* French Hales** A small tree, local in SW England and SE Ireland; planted in a few collections.

S. discolor – see *S. commixta*.

***S. domestica* True Service** Native to cliff-tops near Cardiff as an ancient bush; rather rare as a planted tree to date. Wotton House, Surrey (pyriform) 15x88 (2000 OCJ); Borde Hill (pyriform) 17x86 (1995 OCJ); Dryads Hall, Essex 22x62 (1979 AFM); Powis Castle, Powys (pyriform) 21.5x60 (2002).

S. eminens The Wye Valley and the Avon Gorge; stunted in the wild. Young trees are in a few collections.

S. esserteauana – see *S.* x *kewensis*.

***S. folgneri* Folgner's Whitebeam** C China, 1901. Very rare. Caerhays 18x38 (1984 AFM).

S. 'Ghose' (*aucuparia* x KW7746?, by 1960) In some big gardens. Hillier Gardens 9x41@0.6m (2001 Harry James).

***S. glabrescens* White Hubei Rowan** C China, 1910 (*S. hupehensis* in part; see also *S. oligodonta*, from which most measured trees were not differentiated). Rather rare. Borde Hill 13x52@1.1m (1995 OCJ); Dyffryn Gardens, Glamorgan 16x32 (1997 OCJ) – drawn up.

S. 'Golden Wonder' (*pohuashanensis* x *reticulata* ssp. *pekinensis*?) Very rare. Westonbirt NA 13x27@1m (2002 OCJ).

***S. graeca* Grecian Whitebeam** E Europe, 1830. Small plants in one or two collections. (Albury Park, Surrey 11x27 (1986 AFM).)

S. hedlundii E Himalayas. Very rare. Winkworth Arboretum, Surrey 10x37@1.2m (2000 OCJ); Windsor (Valley Gardens) 14x35 (2000 OCJ).

S. hibernica Central Ireland; a bush in the wild. Young trees are in a few collections: Speech House, Glos. 7x25@? (1987 JW), p1963.

S. hupehensis – see *S. glabrescens*, *S. oligodonta*.

S. hybrida (*aucuparia* x *rupicola*) Scandinavia. Occasional (usually as the clone 'Gibbsii'). Birr Castle 15x69 (2000 TROI).

***S. intermedia* Swedish Whitebeam** NW Europe. Abundantly planted but short-lived; rarely naturalising; prefers a continental climate. Glenorchy, E Lothian 16x90 (1999); Malt House, W Sussex 20x74@1.2m (1997 OCJ).

***S. japonica* Japanese Whitebeam** Japan, Korea. In a few collections. Wakehurst Place 7x28 (1997 OCJ); Edinburgh RBG (var. *calocarpa*) 11x22 (1997).

***S. 'Joseph Rock'* Joseph Rock's Rowan** W China? Occasional. Windsor (Valley Gardens) 12x52@1m on short bole (2000 OCJ), with mistletoe; Hydon Nurseries, Surrey 11x40 (2000 OCJ); Stagshaw Garden, Cumbria 13x25 (1995 DH).

S. keissleri W China, 1907. Westonbirt NA 15x84@0.3m under forks (2002 OCJ) – very spreading.

***S.* x *kewensis*.** Rare; most larger trees grown as *S. pohuashanensis* (qv.) and *S. esserteauana* are likely to belong in this group of hybrids with *S. aucuparia*; the largest, at Carberry Tower, E Lothian 15x67 (1985 AFM), was recorded as *S. pohuashanensis*.

S. lancastriensis S Cumbria. Stunted in the wild; young trees in one or two collections.

***S. latifolia* Service Tree of Fontainebleau** Ile de France. Occasional. Wells House, Wexford 15x99 (2000 TROI); Aldenham Park, Herts. 21x53 (2002 OCJ).

S. 'Leonard Messel' (*aucuparia* x *harrowiana*) In a few big gardens. Hillier Gardens 11.5x30 (2000 H M Brown).

***S. leyana* Ley's Whitebeam** Taff Valley, Wales: one of the world's rarest trees. Typically a bush, but a shapely small tree at the Garwnant Visitor Centre, Glamorgan.

S. matsumurana – see *S. commixta*.

S. minima Confined to near Crickhowell, Powys. Typically a bush; young trees in a few collections.

***S. mougeotii* Mougeout's Whitebeam** Alps, Pyrenees, 1880. In some big gardens. Norney Grange, Surrey 14x47@1m under scar, and 13x40+39 (2002 OCJ).

***S. oligodonta* 'Rosea' Pink Hubei Rowan** C China (*S. hupehensis* in part; and see *S. glabrescens*, from which most measured trees were not differentiated). Occasional; small-growing. Windsor (Valley Gardens) 9x36 (2000 OCJ); Borde Hill 12x31 (1995 OCJ).

S. pallescens W China, 1908. Very rare. Westonbirt NA 12x68@1.2m (2002 OCJ), p1945; Borde Hill 16x51 (1995 OCJ). Both are fine trees from Forrest 29044.

The Wild Service (*Sorbus torminalis*) is one of our most colourful native trees. It is restricted to heavy clays in southern and midland England and Wales, and is nowhere abundant: the seeds need plenty of summer heat to be fertile, so it tends to reproduce only by suckers in old hedges and ancient woods. The berries, which are tasty when over-ripe (a cross between pears and dates), used to be brewed into an alcoholic drink, and one of the plant's other names – the Checkers Tree – may have been the origin of the popular pub name, 'The Chequers'. Trees stand out in late spring, when laden with plates of creamy blossom, and again in autumn when their uniquely-shaped leaves may turn blood-red. It can grow big, but the champion at Hall Place, Kent, is exceptional for its great, pillar-like bole.

S. pohuashanensis N China, 1883. Rare (and when large always likely to be *S.* x *kewensis*, qv.). Edinburgh RBG 7x45@1m (1985 AFM), p1924; Borde Hill 16x36@1m (1995 OCJ).

S. porrigentiformis N Devon, the Mendips and S Wales. Stunted in the wild; young trees are in one or two collections.

S. pseudofennica Arran Service N Arran. Stunted in the wild; young trees are in a few collections.

S. reflexipetala – see *S. commixta*.

S. reticulata ssp. pekinensis (*S.* x *pekinensis*) N China. In a few big gardens. Wallington, Northumberland 7x27 (1992 AFM).

S. rupicola Cliff Whitebeam Native to limestone uplands, where always stunted; young trees are in a few collections. (Westonbirt NA 15x30 (2002 OCJ) – shapely slender tree, blown that autumn.)

S. sargentiana Sargent's Rowan W China, 1908. Rather rare; often a bush. Trewithen, Cornwall 9x51 above graft (1985 AFM).

S. 'Savill Orange'. Windsor (Valley Gardens) 8x36 (2000 OCJ) – larger of two.

S. scalaris Ladder-leaf Rowan W China, 1904. Rare; often bushy. Borde Hill 10x54@0.4m and 12x36@0.9m (1995 OCJ).

S. subcuneata Exmoor Service Native to Exmoor, where always stunted; young trees are in a few collections: Birr Castle 14x28 (1990 AFM).

S. thibetica E Himalayas, 1953. In a few big gardens. Wakehurst Place 10x32 (from Kingdon Ward 20834) and 13x29 (1997 OCJ).

'John Mitchell' 1938. Now occasional. Alexandra Park, E Sussex 17x64 (2001 OCJ). A fine 'double' to the original (lost) at Westonbirt NA.

S. x thuringiaca Bastard Service (*aria* x *aucuparia*). Very rarely found in the wild, but frequently planted (as 'Fastigiata'). Seton Collegiate Church, E Lothian 18.5x91 (1998 Donald Rodger).

S. torminalis Wild Service Native to heavy clays in S England (but tending to grow biggest on lighter sands); scattered in the wild but now more widely planted. Parsonage Farm, Udimore, E Sussex 15x146@0.6m under fork (2002 OCJ) – about 180 years old, and half collapsed in 2000; Hall Place, Kent 20x125 (1999 OCJ) – columnar bole; Markshall estate, Essex x124 (1995) – bole 7.5m in 1984; Kites Nest Wood, Glos. 23x63 (1995 Professor Lambert).

S. umbellata Balkans to the Caucasus. In one or two collections. Winkworth Arboretum, Surrey (?) 8x26 (2000 OCJ).

S. x vagensis (*aria* x *torminalis*) A very rare wild hybrid; in a few collections. Edinburgh RBG 17x74 (1991 AFM).

S. vexans N Devon. Always stunted in the wild; young trees are in a few collections.

S. vestita Himalayan Whitebeam (*S. cuspidata*) 1820. Rare. Borde Hill 17x90 (1995 OCJ), p1907; Clarence Park, Herts. 17x74@1.3m (2002 OCJ). Both have broad leaves and may be hybrids with *S. aria*.

S. vilmorinii Vilmorin's Rowan W China, 1889. Rather rare; usually a bush in lowland areas. Crarae, Argyll 11x47@? (1994 VES); Leckmelm, Highland 14x24 (1991

Stuartia sinensis is too rare for anyone to have given it a familiar English name, but it is a tree whose only sin is that is choosy about where it grows. It holds dainty tiers of fresh-green leaves, which turn crimson and gold in autumn. In high summer, it is studded with white, camellia-like flowers. And its greatest glory is its bark – stone-cold, skin-pink and as smooth as porcelain. Through the year it darkens, before peeling in tissue-thin layers to reveal a bone-white under-surface. The few good trees are in sheltered woodland gardens, with light acid soils and warm summers, as here at Tilgate Park, West Sussex.

AFM).

S. 'Wilfrid Fox' (*aria* x *vestita*) Rare. Windsor (Valley Gardens) 11x68@0.3m under branching (2000 OCJ); Innes House, Moray 13x41 (1991 AFM).

S. wilmottiana Avon Gorge, Bristol. Stunted in the wild; young trees are in a few collections.

Staphylea holocarpa Chinese Bladder-nut 1908. In a few big gardens; usually a bush. Briggens, Herts. 9x27+++ (2002 OCJ).

Stuartia monadelpha Japan, Korea, 1903. Very rare. High Beeches Garden 11x24 (1994 VES) – lovely tree.

S. pseudocamellia Deciduous Camellia Japan, by 1878. Rare; does best in woodland soils with warm summers. Killerton, Devon 15x51 (2001 OCJ) – very shapely.

S. pteropetiolata W China, 1912. Tender. Caerhays

20x50@1m and 24x29+24 (1984 AFM).

***S. sinensis* Chinese Stuartia** 1901. A rare but beautiful tree, needing shelter and warm summers. Trewithen, Cornwall 14.5x63@0m (1995); Tilgate Park, W Sussex 12x41 (2002 OCJ) – dying back.

***Styrax hemsleyana* Hemsley's Storax** W China, 1900. Rare; in warm areas. Windsor (Valley Gardens) 5x36 (2000 OCJ); Wakehurst Place 12x20 (1997 OCJ).
S. hookeri The Himalayas. Caerhays 9x28 (1984 AFM).
***S. japonica* Snowbell Tree** Japan, Korea, 1862. Occasional. Tregothnan, Cornwall 13x46 (1989 AFM).
***S. obassia* Big-leaved Storax** Japan, 1879. Rare; in warm areas. Penrhyn Castle, Gwynedd 11x31@1.3m? (1989 AFM); Ramster, Surrey 12x30 (1994 VES).

***Syagrus romanzoffiana* Queen Palm** Brazil. An established tree in Fox Rosehill Gardens, Cornwall.

***Syringa reticulata* ssp. *amurensis* Amur Lilac** NE Asia, 1855. Rare. Can reach tree-size: Stanmer Park, E Sussex 9x29+ (2002 OCJ).
***S. vulgaris* Lilac** E Europe; long grown here. Abundant, but a bush except where summers are hottest. Esher, Surrey ('Charles X'?) 7x(35) on single bole (2000 OCJ).

Taiwania cryptomerioides China, Taiwan, 1920. Very rare and never thriving for long: needs mild winters but warm summers. Killerton, Devon 17x38 (2001 OCJ).

***Tamarix gallica* Tamarisk** SW Europe; long grown here. Abundant (along with other very similar species) and naturalised on coasts; nearly always a bush. Sunbury, Surrey

6x(45) on single sprouty bole (2000 OCJ) – pollarded.

Taxodium ascendens – see *T. distichum* var. *imbricatum*.
***T. distichum* Swamp Cypress** SE USA, c1640. Occasional; does best in sandy soils (not necessarily wet ones) where summers are hottest. Deans Court, Dorset (31)x204 among branches (2003 Sir Michael Hanham); Syon Park, London 23x184 under branching (1990 AFM); Burwood Park, Surrey 27x180@1.2m over limb-stump (2000 OCJ) – top lost in 1987; Broadlands, Hants. 36x159 (1986 AFM).
var. *imbricatum* Pond Cypress (*T. ascendens*) 1789. Rare; less hardy. Knaphill Nursery, Surrey 20x79 (2000 OCJ); Dunster Castle, Somerset (23)x64 (1991 AFM).
***T. mucronatum* Mexican Swamp Cypress** A sturdy tree at Kew RBG: 20x104 (2001 OCJ), p1908.

Taxus Yews

***Taxus baccata* Common Yew** – see feature on p.104
'Adpressa' Rare. Alexandra Park, E Sussex 11x69 on single but branchy bole (2001 OCJ), p1878?; Hawkstone Park, Shropshire 15.5x54+25++ (1978 AFM).
'Adpressa Variegata' Rare. Frensham Hall estate, Surrey 7x32@1m++ (2000 OCJ).
f. *aurea* Golden Yew Frequent; usually as a bush. Frensham Hall estate, Surrey 13x49@1m (2000 OCJ) – shapely.
'Dovastonia' West Felton Yew Rare. Ardgomery, Stirling 15x120 (1988 AFM); West Felton, Shropshire 15x118@0.45m (1997) – original, bought by Mr Dovaston from a pedlar in 1777.
'Dovastonii Aurea' Rare. Highnam Court, Glos. 10x32@? (1991 JW).

Swamp Cypress (*Taxodium distichum*) is the only common tree which will thrive in standing water. It throws up 'knees' to help its roots to breathe and to trap silt around itself. Most of the biggest, however, are away from water.

YEWS

Unlike all our other wild trees, Yews are theoretically immortal – a tree a thousand years old can be as hale and hearty as a sapling. Their wood is so tough and flexible that hollow boles are not a liability – especially if the supporting branches are allowed to settle on the ground and take root. It is hard not to imagine that the British and Irish Wildwood was full of Yews at least as huge and ancient as any left to us today.

But Yew's foliage can be deadly to livestock, and the trees were systematically eradicated, surviving in groves only on steep chalk slopes and remote mountainsides, and individually within the holy sites that were ultimately to become our churchyards. Even here, many 'sacred trees' seem to have been destroyed as new beliefs took hold: ancient churchyard Yews are typical today of tiny, backwater sites in southern England and the Welsh Marches; Scotland and northern England retain scarcely any, and Ireland none. Some of these trees were clearly planted: they stand in lines, squares and circles, or on soils much heavier and wetter than the wild groves.

Until very recently, the antiquity and cultural importance of our ancient Yews was little recognised. Some were burnt down, or felled as 'dangerous'; others were used as sheds or sites for oil tanks. Many have disappeared in historic times: one at Brabourne church, Kent, was x582 in 1655 (John Evelyn), but nothing was known of it by 1888; another stupendous tree at Hamstead Marshall, Berkshire, was x456 at ground level in 1896 (John Lowe). Today, more than 2,000 historic churchyard Yews are on the Tree Register, while repeated measurements continue to provide strong evidence that the oldest are growing extraordinarily slowly and may be as much as 5,000 years old.

The tallest Yews tend to be young trees planted in sheltered woodlands: Luttrellstown Castle, Dublin 25x93 (2003 DGA); Belvoir Castle, Leics. (29)x89 (1987 AFM). Unlike the sprawling veterans, such trees are liable to blow down and may not prove long-lived.

Some of the largest and oldest churchyard Yews:

Fortingall, Perth x548cm in 1769 (Pennant) or x504cm (Daines Barrington) – around two now separate parts.

Ashbrittle, Somerset x388@0m (1992 Percival Morgan) – seven diverging pieces remain.

Llangernyw, Conwy x350@0.1m (1999 Jeroen Pater) – four fragments diverge widely.

Discoed, Powys x272@0.3m (1999 Jeroen Pater).

Bettws Newydd, Monmouth x(300) (1997 Fergus Kinmonth) – fragments surround a younger trunk.

Linton, Herefords. x314@1.3m (1999 Jeroen Pater) – young stem within a hollow shell.

Crowhurst, Surrey 11x306/x283@1.6-2.3m (2000 OCJ) – hollow, slanting bole with a door in it.

Payhembury, Devon 11x338@0.1m (2001 OCJ) – four healed fragments (two male, one now female) diverge widely.

Norbury, Shropshire 15x(320)@0m. Walled in by 1790.

Kenn, Devon 15x332@0m (2001 OCJ) – two massive halves sag outwards.

Defynnog, Powys 9x334@0.3m (1999 Jeroen Pater) – ten fragments from the base.

Tisbury, Wilts. x309 (1999 Jeroen Pater) – very hollow.

Ystradfellte, Powys x350@base (1992 Percival Morgan) – two fragments (one sawn off) in a stone wall.

Clun, Shropshire x330@0m (Tim Hills).

Darley Dale, Derbyshire 16x307 (1994).

Coldwaltham, W Sussex 14x296@1.2-1.5m (1997 OCJ) – very hollow, tapering bole.

Loose, Kent 16x306@0.5-1.5m (1995 OCJ) – very hollow; on a perennial spring.

Llanfaredd, Powys x290@0.6m (Tim Hills).

Loughton, Shropshire x(310)@0.5m (1983 Andrew Morton).

Llanafan Fawr, Powys x308@0m (Tim Hills) – fragments remain.

Mallwyd, Gwynedd x(320)@1m (Tim Hills).

South Hayling, Hants. 12x315 (1987 AFM).

Mamhilad, Monmouth x302@0m (Tim Hills) – half of the trunk long lost.

Staunton, Tewkesbury, Glos. x(310) (1980 Allen Meredith). Two fragments wired together.

Farringdon, Hants. 11x289@0.1m (1996 Tim Hills) – a hollow shell.

Tandridge, Surrey 18x334@0.3-1.5m under fork (2000 OCJ) – long, clean stems.

Ulcombe, Kent 12x315@0m (1999 OCJ) – sprouty, barrel-shaped and scarcely hollow.

Llanfeugan, Powys x288@0m (Tim Hills) – male; largest of 12. Four fragments lean out.

Hambledon, Surrey 13x303@0.1m (2000 OCJ) – clean, hollow bole broadening with height.

Mamhead, Devon 8x303@0m (2001 OCJ) – solid mass of sprouts.

Woolland, Dorset x296@0.3m (1999 Jeroen Pater).

Crowhurst, E Sussex 12x289@0.8-1.5m (1994 OCJ) – very hollow bole sagging apart.

Yew at Crowhurst, Surrey.

Ancient Yew (*Taxus baccata*) at Ashbrittle church, Somerset.

'Fastigiata' Irish Yew Abundant. Ballindoolin, Kildare 15.5x136@0.4m (2002 AF); Beauport Park, E Sussex 14x118@0.7m on distinct, sprouty bole (1997 OCJ); Culzean Castle, Ayr 18x122 (2003 Ian Cornelius); Tregrehan, Cornwall 19m (1979 AFM).

'Fastigiata Aurea' Golden Irish Yew Abundant. Westonbirt School, Glos. 13m (2002 OCJ).

'Lutea' Yellow-berried Yew Very rare; usually bushy.

'Semperaurea' Rare. Calderstones Park, Liverpool 12x49 (1984 AFM).

T. cuspidata Japanese Yew 1855. In a few collections. Borde Hill 11x48 on single bole (1996 OCJ).

T. x media 'Hicksii' Hicks' Yew (*baccata* x *cuspidata*, c1900) Rare. Hertingfordbury church, Herts. 9x77@0.2m (2001 OCJ).

Telopea truncata Tasmanian Waratah 1930. In a few mild gardens. Castlewellan NA 10x36 (1994 VES).

Ternstroemia gymnanthera India to Japan and Borneo. Very rare. Chapel Knap Gardens, Somerset 9x35@? (1993).

Tetracentron sinense Spur-leaf W China, 1901. Very rare. Edinburgh RBG 9x42 (1991 AFM), p1905; Cambridge UBG 13x34+27 (2002 DGA).

Tetradium daniellii Euodia (*Euodia hupehensis*) NE Asia, 1905. Very occasional; grows well everywhere. Glendoick,

Perth 24x109 (1991 VES), p1923. Separate species are sometimes distinguished.

Thuja koraiensis Korean Thuja 1918. Very rare; scarcely to 'tree' size. Headfort, Meath 8.5x28 (1980 AFM). (Hergest Croft 13x22 (1989 AFM).)

T. occidentalis Eastern White Cedar E N America, 1536? Now very occasional; a tough tree but short-lived and seldom happy here. Logie House, Highland 14x71 (1992 AFM); Bedgebury Forest, Kent 17x25 (2002 OCJ). (Wilton House, Wilts. 23.5x116@? (1931).)

'Aurea'. Very rare. Abbeyleix, Laois 9.5x37+34 (2000 TROI).

'Dicksonii'. Bedgebury NP 12x37 (1995 OCJ), p1930.

'Elegantissima'. Bedgebury NP 9x30 (1995 OCJ), p1926.

'Erecta'. Bedgebury NP 11x32 (1995 OCJ), p1935.

'Holmstrup' c1950. Abundant; nominally dwarf. Grayswood Hill, Surrey 9m (1998 OCJ).

'Lutea' Rare; the most vigorous clone here. Dochfour, Highland 17.5x53 (1982 AFM).

'Spiralis' Rather rare. Windsor (Valley Gardens) 12x41 (2000 OCJ); Lythe Hill Park, Surrey 15x33 (2000 OCJ).

'Wintergreen'. Hillier Gardens 9x25 (2002 Ron Holley).

T. orientalis – see *Platycladus orientalis*.

T. plicata Western Red Cedar W N America, 1853. Abundant; happiest in high humidity with cool summers, on richer or limestone soils. Balmacaan, Highland 39x286@0.3m (2002 John Miller) – 5 boles, and 40x197

on a fine bole (1993 AFM); Fortgranite, Wicklow 33x205 (2000 TROI); Belladrum, Highland 42x192 on fine bole (1993 AFM); Ardkinglas, Argyll (46)x176 (1988 AFM), p1875.

'Aurea' Rare, as a vigorous young tree. Windsor (Valley Gardens) 10x42 (2000 OCJ), p1977; Hillier Gardens 13x39 (2001 Ron Holley).

'Cuprea' Rare. Tillypronie, Aberdeen 12x28 (1991 AFM).

'Excelsa' Rare. Bedgebury NP 17x58 (1999 OCJ), p1961.

'Pyramidalis' Occasional. Alexandra Park, E Sussex 24x80@1.2m under branch, and 25x78 (2001 OCJ); Snowdenham Hall, Surrey 26x65 (2000 OCJ); Bedgebury NP 26x62++ (1999 OCJ).

'Semperaurescens' Rare. Whittingehame Tower, E Lothian 22x90 (1987 AFM); Westonbirt NA 23x66 (2002 OCJ), p1939.

'Umbraculifera'. Bedgebury NP 14x(45) (1995 OCJ).

'Wintergold' Occasional as a young tree. Bedgebury NP 11x(28) (1995 OCJ) – growing fast.

'Zebrina' Abundant. Woodstock, Kilkenny ('Irish Gold') 24x125 at fork (1999 Michael Lear); Cefn Onn Park, Glamorgan (27)x55 (1990 AFM).

T. plicata x standishii Vigorous young trees in a few big gardens. Windsor (Valley Gardens) 10x47 (2000 OCJ); Alice Holt, Hants. 18x40 (2001 OCJ).

T. standishii Japanese Thuja 1860. Rather rare; shows only a slight preference for humid areas. Benenden School, Kent 21x98 (1995 OCJ); Powerscourt, Wicklow 23x95 (2000 TROI); Tregrehan, Cornwall 25x79 (2002 Tom Hudson).

Thujopsis dolabrata Hiba Japan, by 1861. Frequent; grows best in warmer humid areas. Many were probably planted as the unstable 'Variegata' – the Tregrehan tree retains some variegation. Tregrehan, Cornwall (21)x102 on good bole (2002 Tom Hudson); Ramsfort, Wexford 24x47 (2000 TROI).

'Aurea' Golden Hiba Very rare. Hillier Gardens 9x26++ (2001 Ron Holley).

var. hondae N Japan. In a few collections. Arduaine, Argyll (21)x51@0.5m (1998).

Tilia Limes

Tilia americana American Lime E N America, 1752. Very occasional in warm areas. Alexandra Park, E Sussex 18x99@1.7m above graft (2001 OCJ); Wye church, Kent 16x83 (1995 OCJ) – gaunt; Derby Arboretum, Derbyshire 23x67 (1988 JW).

'Dentata'. Oare House, Wilts. 21x40 (1994 VES), p1935.

var. vestita In a few collections; more tolerant of cool summers. Dawyck, Scottish Borders (*T. heterophylla*?) 22x103 (1982 AFM); Nymans, W Sussex 24x66 (1997 OCJ).

T. amurensis NE Asia, 1909. Young trees in one or two collections. (Westonbirt NA 26x48 (1989 AFM), p1941.)

T. chinensis China, 1925. In a few collections. Westonbirt NA 15x32 (2002 OCJ).

T. chingiana China. Birr Castle 11.5x27 (2002 AF), p1946.

T. cordata Small-leaved Lime Locally native N to Cumbria; now much planted. Dallam Park, Cumbria (16)x262@0.5m around 'waist' (1994 DH) – shapely parkland tree; Worth, W Sussex 23x247 (2000 OCJ) – old wild pollard; Algarkirk, Lincs. x211@1m (1965 HPG); Arniston House, Midlothian x(194) under a huge limb (Alistair Scott); Brampton Bryan, Herefords. 21.5x186 (1979 AFM) – many gaps in the bole; Haveringland Hall, Norfolk 19x184 (1991 AFM); Turville Heath, Bucks. 27x180 (1983 AFM) – in William Perry's 1740s avenue; Balrath, Meath 22x178@1.3m (2000 TROI); Bell Beck, Rusland, Cumbria 37x120 (1998 DH) – wild tree.

'Greenspire' Very rare to date. Windsor (Savill Garden) 13x38 (2000 OCJ).

'Rancho' Rare to date. Hillier Gardens 11x31 (2002 Harry James).

T. dasystyla Crimean Lime SE Europe to Iran, 1880. In some collections. Westonbirt NA 21x74 (2002 OCJ).

ssp. caucasica One or two trees. Birr Castle (29)x126 (2000 TROI), p1912.

T. x euchlora Caucasian Lime (*cordata* x *dasystyla*? by 1860) Frequent. Flaybrick Memorial Gardens, Liverpool 19.5x103 (1998); Westonbirt NA 20x64 (2002 OCJ).

T. x europaea Common Lime (*cordata* x *platyphyllos*) Abundant. Florencecourt, Fermanagh x341 around 'waist' (2000 TROI) – several stems fused?; Stanway House, Glos. 36x301@0.5-1.3m among sprouts (1982 AFM); New Wardour Castle, Wilts. 27x(300) among sprouts (1977 AFM); Bifrons Park, Kent 19x294@0.5m-1m (1999 OCJ) – three fragments of the bole lean out; Strokestown Park, Roscommon 25.5x290@1.1m (2000); Newstone House, Meath 21x280@1.35m (2001 TROI); Holker Hall, Cumbria 18.5x251@0.7m around fluted 'waist' (2002 DH); Ffynone, Pembrokes. x246@1m under fork (1998 Earl Lloyd George) – burred; Barrow House, Cumbria 45x184 (1995 DH); Duncombe Park, Yorks. 44x159 (1993).

'Pallida'. Thorp Perrow, Yorks. 24x52 (1991 AFM), p1936.

'Wratislaviensis' Golden Lime Strangely very rare, as a young tree. Linton Gardens, E Sussex 10x34 (2001 OCJ), p1981?

T. x flavescens (*americana* x *cordata*?). (Kew RBG 14x43 (1967 AFM), p1906.)

T. 'Harold Hillier' (*insularis* x *mongolica*). Hillier Gardens 12x27 (2001 Harry James).

T. henryana C China, 1901. Very rare. Birr Castle 14.5x37 (2002 AF), p1946.

T. heterophylla White Basswood E USA, 1755 (incorporating *T. monticola*). Very rare. Kew RBG 24x106 (2001 OCJ), from 1872 seed.

T. 'Hillieri'. Hillier Gardens 17x30 (2002 Harry James).

T. insularis Korea, 1919. In a few collections. Kew RBG 13x43 (2001 OCJ); Westonbirt NA 20x40 (2002 OCJ), p1950.

T. intonsa W China, 1903. One or two trees. Wakehurst Place 8x29 (1997 OCJ) – broken.

T. japonica Japan, 1875. In some collections. Westonbirt NA 17x47 (2002 OCJ), p1930.

T. laetevirens W China. Edinburgh RBG 13x36 (1991 AFM), from Farrer 393.

T. mandshurica Manchurian Lime NE Asia, c1860.

LIMES

Pollen grains preserved in lake deposits suggest that Small-leaved Lime was the dominant tree in the wildwood of southern England, until 6,000 years ago. Since then, a slight cooling in the climate has meant that its seed seldom ripens and it has dwindled into a rare and local species of old hedgerows, ancient coppiced woodlands and hillsides too steep for browsing animals to reach it.

The Broad-leaved Lime is even scarcer in the wild: a towering clean-limbed tree adapted to cooler and wetter conditions and limey soils. It is a sign of how few people there are who really look at trees that the several dozen wild stands of giant Broad-leaved Limes in southern England were 'discovered' only in 1989 by the eminent botanist Francis Rose. Meanwhile the champion, at Pitchford Hall in Shropshire, sports a tree-house which is itself believed to date back to the 17th century.

For hundreds of years, trees have been at the mercy of fashions in taste and planting. Broad- and Small-leaved Limes have a hybrid, the Common Lime, which is extremely rare in the wild but around 1600 became the essential tree for avenues and topiary arbours. It is long-lived, and some of the earliest plantings survive, like this haunting and skeletal avenue which stalks across a field on the site of Bifrons Park in Kent (below). Given a lime-rich soil, it has also become our tallest broadleaf, while its wonderful crops of sprouts and whiskers are ideal for nesting birds. But in the later 20th century, the honeydew dropped by the aphids on its leaves onto cars parked underneath suddenly put the Common Lime out of favour: scarcely any nurseries now stock it. (Simultaneously, the Small-leaved Lime became the tree of the moment: its tantalisingly patchy wild distribution has now been largely obscured by indiscriminate plantings.)

Sprouts and buttresses make our biggest Common Limes (*Tilia x europaea*) difficult to compare. Even the most imposing of all, in the park at Florencecourt, Fermanagh, (above) is probably a 'bundle' of separate saplings planted together – especially to confuse tree-recorders three centuries later. There is a similar impostor on the lawn of Cobham Hall School in Kent, but its individual stems, making a circle 350cm across, have not yet perfectly fused.

Champion Small-leaved Lime (*Tilia cordata*) at Dallam Park, Cumbria.

In a few collections. Borde Hill 14x45@1.2m (1995 OCJ); Blackmoor, Hants. 19x29 (1984 AFM).

T. maximowicziana Japan, 1880. In a few collections. Hergest Croft 21.5x62 (1995 VES).

T. miqueliana **Temple Lime** E China, by 1900. In a few collections. Birr Castle 13.5x37 (2000 TROI); Killerton, Devon 14x28 (2001 OCJ) – as label.

T. 'Moltkei' (*americana* x *tomentosa* 'Petiolaris'?) Increasingly rare as an old tree. South Park, Ilford, London 17x87 (2001 OCJ); Glasnevin NBG 22x76 (2003 DGA).

T. mongolica **Mongolian Lime** N China, 1880. Rare to date. Kew RBG 14x62 and 20x47 (2001 OCJ), from 1905 seed.

T. oliveri **Oliver's Lime** C China, 1900. Rare to date. Westonbirt NA 25x64 (2002 OCJ) – fine tree.

T. x petiolaris – see *T. tomentosa* 'Petiolaris'.

T. platyphyllos **Broad-leaved Lime** Native to limestones in England and Wales; abundantly planted. Pitchford Hall, Shropshire 14x236 (1984 AFM) – carries much mistletoe; Buxted Park, E Sussex 20x206 (1994 OCJ) – burry bole; Tulfaris, Wicklow 17x204@1.1m (2000 TROI) – rotting fast; Tottenham House, Wilts. x193 (2000 Jack Oliver) – tiny leaves; Longnor Hall, Shropshire 30x192 (1984 AFM); Grove House, Tipperary 41.5x136 (2000 TROI).

'Aurea' Now very rare. (Kew RBG 23x67 (1979 AFM), sourced 1871.)

'Fastigiata' Rather rare to date. Sussex University Campus, E Sussex 14x50 (2002 OCJ); Penns-in-the-Rocks, E Sussex 14x36 (1994 OCJ) – growing fast.

'Glauca'. Edinburgh RBG 19x62 (1997).

'Laciniata' Cut-leaved Lime Very occasional; usually small-growing. Temple House, Sligo 16x92 (2000 TROI); Jardine Hall, Dumfries & Galloway 15.5x90@1m (1984 AFM); Drumkilbo, Perth (26)x67 (1986 AFM).

'Pendula'. Hillier Gardens 14x51 (2002).

'Rubra' Red-twigged Lime Now rare? Brocket Hall, Herts. (?) 26x147@1m under fork (2002 OCJ); Melbury House, Dorset 31x69 (1989 AFM).

'Tortuosa'. Kew RBG 21x56 (2001 OCJ), sourced 1872.

'Vitifolia' Vine-leaved Lime In a few collections. Kew RBG 18x54 (2001 OCJ), sourced 1872. (Alexandra Park, E Sussex 19x92@1m under branch-spring (1993 OCJ); fell 1999.)

T. tomentosa **Silver Lime** SE Europe, 1767. Quite frequent in warm areas. Buckland Hall, Powys 28x181@? (1987 JW); Tortworth church, Glos. (30)x159 (2000 Ted Palmer) – spread 33m; St Cuthman's School, W Sussex 32x114 (1997 OCJ).

f. *fastigiata* Very rare. Talbot Manor, Norfolk ('Erecta') 10x38 (1978 AFM), p1960.

'Petiolaris' Silver Pendent Lime By 1840. Frequent. Toddington Manor, Beds. 22x152 (2003 DGA) – cut back; Bath BG, Somerset 33x138 (2002 OCJ) – graft at 3m.

'Spectabilis'. Kew RBG 19x61 (2001 OCJ), sourced 1899.

T. tuan C China. In a few collections. Thorp Perrow, Yorks. 16x49 (1991 AFM), p1936.

Toona sinensis **Chinese Cedar** (*Cedrela sinensis*) N China, 1862. Very rare. Does best in humid areas but with warm summers. Glasnevin NBG 15x76 (1992), from

Wilson 185; Hergest Croft 23x70 (1995 VES).

***Torreya californica* Californian Nutmeg** 1857. Rare; best in warm but humid areas. Fota, Cork 18x124@1.2m (1999 TROI), p1852; Tregothnan, Cornwall 22x103 (1989 AFM).

T. nucifera **Naya** Japan, 1764. 20-30 trees? Wakehurst Place 14x35 (1997 OCJ) – dense column.

***Trachycarpus fortunei* Chusan Palm** China, 1830. Occasional away from cold parts; grows best in the mildest areas. Trebah, Cornwall 12x21 (2003 DGA).

T. martianus E Himalayas 1817. A few trees have been grown.

Trochodendron aralioides Japan, Taiwan, Korea, 1894. Rare; to tree size in humid areas. Arduaine, Argyll 17x52@0.5m (1998).

***Tsuga canadensis* Eastern Hemlock** E N America, 1736. Occasional. Oakly Park, Shropshire 25x163@? (1995); Eden Hall, Cumbria 33x95 (1995 DH).
'Albospica'. Kew RBG 9x34 (2001 OCJ), p1932.
'Compacta'. Nominally dwarf. Hillier Gardens 9.6x49@0m (2002 Ron Holley).
'Macrophylla'. Kew RBG 10x31 (2001 OCJ).
'Microphylla' In a few collections. Bedgebury NP 10x30++ (1995 OCJ).
'Pendula' Weeping Hemlock Rather rare. Parkfield, Worcs. 11.5x51 (1993 VES). (Hutton-in-the-Forest, Cumbria x63 (1985 AFM).)
T. caroliniana **Carolina Hemlock** SE USA, 1886. 20-30 trees? Hollycombe, W Sussex 13x45 (1997 OCJ) – leans; Bedgebury NP 13x32+++ (1995 OCJ), p1926; St Clere Pinetum, Kent 13x32++ (1997 Philip Webb).
T. chinensis **Chinese Hemlock** W China, 1900. Perhaps 20 trees. Bodnant, Conwy 18x65 (1990 AFM).
T. diversifolia **Northern Japanese Hemlock** 1861. 100 trees? Dunira, Perth 21.5x(142) and 22.5x113@0.5m under forks (2002 DH).
T. dumosa **Himalayan Hemlock** 1838. 20-30 trees?; grows large only in cool humid areas. Woodstock, Kilkenny (30)x110++ (1999 Michael Lear); Castlewellan NA 17x148@0.9m under fork (1994 VES).
T. heterophylla **Western Hemlock** W N America, 1851. Abundant except in dry areas. Scone Palace, Perth 41x201 on branchy bole (1988 AFM), p1860; Doune Castle, Stirling x200 on branchy bole (1989 AFM) – died back to 37m by 1970; Benmore, Argyll (51)x113 (1991 AFM), p1870.
'Greenmantle'. Windsor (Savill Garden) 15x35 and (Valley Gardens) 17x29 (2000 OCJ).
'Laursen's Column'. Hillier Gardens 12x31 (2001 Harry James).
T. x jeffreyi –see *Hesperopeuce mertensiana* var. *jeffreyi*.
T. mertensiana – see *Hesperopeuce mertensiana*.
T. sieboldii **Southern Japanese Hemlock** 1861. Perhaps 100 trees. Ochtertyre Hotel, Perth 20x87+69 (1987 AFM); Culzean Castle, Ayr 26x40 (2003 Ian Cornelius).

T. yunnanensis **Yunnan Hemlock** W China, 1908. In a few collections. Rowallane, Down 8x32+27 (1991 AFM); Edinburgh RBG 9.4x27 (1997).

Ulmus Elms

***Ulmus* '148'** ('28' x x *hollandica* 'Vegeta') A few plantings in Brighton. Lawn Memorial Cemetery, E Sussex x79 (2001 PJB), p1964.
U. **'202'** (*glabra* 'Exoniensis' x *wallichiana*) 10-20 trees in Brighton. Sussex University Campus, E Sussex 17x57 (2002 OCJ), p1969; Crespin Way, Brighton, E Sussex (21)x38 (1995 PJB), p1964.
U. **'215'**. Lullington, E Sussex (16)x32 (1997 PJB).
U. **'240'** (*minor* var. *minor* x *parvifolia*). Stanmer Park, E Sussex (?) 20x41 (2002 OCJ), p1965.
U. **'260'** (x *hollandica* 'Vegeta' x *pumila*) A few in Brighton. Happy Valley Park, Woodingdean, E Sussex (18)x63 (2001 PJB), p1961.
U. **'297'** (*minor* 'Christine Buisman' self-pollinated). Preston Park, E Sussex (19)x43 (2001 PJB), p1964.
U. alata **Winged Elm** SE USA, 1820. The only known survivor is in East Brighton Park, E Sussex: (13)x31 (2001 PJB), p1959.
U. americana **American White Elm** E N America, 1752. A handful remain. Avondale, Wicklow 20x94 (1991 AFM); Stanmer Park, E Sussex 21x80 (2002 OCJ). (Hyde Park, London 21x118 (1967 AFM).)
U. angustifolia – see *U. minor* var. *goodyeri*.
U. bergmanniana China, 1973. In a few collections. Kew RBG 8x34 (2001 OCJ) – original.
U. carpinifolia – see *U. minor* var. *minor*.
U. castaneifolia China, 1973. In a few collections. Kew RBG 11x26 (2001 OCJ) – original.
U. **'Coolshade'** (*pumila* x *rubra*) Very rare. Tenantry Down Road, Brighton, E Sussex (18)x55 (1998 PJB), p1960; Ryecroft, Brighton, E Sussex (19)x53 (1996 PJB), p1964.
U. coritana – see under *U. minor* var. *minor*.
U. davidiana NE Asia, 1895. Stanmer Park, E Sussex (?) 7x40 (2002 OCJ), p1965; very spreading.
U. x diversifolia – see under *U. x hollandica*.
U. **'Dodoens'** (*glabra* 'Exoniensis' x *wallichiana*, 1973) Rare to date. Westonbirt NA 17x36 (2002 OCJ).
U. x elegantissima – see under *U. x hollandica*.
U. glabra **Wych Elm** Native. Abundant in cool moist areas, though much reduced by its tendency not to sucker when infected; the one indisputably native elm. The odd big tree remains in disease-hit areas. Brahan, Highland 25.5x224 (2002 Donald Rodger), p1735; Rossie Priory, Perth (42)x147 (1985 AFM). (Cassiobury Park, Herts. 30x258 (1904 Elwes & Henry).)
'Atropurpurea'. The only survivor may be at Cottesmore St Mary's School, E Sussex: (18)x51 (1993 PJB).
'Camperdownii' Camperdown Elm 1850. Still occasional, as it tends to withstand DED. Castle Kennedy, Dumfries & Galloway 6.5x87 (1993 VES); Durris House, Aberdeen 15x44 (1987 AFM).
'Crispa' Almost extinct: Birr Castle x29 (2002 AF). (Chiltley Place, Hants. 26x86 (1960 AFM).)
'Exoniensis' Exeter Elm 1826. Still very occasional in some disease-hit areas. Preston House, W Lothian 22x115

Smooth-leaved Elms (*Ulmus minor* var. *minor*) are still part of the East Kent landscape. Stone Chapel, Faversham.

(1987 AFM); Cambridge UBG (15)x72 (1999 PJB). (Bitton Vicarage, Somerset 9x135 (1960 AFM) – topped.)

'Horizontalis' ('Pendula') Still very occasional, as it tends to withstand DED. Fordcombe, Kent 13x116 (1999 OCJ) p1851? – injected with fungicide but sickly by 2000; Rathmullen House, Donegal 6x103 (2000 TROI); Glen Mooar, Isle of Man 14x84 (1998 Frank Harrison).

'Luteovariegata'. Castle Terrace, Edinburgh (18)x62 (1989 PJB).

'Lutescens' Golden Wych Elm Now rare, but still in commerce. Dyke Road Place, Brighton, E Sussex 16x79 and 17x74 (2002 OCJ); Munches, Dumfries & Galloway (31)x79 (1985 AFM) – reverting from 26m.

'Nana' Perhaps extinct. (Alexandra Park, E Sussex 6x38@1m (1980 OCJ).)

'Serpentina' Almost extinct. Jevington church, E Sussex 5x35 (2003 OCJ).

***U.* x *hollandica* Hybrid Elm** (*glabra* x *minor*). The dominant elm in parts of E Anglia in great variety ('*U.* x *diversifolia*'; '*U.* x *elegantissima*'); many mature trees survive in some populations. Bozeat, Northants. ('*U.* x *diversifolia*') 22.5x129 (2000 John Niles).

'Bea Schwarz' Holland, 1948. A few survive in Brighton. Holy Trinity church, Hove, E Sussex (15)x49 (1994 PJB); Crespin Way, Brighton, E Sussex (22)x33 (1998 PJB), p1964.

'Belgica' Belgian Elm Now almost extinct. Donald Hall Road, Brighton, E Sussex (23)x65 (2001 PJB). (Hyde Park, London 18x128 (1967 AFM); North Inch, Perth 34x100 (1983 AFM) – single survivor by 1987.)

'Commelin' ('28' x x *hollandica* 'Vegeta', 1940) Survivors are rare. Sussex University Campus, E Sussex (21)x61 (1995 PJB), p1966; Courtlands, Brighton, E Sussex (23)x52 (1998 PJB), p1967.

'Dampieri' Almost extinct. Threave Garden, Dumfries & Galloway 14x30 (1991 AFM), p1965.

'Dampieri Aurea' Golden Elm (*minor* 'Wredei') Still widely planted; tends to resist DED. South Park Gardens, Wimbledon, London 14x59 (2001 OCJ).

'Dauvessei' A few survive around Brighton. Highleigh, Brighton, E Sussex (23)x76 (1998 PJB).

'Groeneveld' Holland, 1963. Locally occasional as a younger planting, showing good disease resistance. Stanmer Park, E Sussex 18x53 (2002 OCJ).

'Hollandica' Dutch Elm ('Major') Now almost confined to disease control zones. Cedar Gardens, Brighton, E Sussex x133 (2001 PJB); Park Crescent, Brighton, E Sussex (34)x96 (1994 PJB). (Easton Lodge, Essex 43x210 (1956 Maynard Greville).)

'Klemmeri'. Hove Cemetery, E Sussex (19)x73 (2001 PJB).

'Pitteursii' A few survive around Brighton. Benfield Way, Portslade, E Sussex (14)x45 (1998 PJB).

'Scampstoniensis'. Woodvale Crematorium, E Sussex

26x73 (2002 OCJ), p1851 – largest in line.

'Vegeta' Huntingdon Elm Big trees survive in good numbers everywhere. 'The Old Elm Tree', Northants. 28x167 (1999 DGA); Courteenhall, Northants. x166 (1999) – forking at 3m; Queen's College, Cambs. (38)x123 (1999 PJB).

'Wentworthii' Wentworth Elm Almost extinct. Edinburgh RBG (21)x56 (1991 AFM).

U. japonica Japan. Very rare as a disease-resistant young planting. Sussex University Campus, E Sussex ('Jacan') 15x31 (2002 OCJ).

U. laevis European White Elm Possibly native; very rarely surviving as a big, wild tree. Ferry Farm, Harewood, Cornwall 24x178 (1995).

U. 'Lobel' Holland, 1973. Locally occasional as young plantings, showing good disease resistance. Old Oak Common Lane, Acton, London 15x44 (2002 OCJ); Lady Margaret Road, Dormer's Wells, London 15x44 (2002 OCJ); Westonbirt NA 17x27++ (2002 OCJ).

U. minor Field Elm Native, or introduced very early, in a great variety of local forms:

'28' (selection from var. *minor*). Preston Park, E Sussex (20)x46 (2001 PJB), p1964.

'Betulifolia' Birch-leaved Elm Extinct? (Kew RBG 23x73 (1967 AFM).)

'Christine Buisman' Holland, 1937. A few survive in Brighton. Carden Park, E Sussex (13)x33 (1998 PJB); Palmeira Avenue, Hove, E Sussex (16)x33 (2002 PJB).

var. cornubiensis Cornish Elm Much reduced in wild (Cornwall); almost extinct elsewhere as a planted tree. The Great Elm of Rosuic, an ancient pollard, still (?) survives in Rosuic, Cornwall. Preston Park, E Sussex (26)x78 (2001 PJB), p1884. (Enys, Cornwall x196 (1962 AFM) – stump.)

'Dicksonii' Dickson's Golden Elm A very rare small tree, but still in commerce.

var. goodyeri Goodyer's Elm (*U. angustifolia*) No mature trees are now known in wild area (S Hampshire); seems scarcely to have been planted elsewhere. (Bisterne Park, Hants. 27x136 and 30x131 (1896 Elwes & Henry).)

var. lockii Lock's Elm (*U. plottii*) A North Midlands form, much reduced in the wild and rarely planted elsewhere. Romney Gardens, Cumbria (hybrid with Wych Elm?) 28x87 (1996 DH).

'Louis van Houtte' Golden English Elm Now almost confined to disease control zones. Dyke Road Park, E Sussex (17)x61 (1997 PJB); Carden Park, E Sussex (21)x61 (1998 PJB) – reverting at tip.

ELMS

No trees have been and continue to be more unjustly neglected than elms. Eastern England is home to a myriad of distinctive forms (most elms reproduce from suckers rather than seed, so these local traits get passed from generation to generation); few botanists have attempted to study them in depth, and those that have generally fail to come to any consensus about which are species, hybrids or varieties. (A minimal approach has been adopted here, listing only the more widespread variants and corralling them either under 'Field Elms' or hybrids of Field and Wych Elms.)

In the mid 1960s, a new and virulent strain of Dutch Elm Disease (DED) reached Britain, probably on timber imported from North America. (The Americans have it differently, claiming that the disease reached them from Europe.) DED is a fungal infection spread on the mouthparts of boring beetles; to isolate the infection, the tree shuts down its sap-conducting vessels and the crown above the blockage is starved of sap and dies. Most infected elms regenerate from suckers, but these become vulnerable to re-infection as soon as their stems are thick enough to interest the beetles.

People observed the catastrophic spread of DED through the 1970s and 80s; concluded, regretfully, that these most majestic trees were now a thing of the past; and set about planting, recording and writing about oaks and ashes instead. In fact, many individual elms of many different kinds have withstood DED – and, precisely located in numbers on the Tree Register, will be the plants to propagate or breed from to produce resistant stock in future. In East Anglia and East Kent, large and diverse Field Elm populations remain; many local authorities have also had the courage to experiment with various new and beautiful ornament forms. Bark beetles prefer warm dry weather, so infection rates are also low in northern Scotland, western Ireland and the Isle of Man, while the disease has not reached Scilly. In the South Downs from Shoreham to Eastbourne, a rigorously-maintained Disease Control Zone has preserved a wealth of old elms, while Brighton inherits the most adventurous urban plantings of all.

Elms like a nutrient-rich soil, and can thrive on raw chalk. They stand up to coastal exposure like no other tree. Great numbers of often exquisite variegated, golden, purple-leaved, fastigiate and weeping forms have been bred, but very few are now in commerce: several are probably already extinct, and others seem bound to follow.

Keeping track of surviving elm populations is hard for the Tree Register's recorders: much-loved trees may be infected any year, new selections grow up with astonishing vigour, and in much of East Anglia all too little field-work has yet been done. What follows is a simplistic and patchy list which will be out-of-date as soon as it is published, but which does at least show that the elm is not yet dead.

var. *minor* Smooth-leaved Elm (*U. carpinifolia*) Covers many varied clones still abundant as old trees in E Anglia and E Kent (including '*U. coritana*'); occasional planted or regenerated trees survive elsewhere. Most variants are unnamed and little studied; 'Dengie Elm' and 'Boxworth Elm' show considerable disease-resistance. Barnwell Place, Cambs. x191 among burrs (1999) – perhaps a hybrid; Larchfield, Down 33x90 (2000 TROI). (Gilston Park, Herts. 41x102 (1955 Maynard Greville); Great Waltham, Essex 27x232 (1953 Maynard Greville).)

var. *minor* 'Variegata' Variegated Smooth-leaved Elm Now extinct? (Little Parndon, Essex 26x97 (1911 Elwes & Henry).)

'Purpurea' (x *hollandica* 'Purpurea'). Dyke Road Drive, Brighton, E Sussex (15)x38 (1995 PJB).

'Sarniensis' Wheatley Elm Much planted (wild on the Channel Islands); now almost confined to disease control zones. Preston Park, E Sussex 31x126 (2001 PJB), p1884; Paradise Plantation, E Sussex 33x79 (2002 PJB). (Powderham Castle, Devon 38x109 (1970 AFM); Avington House, Hants. 32x186 (1977 AFM).)

'Viminalis' Cut-leaved Elm A rare and obscure wild form; almost extinct as a planted tree. Upper Larkrise Wood, E Sussex (23)x50 (1995 PJB) – wild tree.

'Viminalis Aurea' Garden form; extinct?

'Viminalis Aureomarginatum' Garden form; extinct? (Antony House, Cornwall 10x38 (1971 AFM).)

'Viminalis Marginata' Garden from; almost extinct?

'Viminalis Pulverulenta' Garden form; extinct? (Busbridge Lakes, Surrey ('Albovariegata') 17x90 (1963 AFM).)

var. *vulgaris* English Elm (*U. procera*) Completely reduced to sucker growth outside disease control zones; once the common Field Elm across lowland middle England but the most susceptible form of all to the current form of DED. Preston Park, E Sussex 16x201 and 15x200 (2001 PJB) – 'The Preston Twins', ancient hollow trees; Lullington, E Sussex 27m – in line of surviving wild trees. (East Bergholt, Suffolk x300 (1942); Forthampton, Glos. 46x194 (1895 Elwes & Henry) – blown.)

var. *vulgaris* 'Argenteo-variegata' Variegated English Elm Only some suckers survive. (Stratfield Saye, Hants. 24x92 (1968 AFM); Kenwood House, London 29x90 (1964 AFM).)

'Wredei' – see *U.* x *hollandica* 'Dampieri Aurea'.

U. *parvifolia* Chinese Elm NE Asia, Japan, Taiwan, 1794. Rare; still planted as it often resists DED. Magdala Avenue, London 13x40 (2002 OCJ) – almost dead; Dyffryn Gardens, Glamorgan 13x37 (1997 OCJ). (Glasnevin NBG 16x51 (1974 AFM) – died by 1980.)

U. 'Pinnato-ramosa' (*pumila* var. *arborea*) W Asia? 1894. Rare; usually resists DED. Hergest Croft 22x66 (1995 VES), p1959.

U. 'Plantijn' (*glabra* 'Exoniensis' x *wallichiana* x *minor* x *minor* '28', 1973) Rare as a young planting. (Kensington Gardens, London 16x45 (2001 OCJ).)

U. *plottii* – see *U. minor* var. *lockii*.

U. *procera* – see *U. minor* var. *vulgaris*.

U. *pumila* Siberian Elm N Asia, 1860. Rare, but still planted, as it usually resists DED. Mote Park, Kent 22x66

(1995 OCJ).

var. *arborea* – see *U.* 'Pinnato-ramosa'.

'Aurea' Golden Siberian Elm. Seaford, E Sussex (14)x47 (1997 PJB).

'Den Haag'. Swanborough Drive, Brighton, E Sussex (17)x45 (1994 PJB), p1967.

'Dropmore' A few survive in Brighton. Tenantry Down Road, Brighton, E Sussex (17)x50 (1994 PJB), p1960.

U. 'Regal' (x *hollandica* 'Commelin' x *minor* 'Hoersholmiensis' x *pumila*, 1983) Very rare as a young planting. Exeter Crematorium, Devon (?) 12x41 (2001 OCJ).

U. *rubra* Slippery Elm E N America, 1830. Almost extinct here. Hove Recreation Ground, E Sussex (18)x65 (2002 PJB).

U. 'Sapporo Autumn Gold' (*japonica* x *pumila*, 1973) Frequently planted in the 1970s for its disease-resistance. Wisley 11x53 among branches (2000 OCJ); Clophill Depot, Beds. 18x35 (2002 DGA) – drawn up; bole 8m.

U. x *sarniensis* – see *U. minor* 'Sarniensis'.

U. *turkestanica*. Edinburgh RBG 15x44 (1997).

U. 'Urban' (x *hollandica* 'Vegeta' x *minor* var. *minor* x *pumila*, 1976) A few young plantings. Royal Bath & West Showground, Somerset (12)x26 (1997 PJB), p1981.

U. x *vegeta* – see *U.* x *hollandica* 'Vegeta'.

U. *villosa* Marn Elm W Himalayas, 1935. Survives in a few collections, with one or two plantings in Brighton. Hodshrove Place, Brighton, E Sussex (15)x51 (1999 PJB); Stanmer Park, E Sussex 15x48 (2002 OCJ), p1964. (Kew RBG 29x86 (1991 AFM) – original.)

U. x *viminalis* – see *U. minor* 'Viminalis'.

U. *wallichiana* Bhutan Elm Himalayas. In a few collections since 1960; about 60 municipal plantings in Brighton; usually disease-resistant. Longhill School, E Sussex (17)x57 (1994 PJB), p1965; Brighton University, E Sussex 19x52 (2002 OCJ), p1964.

Umbellularia californica Californian Bay California, Oregon, 1829. Rare; has a slight preference for hot summers. Warnham Court, W Sussex 16x122@0.7m under branching (1997 OCJ); Mount Usher, Wicklow (13)x106 (1989 AFM); Warley Place, Essex 20x62+42 (1996).

Viburnum cylindricum Himalayas, W China, 1881. Rare. Can reach tree size in mild areas. Ashbourne House, Cork 6x27+27 (1987 AFM) – bush; Plas Newydd, Anglesey 10x24+19 (1991 AFM).

V. odoratissimum Malaya, 1818? Very rare. Can reach tree size in mild areas. Singleton Park, Glamorgan 8x25+20+ (2000 OCJ).

Villaresia mucronata – see *Citronella gongonha*.

Weinmannia trichosperma S Andes. In one or two mild gardens. Tregothnan, Cornwall 13x47 (1989 AFM).

Xanthocyparis nootkatensis Nootka Cypress W N America, 1853? Occasional; best in humid areas. Woodbrooke, Wexford 20x129 on single bole (2001 AF); Drenagh, Derry (32)x128 (1983 AFM).

Caucasian Elm (*Zelkova carpinifolia*) is one of the least familiar of really big trees. It is closely enough related to the elms to be an occasional casualty of Elm Disease, but its round-lobed leaves and orange-flaking bark are all its own. So is its shape – in its native Caucasian forests it grows like any other tree but the norm in Britain and Ireland is a besom-broom of innumerable fine branches soaring from a short, fluted trunk. This makes it vulnerable to wind-throw, but a few of today's biggest are probably 1760 'originals'. The champion has been preserved within a housing estate in Worlingham, Suffolk.

'Argenteovariegata' Variegated Nootka Cypress Rare. Bedgebury NP 15x32 (1995 OCJ), p1925; Walcot Hall, Shropshire x68 (1995) – reverted.

'Glauca' Very rare. Thorp Perrow, Yorks. 15x29 (1991 AFM), p1939.

'Lutea' Golden Nootka Cypress Rare. Castlewellan NA 21.5x92 (double stem), and 19.5x73+ (1983 AFM); Bedgebury NP 22x63 (1995 OCJ), p1927.

'Pendula' Weeping Nootka Cypress Rather rare. Wall Hall, Herts. 21x66++ (2002 OCJ), layering; Westonbirt NA 21x64 (2002 OCJ).

Zanthoxylum ailanthoides Japanese Toothache Tree NE Asia, Japan. In one or two collections: the most tree-like *Zanthoxylum*. (Wakehurst Place 7x32+24 (1991 VES).)

Zelkova abelicea Cretan Zelkova (*Z. cretica*) 1924? In a few collections; scarcely reaching 'tree' size.

Z. carpinifolia Caucasian Elm 1760. Very occasional. Park Drive, Worlingham, Suffolk 27x219@0.5m around 'waist' (1990 AFM); New Wardour Castle, Wilts. 35x76 (1977 AFM) – clump of suckers.

Z. schneideriana W China. Young trees in a few big gardens. Kew RBG 7x33 and 8x28@1m (2001 OCJ), from 1977 seed.

Z. serrata Keaki NE Asia, Japan, 1861. Quite frequent as a younger planting. Powerscourt, Wicklow 18x102 (1990 AFM); Kilmacurragh, Wicklow 18x101 (1990 AFM); Lower Sherriff Farmhouse, W Sussex 19x101 on 5m bole (1997 OCJ), from 1890 seed; spread 26.5m; Hergest Croft 23x79 (1995 VES), p1902.

Z. sinica Chinese Zelkova China, 1908. Very rare. Kew RBG 16x75 (2001 OCJ), from 1920 seed.

Z. x verschaffeltii Very rare; often a bush. Crathes Castle, Aberdeen 11x41 (1988 AFM) – with brilliant autumn colour; Edinburgh RBG 14x29+22 (1991 AFM).

Gazetteer

This Gazetteer lists our champion trees by country, by county and then alphabetically by site. Unitary Authorities have been included within their 'old' counties except when they cross county boundaries. The tree's common name is used when extant but, within each site, the trees are ordered alphabetically by their botanical names. Further details about each tree's size, shape, age and origin will be found in the Directory (or 'Record-breaking Trees', p.22). Notable trees that are known to have been lost, but which are mentioned in the Directory, are only included here – in (brackets) – if they are the only tree featured for that site. The year when the tree was last measured is given when it has not been possible to confirm its recent survival. To help locate out-of-the-way trees, Ordnance Survey six-figure grid references are given, as are the catalogue numbers that many big gardens include on all their trees' labels.

A two-star grading system indicates those parks and gardens which will most interest people who are hoping to see a variety of large and rare trees. What follows, however, is not quite a comprehensive list of the best sites for trees: some fine gardens have been excluded as none of their trees currently happen to be champions.

Some indication is given if sites are known to open to the public but as arrangements can alter from year to year these are not intended to be comprehensive. The *Good Gardens Guide*, the NGS's 'Yellow Book' and *Hudson's Historic Houses and Gardens* provide annual details. Many champions in open gardens will not be labelled (and a few will be mis-labelled), while others are hidden in out of the way places, so readers should not be disappointed if they fail to find them. A few gardens have made a particular feature of their champions: at Wisley Gardens and Kew they are specially labelled, while Westonbirt Arboretum floodlight many of theirs in December.

The other sites included here do not open to the general public, and their locations have deliberately not been given too precisely. At least 75% of champions are either in the public domain or accessible on open days; the rest have been entered on the Tree Register partly under the understanding that numbers of readers will not approach their owners asking to visit them.

CHANNEL ISLANDS

The islands' special climate, mild in winter but warm and very sunny in summer, allows gardens in shelter to grow a great range of trees.

Guernsey
Candie Gardens, Candie Road, St Peter Port. Historic public park. Largest Canary Palm.
*Sausmarez Park, Castel. Public park; many tender trees. Largest Akiraho (1995).

Jersey
Les Vaux, Rozel. Largest Bead Tree.
Magnolia Cottage, Rozel. Largest Ulmo and Epaulette Tree.
Trinity Manor, Trinity. One of the largest Lucombe Oaks.

ENGLAND
Bedfordshire
This is the only Midlands county to have been comprehensively explored for champions, though there are rather few stately homes and historic gardens. Woodlands and the best conditions for tree growth are largely confined to the Chilterns in the far south and to a narrow band of Lower Greensand hills.

Clophill (Beds. County Council Depot). Tallest 'Sapporo Autumn Gold' Elm.
Flitwick Manor, Flitwick. One of the largest Alders.
Luton Hoo, Luton. Largest Hybrid Cockspur Thorn (rock garden, overhanging pet cemetery), and Golden Oak (opposite main car park).
Mary Bassett Lower School, Leighton Buzzard. Largest Vine Maple.
Pertenhall Old Rectory. Largest Quince.
Shefford. Largest Stag's-horn Sumach (6, Mayfields).
Shillington. Largest Black Mulberry (91, Church Street).
Stockwood Country Park, Farley Hill, Luton. One of the largest Red Oaks (golf course near Craft Museum entrance).
Swiss Garden, Old Warden Park, Biggleswade. Historic garden restored by Bedfordshire County Council; open daily in summer. Largest *Castanea sativa* 'Aureomarginata'; tallest Hedgehog Holly (in shrubbery).
Tempsford. Largest *Platycladus orientalis* 'Elegantissima'

Champion Golden Oak at Luton Hoo, Bedfordshire.

(St Peter's Church); one of the largest White Willows (Station Road, 200m from railway crossing on right).
Toddington Manor, Toddington. Opens regularly. Largest Silver Pendent Lime.
*Woburn Park, Woburn. The Abbey gardens and deer park are open daily, and comprise the county's only extensive arboretum. Tallest Purple Sycamore (Speedwell Belt); tallest Chosen Maple (Abbey garden, A7); tallest *Fagus sylvatica* 'Rotundifolia'(The Evergreens: top of hill above Pinetum); tallest Japanese Crab (Potters End/Eversholt); largest *Prunus* 'Shogetsu' (Stump Cross Pond); largest *Sorbus aria* 'Majestica' (The Evergreens, by Crawley Road wall).

Berkshire

A small county with a great variety of landscapes. Conifers dominate the poor Bagshot sands in the south-east; stately homes with fine trees cluster along the rich soils of the Thames and Kennet valleys, and have been enveloped in suburban sprawl around Slough. In the west, the high downs have few trees.

Bridge Gardens, Hungerford. Some rare young trees. Largest Prince Rupert's Larch (1995).
Easthampstcad Park College, Bracknell. Tallest *Ilex* x *altaclarensis* 'Hodginsii' (W lawn, 1992).
Eton College. Largest Farges' Catalpa (College Field, E),

White Ash (Triangle Field, NE), and Sand Pear (Triangle Field, S).
Hamstead Marshall church, Kintbury. Largest Yew (lost since 1896).
Reading University. The campus covers part of the grounds of 'Whiteknights', with rare old tree. Largest Shagbark Hickory (the Wilderness).
**Windsor Great Park. Most of the Great Park is in Berkshire, including the Empire Oaks (planted in 1937 near Bishopsgate) and the western half the Valley Gardens above Virginia Water (with open access year-round), including the National Collection of *Ilex*. The older parts of the park to the west still have many medieval oak pollards. (And see Surrey.)
Largest Red Snake-bark Maple (Valley Gardens: High Flyer's hill, S of pine plantation; WGP82076).
Largest Hers' Maple (Valley Gardens: High Flyer's Hill, above birch lawn to W).
Tallest *Betula* x *koehnei* (Valley Gardens: High Flyer's Hill, top of birch lawn).
Largest Medwediew's Birch (Valley Gardens: High Flyer's Hill, birch lawn).
Largest Himalayan Sea Buckthorn (Valley Gardens: Heather Garden, W).
Largest *Magnolia stellata* 'Norman Gould' (Valley Gardens: High Flyer's Hill, W of pine plantation; WIS82080).
Largest *M. officinalis* (Valley Gardens: Breakheart valley, E bank; HIL82067).
Largest *Picea asperata* var. *retroflexa* (Valley Gardens: pinetum valley, near bottom).
Tallest Limber Pine (1990).
Largest *Prunus cerasifera* 'Lindsayae' (Valley Gardens: Breakheart valley, E side, bottom).
Tallest Water Oak (Empire Oaks: Western Pacific Territories).
Largest Moscow Oak (Empire Oaks: Zanzibar).
One of the largest English Oaks (near Cranbourne Tower, E side of drive from Forest Gate; SU94037298).
Tallest Chinese Cork Oak (Valley Gardens: Breakheart valley, up E bank, mid).
Largest *Sorbus* 'Wilfrid Fox' (Valley Gardens: High Flyer's Hill, above maple lawn).
Largest *Thuja occidentalis* 'Spiralis' (Valley Gardens: pinetum valley, W side, upper).
Tallest *Tsuga heterophylla* 'Greenmantle' (Valley Gardens: pinetum valley, W side, top; WGP86250).
Windsor Home Park, Windsor. (Only recorded Water Elm, lost since 1972.)
Wokingham Road Cemetery, Reading. Largest Weeping Beech.
Woodley, Reading. Largest Stone Pine (public land by South Lake).

Bristol area

Bristol Zoo Gardens, Clifton. Open daily. Established in 1835 as a combined zoo and arboretum. Largest *Magnolia* x *loebneri* (near N wall).
Churchill Hall. Churchill College; large arboretum developed since 1961. Largest *Paulownia fargesii* (1991).
Homes Garden, Stoke Bishop. Largest Hybrid Laburnum (gate; 1991).

Buckinghamshire

Woodland is concentrated in the Chilterns in the southeast; the fringes of Greater London have the greatest number of old parks. The clay vale in the north has little woodland and the few notable gardens tend to cluster on the sandier hills.

*Ascott House, Wing, Leighton Buzzard. NT; open most days except winter. Fine and unusual trees. Largest Weeping Purple Beech (by Venus Fountain).

Bellingdon Wood, Chesham. Tallest Rowan (drawn up in beech plantation, 1995).

Bulstrode Park, Oxford Road, Gerrards Cross. Historic gardens. Largest *Prunus* 'Shirofugen' (S of house); one of the largest Turkey Oaks (off Lime Avenue).

Burnham Park, Slough. Public park. Largest *Acer pseudoplatanus* 'Simon-Louis Frères' (S of The Priory).

Chesham Bois, Chesham. The Woodland Trust. Tallest Whitebeam (far top corner, E side of A416, near fence and footpath).

*Cliveden, Taplow, Maidenhead. NT; historic gardens open daily. National collection of *Catalpa*. Tallest Butternut (just W of house).

Fawley Court, Henley. Regularly open in summer. Largest Female Lombardy Poplar (Ornamental Water, N; 1985).

Gayhurst, Newport Pagnell. Largest Walnut (park).

Hampden House, Great Hampden. One of the largest Cedars of Lebanon (1999).

Priestfield Pinetum, Little Kingsmill. The arboretum has been restored entirely by volunteers and has regular open days. Largest *Malus kansuensis* (1984).

Priestwood, Little Kingsmill. Tallest *Chamaecyparis lawsoniana* 'Rosenthalii' (1984).

Stowe Landscape Gardens, Buckingham. NT; open daily except in winter. A range of unusual trees in this historic parkland. Largest X *Cupressocyparis leylandii* 'Stapehill' (by shop; 1986).

Taplow House Hotel, Berry Hill, Taplow, Maidenhead. Fine old trees; one of the largest Tulip Trees (foot of lawn).

Turville Heath, Stonor. 1740s avenue of Small-leaved Limes along lane (once the drive to Turville Park).

Wexham Place, Wexham Street, Slough. Residents' garden. Tallest Golden Chestnut (in 1978).

Cambridgeshire and Peterborough

Trees and gardens cluster in the south and east around the fringes of the drained levels – whose rich soils are almost exclusively devoted to agriculture. A variety of elm clones have largely survived DED. The climate is the most 'continental' in England, with dry, hot summers but frosty winters.

*Anglesey Abbey, Lode. NT; open most days except in winter; range of rare trees. Largest *Pinus sylvestris* 'Argentea' (pinetum).

Barnwell Place, Buckden Road, Brampton. Largest Smooth-leaved Elm (back garden; ?; 1999).

Bedford Purlieus, Rockingham Forest, Wansford. FC; Ancient Woodland nature reserve which is perhaps the richest in Britain for its flora. Tallest Wild Crab (stream at TL040995?; 1990).

Bishop's Palace, Ely. NGS open days. Largest London Plane.

**Cambridge University Botanic Garden, Trumpington Road, Cambridge. Open daily; 18ha with a great range of trees and special collections of native species. Largest Caucasian Alder (N side of South Walk, near junction with Middle Walk).

Largest Paper Mulberry (SE; 1991).

Largest Pecan.

Largest *Catalpa* x *erubescens* 'Purpurea' (Rock Garden).

Largest *Celtis jessoensis* (W boundary; 10005286 A).

Largest Altai Mountain Thorn (Order Beds, 1991).

Largest *Crataegus monogyna* 'Nordica Splendens' (1994).

Largest Chinese Honey Locust (Gleditsia collection).

Largest *Juglans elaeopyren* (by Gilbert-Carter Memorial Garden).

Largest *Lonicera maackii* (near the Cambridge Oak).

Largest *Morus mongolica* (10005288A).

Largest Chilgoza Pine (near Terrace Garden; 10005001A).

Largest Single-leaved Nut Pine (among pines S of fountain).

Tallest Mountain Pine (ssp. *uncinata*) (Old Pinetum; 1995).

Largest *Populus* x *acuminata* (1989).

Largest *P. simonii* 'Fastigiata' (1989).

Largest *Pyrus betulifolia* (1984).

Largest Cambridge Oak (Gilbert-Carter Memorial Garden).

Largest Varnish Tree (lake, N).

Largest Golden Willow (lake/Bog Garden).

Tallest Spur-leaf.

Largest surviving Exeter Elm (82.0162; 1999).

Emmanuel College, Cambridge. Open daily; many fine trees. Tallest Golden Robinia (1990).

The Fen, Cambridge. Public park. Tallest Lombardy Poplar (Coe's Fen; 1991).

Holywell-cum-Needingworth, St Ives. One of the largest White Willows, on farmland (1994).

Pampisford House, Sawston (1988). Variety of rare trees. Tallest *Acer* x *coriaceum* and Swamp White Oak.

Peckover House, North Brink, Wisbech. NT; large town garden open most days except in winter. Tallest Box Elder (1984); largest Cornelian Cherry (1997).

Queen's College, Cambridge. Tallest Huntingdon Elm (in grove).

Ramsey Abbey School, Ramsey. Largest Weeping Whitebeam (S lawn).

St Neots. Largest and tallest Almond Willows (by River Ouse and in the Riverside Gardens, 1990).

Wicken Fen, Wicken, Ely. NT; National Nature Reserve; one of the few remaining fragments of undrained Fen. Largest Buckthorn and Bay Willow (TL558705?; 1989).

Cheshire

The heavy soils of the Cheshire plain tend not to promote tree growth, but many old estates have yet to be studied for their trees. Notable gardens tend to cluster on the high ground to the south and east, where New Red Sandstone soils provide excellent conditions.

*Jodrell Bank Arboretum, Jodrell Bank Science Centre, Macclesfield. Manchester University; open most days. Extensive arboretum developed since 1972; National Collections of *Malus* and *Sorbus*. Largest *Acer pseudoplatanus* 'Erectum', Weeping Grey Alder, and *Alnus lanata*.

Marton, Congleton. Largest Sessile Oak (framentary), in garden in Oak Lane.

*Ness Botanic Gardens, Neston Road, Ness. University of Liverpool; open daily. A great variety of younger trees, especially *Betula*, *Salix* and *Sorbus*.

Tatton Park, Knutsford. NT; open most days. Large historic gardens and arboretum. Tallest Bay Willow in 1983.

Cornwall and Scilly

The mild winters but comparatively warm, sunny summers of the south coast offer special conditions for tree growth, and the gardens clustering in the shelter of the wooded inlets here have specialised in growing tender species since the 18th century. The north and interior of the county have little woodland and few notable gardens. Most conifers thrive in the high humidity but there is seldom enough depth of shelter for them to grow tall. The list here if anything underestimates the horticultural importance of the county's gardens, many of which have not had their rare trees comprehensively measured for some years.

Alverton, Penzance. Largest Pindo Palm (private garden).

*Antony House, Torpoint, Plymouth. NT and Carew Pole Garden Trust; open most days except winter. Extensive woodland garden. Largest Loquat (4403; 1991); tallest *Magnolia campbellii* 'Charles Raffill' (1991); tallest Cork Oak (1988).

*Boconnoc, Lostwithiel. Woodland garden (open most days), and one of the most important surviving deer parks. Largest Japanese Red Cedar and Japanese White Pine (cricket field).

Bosahan, Manaccan, Helston. Open by arrangement. Mature valley garden with tender trees. Tallest Tarata; largest and tallest Variegated Taratas; largest *Prunus* 'Gyoiko' (1985).

**Caerhays Castle, Gorran, St Austell. Open on weekdays in spring. The biggest collection of very rare and tender trees in Britain (mainly collected in China early in the 20th century), filling woodlands which stretch down to the sea. National Collection of *Magnolia*.
Largest Campbell Maple (26545; 1991).
Largest and tallest Forrest's Maples (26918 and 26919; 1991).
Tallest Giraldi's Maple (Pound Corner, 1984).

Largest Henry's Maple (1984).
Largest Maximowicz's Maple (1984).
Largest Wilson's Horse Chestnut (1991).
Largest and tallest trees of *Castanopsis concolor* (1984).
Tallest *Emmenopterys henryi* (1991).
Largest and tallest trees of *Ilex kingiana* (1984).
Largest *I. perado* var. *platyphylla* (1984).
Largest *Ligustrum confusum* (1984).
Tallest *Lindera megaphylla* (1984).
Largest and tallest trees of *Lithocarpus cleistocarpus* (1984).
Largest *L. henryi* (1975).
Largest *L. pachyphyllus* (1984).
Tallest Chinese Evergreen Magnolia (1993).
Largest *Magnolia nitida* (Donkey Field, 1984).
Tallest Willow-leaved Magnolia (26441; 1991).
Tallest Sargent's Magnolia (1984).
Largest *M. sargentiana* var. *robusta* (1984).
Largest Sprenger's Magnolia (1984).
Tallest Veitch's Magnolia (1984).
Largest *Manglietia hookeri* (1984).
Largest *M. insignis* (1984).
Largest *Meliosma beaniana* (1984).
Largest *M. pungens* (1984).
Largest *Michelia doltsopa* (26797; 1991).
Largest *Neolitsea sericea* (1984).
Largest Silver Beech (1984).
Largest Giant Osmanthus (1984).
Largest Maritime Pine (1984).
Largest Japanese Evergreen Oak (26417; 1991).
Tallest *Quercus crassifolia* (1984).
Largest *Q. glauca* (1984).
Largest and tallest trees of *Q. lamellosa* (1984).
Largest *Q. oxyodon* (1984).
Tallest *Q. phillyreoides* (1984).
Largest Folgner's Whitebeam (1984).
Largest and tallest trees of *Stuartia pteropetiolata* (1984).
Largest *Styrax hookeri* (1984).

*Carclew, Perran-ar-Worthal, Falmouth. NGS open days. Fine old trees: largest Golden Larch; tallest Lucombe Oak (1989).

*Chyverton, Zelah. Open by appointment in summer. Many rare plantings, including magnolias bred by the owners, the Holman family. Largest *Magnolia* 'Buzzard', *M. dawsoniana* 'Chyverton' and *M.* 'Treve Holman'.

Coldrennick, Menheniot. One of the largest Cork Oaks (1992).

Enys, Penryn, Falmouth. Largest Mockernut Hickory; tallest Totara.

Ferry Farm, Harewood, Calstock. Largest European White Elm (1995).

Planes are the only trees which after 300 years can still look youthful. All appreciate a rich, moist soil. Old Oriental Planes are at once grotesque and delicate, with fresh-green snowflake-shaped leaves and bulging boles flaking in jigsaw patterns. The London Plane is more exclusive as a big tree to the hottest areas. (Its American parent, the Buttonwood, is scarcely cultivable in the short, uncertain summers of northern Europe.) The oldest, like the 1680 original at the Bishop's Palace, Ely, Cambridgeshire, are continuing to grow with undiminished vigour.

The tallest Chusan Palms, at Trebah gardens, Cornwall.

*Fox Rosehill Gardens, Melville Road, Falmouth. Small public park. Largest Queen Palm.

*Glendurgan, Mawnan Smith, Falmouth. NT; open most days through summer. Sub-tropical gardens developed since the 1820s. *Populus* 'Androscoggin' – fastest tree to 24m.

*Heligan, St Ewe. 'The Lost Gardens', restored since 1991; open daily. Largest Dove Tree (walled garden), Japanese Black Pine and Totara.

Lamorran House, Upper Castle Road, St Mawes. Regular open days. (Largest Oriental Thuja in 1928.)

*Lanhydrock, Bodmin. NT; open daily. Many rare trees have been grown here since 1634. Largest *Magnolia campbellii* ssp. *mollicomata* (in front of thatched cottage).

Menabilly, St Austell. Largest Heart-leaved Silver Gum (1984).

Mount Edgcumbe Country Park, Cremyll, Torpoint. One of the largest Cork Oaks (300m E of House).

*Pencarrow, Washway, Bodmin. Open daily in summer. The remnants of a pinetum with some very early plantings (1995). Largest Chinese Fir (504) and Tiger-tail Spruce (181).

Penjerrick, Budock, Falmouth. Regularly open; rare trees in the Upper Garden. (Largest Mourning Cypress in 1928.)

Rosuic, Coverack. The Great Elm of Rosuic (Cornish Elm), in the hamlet (1995.)

Scorrier House, Redruth. Open by appointment. Largest Summit Cedar (Walled Garden).

*Trebah, Mawnan Smith, Falmouth. Open daily. Spectacular valley garden, running down to the sea and developed since the 1840s. Largest Hardy Tree Fern (middle of fernery between Beach Path and Zigzag); tallest Peruvian Nutmeg (198); one of the largest Totaras (150); tallest Chusan Palm (uppermost of three in valley).

Tregothnan Botanic Garden, Truro. Open to parties by appointment. Many rare and tender trees. Largest Cretan Maple; largest *Euonymus fimbriatus*; tallest *E. lucidus*; largest Monterey Pine (New Drive); largest Snowbell Tree; tallest Californian Nutmeg; largest *Weinmannia trichosperma*.

**Tregrehan, Par. Open most days in spring. A woodland garden with a great variety principally of conifers.
Largest *Abies alba* f. *pyramidalis* (5173).
Tallest *Chamaecyparis obtusa* 'Lycopodioides' (5163).
Tallest *C. o.* 'Tetragona Aurea' (Loderi Walk, 5150).
Largest Golden Thread Cypress (5128).
Largest *Cryptomeria japonica* 'Viminalis' (5168).
Largest Chinese Fir (5203).
Largest *Cupressus lusitanica* var. *benthamii* (valley; 5154).
Largest Dove Tree (5123).
Largest and tallest Nymans Eucryphias (5143 and 5134).
Tallest Maidenhair Tree (bridge; 5209).
Tallest Red Beech (5140).
Tallest Black Beech (5131).
Largest Sargent Spruce (5222).
Largest Jelecote Pine (5164).
Tallest Totara (5151).
Tallest *Podocarpus totara* var. *hallii* (5170).
Tallest Algerian Oak (5064).
Tallest Lea's Oak (Yew Walk, 5029).
Largest *Quercus semecarpifolia* (5061).
Tallest Cork Oak (garden).
Tallest Irish Yew (sixth from N end in Yew Walk).
Tallest Japanese Thuja (5157).
Largest Hiba (5055).

*Trelissick, Feock, Truro. NT; open most days. Many rarities in the garden dell. Tallest Hardy Tree Fern (19230; 1991).

*Trengwainton, Penzance. NT; open most days. A range of tender trees. Largest Campbell's Magnolia, and 'Charles Raffill'.

*Tresco Abbey, Tresco, Scilly. Open daily. Spectacular range of tender plants; many of the larger trees were blown down in the January 1990 storm. National collection of *Acacia*. Tallest Chilean Myrtle; largest and tallest New Zealand Christmas Trees (Eucalyptus terrace and Table Stone) – in 1987.

Trevorick, Perran-ar-Worthal, Falmouth. Largest Pignut (pond).

Trewidden, Buryas Bridge, Penzance. Open most days in spring; a range of rare trees. Largest Japanese Big-leaved Magnolia.

**Trewithen, Grampound Road, Truro. Open daily through summer. 'Trewithen' means 'the house of the trees', and the gardens are famed for their many rare specimens.
Tallest *Acer campbellii* ssp. *flabellatum* var. *yunnanense* (1985).
Largest *A. laxiflorum* (1987).
Largest *A. rubescens* (1987).

Veteran stool of Common Alder in Geltsdale, Cumbria.

Largest *Eucryphia moorei* (1987).
Largest *Ilex cyrtura* (1985).
Largest *Magnolia campbellii* ssp. *mollicomata* (1995).
Largest Sargent's Magnolia (1987).
Largest Sprenger's Magnolia (1995).
Largest *Quercus leucotrichophora* (1993).
Largest Rehder Tree (1987).
Largest Sargent's Rowan (1985).
Largest Chinese Stuartia (1995).

Cumbria

Derrick Holdsworth's thorough study of Cumbria's notable trees show the champions clustering in the well wooded Furness Fells in the far south, where the Lakeland scenery attracted many Victorian gardeners. The coasts are mild, while the Lakes' high rainfall is ideal for many conifers (though as shelter is at a premium there are few very tall trees). The wilder countryside across the north of the county has little old woodland and few big estates.

Barrow House, Borrowdale, Keswick. Youth Hostel. Tallest Common Lime.
Bell Beck, Rusland, Newbybridge. Tallest Small-leaved

Lime (E bank, 100m from road, at SD331894).
Brathay Hall Outdoor Centre, Ambleside. Tallest Cock's Comb Beech.
Dalemain Historic House and Garden, Dacre, Penrith. Open most days. Largest Grecian Fir (end of terrace).
Dallam Park, Milnthorpe. Open access. Largest Small-leaved Lime (SD493810).
Eden Hall, Penrith. Largest Cedar of Lebanon; tallest Eastern Hemlock.
Geltsdale Castle, Castle Carrock. Largest coppiced Alder (NE bank of River Gelt, at NY577537).
High Close, Grasmere; NY338052. NT. Largest Siberian Spruce (unconfirmed).
*Holker Hall, Cark. Open most days (pronounced 'Hooker'). The woodland garden contains many rare trees and the National Collection of *Styracaceae*. Largest Tarajo (garden just W of Hall); largest *Robinia kelseyi* (garden, E corner); one of the largest Common Limes (garden, SW corner).
Hopefield House, Lowick, Ulverston. Tallest Cut-leaved Walnut (roadside).
*Hutton-in-the-Forest, Penrith. Open most days; one

of the few notable gardens north of the Lakes. Tallest Eugene's Poplar, 'Robusta' Poplar, and Cricket-bat Willow.

Lancrigg Hotel, Easedale, Grasmere. Tallest Golden Moon Maple (house end, above path), and *Chamaecyparis obtusa* 'Crippsii' (by water).

Lingholm, Keswick. Largest Norway Spruce.

Monk Coniston, Coniston. HF Holidays. Some big old conifers. Tallest Pindrow Fir; largest Chinese Red Cedar (above gate).

*Muncaster Castle, Ravenglass. Open daily. Mild coastal garden most noted for its rhododendrons; many unusual trees.
Largest *Castanopsis cuspidata* (A595 near church).
Largest *Cryptomeria japonica* 'Spiralis' (drive fork near stables).
Largest *Eucryphia moorei* (W of Castle).
Tallest *Ilex* x *altaclarensis* 'Hendersonii' (1991).
Largest Fishtail Magnolia (drive, mid).
Largest *M.* x *veitchii* 'Isca' (W of Castle).
Largest and tallest Coigues (SW of Castle).
Tallest Roblé Beech (grove near Castle).
Largest Mountain Beech (steps near plant centre).
Tallest *Rhododendron falconeri* (W from maze).

Patterdale. Tallest and largest Mountain Pines (St James' church).

Penny Bridge, Ulverston. One of the largest Ashes (at SD306840).

Romney Gardens, Kendal. Public park. Largest Lock's Elm (hybrid?; riverbank, first from Romney Bridge).

Rydal Hall, Ambleside. 'The Rydale Chestnut' – one of the largest Sweet Chestnuts.

Rydal Mount, Ambleside. Open daily; William Wordsworth's last home. Tallest Fern-leafed Beech.

Sedgwick House, Kendal. Tallest *Ilex aquifolium* 'Crispa'.

Stagshaw Garden, Ambleside. NT; open daily in spring. Tallest *Sorbus* 'Joseph Rock'.

Storrsthwaite, Bowness-on-Windermere. Largest Fern-leafed Beech.

Thirlmere, Keswick. Tallest Common Silver Fir (W side of the road under the shelter of High Seat, at NY304171 near the forestry car park), and also one of the largest (follow the signs to the 'Giant Tree').

White Crags, Ambleside. Tallest Blue Douglas Fir.

White Moss Common, Grasmere. Tallest Elder (NY346062).

Winderwath, Penrith. Late Victorian gardens; NGS open days. Tallest Bird Cherry.

Wray Castle, Low Wray, Ambleside. NT; gardens open daily. Largest Cock's Comb Beech.

Derbyshire

Old estates such as Melbourne and Kedleston cluster in the southern lowlands; on the sheltered side of the Peak District, only Chatsworth boasts rare and mature trees. Historically, industrial pollution has limited the growth of the conifers that would otherwise thrive on the higher ground.

*Chatsworth House, Edensor, Bakewell. Open daily through summer; 40ha of historic gardens under the shelter of the Peak District. Tallest Bosnian Pine (near Grotto Pond, behind seat), and Macedonian Pine (pinetum).

Darley Dale church. One of the largest Yews (S of church).

Derby Arboretum, Arboretum Square, Derby. Public park: Britain's first to be designed as a tree collection, in 1839. Tallest American Lime (N of fountain; 10 on tree trail).

Elvaston Castle Country Park, Borrowash Road, Elvaston. On the site of vast early 19th century gardens. (Weeping Ash grafted at 27m, 1906).

Devon

A large and diverse county with a great range of champions. Sheltered coves along the 'Riviera coast' in the south are exceptionally mild. In the relatively warm and sunny east around Exeter and Sidmouth, partly protected by Dartmoor, the rich New Red Sandstone soils and Jurassic limestones grow parkland trees and field oaks of exceptional size, and there is a concentration of notable old gardens. Huge conifers, notable hereabouts in the mid 20th century, are now largely confined to wooded valleys on the wetter south and west slopes of Dartmoor and Exmoor – a rolling, deeply rural countryside with few big estates. The north coast is comparatively rugged, with less shelter.

Balfour Manor, Sidmouth. (The garden has since been developed.) Tallest Momi Fir in 1979.

Bickham House, Kenn. NGS open days. Largest *Eucalyptus acaciaformis* (walled garden).

*Bicton College, East Budleigh, Exmouth. Arboretum open daily. Agricultural College, approached through historic parkland along the celebrated 1844 Monkey Puzzle avenue; the 1960s arboretum has many rare trees. National Collection of *Pittosporum*. Largest *Eucalyptus mooreana* (lower arboretum); largest *Populus* x *canadensis* 'Serotina de Selys' (top of Aldergrove nature area).

**Bicton Park Botanical Gardens, East Budleigh, Exmouth. Open daily. Included in the gardens are Bicton's formal gardens, its old pinetum and the Edwardian

---

The Turkey Oak has made itself very much at home here, preferring lighter sandy soils than most oaks but growing happily on chalk and in maritime exposure. It has now found its way into conservationists' bad books by hosting alternate generations of the Knopper-gall Wasp, which lays its eggs in the acorns of English Oak and turns the acorns into inedible, infertile galls – to the misfortune of animals like Jays and Badgers for whom acorns are a staple. The biggest Turkey Oaks, such as the champion at Knightshayes, are in south-east Devon, where deep acid soils combine with warm summers and reasonable humidity.

extension which grows many of Ernest Wilson's original introductions from China.

Tallest Grecian Fir (Pinetum valley; 320).

Largest *Chamaecyparis obtusa* 'Albospica' (Pinetum/Italian Garden; 316).

Tallest and largest *C. o.* 'Aurea' (bonfire site by Wilson Collection; 389, and Italian Garden; 160).

Largest Golden Leylandii (in hedge below gate).

Largest Gowen Cypress (Wilson Collection, top; 441).

Largest *Cupressus macrocarpa* 'Coneybearii' (Dwarf Conifers – above cascade; 858).

Largest *Liriodendron tulipifera* 'Cortortum' (American Garden; 74).

Largest Tupelo (American Garden; 70).

Tallest *Picea abies* 'Clanbrassiliana' (Pinetum/dam; 372).

Tallest Durango Pine (Pinetum above crazy golf; 775).

Largest Short-leaf Pine (Pinetum, top; 552).

Largest Bosnian Pine (Pinetum, top; 560).

Largest Loblolly Pine (Pinetum, top; 533).

Largest Scrub Pine (Pinetum above crazy golf; 768).

Largest Mexican Douglas Fir (roadside by chapel; 2).

Largest Oregon Oak (Oak Grove; 734).

Tallest Holm Oak (Oak Grove – back fence; 714).

Largest Weeping Pyranean Oak (Oak Grove – back fence; labelled *Q. cerris*; 715).

Castle Hill, Filleigh, South Molton. Some very big conifers. Largest Sitka Spruce (1989).

Cockington Court, Cockington, Paignton. Extensive arboretum. Largest Tarata (1984).

*Coleton Fishacre, Brownstone Road, Kingswear. NT; open most days except in winter. This mild coastal garden was begun in 1925 and includes many rare trees. Largest Waterer's Cotoneaster.

Combe House Hotel, Gittisham. Small wild garden. Largest Chinese Necklace Poplar; tallest Variegated Turkey Oak (reverting).

Dartington Hall, Dartington. Dartington Hall Trust; open daily. Tallest *Prunus* 'Ichiyo' (1995).

Eggesford Forest, Lapford, Crediton. FC. Largest Douglas Fir (near the ruins of Eggesford House).

**Endsleigh, Milton Abbot, Tavistock. Endsleigh Charitable Trust; regularly open; the house is a hotel. Many rare and exceptionally large trees in the wooded valley of the Tamar under Dartmoor.

Largest Caucasian Fir (New Piece, 35; 1990).

Largest Oliver Maple (Upper Georgia, 1990).

Largest Chinese Red Birch (garage, 41; 1990).

Largest and tallest Himalayan Birches (?; 1995).

Tallest Golden Deodar (pondside, 1995).

Tallest Katsura (Carriage Drive, 1995).

Largest Fern-spray Cypress (1991).

Largest Thread Cypress (1991).

Tallest Japanese Red Cedar (North Georgia, S; 1995).

Tallest Weeping Beech (1995).

Tallest Mountain Snowdrop Tree (Rockery, 23; 1990).

Largest Weeping Holly (Upper Georgia; 1990).

Largest Castor Aralia (west of pair by stream, 9; 1995).

Tallest Yulan (1995).

Largest *Picea abies* f. *monstrosa* (1995).

Largest Serbian Spruce (New Piece, 1990).

Tallest Japanese White Pine (hotel; 1995).

Escot Country Park and Gardens, Feniton. Open daily through summer. Largest Japanese Maple (N of adventure playground); tallest Tree of Heaven (private lawn); largest *Chamaecyparis lawsoniana* 'Albomaculata' (private garden bank).

Exeter Crematorium, Topsham Road, Exeter. Largest *Ulmus* 'Regal' (?).

*Exeter University, Exeter. Open access. In the centre of the campus, the gardens of Reed Hall were planted with many rare trees in the 1860s. Largest Santa Lucia Fir (bank behind Reed Hall).

Gnaton Hall, Yealmpton. Tallest Hondo Spruce (in 1978).

Grey Timbers, Chapple Lane, Bovey Tracey (Eucalyptus nursury in 1979). Tallest Broad-leafed Sally.

Haldon Grange, Dunchideock. Largest Bhutan Pine.

Honiton. Original *Aesculus hippocastanum* 'Honiton Gold' (Offwell lane hedge just above A35, at ST174002).

Kenn church. One of the largest Yews (SE of church).

*Killerton, Silverton, Exeter. NT; open daily. A large historic garden with many fine and rare trees, set in ancient parkland. Largest *Betula platyphylla* (top of garden slope, 11968); largest *Castanea* x *neglecta* (garden, lower W; 12195); largest Chinese Sweet-gum (garden, C; 12069); tallest Tulip Tree (Chapel; 40707); largest *Magnolia campbellii* 'Lanarth' (garden, E edge; 11916); tallest Hop Hornbeam (Chapel); tallest *Photinia serratifolia* (upper garden slope; 11936); largest Deciduous Camellia (garden, C; 12076); largest *Taiwania cryptomerioides* (garden, C; 2798); tallest *Tilia miqueliana* (garden, C).

*Knightshayes, Bolham, Tiverton. NT; open daily through summer. Many unusual trees. Largest *Acer platanoides* 'Schwedleri' (Park; 14089); tallest Paper-bark Birch (below terrace, 14104); largest *Cornus* 'Norman Hadden' (14301); tallest Turkey Oak (24476).

Lindridge Park, Bishopsteignton. Residential development. Tallest Tansy-leaved Thorn (centre of old garden), and Wentworth Weeping Ash (old garden, mid S).

Lower Coombe Royal, Kingsbridge. A historic garden with many early plantings. Largest *Chamaecyparis pisifera* 'Squarrosa', Butternut, and Yulan.

Mamhead, Kenton, Exeter. Tallest *Prunus sargentii* 'Fastigiata' (plantation SE of church); one of the largest Yews (NW of the private church).

*Marwood Hill, Marwood, Barnstaple. Open daily. 6-ha garden full of rare plants; large plantings of *Betula*, *Eucalyptus*, *Magnolia* and *Salix*. Largest Japanese Angelica Tree.

Overbecks Museum and Garden, Sharpitor, Salcombe. NT; open daily. A coastal garden with many tender trees. Largest Camphor Tree (Statue Garden).

Paignton Zoo Environmental Park, Totnes Road, Paignton. Whitley Wildlife Trust; open daily. Developed since the 1940s as a combined zoo and botanic gardens. Tallest Loquat (1984).

Payhembury church. One of the largest Yews (NE of church).

Phear Park, Exmouth. Public park – old parkland with

The London Planes of Bryanston School, Dorset, are exceptional for their height.

huge oaks. Largest Lucombe Oaks.

Powderham Castle, Kenton, Exeter. Castle grounds open most days. (Tallest Wheatley Elm in 1970.)

Rockbeare Park, Rockbeare, Exeter. Largest White Poplar (stream at SY028941).

*Rosemoor Garden, Great Torrington. RHS; open daily; 18ha of rare plants. National Collections of *Cornus* and *Ilex*.

Saltram House, Plympton, Plymouth. NT; open most days. Large historic gardens. Largest *Acer palmatum* 'Osakazuki' (1984).

Shute Barton, Shute, Axminster. NT; manor house open regularly except in winter. Largest Turkey Oak (N drive, on footpath).

Sidbury Manor, Sidbury. Many rare trees planted from the late 19th century. Largest Cider Gum, Sikkim Spruce,

and Endlicher Pine.

*Stone Lane Gardens, Chagford. National Collections of wild-collected Alders and Birches, developed over the last two decades.

Strete Ralegh House, Whimple, Exeter. One of the largest Monterey Cypresses (back lawn).

Teigngrace. One of the largest English Oaks – 'the Prince of Orange's Oak' (lane in village).

Thorn House, Wembury. Tallest Chinese Tree Privet (in 1977).

Westbrook House, Bampton, Tiverton. One of the largest London Planes (1986).

Westlake, Paignton. Largest Oyster Bay Pine (?) and tallest Camphor Tree (1984).

Whitcombe, Kenn, Exeter. Largest Narrow-leaved Black Peppermint (opposite house).

Woodhouse, Uplyme, Lyme Regis. Remnants of a pinetum which grew many conifers of great height. Tallest Prince Albert's Yew.

Woolborough Hill, Newton Abbott. Largest Yellow-wood (garden).

Dorset

Chalk downland is the dominant landscape feature, but many of the finest trees are concentrated in old estates on congenial sandy soils in the south-east, around Wimborne Minster and Wareham; in the west, towards Bridport and Beaminster; and between the downs and the Blackmoor Vale in the north. Abbotsbury is the only large gardens along the mild but often exposed coast.

*Abbotsbury Subtropical Gardens, Abbotsbury. Open daily. Many tender trees in a sheltered valley by the sea. Largest *Ilex fargesii* (dog's grave, 1980); largest *Photinia nussia* (1980); largest *Picconia excelsa* (dog's grave, 1993); largest Karo (1993); tallest Caucasian Wingnut (valley, 1993); tallest *Pyrus elaeagrifolia* (Eucalyptus Walk, 1980).

Bryanston School, Blandford Forum. Tallest London Planes.

Canford School, Wimborne Minster. National Collections of *Cercidiphyllum* and *Juglans*. Largest Sweet Chestnut; tallest Japanese Walnut (far end of arboretum); tallest Texan Walnut (far end of arboretum).

Carey House, Wareham. Largest Maritime Pine (Middle Copse Cottage).

*Central Gardens, Bournemouth. Series of public parks running along the valley through Bournemouth. A golden Chinese Privet (in 1985).

Cerne Abbey, Cerne Abbas. Largest Golden Giant Sequoia (1996).

Deans Court, Wimborne Minster. Open days. Largest Swamp Cypress.

Duntish Court, Duntish. One of the largest Oriental Planes (1986).

*Forde Abbey, Chard. Open daily. Large gardens and arboretum. Largest and tallest Table Dogwoods (Arboretum); tallest *Populus* 'TT37' (field, W).

Gaunts, Wimborne Minster. Tallest Bull Bay in 1973.

Hurn Court (Heron Court) Hurn, Christchurch. One of the largest Hornbeams (house front, 1985).

*Melbury House, Melbury Sampford, Yeovil. Occasional open days. Historic arboretum and deer park. Tallest Wilson's Horse Chestnut (Pleasure Grounds); largest Caucasian Wingnut (Valley Garden); tallest Algerian Oak (Pleasure Grounds); largest Caucasian Oak (Pleasure Grounds); tallest Downy Oak (Valley Garden, N edge); one of the largest English Oaks (park; 'Billy Wilkins'); tallest Red-twigged Lime (Pleasure Grounds).

*Minterne, Minterne Magna, Dorchester. Open daily; large historic garden with varied younger plantings. Tallest Thread Cypress (1996).

Silton, Gillingham. 'Wyndham's Oak' – one of the largest English Oaks (1982).

Stapehill Nursery, Stapehill, Wimborne Minster. Largest X *Cupressocyparis leylandii* 'Skinner's Green' (1984).

Woolland church. One of the largest Yews (S of church).

Durham

A rather cold, dry county with few traditions of arboriculture; the rather ad hoc industrial sprawl in the east has no large public parks.

Brignall, Barnard Castle. One of the largest Ashes (field corner above ruins of old church).

Croxdale Hall Park, Spennymoor. Largest Wild Crab (middle of field NE of Hall near footpath, at NZ273380).

East Durham and Houghall College, Durham. Unusual 1960s plantings. Largest Yellow-berried Rowan (1987).

Thwaite Hall, Cotherstone, Barnard Castle. One of the largest Sycamores (garden).

East Sussex

The windswept downs owe less to trees than almost any other southern English landscape, but feature prominently in the list of champions thanks to the Dutch Elm Disease Control Zone established by the County Council between Eastbourne and Portslade in the late 1960s. The sandy hills of the High Weald are densely wooded, with some fine collections. Brighton and Hastings both enjoy remarkable traditions of municipal arboriculture.

*Alexandra Park, Hastings. Probably Britain's finest public park for trees, developed since 1864 along 3km of sheltered valleys; notable oak collection. Many rarities planted in Thorpe's Wood in 1935.
Largest *Alnus glutinosa* 'Quercifolia' (pumping station/ miniature railway).
Largest Japanese Silver Birch (Thorpe's Wood, W fence).
Largest Fastigiate Birch (Oak Bank).
Largest *Crataegus* x *grignonensis* (Thorpe's Wood, mid).
Largest *Fagus sylvatica* f. *latifolia* (beech collection, Harmer's Ponds).
Largest *Prunus* 'Shibayama' (W from bandstand, over bridge).
Tallest Wild Pear (S bank W of bandstand).
Largest *Sorbus thibetica* 'John Mitchell' (above swings in Shornden Wood).
Largest *Taxus baccata* 'Adpressa' (under Buckshole dam).
Largest trees of *Thuja plicata* 'Pyramidalis' (Shornden

Avenue, and Dordrecht Way SW gate).
Largest American Lime (bowling green bank).

Ashburnham Place, Ninfield, Battle. Ashburnham Christian Trust; NGS open days. Ancient wooded park with some rare Victorian plantings. Tallest Snowy Mespil (Burrage Wood lakeside path, mid); tallest Maritime Pine (outside Winter Garden, S).

Banks Farm, Barcombe. NGS open days. Largest Osier (garden).

Beauport Park, Battle Road, St Leonards-on-Sea. One of Britain's most ambitious Victorian arboreta; long neglected and overgrown and traversed by one footpath. Largest Cut-leaved Hornbeam (behind Riding School); one of the largest Monterey Cypresses (behind 13th tee); one of the largest Irish Yews (13th tee/Swan Pond).

Benfield Way, Portslade. Largest *Ulmus* x *hollandica* 'Pitteursii' (street tree; 1998).

Brede. One of the largest Hornbeams (hedge just N of village, at TQ830192).

Brighton University. Tallest *Ulmus wallichiana* (S of Cockcroft Building, Moulsecoomb; largest survivor in group).

Broadstone Warren, Wych Cross. Many old pollards. Largest Beech (left of footpath from Ashdown Forest Centre toward Forest Row, at TQ433328).

Buxted Park, Buxted, Uckfield. Victorian Hotel garden; footpaths cross the ancient deer park. Largest *Ilex aquifolium* 'Aurea Marginata' (garden, SE); largest Hungarian Oak (park by lake); one of the largest Broad-leaved Limes (park S of lake).

Carden Park, Carden Avenue, Brighton. Public park. Largest *Ulmus minor* 'Christine Buisman' (near playground, 1998); tallest Golden English Elm (N side of football pitch, 1998).

Cedar Gardens, London Road, Brighton. Largest Dutch Elm (street tree).

Charleston Manor, Litlington. Largest Filbert.

Cottesmore St Mary's School, Upper Drive, Hove. Largest *Ulmus glabra* 'Atropurpurea' (near entrance, 1993).

Courtlands, Ashton Rise, Brighton. Tallest *Ulmus* x *hollandica* 'Commelin' (municipal planting; 1998).

Crespin Way, Brighton. Linear arboretum of rare elm clones planted above the railwayline in the 1960s. Tallest *Ulmus* '202' (1995) and *U.* x *hollandica* 'Bea Schwarz' (1998).

Crowhurst church. One of the largest Yews (S of church).

Donald Hall Road, Bristol Gate, Brighton. Largest Belgian Elm (third street tree, 2001).

Dyke Road Drive, Brighton. Largest *Ulmus minor* 'Purpurea' (street tree, 1995).

Dyke Road Park, Dyke Road Drive, Hove. Public park. Largest Golden English Elm (1997).

Dyke Road Place, Brighton. Largest Golden Wych Elms (bottom street trees in avenue).

Eastbourne. Largest White Almond (front garden of 18, Rosebery Avenue).

East Brighton Park, Wilson Avenue, Whitehawk. Public park. Largest Winged Elm (SW entrance; 375).

Eridge Park, Eridge Green, Tunbridge Wells. Tallest Wild Crab (pinetum).

Our largest known Beech grows in private woodland in Frant, East Sussex.

Firle Park, Firle, Lewes. Largest Mandshurian Walnut (park below House, on footpath, 1994).

Frant. Largest Beech (private woodland at TQ572352).

Happy Valley Park, Woodingdean, Brighton. Public park. Largest *Ulmus* '260' (S central group, at TQ358047, in 2001).

Haremere Hall, Etchingham. One of the largest Ashes (field hedge at TQ721254).

Hastings. Largest Double Cherry Plum (back garden in Linton Road).

Hastings Cemetery, The Ridge. Largest *Sorbus decipiens* (Ivyhouse Lane fence).

Herstmonceux Castle, Herstmonceux. Queen's University, Ottawa; open most days. Old parkland; unusual trees planted in the 1950s. Largest *Cotoneaster frigidus* 'Cornubia' (N, by belvedere); largest Black Gums (line by moat).

Higham House, Salehurst. (Largest Cedar of Lebanon, blown 1987.)

Highleigh, Grove Hill, Brighton. Largest *Ulmus* x *hollandica* 'Dauvessei' (municipal planting; 1998).

Hodshrove Place, Brighton. Largest *Ulmus villosa* (municipal planting; 1999).

Holy Trinity church, St Helier's Avenue, Hove. Largest *Ulmus* x *hollandica* 'Bea Schwarz' (1994).

Hove Cemetery, Old Shoreham Road. Largest *Ulmus* x *hollandica* 'Klemmeri' (2001).

Hove Recreation Ground, Old Shoreham Road.

Various rare elms surround the ground. Largest Slippery Elm (first elm opposite and W of Bishop's Road junction, at TQ292061).

Jevington church. Largest Ulmus glabra 'Serpentina'.

Lawn Memorial Cemetery, Woodingdean, Brighton. Elm clones planted in the 1960s. Largest *Ulmus* '148' (W entrance, 2001).

Linton Gardens, Linton Road, Hastings. Public park. Largest Golden Lime (in line).

Longhill School, Falmer Road, Rottingdean. Largest *Ulmus wallichiana* (Nursery centre, 1994).

Lullington. Largest *Ulmus* '215' (in Long Bridge Road Elm line, at TQ524033; 1997); tallest English Elm (Long Bridge Road).

Newick Park, Buxted. Largest Black Cherry (SW bank of dell).

Oaklands House, Pestalozzi Children's Village, Sedlescombe. Largest False Acacia (back lawn).

Old Malling Deanery, Lewes. Two of the largest Wild Black Poplars (arboretum field by river, viewable from far bank).

Old Roar Ghyll, St Helens Road, St Leonards-on-Sea. Public woodland. Tallest Alder (in group on E bank, 200m N of road bridge).

Palmeira Avenue, Hove. Tallest *Ulmus minor* 'Christine Buisman' (street tree, by new flats S of 27).

Paradise Plantation, Paradise Drive, Eastbourne. Public downland. Tallest Wheatley Elm (by road).

Park Crescent, Brighton. Residents' garden. Tallest Dutch Elm (1994).

Parsonage Farm, Udimore. Largest Wild Service (field by drive at TQ872188, visible from road).

Pashley Manor, Ticehurst. Open most days. Tallest *Prunus* 'Kanzan' (back lawn, 1994).

Penns-in-the-Rocks, Lye Green, Groombridge. NGS open days. Tallest *Tilia platyphyllos* 'Fastigiata' (behind house, 1994).

*Preston Park, London Road, Brighton. Historic public park; magnificent line of Wheatley Elms. Largest *Ulmus* '28' (E copse, 1.031); largest *U.* '297' (E copse, 1.033); tallest Cornish Elm (W line, 1.113); largest Wheatley Elm (in W line, 1.123); largest English Elms, 'The Preston Twins' (London Road side).

Robertsbridge. Largest recorded Bat Willow (felled 1902).

Ryecroft, Whitehawk Road, Brighton. Tallest *Ulmus* 'Coolshade' (municipal planting; 1996).

St Leonards-on-Sea. Largest Winter Cherry (front garden of 10, Combermere Road).

Seaford. Largest Golden Siberian Elm (garden in Downsview Road, 1997).

*Sheffield Park, Fletching. NT; open most days. Large landscaped gardens; most of the rare trees were planted from 1909-34, with an emphasis on autumn colour. Largest Young's Weeping Birch (SE of waterfall); largest *Cedrus libani* 'Comte de Dijon' (S drive near cottages); largest *Chamaecyparis lawsoniana* 'Filiformis' (Conifer Walk, NE); tallest Tupelo (E Park); tallest Maritime Pine (N shore of Second Lake). One of the largest Cider Gums grows over the private House's fence.

The veteran English Oak in the centre of Great Yeldham, Essex, died in 1949 but was preserved in masonry. The oak planted to commemorate Prince Edward's marriage in 1863 is now taking its place.

*Stanmer Park, Falmer. Public park. Old parkland and ancient woods; extensive arboretum planted in 1964-5 to test tree-growth on raw chalk. National Collection of *Ulmus*. Largest *Crataegus monogyna* 'Multiplex' (Arboretum, thorns); tallest X *Cupressocyparis leylandii* 'Stapehill' (Arboretum, elms, lower); largest Chinese Ash (Arboretum, ashes); largest Amur Lilac (Arboretum; top, mid); largest *Ulmus* '240' (Arboretum; top path above elms); largest American White Elm (Arboretum: under top path, mid); largest *U. davidiana* (Arboretum, elms, lower; ?); largest *U.* x *hollandica* 'Groeneveld' (S of mansion by drive); tallest *U. villosa* (Arboretum, elms, W).

Sussex University Campus, Stanmer Park, Falmer. Largest *Tilia platyphyllos* 'Fastigiata' (Refectory Road, by junction of Arts Road, 796), *Ulmus* '202' (S of Arts Building 'A'), *U.* x *hollandica* 'Commelin' (Great Wilkins, 1995) and *U. japonica* 'Jacan' (W of Bramber House).

Swanborough Drive, Brighton. Largest *Ulmus pumila* 'Den Haag' (street tree; 1994).

Tenantry Down Road, Brighton. Roadside plantings of rare elms. Largest *Ulmus* 'Coolshade' (1998) and *U. pumila* 'Dropmore' (1994).

Upper Larkrise Wood, Folkington, Polegate. Largest Cut-leaved Elm (TQ557039, 1995).

Winchelsea church. Largest *Crataegus laevigata* 'Punicea Flore Pleno' (S).

Woodvale Crematorium, Lewes Road, Brighton. Largest *Ulmus* x *hollandica* 'Scampstoniensis' (central drive).

Essex

An agricultural landscape with many old estates, but the uniformly clay soils and low rainfall have attracted few horticulturalists. Wild elms survive in great variety, but, like the county's other trees, have been under-studied in recent years.

Audley End, Saffron Walden. English Heritage; open most days except in winter. Fine old trees include the original Audley End Oak.

Barrington Hall, Hatfield Broadoak. 'The Great Oak' – one of the largest English Oaks (drive, 1995).

Boreham. Bat Willow – fastest tree to x170cm (plantation near village; felled).

Downham church. Largest Field Maple (1992).

Dryads Hall, Loughton. Many fine trees. Tallest True Service.

Easton Lodge, Little Easton, Great Dunmow. Gardens regularly open; in the mid 20th century the park with its ancient pollards was the home of the noted dendrologist Maynard Greville. One of the largest English Oaks (aerodrome site, 1987).

Great Waltham. (Largest Smooth-leaved Elm in 1953.)

Hatfield Forest, Bishop's Stortford. NT. Remarkable working example of a medieval forest with ancient hornbeam pollards and coppices. Tallest Black Walnut (the Warren).

Little Parndon. (Largest Variegated Smooth-leaved Elm, 1911.)

Markshall estate, Coggeshall. One of the largest Wild Services (avenue, W; 1995).

Mill House, Mill Lane, Dedham. Tallest Black Mulberry.

Terling Place, Terling, Witham. Fine tree collection. Largest Crack Willow in 1977.

Warley Place, Great Warley, Brentwood. Garden created by Ellen Willmott. Tallest Californian Bay (1996).

Writtle Park, Loves Green, Writtle. (Largest Sweet Chestnut in 1758.)

Gloucestershire

The sheltering valleys and deep soils of the Cotswolds create fine growing conditions for many taxa, and there is a great concentration of big gardens especially in the south, while the champions of several commoner trees cluster under the scarp around Stroud. In contrast, the higher humidity and acid soils of the Forest of Dean and Wye Valley in the west grow magnificent conifers. The warm and fertile vales of Berkeley and Gloucester are intensively farmed, but include the notable arboreta at Tortworth and Highnam.

Abbotswood, Cinderford, Forest of Dean. FC. (Not to be confused with Lutyens' gardens at Abbotswood near Stow.) Largest Min Fir (Blaize Bailey, at SO667119).

Ashwicke, Marshfield, Bath. Largest Siberian Crab (?; 1995).

****Batsford Arboretum**, Moreton-in-Marsh. Open daily except in winter. 20ha arboretum on the sheltered slopes of the Cotswolds, expanded in the 1960s and now with over 1500 tree and shrub taxa, immaculately labelled. National Collection of Flowering Cherries.
Largest *Acer palmatum* 'Higasayama' (upper stream; 944, G2).
Largest *A. platanoides* 'Reitenbachii' (icehouse bank; 2451, N4).
Largest *A. turkestanicum* (above lake; 544, D11).
Tallest *Betula pendula* 'Tristis' (Buddha; 1487, H1).
Largest *B. rockii* (hybrid?; above E drive; 2681, O7).
Largest *Cupressus bakeri* ssp. *matthewsii* (S of house; 636, D12).
Largest *C. corneyana* (above entrance; 796; F3).
Largest *Eucalyptus gunnii* var. *divaricata* (nursery lawn; 43, W2).
Largest Spinning Gum (S of house; 531, D11).
Tallest White Ash (bank, mid; 1712, I4).
Largest Syrian Juniper (Japanese Rest House).
Tallest Prince Rupert's Larch (above entrance; 818, F9).
Largest *Malus* 'Elise Rathke' (?; above Thatched Cottage; 1686, J1).
Tallest Siberian Spruce (above icehouse; 2349, N2).
Tallest Northern Pitch Pine (above entrance; 823, F4).
Largest *Populus lasiocarpa* var. *tibetica* (above entrance; 834, F4).
Largest *P. wilsonii* (S of Daphne; 2002, M1).
Tallest *Prunus* 'Benden' (above E drive; 2579, O4).
Tallest Valonia Oak (above icehouse; 2284, N2).

Cannop, Forest of Dean. FC. Tallest Weymouth Pine (SO605127).

Cerney House Gardens, North Cerney, Cirencester. Occasionally open. Tallest Aspen (bottom of grounds).

Chaceley. One of the largest English Oaks (in a field SW of the lane to Chaceley Stock, on the NW bank of the Severn at SO861300).

Chargrove House, Main Road, Shurdington, Cheltenham. Tallest Pear (1988).

Cheltenham College, Cheltenham. Tallest Judas Tree (right of reception, viewable from Bath Road).

Cirencester Abbey Park. Public park. Largest Golden Atlas Cedar (1989).

***Cirencester Park**. Open access to most of this huge landscaped parkland. One of the tallest Sycamores (Broad Ride); one of the tallest Ashes (Broad Ride, N, at SP014022); tallest Japanese Red Pine (Eve Pens, at SO999025) – all 1989.

Cirencester Royal Agricultural College. Largest Broad-leaved Cockspur Thorn (rugby field); largest Pissard's Plum (E of house, 1989).

Coleford, Forest of Dean. ('The Newland Oak', the largest English Oak, at Spout Farm, Newland; collapsed May 1955.)

***Colesbourne**, Cheltenham. Occasional open days. Former home of the noted dendrologist H J Elwes; many rare mature trees. Tallest Fastigiate Hornbeam; largest Eugene's Poplar; tallest Balsam Poplar.

Dyrham Park, Chippenham. NT. Historic landscaped park open daily; garden open except in winter. Largest *Fraxinus pennsylvanica* 'Aucubifolia' in 1976.

Eastwood Park, Falfield, Thornbury. One of the largest English Oaks.

Edge, Painswick. One of the largest English Oaks (field near village).

Forthampton. (Tallest English Elm, blown 1895.)

Haresfield, Hardwicke. Largest Lombardy Poplar and Pear (near village, 1993).

***Hidcote Manor Garden**, Hidcote Bartrim, Chipping Campden. NT; open most days. One of the country's most famous gardens, created by Lawrence Johnston early in the 20th century; many unusual trees. Largest Indian Horse Chestnut (stream, 1993); tallest Armenian Oak (1983).

***Highnam Court**, Highnam, Gloucester. NGS open days; the pinetum in Highnam Woods is independently owned (Churcham Pinetum). Large mature arboretum. Largest *Fagus sylvatica* 'Luteovariegata' (1992); largest Golden Ash (1992); largest Red Ash (park, N; 1988); tallest Blue Colorado Spruce (W of house, 46; 1989); largest *Populus grandidentata* (lake, 1996); largest Japanese Chestnut Oak (1988); largest and tallest trees of *Sequoia sempervirens* 'Adpressa' (Churcham Pinetum, 1984); largest *Taxus baccata* 'Dovastonii Aurea' (front of house, 1991).

Horton Court, Horton, Chipping Sodbury (1989). NT; the house is regularly open. Largest Variegated Oak; tallest Buckthorn.

Kites Nest Wood, Gloucester. Tallest Wild Service (SO766203; 1995).

***Lydney Park**, Lydney. Frequently open. Ancient parkland and fine gardens. One of the largest London Planes (drive; 1983).

Moreton-in-Marsh. Largest *Robinia pseudoacacia* 'Aurea' (St David's School; wall by playing field).

Painswick. The Rococo Gardens in the estate are open

most days. Largest Bullace (Holcombe Folly garden, 1992).

Painswick Lodge, Sheepscombe, Painswick. One of the largest Alders (SO879105; 1999).

Pitville Park, Evesham Road, Cheltenham. Public park. Tallest Thurlow Weeping Willow (1995).

Sandford Park, College Road, Cheltenham. Public park. Tallest Mop-head Acacia (1989).

Sezincote, Moreton-in-Marsh. Regularly open. Largest Weeping Hornbeam.

Shurdington. One of the largest Beeches (by footpath off A46 in parkland behind the Greenway Hotel, 1998).

*Speech House Arboretum, Coleford, Forest of Dean (Cyril Hart Arboretum). FC; arboretum and forest plots developed since 1916. Largest Cilician Fir; largest Cascara Sagrada (plot 86); largest *Sorbus hibernica* (plot 58).

Standish Hospital, Stroud Green, Stonehouse. Largest Cork Oak.

Stanway House, Stanway, Winchcombe. Historic gardens; regularly open. Tallest Female Lombardy Poplar (middle of field to W), and one of the largest Common Limes (edge of prospect) – 1982.

Staunton church, Tewkesbury. One of the largest Yews (W of church).

*Stratford Park, Stratford Road, Stroud. Public park with many fine trees. Largest Golden Deodar (riverside, 1991); largest *Prunus padus* 'Watereri' (lake, 1991); tallest *Sorbus commixta* 'Embley' (1984).

Tortworth church, Stroud. Two of the largest Sweet Chestnuts ('the Tortworth Chestnut'), and Silver Limes.

**Tortworth Court, Tortworth, Wotton-under-Edge. The remains of a huge arboretum developed through the 19th century by Lord Ducie in rivalry with his friend Lord Holford at Westonbirt. Most of the trees are accessible to the public in Leyhill Prison's arboretum (open daily) and the Tortworth Court Hotel's garden.

Largest Nikko Maple (Hotel drive, 116; 1993).

Largest Mono Maple (Market Garden area of Prison, 1988).

Largest Italian Maple (1992).

Largest Trautvetter's Maple (top of Dell, 9422; 1988).

Largest Californian Horse Chestnut (Dell, 12/610; 1988).

Largest Dawyck Beech (3/372, 1992).

Tallest Narrow-leaved Ash (Dell, 12/739; 1988).

Largest *Fraxinus paxiana* (Dell, 9/433; 1988).

Largest Phoenicean Juniper (bank, 1980).

Largest Sakhalin Cork Tree (Market Garden area of Prison, 1992).

Largest *Platanus* x *hispanica* 'Augustine Henry' (conservatory, 1973).

One of the largest Scarlet Oaks (3/370, 1987).

Tallest *Quercus faginea* (Hotel arboretum, 1973).

Largest Californian Black Oak (Market Garden area of Prison, 1988).

Largest Black Jack Oak (bank, S; 1973).

The Warren, Clanna, Hewelsfield. Tallest Hazel (1992).

Westbury Court, Westbury-on-Severn. NT; open most days except in winter. Largest Holm Oak (1993).

**Westonbirt National Arboretum, Tetbury. FC; open daily. The arboretum was begun in open farmland in 1829 by Robert Holford, utilising a pocket of sandy soils in the limestone Cotswolds. It was developed and expanded by the Holford family and then threatened with destruction until taken over by the Forestry Commission in 1956. A huge range of trees of all kinds and ages now contributes to the dramatic landscaping of the many drives and avenues. Most notable for *Acer*, *Betula* and *Sorbus*, and for the exceptional growth of many common trees; National Collection of *Salix*. An ancient woodland nature reserve within Silk Wood contains perhaps the country's oldest stool of Small-leaved Lime.

Tallest Cheng Fir (mid Willesley Drive, S, labelled *A. forrestii*; 33.1).

Largest Manchurian Fir (W Willesley Drive, S, 36.146).

Largest Sakhalin Fir (W Willesley Drive, N, 37.69).

Tallest *Acer acuminatum* (N Circular Drive, N; 20.3).

Largest *A. campestre* 'Schwerinii' (E Waste Drive, N, up slope; 45.94).

Tallest *A. cappadocicum* var. *sinicum* (shop window/Mitchell Drive; 2.66).

Largest Hornbeam Maple (W Main Drive, S; 18.64).

Tallest and largest Vine-leafed Maples (mid Mitchell Drive, N; 14.0069; N Morley Ride, W; 7.108).

Largest *A.* x *coriaceum* (E Willesley Drive, N; 40.122).

Largest Balkans Maple (mid Broad Drive, W; 43.78).

Tallest Lobel's Maple (Clay Island; 16.206).

Tallest Oregon Maple (Hollybush Gate; 23.234).

Tallest Nikko Maple (E Mitchell Drive, S; 2.22).

Largest *A. palmatum* 'Hagoromo' (Main Drive, S, by Mitchell Drive; 14.48).

Largest and tallest Moosewoods (W of shop window, 9.147, and NE of Savill Glade, 25.75).

Tallest *A. platanoides* 'Cucullatum' (mid Broad Drive, W (S tree); 43.75).

Tallest *A. p.* 'Globosum' (mid Broad Drive, W).

Tallest *A. p.* 'Schwedleri' (E Mitchell Drive/Loop Walk, labelled as the type; 3.215).

Tallest Silver Maple (Willesley Drive by Byhams Ride).

Largest Chalk Maple (S Broad Drive, E; 38.38).

Largest Birch-leaved Maple (mid Willesley Drive, S; 33.105).

Tallest Chosen Maple (Holford Ride/Specimen Avenue; 11.68).

Tallest Van Volxem's Maple (E Willesley Drive, N; 32.134).

Tallest *Aesculus* x *carnea* 'Briotii' (picnic site; 26.180).

Tallest Indian Horse Chestnut (far W Loop Walk, S; 19.170).

Largest Sunrise Horse Chestnut (offices; 23.44).

Largest and tallest Japanese Horse Chestnuts (NW Circular Drive, N; 21.0012; Clay Island/Specimen Avenue, W; 16.34).

Tallest Italian Alder (Skillings Gate; 30.111).

Largest *Alnus inokumae* (Skillings Gate; 30.107).

Tallest *Betula albo-sinensis* var. *septentrionalis* (N Circular Drive, N; 20.6).

Largest Erman's Birch (W Mitchell Drive, N; 15.148).

Largest Alaskan Birch (Circular Drive/Savill Glade, W; 24.239).

Largest *B. occidentalis* (shop window; 2.72).

Largest and tallest Grey Birches (shop window; 2.243 and 2.73).

Tallest Downy Birch (W of Jackson Avenue, mid; 4.943).

Largest American Hornbeam (Clay Island, by Specimen

Erman's Birch has already shown willing to become the biggest birch in cultivation. The champion grows on fertile limestone at Westonbirt National Arboretum.

Avenue; 16.199).

Largest *C. henryana* (N Morley Ride, E; 4.111).

Tallest Mockernut Hickory (shop window, W; 9.48).

Tallest Cut-leaved Sweet Chestnut (W Circular Drive, E, labelled as the type; 24.814).

Largest *Castanea sativa* 'Laciniata' (E Willesley Drive, S, labelled 'Aspleniifolia'; 31.784).

One of the largest Lawson Cypresses (W Main Drive, S; 18.78).

Tallest *Chamaecyparis lawsoniana* 'Blue Jacket' (E Willesley Drive, S; 31.309).

Largest *C. l.* 'Smithii' (W Main Drive/Loop Walk).

Largest *Cotoneaster multiflorus* (mid Main Drive, W; 18.19).

Largest *Crataegus schraderiana* (Pool Gate; 17.62).

Largest *C. spathulata* (mid Willesley Drive, S; 33.56).

Tallest X *Cupressocyparis notabilis* (Savill Glade, mid W; 24.322).

Tallest X *C. ovensii* (E Willesley Drive, S/Byhams Ride; 31.799).

Largest Date Plum (E Mitchell Drive, S; 2.44).

Tallest Jounama Snow Gum (S of Silk Wood ash collection; 54.21).

Tallest *Eucalyptus rodwayi* (S of Silk Wood ash collection; 54.84).

Tallest Engler's Beech (W Willesley Drive, N; 37.62).

Largest Golden Beech (The Downs, near Downs Gate; 28.114).

Largest Pumpkin Ash (E Main Drive, S; 14.16).

Tallest *Ilex macrocarpa* (W Pool Avenue, S; 12.76).

Tallest Temple Juniper (mid Specimen Avenue, N; 12.192).

Largest Meyer's Juniper (W Willesley Drive, S).

Largest Adam's Laburnum (W Waste Drive, N; 45.320).

Largest *Ligustrum sinense* (N of Waste Drive, mid; in group; 45.282.)

Largest *Magnolia campbellii* x *sprengeri* (Clay Island, W; 16.331).

Tallest Sikkim Crab (E Main Drive, S; 14.25).

Tallest Pillar Apple (N Morley Ride, W; 7.58).

Tallest *Malus* x *zumi* (E Main Drive, N; 10.133).

Tallest *Nothofagus* x *alpina* (S Palmer Ride, E; 40.29).

Tallest Ironwood (E Main Drive, S; 15.113).

Tallest Persian Ironwood (N Broad Drive, E; 43.394).

Tallest Golden Norway Spruce (E Specimen Avenue, N; 11.43).

Largest trees of *Picea abies* x *asperata* (W Willesley Drive, S; 36.1 and 2).

Largest *P. asperata* x *koyamae* (W Willesley Drive, S; 36.3).

Largest *P.* x *hurstii* (Concord Glade/Palmer Ride, W; 32.291).

Tallest *P. maximowiczii* (E Specimen Avenue, N; 11.48).

Tallest *P. purpurea* (mid Specimen Avenue, N; 12.210).

Largest Lodgepole Pine (W Pool Avenue, N; 13.103).

Largest and tallest trees of *Pinus cooperi* (Byhams Ride, W).

Tallest Holford's Pine (E Holford Ride, S; N tree in group).

Largest *Prunus* 'Benden' (Cherry Glade, E; 39.297).

Largest Himalayan Bird Cherry (mid Broad Drive, W; 38.300).

Largest *P.* 'Gyoiko' (mid Willesley Drive, S; 33.88).

Largest *P. hirtipes* (W Waste Drive, S; 44.286).

Largest Fuji Cherry (E Waste Drive, S; 41.291).

Largest *P. padus* 'Watereri' (mid Willesley Drive, S; 33.49).

Largest *P. pilosiuscula* (W end of Waste Drive, S; 56.155).

Largest Weeping Yoshino Cherry (far W Willesley Drive, N.)

Tallest Hybrid Wingnut (Main Drive by Pool Gate; 18.1).

Largest *Pyrus syriaca* (Green Lane, E side; 36.340).

Tallest Caucasian Oak (mid Mitchell Drive, N; 14.66).

Largest Weeping Pyranean Oak (Willesley Drive/Byhams Ride; 31.871).

Largest *Rhus sylvestris* (Concord Glade; 32.109)

Largest *Salix* x *dasyclados* (Willow collection; 50.78).

Largest Coyote Willow (Willow collection, W).

Largest Scouler Willow (Willow collection; 50.116).

Largest and tallest Bristol Services (S Broad Drive, W; 38.150 and 149).

Tallest Japanese Rowan (mid Broad Drive, W).

Largest *Sorbus decora* (W Main Drive, S; 18.88).

Largest *S.* 'Golden Wonder' (W of Shop Window; 9.270).

Largest *S. keissleri* (W Waste Drive, S; 44.209).

Largest *S. pallescens* (N Broad Drive, W; 43.238).

Tallest *Thuja plicata* 'Semperaurescens' (far W Willesley Drive, N; back of group; 37.188).

Largest *Tilia chinensis* (W Mitchell Drive, N; 15.63).

Largest Small-leaved Lime stool (Silk Wood nature reserve).

Tallest Crimean Lime (W Holford Ride, N).

Largest Caucasian Lime (E Willesley Drive, S; 31.270).

Tallest *T. insularis* (E Pool Avenue, N).

Largest *T. japonica* (mid Pool Avenue, S; 12.142).

Largest Oliver's Lime (Specimen Avenue, path to Main Drive; 16.17).

Largest *Ulmus* 'Dodoens' (Rattrays, N of Loop Walk).

Tallest *U.* 'Lobel' (Rattrays, N of Loop Walk).

Tallest *Xanthocyparis nootkatensis* 'Pendula' (mid Waste Drive, S; 44.92).

*Westonbirt School, Tetbury. Regularly open in summer; the gardens were developed by the Holford family in conjunction with the Arboretum. Largest *Acer acuminatum* (E of lake, near amphitheatre); largest *A. palmatum* 'Osakazuki' (W of lake); tallest Rough Arizona Cypress (lower garden); largest *Malus* x *gloriosa* 'Oekonomierat Echtermeyer' (N bank of lake); tallest Golden Irish Yew (SE lawn, towards Italian Garden).

Hampshire

Champions are almost absent from the swathe of rolling downland which crosses the county. They cluster instead in old estates along the fertile Test valley, and on the well-wooded sandstones of the south and the far north and east. The New Forest is notable for its giant conifers, while north from Petersfield is a ridge of Lower Greensand, a soil which grows many of England's finest trees. The trees of Hampshire's town parks and smaller gardens have been understudied to date.

Aldershot Cemetery, Redan Road, Aldershot. Largest *Chamaecyparis pisifera* 'Plumosa' (N, near road, by path).

*Alice Holt Forest, Farnham. FC. Ancient woodland on poor, acid clay; now largely coniferised. National Collections of poplars were established in the 1950s on 4 sites: the 15 Acre Field by the A325 next to 'Bird World', the Vista Field and Maple Field S and E of the Forest Research Station at Alice Holt Lodge (whose gardens are not open to the public), and the Lodge Pond Field E of the A325. Compartment 31 (N of the drive to Bentley Station) has varied rare plantings.

Largest *Alnus matsumurae* (Lodge garden/Gravel Hill road).

Largest Oregon Alder (Lodge garden/Gravel Hill road; labelled *incana*).

Tallest X *Cupressocyparis leylandii* 'Naylors Blue' (back of Intensive Nursery, 1997).

Tallest X *C. l.* 'Skinner's Green' (back of Intensive Nursery).

Largest X *C. notabilis* (back of Intensive Nursery).

Largest X *C. ovensii* (back of Intensive Nursery).

Largest *Nothofagus* x *alpina* (Lodge garden lawn).

Largest *Pinus* x *schwerinii* (bottom of compartment 31).

Tallest Scrub Pine (top corner of compartment 31, by Station Ride).

Largest *Populus* x *canadensis* 'Casale 78' (15 Acre Field, S corner).

Largest *P.* x *c.* 'Florence Biondi' (15 Acre Field, back).

Largest *P.* x *c.* 'Gelrica' (Lodge garden/Gravel Hill road).

Largest *P.* x *c.* 'Ghoy' (15 Acre Field, back).

Largest *P.* x *c.* 'Heidemij' (Lodge garden, by Gravel Hill road).

Largest *P.* x *c.* 'Lloydii' (15 Acre Field, N edge).

Largest *P.* x *c.* 'Pacheri' (15 Acre Field, N corner).

Largest Eastern Cottonwood (15 Acre Field, N corner).

Largest *P.* 'Frye' (15 Acre Field, Bird World side).

Largest *P.* 'Geneva' (15 Acre Field, Bird World side).

Largest *P. laurifolia* x *nigra* (15 Acre Field, Bird World side).

Largest *P. nigra* 'Charkowiensis' (Vista Field).

Largest *P. n.* 'Criollo' (Vista Field).

Largest *P. n.* 'Vereecken' (Vista Field).

Largest *P. nigra* x *trichocarpa* (15 Acre Field, road side).

Largest *P.* 'OP265' (15 Acre Field, back).

Largest *P.* 'OP66' (15 Acre Field, back).

Largest Great Plains Cottonwood (Maple Field).

Largest *P. suaveolens* (?; Vista Field).

Largest *P. tomentosa* (Maple Field).

Largest *P.* 'TT37' (Lodge Pond Field).

Tallest *Thuja plicata* x *standishii* (compartment 31; Thuja Bank, W).

Ashford Chace, Ashford Lane, Steep, Petersfield. Edwardian gardens. Largest *Acer palmatum* 'Aureum' (rockery), Kentucky Coffee Tree (under Bees Cottage) and Chinese Tulip Tree (under walled garden).

Avington House, Itchen Abbas. (Largest Wheatley Elm in 1977.)

Bisterne Park, Bisterne. (Largest Goodyer's Elms in 1896.)

Blackmoor, Liss. Large mature arboretum. Tallest Manchurian Lime (Drift Road, 1984).

Bolderwood Holms, New Forest. Largest Rowan (open heath at SU23740867).

Bransgore House, Bransgore. Tallest Sorrel Tree.

Broadlands, Romsey. Open daily in summer; fine old trees. Tallest Swamp Cypress (river, W; 1986).

Chiltley Place, Liphook. The historic gardens have now been developed. (Largest *Ulmus glabra* 'Crispa', 1960.)

Cuffnells, Lyndhurst. Some notably tall conifers in a clay hollow in the New Forest. Tallest Morinda Spruce (1992).

*Exbury Gardens, Exbury, Beaulieu. Open daily except in winter. Many rare trees. (Largest *Picea farreri*, died 1995.)

Farleigh School (Red Rice College), Goodworth, Andover. Victorian pinetum: tallest Vilmorin's Fir (1982).

Farringdon church. One of the largest Yews (W of church).

Heckfield Place, Heckfield. Historic arboretum. Largest *Chamaecyparis pisifera* 'Plumosa Aurea' (lower lake, S; 1982).

*Highclere Castle, Highclere, Newbury. Landscaped parkland open daily in summer; a long tradition of rare plantings. Tallest Cork Fir in 1978.

Hurstbourne Priors, Whitchurch. Largest Horse Chestnut (field near church, 1993).

Jenkyn Place, Bentley, Alton. Largest Grecian Strawberry Tree.

Kingsmere, Shawford, Winchester. Largest Chinese Tree Privet (in 1977).

Kingsway Gardens, Chandler's Ford. Public park on the site of Hilliers' old nursery. Largest Fastigiate Atlas Cedar (1983).

The Knowles, Holmhill Enclosure, New Forest. One of the largest Beeches (at SU266086).

Merrie Cottage, Woodgreen, Fordingbridge. NGS open days. One of the largest Maidenhair Trees.

Mottisfont Abbey, Mottisfont, Romsey. NT; open daily

except in winter; some big trees in the rich soils beside the river Test. National Collection of *Platanus*. Largest London Plane; 'The Oakleigh Oak', one of the largest English Oaks, by bridge to Oakleigh Farm near river.

*Rhinefield Ornamental Drive, New Forest. Public. Avenue of unusual Victorian conifers along the old drive to Rhinefield House. Largest Red Spruce (1992) and Weymouth Pine.

Shirley, Southampton. Largest Nettle Tree (private garden in Grove Road, 1993).

**The Sir Harold Hillier Gardens and Arboretum, Jermyns Lane, Ampfield. Hampshire County Council; open daily. Arboretum begun by the nurseryman Sir Harold Hillier around his home in 1953, now extending to 80ha and one of the most comprehensive in the world. National Collections include *Carpinus*, *Cornus*, *Corylus*, *Lithocarpus*, *Pinus* and *Quercus*.

Largest *Abies borisii-regis* x *bornmulleriana* (at TW500; 1978.2778*S).

Largest Cheng Fir (at TW140; 1978.2826*U).

Largest *A. lasiocarpa* var. *arizonica* 'Compacta' (at PN740; 1977.0849*R).

Largest Sacred Fir (at BL350; 1976.5806*U).

Largest *Acer* x *bornmuelleri* (at AV400; 1977.2111*Z).

Largest *A. campbellii* ssp. *flabellatum* var. *yunnanense* (1978.0017).

Tallest *A. campestre* 'Schwerinii' (at TW300; 1978.1819*R).

Largest *A. davidii* x *rufinerve* 'Hatsuyuki' (at TW300; 1978.2841*Z).

Largest *A. divergens* (at NW200; 1977.7511*Z).

Largest Canyon Maple (at TP800; 1977.8031*Z).

Largest *A. heldreichii* ssp. *visianii* (at OF630; 1977.5309*R).

Largest *A.* x *hillieri* 'West Hill' (at AA100; 1976.1034*W).

Tallest *A. macrophyllum* 'Seattle Sentinel' (at AV300; 1977.0754*W).

Largest Coral-barked Maple (at JH270; 1976.0268*S).

Largest *A. pectinatum* (at TW400; 1978.1840*Q).

Largest *A. platanoides* 'Cleveland' (at OF620; 1977.5471*Z).

Largest Cut-leaved Norway Maple (at TW630; 1978.5207*T).

Largest *A. platanoides* x *truncatum* (at PN720; 1977.0805*V).

Largest *A. pseudoplatanus* 'Nizetii' (at TP800; 1977.8022*Y).

Largest trees of *A. pycnanthum* (at BU450; 1976.9950*Q, and at BH330; 1976.6173*X).

Largest *A. rubrum* 'Columnare' (at TE310; 1978.0049*R).

Largest *A. r.* 'Scanlon' (at TW300; 1978.1811*Z).

Largest *A. saccharum* 'Newton Sentry' (at TW500; 1978.2734*W).

Tallest Shirasawa's Maple (at TE700; 1978.0879*Q).

Largest Tartar Maple (1978.0017).

Largest *Ailanthus altissima* 'Pendulifolia' (at TW500; 1978.2123*X).

Largest *Alnus incana* 'Ramulis Coccineis' (at TP200; 1977.4507*T).

Largest *A. rugosa* (at PN400; 1982.0554*A).

Largest Sitka Alder (at TW210; 1978.1724*W).

Largest *Betula chinensis* (at HG200; 1976.2209*R).

Largest Japanese Cherry Birch (at PB200; 1977.2149*R).

Largest *B.* x *intermedia* (at PB100; 1978.4714*W).

Largest *B.* x *koehnei* (at NW500; 1977.7132*Y).

Tallest Japanese Silver Birch (at NW500; 1977.7139*R).

Largest *B. utilis* 'Jermyns'(at TE600; 1978.0233*X).

Largest *Carpinus betulus* 'Columnaris' (at TP200; 1977.4500*Q).

Largest *C. b.* 'Pendula Dervaes' (at TW500; 1977.4500₊Q).

Tallest American Sweet Chestnut (at PB200; 1977.0695*V).

Largest Chinquapin (at TP300; 1977.4408*S).

Largest Weeping Deodar (at TP600; 1977.4676*U).

Largest *Cedrus libani* ssp. *stenocoma* (at PN760; 1977.0923*X).

Tallest *Cercis racemosa* (at TW200; 1978.1497*T).

Largest *Chamaecyparis lawsoniana* 'Pembury Blue' (at TW14; 1978.2834*W).

Largest *C. pisifera* 'Boulevard' (at TW500; 1978.2112*Y).

Largest *C. p.* 'Gold Spangle' (at NW025; 1977.8874*W).

Tallest Pacific Dogwood (1976.0857).

Tallest *Crataegus* x *dippeliana* (at TP200; 1977.4471*Z).

Tallest *C. laevigata* 'Plena' (at TE510; 1978.0447*T).

Largest *Crataegus punctata* f. *aurea* (at TW140; 1978.2842*Y).

Largest *Cryptomeria japonica* 'Yoshino' (at PN450; 1977.0311*Z).

Largest *Cupressus arizonica* var. *glabra* 'Aurea' (at PB10; 1978.4056*U).

Largest *C. a.* var. *stephensonii* (at PB200; 1978.3906*U).

Largest Modoc Cypress (at TW540; 1978.2789*R).

Largest Santa Cruz Cypress (at BH300; 1976.6737*T).

Largest *C. lusitanica* x *macrocarpa* (1976.6756).

Largest *C. macrocarpa* 'Golden Pillar' (1977.1126).

Tallest Glencormac Cypress (1977.4232).

Largest Small-leaved Gum (at PB200; 1977.0685*V).

Largest *Fagus sylvatica* 'Cockleshell' (at TP900; 1977.4298*S).

Largest Golden Dawyck Beech (at FD400; 1976.0716*U).

Largest Purple Dawyck Beech (at AB200; 1976.0809*R).

Tallest *F. s.* f. *latifolia* (at TP800; 1977.4275*V).

Largest *F. s.* 'Rohan Gold' (at NW060; 1977.8818*S).

Largest *F. s.* 'Rohan Pyramid' (at NW 040; 1977.8814*W.)

Tallest *F. s.* 'Tortuosa' (at TP800; 1977.8023*X).

Largest *Fraxinus excelsior* 'Erosa' (1977.4461).

Tallest Carolina Snowdrop Tree (at NW100; 1977.7790*Q).

Largest *Juniperus virginiana* 'Burkii' (at JH270; 1976.0470*Q).

Largest *Larix kaempferi* 'Pendula' (at AA; 1976.1069*R).

Largest *Liquidambar styraciflua* 'Variegata' (at TE700; 1978.0847*T).

Largest Italian Crab (at TE400; 1978.0074*W).

Largest *Malus* 'Golden Gem' (at TW400; 1978.3681*Z).

Largest *M. lancifolia* (1978.1204).

Largest *M. orthocarpa* (at TE700; 1978.0821*Z).

Largest *M. prunifolia* var. *rinki* (1978.1209).

Largest *M.* x *sublobata* (1978.1695).

Largest Cut-leaved Crab (at TE500; 1978.0112*Y).

Largest *Picea abies* 'Argentea' (at PN100; 1977.0066*U).

Largest *P. a.* 'Cincinnata' (at PN740; 1977.0877*T).

Largest *P. a.* 'Cranstonii' (at NW200; 1977.7610*Q).

Largest *P. a.* 'Cupressina' (at PN400; 1977.0157*T).

Largest *P.* x *mariorika* (at JH290; 1977.0009*R).

Largest *Pinus ayacahuite* var. *veitchii* (at TE400; 1978.0569*R).

Largest Slash Pine (at BL100; 1976.4532*Y).

Largest *P. strobus* 'Contorta' (in pinetum, C17 U36; 1977.0990).

Largest Picart's Poplar (at NW500; 1977.7153*X).

Largest *Populus lasiocarpa* x *wilsonii* (at TW200; 1978.1543*X).

Largest *Prunus* x *amygdalo-persica* (at TE600; 1978.0195 V).

Largest *P. avium* 'Decumana' (at TP400; 1977.4612*Y).

Largest *P. canescens* x *serrula* (1978.0995).

Largest *P. cuthbertii* (at NW200; 1977.7336*U).

Largest *P.* x *fontanesiana* (at NW200; 1977.7491*Z).

Largest *P. incisa* 'February Pink' (at TE100; 1978.1261*Z).

Largest *P. padus* var. *commutata* (at TP300; 1977.4379*R).

Largest *P. pendula* var. *ascendens* 'Flore Pleno' (at TW500; 1978.2770*Q).

Largest Hubei Hill Cherry (at TW500; 1978.2787*T).

Largest *Pseudotsuga menziesii* 'Brevifolia' (at AA; 1976.0946*U).

Largest *P. m.* 'Moerheimii' (at RD100; 1976.1000*Q).

Largest *Pyrus* x *canescens* (at NW500; 1977.7162*Y).

Largest *P. caucasia* (1977.2195).

Tallest Ussurian Pear (1977.3150).

Largest *Quercus acutissima* ssp. *chenii* (at NW100; 1977.7735*V).

Largest *Q.* x *bebbiana* (at TW200; 1978.1502*Y).

Largest *Q.* x *benderi* (at BH335; 1976.6150*Q).

Largest *Q.* x *bushii* (at PN510; 1977.0538*S).

Largest *Q. canariensis* x *faginea* (at TE500; 1982.1199*A).

Largest *Q.* x *capesii* (at TW100; 1978.1324*W).

Largest *Q. castaneifolia* 'Green Spire' (Spring border, E, at SW250; 1983.3081*A).

Largest *Q. c.* x *libani* (at PG950; 1977.8963*X).

Largest *Q. emoryi* x *hypoleucoides* (at TG; 1976.1579*R).

Largest Georgia Oak (at AV002; 1979.0226*A).

Tallest *Q. hartwissiana* (at BH150; 1976.8672*Y).

Largest *Q. infectoria* ssp. *veneris* (at OF455; 1977.2200*Q).

Largest *Q. ithaburensis* (at OF470; 1977.2237*T).

Largest *Q. macranthera* x *petraea* (at OF621; 1977.2265*V).

Largest *Q. nuttallii* (at AV002; 1979.0224*A).

Largest *Q. petraea* 'Acutifolia' (at N200; 1977.6022*Y).

Largest Fastigiate Sessile Oak (at TP400; 1977.4415*V).

Largest *Q.* 'Pondaim' (1977.0489).

Largest *Q. rhysophylla* (at BH400; 1976.7826*U).

Largest *Q.* x *viveri* (at TW500; 1978.2785*V).

Tallest *Q. wislizenii* (at TW140; 1978.2838*S).

Largest *Salix daphnoides* 'Aglaia' (at TP200; 1977.4514*W).

Largest *Sequoia sempervirens* 'Cantab' (at TW200; 1978.1513*X).

Largest *Sequoiadendron giganteum* 'Glaucum' (at NW200; 1977.7597 T).

Tallest X *Sorbaronia alpina* (at TW200; 1978.1552*Y).

Largest Golden Whitebeam (at TP600; 1977.4673*X).

Largest *S. aucuparia* 'Sheerwater Seedling' (at TP800; 1977.8012*Y).

Largest *S.* 'Ghose' (at TW800; 1978.3254*W).

Largest *S.* 'Leonard Messel' (Pond, at BG400; 1977.8427*T).

Largest *Thuja occidentalis* 'Wintergreen' (at NW025; 1977.8858*S).

Tallest *T. plicata* 'Aurea' (at NW200; 1977.7468*S).

Largest *Thujopsis dolabrata* 'Aurea' (at JH270; 1976.0368*S).

Largest *Tilia cordata* 'Rancho' (at PN510; 1981.0049*A).

Largest *T.* 'Harold Hillier' (at TE110; 1978.1103*X).

Largest *T.* 'Hillieri' (at PN500; 1977.0521*Z).

Largest *T. platyphyllos* 'Pendula' (at TP200; 1977.4503*X).

Largest *Tsuga canadensis* 'Compacta' (at BL300; 1976.5753*X).

Largest *T. heterophylla* 'Laursen's Column' (at TW610; 1978.3225*V).

South Hayling church. One of the largest Yews (S of church).

Southsea Castle Gardens, Portsmouth. Public park. Tallest Mount Etna Broom (1989).

*Staunton Country Park, Middle Park Way, Havant. Open daily. The old gardens of Leigh Park contain a variety of large and rare trees. Tallest Yellow-berried Holly (1985); one of the largest Tulip Trees (1998).

*Stratfield Saye, Tadley. The historic grounds are regularly open; many fine trees. Largest Sweet Gum (N Arboretum, 1996).

Waterlooville, Portsmouth. One of the largest Tulip Trees (Stakes Hill recreation ground).

West Hill, Winchester. Former Hilliers' nursery site. (Largest *Ligustrum lucidum* 'Tricolor' in 1960s.)

West Kingsclere Farm, Kingsclere. Largest Golden Weeping Willow (near house, 1987).

Herefordshire

The Old Red Sandstone soils are some of the finest in Britain for tree growth; the rolling, rural country has few large gardens, but many enormous field oaks and churchyard Yews. Most of the notable trees stand around the edges of the county – along the Welsh Marches where the shelter and humidity allows conifers to thrive, and at the foot of the Malverns in the east. Many outstanding specimens probably await discovery.

Brampton Bryan, Knighton. Medieval parkland. One of the largest Small-leaved Limes (1979).

Brobury House, Bredwardine. NGS open days. Largest Western Balsam Poplar (N bank of Wye).

Brockhampton Park, Bromyard. NT; woodland walks around the estate. Tallest Blue Atlas Cedar (field sloping up to A44).

Cowarne Court, Much Cowarne. One of the largest English Oaks (1976).

*Croft Castle, Leominster. NT. The park with its ancient oaks and Sweet Chestnut avenues is open year-round; the garden opens most days except in winter. Two of the largest Sessile Oaks (quarry) and English Oaks ('Waggoners' Oak').

Easthampton Farm, Shobdon. The Shobdon Oak, one of the largest Sessile Oaks (opposite Easthampton Farm house, at SO410632).

*Eastnor Castle, Ledbury. Large old arboretum, regularly open. Largest Blue Atlas Cedar (SE bank, top of line; 1984); tallest Deodar (woods, NE; 1984); largest Cucumber Tree (playground near castle; 2 on tree trail); tallest Dragon Spruce (below drive; 34 on tree trail).

**Hergest Croft, Kington. Open daily except in winter. (Pronounced 'Harg-est'.) One of the most extensive private arboreta in Britain, situated more than 200m up in the

Several magnificent Blue Atlas Cedars are a feature of the grounds of Eastnor Castle, Herefordshire.

Welsh Marches. Many of the trees are in Park Wood, a 1km walk across the park from the main garden. National Collections of *Acer*, *Betula* and *Zelkova*.
Tallest Korean Fir (Park Wood; 151).
Largest Vejar Fir (Park Wood; 2892).
Largest Fan-leaved Maple (?; Corner Cap, 3359).
Largest Horned Maple (Park).
Largest Heldreich's Maple (713).
Largest Mono Maple (Rockery).
Tallest Japanese Maple (by old garden; 445).
Tallest Coral-barked Maple (Rockery; 618).
Tallest Golden Norway Maple (Well Meadow; 2455).
Tallest Downy Tree of Heaven (Azalea Garden; 733).
Tallest Madrone (Azalea Garden; 671).
Largest Chinese Red Birch (Park Wood; 1000).
Largest *Betula luminifera* (1128).
Largest and tallest Sichuan Birches (garden, 1116; and by paddock, N, 1110).
Largest *B. utilis* var. *prattii* (Park Wood; 1123).
Tallest Cedrus libani 'Comte de Dijon' (Rockery; 4861).
Largest Taiwan Cypress (Park Wood).
Largest *Corylus* x *vilmorinii* (Azalea Garden, S of Avenue; 4775).
Two of the largest Dove Trees (Daisy Border, var. *involucrata*, 574; and 765, var. *vilmoriniana*).
Tallest Hardy Rubber Tree (Daisy Border; 593).
Largest Carolina Snowdrop Tree (garden; 661).
Largest Chinese Walnut (Corner Cap; 815).
Largest *Juglans* x *intermedia* (Azalea Garden, S of Avenue; 1042).
Largest Cut-leaved Walnut (Corner Cap; 825).
Tallest Cox's Juniper (Park Wood; 3287).
Tallest Dahurian Larch (Park Wood; 1018).
Tallest Sakhalin Cork Tree (Park Wood, Chinese Path; 3276).
Largest Dragon Spruce (Park Wood; 152).
Tallest Brewer Spruce (Park Wood, SW Bank; 134).
Largest *Picea purpurea* (Park Wood; 164).
Largest *Pinus cembra* 'Aurea' (Rockery).
Tallest Medlar-leaved Oak (Azalea Garden; 730).
Largest Chestnut Oak (Corner Cap; 833).
Tallest Macedonian Oak (Haywood Common; 1972).
Tallest *Sorbus aria* 'Lutescens' (Azalea Garden; 2521).
Tallest *S. commixta* var. *rufoferruginea* (Azalea Garden; 3564).
Largest *Tilia maximowicziana* (Park, Corner Cap; 805).
Tallest Chinese Cedar (Azalea Garden; 700).
Largest *Ulmus* 'Pinnato-ramosa' (Hergest Croft garden).
Tallest Keaki (Azalea Garden; 761).
Kentchurch Court, Kentchurch, Ewyas Harold. Largest Orchard Apple (1975); one of the largest English Oaks – 'Jack Kemp's Oak' (1998).
Kington recreation ground. Largest Fern-leaved Alder (1995).
Linton church, Ross-on-Wye. One of the largest Yews (NW of church).
Moreton on Lugg, Hereford. One of the largest White Willows (grounds of former RAOC Training Centre, 1989).
*Whitfield, Allensmore, Thruxton. NGS open days; many fine trees. Largest Himalayan Alder; tallest Atlas Cedar; largest Maidenhair Tree (kitchen garden); largest Weeping Oak (garden) – all 1995.

Hertfordshire

In common with the other counties around London, Hertfordshire is crowded especially in the south with estates where rare trees have long been grown; but the dry climate has been relatively unkind especially to the conifers. The rich soils of the many river valleys, however, seem to suit poplars and willows in particular, along with heat-loving broadleaves such as walnuts. Little remains of the varied elm populations which once dominated the landscape.

Abbey Gate House, Abbey Mill Lane, St. Albans. Largest Pagoda Tree (viewable from road).
Aldenham church. Largest *Betula* x *caerulea* (?).
Aldenham Park, Elstree. Aldenham Park was of the country's largest and most famous private gardens until 1932, when Lord Aldenham's death led to many of the plants being sold off. The Manor is now part of the Haberdashers' Aske's School (qv), while many rare trees survive in the woods.
Tallest Ohio Buckeye (woods by footpath, off Sargent's Drive).
Tallest Big Shellbark Hickory (woods: Elwes Drive near Gerald's Drive).
Tallest Oregon Ash (woods: S of Elwes Drive, W of Walter's Drive).
Largest Berlin Poplar (park just S of School).
Largest *Populus* x *canadensis* 'Robusta' (bridge SE of woods).
Largest *Pyrus* x *lecontii* (woods; Edith's Drive/Sargent's Drive).
Tallest *P. pashia* (woods: Alban's Drive/Elwes Drive).
Largest Sand Pear (woods near School fence).
Largest Orange-berried Service (woods N of Sargent's Drive, W of Vicary's Walk).
Tallest Service Tree of Fontainebleau (woods; Elwes Drive off Vicary's Walk).
Batford Springs Local Nature Reserve, Harpenden. Largest Cricket-bat Willow (S tree of three by Marquis Lane Play Area, at TL146149).
Bayfordbury, Bayford. Remants of two Victorian pineta; the Clinton Baker Pinetum (University of Hertfordshire) is open by appointment. Tallest MacNab Cypress (Bells Wood, 1985); tallest White Mulberry (old entrance drive by junction with Victoria Mews); largest Bristlecone Pine (Bells Wood, 1985); one of the largest Western Yellow Pines (Clinton Baker Pinetum).
Brickendon Grange Golf Club, Brickendon, Hertford. The remains of a Victorian pinetum. Tallest Syrian Juniper (SW, on footpath).
Briggens Hotel, Hundsdon, Ware. Notable old gardens. Largest Persian Ironwood (S of walled gardens), *Prunus cerasifera* 'Hessei' (S of walled garden), and Chinese Bladder-nut (garden, SE edge).
Brocket Hall, Welwyn Garden City. Many exceptional trees. One of the largest Hornbeams (under reservoir, 593); largest Medlar-leaved Oak (15th tee); largest Silver Willow (16th fairway); largest Red-twigged Lime (above 15th tee, near footpath).

Cassiobury Park, Watford. Public park; fine parkland trees. (Largest Cut-leaved Alder and Wych Elm in 1904.)
Cheslyn Gardens, 54, Nascot Wood Road, Watford. Suburban garden with many rare plants, bequeathed to Watford Council in 1965. Largest *Cephalotaxus harringtonia* (entrance).
Clarence Park, St Albans. Public park; various fine trees. Largest *Malus x soulardii* (S of central avenue); tallest Himalayan Whitebeam (SW).
Fanhams Hall, Ware. Tallest Hybrid Bean; largest Weeping Hazel.
Gilston Park Hotel, Gilston, Harlow. (Tallest Smooth-leaved Elm in 1955.)
The Haberdashers' Aske's School, Butterfly Lane, Elstree. The grounds were formerly part of the Aldenham Park (qv); many rare trees survive. Largest *Crataegus laevigata* 'Gireoudii' (drive N of bridge), Osage Orange (woodland NW of drive bridge), *Morus alba* 'Venosa' (garden S of Manor), *Pyrus pashia* (wood edge behind Manor) and Variegated Pagoda Tree (carpark edge N of school buildings).
Hertingfordbury church, Hertford. Largest Hicks' Yew (NW).
High Canons, Borehamwood. A Victorian pinetum; largest Grecian Juniper.
Kings Walden Park, Kings Walden. One of the largest English Oaks, The Kings Walden Great Oak (TL163234).
Knebworth House, Knebworth. Gardens open regularly in summer. Largest and tallest Swedish Birches (Wilderness).
Much Hadham Old Rectory, Bishop's Stortford. Some huge old trees planted by the Bishops of London. Tallest Yellow Buckeye; largest Black Walnut; tallest Crack Willow (far side of river, house end).
Munden, Watford. Tallest Golden Poplar (River Colne by footpath bridge, at TQ133998).
Putteridge Bury, Luton. University of Luton; open daily. A restored Lutyens and Jekyll garden. Largest *Ilex aquifolium* 'Pyramidalis' (SE woodland garden, 5).
St Albans. Largest White Poplar (S woodland edge in Verulam Park, at TL136067).
Sawbridgeworth. Largest *Quercus x turneri* 'Spencer Turner' (front lawn of 3, High Tree Close, on the site of Thomas Rivers' Nursery).
Stanborough Park, Welwyn Garden City. Public park. Largest Balm of Gilead (by river; ?).
Wall Hall, Aldenham. University of Hertfordshire (Watford Campus). Largest *Xanthocyparis nootkatensis* 'Pendula' (E end of old pinetum below mansion).
Welwyn Garden City. Imaginative street plantings. Largest *Malus x purpurea* 'Eleyi' (Stanborough Green, by 24-30 flats).

Isle of Wight
*Osborne House, Osborne, East Cowes. English Heritage; open daily through summer. Queen Victoria's garden, with many notable trees. One of the largest Cork Oaks (private valley walk)
*Ventnor Botanic Gardens, The Undercliffe Drive, Ventnor. Open access; many rare and tender plants.

Kent
Many different soils cross the county in narrow bands, creating varied landscapes. In the south-east, the wooded and sheltered valleys of the High Weald are thronged with fine trees, and are England's easternmost outpost for many moisture-demanding conifers. Another sandy outcrop, the Lower Greensand, encompasses a great concentration of notable gardens, while the lowland fringes of the Downs in the north also provide outstanding growing conditions. By contrast, exceptional trees are almost absent from the clays of the Low Weald, and from the bleak and windswept Thameside levels.

Abbey School, London Road, Faversham. Largest *Prunus* 'Shirotae' (entrance path).
Aldon Old Rectory, Aldon Lane, Addington. Largest Apricot.
Bedgebury Forest, Goudhurst. FC. Forest plots of many rare taxa were established from 1929 to 1970, and mostly blown down in 1987. Tallest Eastern White Cedar (plot 62).
**Bedgebury National Pinetum, Lady Oak Lane, Goudhurst. FC; open daily. Established by the Royal Botanic Gardens from 1921 in the grounds of Bedgebury House as a home for conifers then being killed by air pollution at Kew, and now probably the largest assemblage of temperate conifers in the world. National collections of *Juniperus*, *Taxus*, *Thuja*, Leyland Cypresses and Lawson Cypress cultivars.
Largest *Abies cephalonica* x *nordmanniana* (Firs, E; 9/162).
Largest Khinghan Fir (Firs, S; 9/196).
Tallest *Betula* x *caerulea* (Thorn Hill; 5/314).
Largest Japanese Sweet Chestnut (bottom of Thorn Hill; 4/348).
Tallest Fastigiate Atlas Cedar (Cedar Bank; 7/33).
Largest *Chamaecyparis lawsoniana* 'Blue Jacket' (Cypress Valley, N; 11/212).
Largest *C. l.* 'Columnaris' (Cypress Valley, S; 11/56).
Tallest *C. l.* 'Filifera' (Cypresses; 11/34).
Largest *C. l.* 'Fletcheri' (Cypesses, by Hills Avenue; 11/250).
Largest *C. l.* 'Golden King' (Yew Bank; 13/274).
Largest *C. l.* 'Green Pillar' (Hills Avenue E, S; 11/150).
Largest *C. obtusa* 'Erecta' (Cypress Valley, W; 10/366).
Largest and tallest trees of *C. o.* 'Magnifica' (Cypress Valley; 10/317 and 10/398).
Largest *C. p.* 'Plumosa Flavescens' (Cypress Valley; 10/414).
Largest *C. p.* 'Pygmaea' (Cypress Valley; 10/410).
Tallest *C. p.* 'Squarrosa Intermedia' (Cypress Valley; 10/545).
Largest *C. thyoides* 'Glauca' (Cypress Valley, N; 11/239).
Largest *Cryptomeria japonica* 'Gracilis' (above Thujas, in group of type; 7/372).
Largest X *Cupressocyparis leylandii* 'Robinson's Gold' (S of Cypress Valley; 30/256).
Tallest X *C. l.* 'Variegata' (National Collection, far fence; 20/100).
Largest Piute Cypress (S of Cedar Bank; 21/104).
Tallest *Juniperus chinensis* 'Kaizuka' (Juniper Bank; 6/210).

Tallest *J. c.* 'Keteleeri' (Juniper Bank; 6/34).

Largest *J. c.* 'Leeana' (Juniper Bank; 6/234).

Largest Temple Juniper (Juniper Bank; 6/45).

Largest *J. virginiana* 'Burkii' (Juniper Bank; 6/273).

Largest and tallest trees of *J. v.* 'Canaertii' (Juniper Bank; 6/338 and 6/331).

Largest Polish Larch (Larches; 8/70).

Tallest Weeping Larch (Larches; 8/114).

Largest *Picea abies* 'Pyramidata' (Thorn Hill, N; 4/310).

Largest *P. meyeri* (Spruce Valley; 3/244).

Largest *P. orientalis* 'Gracilis' (Spruce Valley, N; 3/78).

Largest Knobcone Pine (Pine Hill; 15/101).

Largest and tallest trees of *Pinus ayacahuite* x *peuce* (Pine Hill, SE; 16/198 and 197).

Largest Bolander Pine (Pines, behind Glory Hole; 15/242).

Largest Durango Pine (below North Avenue; 15/212/3).

Largest and tallest trees of *P. echinata* x *rigida* (Thorn Hill, 5/248, and Glory Hole, 15/197).

Largest Two-leafed Nut Pine (SW Cypress Valley; 30/157).

Largest *P. kochiana* (Pine Hill; 16/186).

Tallest Mountain Pine (North Avenue, E).

Largest Red Pine (below North Avenue; 15/46).

Largest *P. sylvestris* 'Alba' (Hills Avenue E, N; 15/37).

Tallest Loblolly Pine (North Avenue, W; 15/91).

Largest Big-cone Douglas Fir (Douglas Firs; 7/293).

Largest Arizona Douglas Fir (Thorn Hill, E; 4/267).

Tallest Lebanon Oak (below Park House; 14/104).

Largest *Quercus* x *sargentii* (opposite Holy Ground; 7/361).

Tallest Bollwyller Pear (Thorn Hill, SW fence; 5/12).

Largest *Thuja occidentalis* 'Dicksonii' (Thujas; 10/128).

Largest *T. o.* 'Elegantissima' (Thujas; 10/143).

Largest *T. o.* 'Erecta' (Thujas; 10/51).

Largest *T. plicata* 'Excelsa' (Thujas; 10/492/3).

Tallest *T. p.* 'Pyramidalis' (Cypress Valley).

Largest *T. p.* 'Umbraculifera' (Thujas).

Largest *T. p.* 'Wintergold' (Thujas).

Largest *Tsuga canadensis* 'Microphylla' (Hemlocks, S; 10/384).

Tallest Carolina Hemlock (Hemlocks, S; 10/383).

Largest Variegated Nootka Cypress (Cypress Valley; 11/169).

Tallest Golden Nootka Cypress (Cypress Valley, S; 160).

Bedgebury Upper School, Goudhurst. Occasional open days. The original gardens of Bedgebury House. Largest Weeping Ash (N side of school); tallest Chinese Juniper (above lake).

Beech Court, Challock Lees. Open most days in summer. A woodland garden established in the 1940s high on the North Downs. Largest *Prunus* 'Pink Perfection' (SE).

Benenden School, Benenden. Old parkland and a Victorian pinetum. Tallest Umbrella Pine (N lodge, by public footpath); largest Japanese Thuja (Pleasure Grounds).

Betteshanger. One of the largest Sycamores (field S of Northbourne Park School, at TR310523).

Bidborough. Original Dallimore's Chestnut (High Street, by Bidborough Ridge, at TQ564434).

Bifrons Park, Patrixbourne. Relic parkland. One of the largest Common Limes (avenue, W end, S).

Boughton Place, Boughton Monchelsea. The gardens are regularly open. Largest *Populus* x *generosa* (park by churchyard wall, 1999).

Brabourne church. (Largest Yew, 1655.)

Brenchley Old Parsonage. One of the largest English Oaks (beside house).

Broom's Down, Mill Lane, Wateringbury. Largest Honey Locust (Rose Garden).

Burrswood, Langton Green, Tunbridge Wells. Largest Cappadocian Maple (above pond).

Bushy Ruff Wild Park, Kearsney, Dover. Public park. Largest *Malus prunifolia* (by path from Russell Gardens).

Charlton Park, Bishopsbourne. Largest Oak-leaved Beech (wood edge N from house, 1999).

Chilham Castle, Chilham. Open most days in summer; historic gardens. Largest Hybrid Bean (under ha-ha); tallest Filbert (E from lake); one of the largest Holm Oaks (S of Keep).

Chilston Park, Lenham. One of the largest Field Maples (by footpath at TQ892497).

Cobham Hall School, Cobham. Open sometimes. Rare trees have been grown here since the 16th century. Largest Alpine Cider Gum (Dickens Chalet Hollow).

*Collingwood Grange, Benenden. The garden until his death at 101 of the noted cherry expert Collingwood Ingram; occasional open days. Largest *Acer monspessulanum* ssp. *microphyllum* (SW of big lawn); largest Siebold's Maple (lawn-edge by house); largest Umbrella Tree (SW of big lawn); tallest *Malus baccata* var. *mandshurica* (SE edge); largest Hill Cherry (SE of lawn); largest Korean Hill Cherry (central bed in lawn); largest *Pyrus cossonii* (fieldside over lane from garden; ?); largest Moroccan Oak (SW).

Court Lodge Farm, Aldington. One of the largest Elders (farmyard, at TR074362).

Cowden. One of the largest Alders (stream just S of Cowden Station, by footpath, at TQ480414).

Crittenden, Matfield, Paddock Wood. Gardens developed by the late Ben Tompsett. Largest *Crataegus monogyna* 'Pink May' (gate), *Malus* 'Crittenden' (front, E), and *M.* x *schiedeckeri* 'Red Jade' (top of drive).

Dane John Gardens, Canterbury. Public park. Largest *Fagus sylvatica* 'Miltonensis' (rampart bank).

Doddington Place, Doddington, Sittingbourne. Garden regularly open. Tallest Winter Cherry (E, 1995).

Fairlawne, Plaxtol, Tonbridge. Largest Field Maple (W of top lake) and Red Horse Chestnut (house front).

Farningham. Largest Dallimore's Chestnut (river-bank by Lion Hotel).

Faversham Recreation Ground, Whitstable Road. Largest Oriental Thorn (S, mid); tallest Red May (NE corner).

Fordcombe, Penshurst. Largest *Ulmus glabra* 'Horizontalis' (garden of the Chafford Arms; 1999).

Champion Weeping Ash at Bedgebury School, Kent.

Fredville Park, Nonington. One of the largest English Oaks – 'Majesty' (old house site).

Frensham Manor, Rolvenden Layne, Rolvenden. Largest Hybrid Wingnut.

Godinton Park, Ashford. Ancient parkland; the garden opens most days in summer. Largest Red Horse Chestnut (N Park carpark); largest *Ilex* x *altaclarensis* 'Golden King' (Wild Garden); largest Great White Cherry (garden); one of the largest Pin Oaks (park N of carpark).

Great Comp, Platt, Borough Green. Open daily in summer. Large garden created since 1957 by the late Roderick Cameron. Largest Manchurian Cherry (S; area 38).

Hadlow College, Hadlow. The Broadview Gardens open most days in summer. Largest *Pyrus calleryana* 'Bradford' (drive N of Broadview Gardens carpark).

*Hall Place, Leigh, Tonbridge. NGS open days. A magnificent Victorian garden set in old parkland. Largest *Malus* x *zumi* 'Golden Hornet' (NE of lake); largest Willow-leafed Pear (S of lake); three of the largest Pin Oaks (E of lake, 1994), Red Oaks (W Park) and Wild Services (S park by drive).

Hawkinge Cemetery, Aerodrome Road, Hawkinge, Folkestone. Largest *Crataegus chrysocarpa* (E gate).

*Hever Castle, Hever. Open daily through summer. Spectacular Edwardian gardens. Largest *Acer palmatum* 'Linearilobum' (carpark/ghyll); tallest *Fagus sylvatica* 'Luteovariegata' (SW of Italian Garden); largest Clammy Locust (Anne Boleyn's Walk, far E) – all 1995.

Horse Pasture Wood, Pembury. Tallest Grey Sallow (footpath at TQ641423).

Howletts Zoo Park, Bekesbourne, Canterbury. Open daily. One of the largest Sweet Chestnuts, 'the Howletts Chestnut' (E of House, on private lawn).

Hunton, Maidstone. Largest *Salix* x *meyeriana* (laneside copse at TQ714503).

Ickham church. Largest Hedgehog Holly (E side).

Joyce Green Hospital, Joyce Green Lane, Dartford. Many unusual trees in the grounds, which have since been developed. Largest *Euonymus bungeanus* in 1997.

Kearsney Manor Nursing Home, River, Dover. One of the largest Aspens (W bank of lake, N of pair).

*Knole Park, Sevenoaks. NT. Deer park (open access) with very tall native trees; garden open regularly. One of the tallest Hornbeams (S, up hill); tallest Sessile Oak (NW, in wood); largest Cypress Oak (garden, S).

*Leeds Castle, Leeds, Maidstone. Open daily. Many fine trees. Tallest Golden Cappadocian Maple (by stream; one of many).

Littlehall Pinetum, Little Hall Wood, Tyler Hill, Canterbury. The remains of one of the most ambitious Edwardian pineta. Largest *Pinus strobus* 'Aurea' (N side, 1995).

Loose church. One of the largest Yews (SW of church).

Luddesdown church, Strood. Largest Phillyrea.

Lullingstone Park. Swanley. Country Park; ancient pollards including two of the largest Hornbeams (Upper Beechen Wood, top N; 29) and Sessile Oaks (golf course N of groundsmen's hut; 228).

Lydd church. Largest Plum (S).

Meadow Wood, Penshurst. NGS open days. Largest *Hoheria angustifolia* (1995).

Mereworth church, Maidstone. Tallest *Platycladus orientalis* 'Elegantissima' (N side).

Merlewood, Mount Harry Road, Sevenoaks (development on the site of a notable 1940s garden). Largest Hodgins' Holly.

Mill House, Shoreham. Largest Turkish Apple.

*Mote Park, Maidstone. Historic public park with large and rare trees. One of the largest Black Walnuts (slope below house); largest Rose-bud Cherry (S of lake); largest Yoshino Cherry (S of lake); tallest Siberian Elm (SW, by drive).

Penshurst Place, Penshurst. One of the largest English Oaks, 'Sir Philip Sidney's oak' – by footpath N of Lancup Well at TQ527447).

Petham, Canterbury. Largest Scarlet Oak (hedge opposite Kenfield Hall, at TR119527).

Preston Hall Hospital, Aylesford, Maidstone. Largest *Prunus* 'Ojochin' (E of front lawn).

Riverhill House, River Hill, Sevenoaks. Regularly open. A notable Victorian woodland garden (much damaged in the 1987 storm). Largest Saucer Magnolia (above house).

Rookery Wood, Penshurst. Largest Silver Birch (N slope at TQ538459); one of the largest Hazels (nearby); one of the largest English Oaks (valley floor at TQ539460).

St Clere Pinetum, Kemsing. Edwardian pinetum high on the North Downs. (St Clere House in the valley below, with further rare plantings, opens under the NGS.) Largest *Chamaecyparis lawsoniana* 'Rosenthalii'; largest Whitebeam coppice; tallest Carolina Hemlock.

St Nicholas at Wade. Largest Cheal's Weeping Cherry (front garden of 4, Bridges Close).

St Ronan's School, Hawkhurst. Remains of a large Edwardian pinetum. Tallest Golden Box Elder (behind nurseries, 1995).

Sandling Park, Saltwood. Many rare young trees. Largest *Populus ciliata* (W side).

Scotney Castle, Lamberhurst. NT. Open most days through summer. Tallest *Sorbus aucuparia* 'Beissneri' (moat, SW).

Sevenoaks. Largest Whitebeam (front garden of 98, Oak Hill Road).

Shoreham. One of the largest Crack Willows (Darent bank at TQ520622).

Spa Hotel, Manor Park, Tunbridge Wells. Largest Weeping Larch (front lawn, N).

Squerryes Park, Westerham. One of the largest Alders (field edge at TQ444522).

Torry Hill, Milstead, Sittingbourne. (The gardens open under the NGS.) Largest *Quercus cerris* 'Marmorata' (Park Farm field at TQ903571).

Tunbridge Wells. Largest Medlar (verge of The Midway, outside 'Albury', Nevill Park).

Twydall, Gillingham. Largest *Prunus* 'Ichiyo' (Doddington Road street tree, near Beeching Way).

Ulcombe church (pronounced 'Oolcombe'). One of the largest Yews (SW).

Updown House, Betteshanger. Largest Almond (NW of walled garden).

Autumn brilliance of the champion Pin Oak at Godinton Park, Kent.

Vernon Grange, Old London Road, Canterbury. Largest Judas Tree (front garden).

Vernon Holme School, Harbledown, Canterbury. Remnants of an ambitious Edwardian pinetum. Tallest *Picea orientalis* 'Aurea' (back lawn, 1995).

Viceroys Wood, Penshurst. Penshurst Off-Road Cyclists' Club; open access. The Seven Sisters Chestnut – largest Sweet Chestnut coppice, at TQ513426).

Westgate Gardens, St Peter's Place, Canterbury. Public park. One of the largest London Planes (by Tower House).

Wincheap playground, Wincheap, Canterbury. Largest *Fagus sylvatica* 'Miltonensis'.

Withersdane Hall, Coldharbour Lane, Wye. Imperial College at Wye; NGS open days. Tallest X *Cupressocyparis*

The Seven Sisters Chestnut in Viceroys Wood, Kent, is one of the most mysterious of big trees. The seven trunks (two fused, and one forking low down), make a circle 5 metres wide, around an earth mound. Were seven trees planted to grow together and look like one? If so, their growth and habits are astonishingly uniform. Or, more than 200 years ago, did a big old Chestnut die and seven sprouts from the base grow up?

leylandii 'Variegata' (SW of buildings); largest Malus 'Wisley' (N path to formal gardens); largest Black Mulberry (formal gardens).

Wye church. One of the largest American Limes (N fence).

Lancashire

Intensive agriculture in the west, industrial pollution in the south, and wild, and windswept fells in the west mean that Lancashire is not noted for its trees, though fine examples in urban parks probably await discovery. The champions in Silverdale belong with the concentration of big gardens in south Cumbria.

Ellel Grange, Ellel, Lancaster. Largest Acer pseudoplatanus 'Leopoldii'.

Hazelwood Lodge, Silverdale. Tallest Weymouth Pine.

Yealand Manor, Silverdale. Tallest Weeping Ash.

Leicestershire

An agricultural county where gardening and silviculture have seldom been a priority. Growth conditions are probably best among the hills in the east and in Charnwood Forest to the north-west, where soils are less sticky.

Belvoir Castle, Belvoir, Grantham. (Pronounced 'Beaver'.) Open daily through summer. One of the tallest English Oaks (road to garden), and Yews (path to garden) in 1987.

Knighton Park, Knighton, Leicester. Largest Crataegus mollis (1985).

*Leicester University Botanic Garden, Stoughton Drive South, Oadby. 7ha gardens with fine and rare trees. National Collection of Lawson Cypress cultivars. Largest Prunus 'Hokusai' (1985).

Willesley Park, Measham Road, Ashby-de-la-Zouch. One of the largest Sweet Chestnuts (golf club, near practice range).

Lincolnshire

Woodland, across much of the county, is almost confined to large, old parks, a few of which have specialised in growing rare trees. These trees have seldom been thoroughly recorded. Summers are warm, but winters cold and dry, restricting the species that will thrive.

Algarkirk, Kirkton. One of the largest Small-leaved Limes in 1965.

Belton House, Belton, Grantham. NT. Open access to

the landscaped park; gardens open most days through summer. Largest Sugar Maple (paddock, 1991); tallest Silver Willow (meadow edge, 1978); tallest Weeping Beech (W of walk, 1978).

Boultham Park, Lincoln. Tallest Railway Poplar (1993).

Bowthorpe Park Farm, Witham-on-the-Hill. Largest English Oak (field behind house; viewable for small charge).

Brocklesby Park, Great Limber, Grimsby. The only ambitious, mature tree-collection near the Humber estuary. Tallest Turkish Hazel.

Spalding Cemetery. Tallest *Prunus cerasifera* 'Nigra' (1991).

Spalding Grammar School. Largest *Alnus incana* 'Aurea' (1991).

Stoke Rochford Hall, Grantham. Tallest Tree of Heaven (garden gate, 1978).

Syston Park, Syston, Grantham. Largest Bitternut and Copper Beech.

Witham Hall School, Bourne. Largest Varnish Tree.

Liverpool and Wirral

A series of fine public parks rings inner Liverpool. Industrial pollution has not helped tree growth, but some notable specimens presumably await recording.

*Calderstones Park, Calderstones, Liverpool. One of the country's finest public parks; wide range of unusual trees. Largest *Ilex* x *altaclarensis* 'Hodginsii' (1988) and *Taxus baccata* 'Semperaurea' (1984).

Flaybrick Memorial Gardens, Tollemache Road, Birkenhead. Victorian cemetery. Largest Caucasian Lime.

Royden Park, Frankby Road, Frankby. Public park. Largest Madrone.

London

London is one of the world's great cities for trees, almost entirely for demographic reasons. Neither heavy London Clays nor poor gravelly sands are ideal for tree growth; the climate is too dry to suit most conifers and until the mid 20th century air pollution was severe, though the very warm summers do benefit most taxa. There is an enthusiasm for planting trees wherever space allows, and a wealth of imaginatively planted public parks, many developed from old estates where rarities were already being grown.

Acton Park, The Vale, Acton. Public park. Largest Chinese Weeping Poplar (SE), *Prunus* 'Kanzan' (S) and *Robinia pseudoacacia* 'Bessoniana' (mid W).

Archbishop Park, Lambeth Road, Lambeth. Public park. Largest St Lucie Cherry (SW).

*Avenue House, East End Road, Finchley. Historic public park with rare trees. Tallest Hawthorn (SW of Bothy, 7175).

Barnes. One of the largest London Planes (Old Ranelegh Club grounds at TQ239766 – over concrete bridge behind the Barn Elms Playing Fields public athletics track, opposite the Wildfowl Centre entrance in Queen Elizabeth Walk).

Barra Hall Park, Hayes, Hillingdon. Largest Common Laburnum (by Hall).

*Battersea Park, Battersea. Large public park with many unusual plantings. Largest Lobel's Maple (SW); largest Hybrid Strawberry Tree (Subtropical Gardens/peninsular); tallest Black Walnut (W side, mid); one of the largest Chinese Tree Privets (Central Avenue, mid E).

Beckenham Place Park, Beckenham. Public park in old parkland. One of the largest Turkey Oaks (NE – off path through golf course, at TQ380708).

Brockley Cemetery, Brockley Road, Lewisham. Largest Plantier's Lombardy Poplar (War Memorial/central roundel, mid NW).

Brockwell Park, Brixton. Large and historic public park. Largest Snowy Mespil (E of lower pond).

Buckingham Palace. Largest Golden Norway Maple (visitor tent, service side; 1874), Chinese Sweet Chestnut (NE of lake) and Weeping Thorn (E of tennis court).

*Bushy Park, Hampton Wick. The Royal Parks. Ancient deer park; rare plantings in the Waterhouse Woodland Garden and Bushy House garden. Tallest Montpelier Maple (Waterhouse Woodland Garden, Crocodile Glade); largest Cut-leaved Sweet Chestnut (Bushy House, SW); tallest *Populus* 'Balsam Spire' (Waterhouse Woodland Garden, N of stream); largest *Salix* x *ehrhartiana* (NE bank of Heron Pond).

*Cannizaro Park, West Side, Wimbledon Common. Historic public park; many rare trees. Largest Full Moon Maple (S end of Maple Avenue); tallest *Acer platanoides* 'Olmsted' (main lawn near pond; ?); largest Sassafras (Birch Grove).

Capel Manor, Bullsmoor Lane, Enfield. Capel College; show gardens open daily. Tallest Spire Cherry (W of South Lawn).

Cator Park, Lennard Road, Beckenham. Public park. Largest Japanese Crab (Aldersmead Road chalet).

Central Park, High Street, East Ham. Historic public park. Largest *Ilex* x *altaclarensis* 'Belgica Aurea' (gardens, E); largest *Prunus* 'Choshu-hizakura' (park, mid S).

Charlton Park, Charlton Road, Charlton. Historic public park. Largest Hackberry (SW corner, by Canberra Road).

Chelsea. Largest Mimosa (front garden of 62, Christchurch Terrace).

*Chelsea Physic Garden, Swan Walk, Chelsea. Regularly open. Largest *Malus* x *adstringans* 'Simcoe' (Embankment edge, E), Olive (NE) and *Rhus punjabensis* (Swan Walk edge; ?).

Church House Gardens, Church Road, Bromley. Public park. Largest Hillier's Cherry (cherry group on hill, W).

*City of Westminster Cemetery, The Broadway, Hanwell. A remarkable range of rare trees. Tallest *Carpinus betulus* 'Columnaris' (NE corner); largest *Crataegus oliveriana* (E edge, N); largest Pin Cherry (mid NE); largest *Pyrus* x *michauxii* (NE).

Clancarthy Road, Parsons Green, Fulham. Tallest *Pyrus communis* 'Beech Hill' (street tree, by 39).

Clifford's Inn, Chancery Lane, Holborn. Tallest Fig (behind museum railings).

Clissold Park, Green Lanes, Stoke Newington. Historic public park. Largest *Crataegus pinnatifida* (mid E); largest Caucasian Ash (bowling green).

Croydon Cemetery, Thornton Road, Croydon. Largest

Purple Crab (W corner of Crematorium; dying?) and Coral-bark Willow (behind memorial water gardens).

Danson Park, Danson Road, Bexleyheath. Historic public park. Tallest Violet Willow (S of lake, W tree).

Fassnidge Park, Uxbridge. Public park. Tallest Golden Weeping Willow (canal side, N).

Finsbury Park, Seven Sisters Road. Public park. Largest Chinese Crab (NE).

Foots Cray Lane, Sidcup. Largest *Acer platanoides* 'Olmsted' (municipal planting, next to Rutland Shaw).

Franks Park, Halt Robin Road, Belvedere. Public park; old wooded parkland. Largest sport of *Quercus petraea* 'Cochleata' (SE, in woods).

Gladstone Park, Dollis Hill Lane, Willesden. Public park. Largest Box Elder (S of tennis courts); tallest *Crataegus laevigata* 'Punicea Flore Pleno' (Kendal Road border, mid); largest Violet Willow (pond, E).

Golders Hill Park, North End Road, Hampstead. Public park. Tallest *Crataegus pedicellata* (E of water garden, in valley).

Goodmayes Park, Green Lane, Goodmayes. Public park. Largest *Crataegus ellwangeriana* (Aberdour Road, W boundary) and *Ligustrum lucidum* 'Aureovariegatum' (Abbotsford Road, N boundary).

*Greenwich Park, Greenwich. The Royal Parks. Largest *Betula* x *koehnei* (Flower Gardens, near mid W gate; labelled *B. maximowicziana*), Hungarian Thorn (Flower Gardens, N) and Castor Aralia (Flower Gardens; W border, N).

Gunnersbury Cemetery, Gunnersbury Avenue. Largest and tallest Variegated Box Elders (W).

*Gunnersbury Park, Gunnersbury Avenue. Historic public park. Largest Variegated Tulip Tree (N of Small Mansion) and Daimyo Oak (walled garden).

*Hall Place, Bourne Road, Bexley. Historic public park. Largest *Prunus pendula* 'Pendula Rubra' (river bridge).

Hammersmith Cemetery, Margravine Road, Hammersmith. Tallest Almond (NE).

Hammersmith Cemetery, Clifford Avenue, North Sheen. Largest Golden Bean Tree (NE).

*Hampstead Heath. Largest Spotted Thorn (Café by bandstand SE of Parliament Hill) and Wentworth Weeping Ash (Highgate Ponds, mid W).

*Hampton Court, Hampton Wick. Open access to the gardens and ancient parkland. Largest trees of *Paulownia fortunei* (Lion Gate border); largest Golden Poplar (North Canal); one of the largest English Oaks, 'The Medieval Oak' (park S of Long Canal, mid).

Havelock Cemetery, Havelock Road, Southall. Largest *Prunus* 'Fugenzo' (gates).

Hendon Park, Queens Road, Hendon. Public park. Largest Japanese Maple (walk W of Holocaust Memorial Garden).

Holborn. Largest *Crataegus laevigata* 'Punicea' (St Andrew's churchyard).

*Holland Park, Abbotsbury Road, Kensington. Historic public park. Largest *Alnus sibirica* (Oak Enclosure; ?); tallest *Gleditsia triacanthos* 'Nana' (Azalea Walk); largest Almond-leaved Pear (Arboretum by North Lawn); tallest *Pyrus communis* 'Beech Hill' (North Lawn); tallest *P.* x *michauxii* (Oak Enclosure); tallest Willow-leafed Pear (Theatre/sports field, E tree); tallest Burr Oak (Oak Enclosure/Kyoto Garden).

Horniman Gardens, London Road, Forest Hill. Public park. Largest Weeping Narrow-leaved Ash (Horniman Drive gate, labelled *F. excelsior* 'Pendula').

*Hyde Park, Kensington. The Royal Parks. Some rare trees. Tallest Hybrid Buckeye (carpark opposite Magazine); largest and tallest Pin Oaks (dell N of police house).

Inner Temple Garden, Temple. Open lunchtimes. Largest Indian Bean Tree; largest Willow-leaved Magnolia.

*Kensington Gardens, Kensington. The Royal Parks. Many unusual trees. Largest Honshu Maple (Queen's Gate); largest and tallest *Fraxinus angustifolia* 'Veltheimii' (N of Round Pond); tallest *F. pennsylvanica* 'Variegata' (North Flower Walk); largest *Ligustrum lucidum* 'Excelsum Superbum' (Peter Pan); largest Swamp White Oak (S of Marlborough Gate); largest American Rowan (SE of Bandstand, in group of three).

Kensington Palace, Palace Green, Kensington. Largest Red May (NW tree by Orangery).

Kenwood House, Hampstead Lane, Highgate. Open access. (Largest Variegated English Elm, 1964.)

King George's Park, Buckhold Road, Wandsworth. Small public park. Largest Purple Crab (N of tennis courts).

Kings Avenue, Dormer's Wells. Largest Spire Cherry (street tree, by 89).

Lady Margaret Road, Dormer's Wells. Largest *Ulmus* 'Lobel' (street tree, by 333).

Lesnes Abbey, Abbey Road, Belvedere. (Pronouced 'Leznez'.) Open access. Largest *Acer davidii* 'Ernest Wilson' (SW).

Lincoln's Inn, Holborn. Tallest Golden Robinia (New Square).

Lordship Recreation Ground, Lordship Lane, Tottenham. Largest *Catalpa bignonioides* 'Nana' (ornamental walk, SE) and Myrobalan Plum (above ornamental walk).

Magdala Avenue, Highgate. Largest Chinese Elm (street tree; 2002).

*Marble Hill Park, Richmond Road, Twickenham. English Heritage; open access. Notable plantings dating back to the 1720s. Tallest Italian Alder (SW corner); one of the largest Black Walnuts (mid, by river); tallest Bolle's Poplar (NW, near café).

Marsworth House, Whitton Road, Haggerston. Largest *Sorbus aucuparia* 'Beissneri' (?).

Maryon Park, Woolwich Road, Charlton. Public park with rare plantings. Tallest *Crataegus pinnatifida* var. *major* (S edge) and Fastigiate Robinia (S edge).

Mayow Park, Mayow Road, Lower Sydenham. Public park. Largest Cut-leaved Rowan (W side).

Mill Hill School, Mill Hill. Home in the 18th century of Peter Collinson, who pioneered the cultivation of many American trees. Largest Pin Oak (mansion front).

Morden Cemetery, Lower Morden Lane. Largest Lombardy Poplar (N from chapel, by crematorium lawn).

Mortlake Green. Largest Midland Thorn.

*Myddelton House, Bulls Cross, Enfield. Open most days. E A Bowles' garden, now restored. Tallest Caucasian Ash (sports field); largest Myrtle-leaved Holly (S of house).

Notting Hill. One of the largest Bays (front garden of

15, Lansdowne Crescent).

Old Oak Common Lane, Acton. Largest *Ulmus* 'Lobel' (street tree, on corner of Long Drive).

Orleans House Gallery, Orleans Road, Twickenham. Public grounds. Tallest Golden Bean Tree (back garden).

*Osterley Park, Osterley. NT; open access to the old parkland and gardens. Tallest Fastigiate Norway Maple (Station Lodge, 49007); largest Variegated Sweet Chestnut (Great Meadow near house); tallest Chinese Crab (SE of Garden Lake, in group).

Palace Yard, Houses of Parliament. Largest Indian Bean Trees (in line of six).

Parliament Square, Westminster. Tallest *Catalpa* x *erubescens* 'Purpurea'.

Parsloes Park, Ivyhouse Road, Dagenham. Public park. Largest Chanticleer Pear (S).

Pembroke Lodge Gardens, Petersham Park. Open access. Largest *Crataegus flabellata* (S side of Lodge).

Petersham Lodge woodlands, River Lane, Richmond. Open access. Tallest Oriental Plane (mid).

Preston Park, Montpelier Rise, Preston. Public park. Largest *Populus alba* 'Richardii' (central path).

Pymmes Park, Sterling Way, Edmonton. Historic public park. Tallest *Crataegus pinnatifida* (S of lake, mid).

Radnor Gardens, Cross Deep, Twickenham. Small public park. Largest Western Catalpa.

Ranelagh Gardens, Royal Hospital Road, Chelsea. Royal Chelsea Hospital; open except lunchtimes. Largest *Acer davidii* 'George Forrest' (central shelter).

Ravenor Park, Ruislip Road, Greenford. Public park. Largest *Populus alba* 'Raket' (lowest tree on S side in avenue).

Rectory Park, Ruislip Road, Yeading. Public park. Tallest *Populus alba* 'Raket' (in series S of play area).

*Regent's Park, Paddington. The Royal Parks. Many rare trees. Tallest Fastigiate Horse Chestnut (E of Broad Walk, S); largest Midland Thorn (S of lake, E of Clarence Gate); largest Oregon Ash (Outer Circle opposite Hanover Terrace); largest Wisconsin Weeping Willow (Lake by Hanover Gate); largest Salamon's Weeping Willow (E of Broad Walk, S).

Richmond Cemetery, Lower Grove Road. Largest *Prunus* 'Pandora' (S cemetery, near gate); largest *P. serrulata* 'Albi-plena' (East Sheen Cemetery, mid S); largest Thurlow Weeping Willow (S cemetery, NE).

Richmond Park. The Royal Parks. Ancient deer park; rare trees in the Isabella Plantation. Tallest Umbrella Tree (Isabella Plantation; top of Acer Walk).

**The Royal Botanic Gardens, Kew. Open daily. The light sandy soils are not especially conducive to tree growth, and until recently air pollution was detrimental to most conifers, but 240 years of planting means that Kew remains by far the richest gardens for champions in Britain or Ireland. The 100ha arboretum is primarily laid out genus by genus.
Largest Golden Cappadocian Maple (NW of Palm House).
Largest *Acer* x *rotundilobum* (Maples, SW; 46802).
Largest *A. c.* var. *sinicum* (Maples, by Marianne North Gallery, 29201).
Largest and tallest Dieck's Maple (Maples, SW, 16978, and E side of Marianne North Gallery, 7101).

Largest *A. divergens* (Maples, SW; 38501).
Largest Okamoto's Maple (Woodland Glade, 8229).
Largest *A. opalus* var. *obtusatum* (N of Princess of Wales Conservatory, 10329).
Largest *A. platanoides* 'Globosum' (Maples, opposite Marianne North Gallery; 52802).
Largest *A. p.* 'Maculatum' (Maples, N of Tea Pavilion; 12501).
Largest *A. p.* 'Pyramidale Nanum' (Maples, NW; 52803).
Largest *A. p.* 'Rubrum' (Maples, N; 10355).
Largest *A.* x *pseudoheldreichii* (Bluebell Wood; 98001).
Tallest Sugar Maple (Hornbeam collection, labelled *A. platanoides*; 13054).
Largest *A. sterculiaceum* ssp. *thomsonii* (Maples, SW).
Largest Shandong Maple (S of Nursery, by Woodland Glade; 11901).
Largest Caucasian Maple (Maples, NE; 10387).
Largest Assam Horse Chestnut (Tea Pavilion/Pagoda Vista, 1601).
Largest *Aesculus* x *bushii* (Tea Pavilion/Pagoda Vista, 32801).
Largest Chinese Horse Chestnut (White Peaks, 52815).
Tallest Virginian Buckeye (E of Orangery, labelled as the type; 10440).
Largest Ohio Buckeye (E Tea Pavilion).
Largest White-bark Buckeye (N of Tea Pavilion, 66401).
Largest *A. hippocastanum* 'Incisa' (Pagoda Vista/Apples, 18615).
Largest *A. h.* 'Memmingeri' (Pagoda Vista/Apples).
Largest Fastigiate Horse Chestnut (N of Tea Pavilion, 57102).
Largest *A. indica* 'Sydney Pearce' (behind Orangery, 11434).
Largest *A.* x *marylandica* (Boathouse Walk, mid; 10428).
Largest *A. sylvatica* (woods by Holly Walk, 10433).
Largest Downy Tree of Heaven (Broadwalk, by sundial; 51002).
Largest *Alnus glutinosa* var. *barbata* (Boathouse Walk, dam end; 17437).
Tallest Caucasian Alder (SE of Lake, 10868).
Largest *Aphananthe aspera* (Elms, 6704).
Largest *Betula obscura* (Heath Garden by Pagoda, 11604).
Largest Fastigiate Hornbeam (Hornbeams, 22602).
Tallest Weeping Hornbeam (Cedar Avenue/Bluebell Wood, 74601).
Largest Purple Hornbeam (Hornbeams, 20705).
Largest *Carpinus caucasica* (Hornbeams, 39001).
Largest *C. fargesiana* (Elms/Rhododendron Dell; ?; 19660).
Tallest *C. henryana* (Hornbeams, 66409).
Largest Oriental Hornbeam (Hornbeams, 13501).
Tallest Chonosuki's Hornbeam (Hornbeams, 58904).
Tallest *C. viminea* (Hornbeams, 5209).
Largest Red Hickory (Robinias/Heath Garden, 11814).
Tallest Chinese Sweet Chestnut (Chestnuts, 65040).
Largest *Castanea sativa* 'Gros-Merle' (Chestnuts, N; 07614).
Largest and tallest *C. s.* 'Marron de Lyon' (Chestnut Walk, 44215, and ('Macrocarpa') 11966).
Largest *C. s.* 'Monstrosa' (Chestnuts, N edge; 7611).
Largest *C. s.* 'Pyramidalis' (Chestnuts, N; 10001).
Largest *Catalpa bungei* (N of Water Lily House, 901).
Largest Farges' Catalpa (E Holly Walk, N of Temperate House; 8804).

Largest Caucasian Nettle Tree (Hackberries, 15601).

Largest *Celtis laevigata* var. *smallii* (Hackberries, 66410).

Largest *C. sinensis* (Bluebell Wood, 6133).

Largest *C. tenuifolia* (Hackberries, 47019).

Tallest *Chamaecyparis lawsoniana* 'Hillieri' (Cypress Walk, 62402).

Largest *C. l.* 'Lycopodioides' (Cypress Walk/glade, 10927).

Largest Chinese Fringe Tree (N of Temperate House, 19601).

Largest Yellow-wood (E of Tea Pavilion, 63102).

Largest *Cladrastis platycarpa* (White Peaks, 14816).

Largest Chinese Yellow-wood (E of Orangery, 16289).

Tallest Cornelian Cherry (Kew Roadside S of Flagstaff, 16561).

Largest *Cornus officinalis* (King William's Temple, S; 12627).

Largest *Corylus* x *colurnoides* (Nut Walk, 12909).

Largest Chittam Wood (Temple of Bellona, 12584).

Largest Glastonbury Thorn (S of Palm House, 3302).

Largest *Crataegus pentagyna* (Apples, border; 11401).

Largest *C. persimilis* (Apples, 19501).

Largest *Cryptomeria japonica* 'Kusari-Sugi' (Cypress Walk, 25205).

Tallest X *Cupressocyparis leylandii* 'Silver Dust' (Cypress glade, 6628).

Largest *Cupressus gigantea* (Boathouse Walk/nursery, mid; 59801).

Tallest Sargent Cypress (Cypress glade, 4571).

Largest Kakis (SE of Broadwalk, 13677, and W of King William's Temple, 14153; var. *lycopersicon*).

Largest Persimmon (N of Temperate House, 50001).

Largest *Ehretia acuminata* var. *obovata* (W of Main Gate, 52526).

Largest *E. dicksonii* (King William's Temple, W; 10242).

Largest *Eucalyptus chapmaniana* (Poplars, 8117).

Largest *E. neglecta* (Marianne North Gallery, 36405).

Largest *E. rodwayi* (Zimbabwean huts, 4150).

Largest Hardy Rubber Tree (N of Berberis Dell, 91101).

Largest American Beech (Japanese Gateway/Pinetum, 13040).

Largest *Fagus sylvatica* 'Bornyensis' (Beeches, near Bamboo Garden, 14901).

Largest *F. s.* 'Grandidentata' (Beeches near lake, 44203).

Largest *F. s.* 'Remilyensis' (Beeches near lake, 7601).

Largest Narrow-leaved Ash (Ashes, above head of lake, 14480).

Largest *Fraxinus angustifolia* ssp. *syriaca* (Ashes/Magnolias, 13403).

Largest *F. excelsior* 'Concavifolia' (Ashes/Magnolias, 361?).

Tallest Weeping Single-leaved Ash (Ashes, N; 47006).

Largest *F. e.* 'Scolopendrifolia' (Ashes, N edge; 47007).

Largest *F. e.* 'Stricta' (Ashes, N; 14498).

Tallest *F. e.* 'Verrucosa' (Ashes, towards Magnolias; 48202).

Largest *F. holotricha* (Ashes/Magnolias; 12903).

Largest Pallis' Ash (Ashes, N; 13052).

Largest Blue Ash (Ashes, by Holly Walk; 19909).

Largest *F. velutina* var. *toumeyi* (Ashes, lake end; 11402).

Tallest Afghan Ash (Ashes, by Princess Walk; 16128).

Largest and tallest Caspian Locusts (Robinia Avenue, E side near Tea Pavilion, 11949, and Acacias, NE, 23705).

Largest and tallest Japanese Honey Locusts (Acacias near Tea Pavilion, 11972, and Acacia Avenue, by Tea Pavilion,

59902).

Tallest *Gleditsia macracantha* (E of Tea Pavilion, 16102).

Tallest Golden Honey Locust (head of lake, 16816).

Tallest Sea Buckthorn (S of Secluded Garden, 6380).

Largest *Ilex aquifolium* 'Contorta' (S of Princess of Wales Conservatory).

Largest Leather-leaf Holly (Holly Walk, mid; 13396).

Largest Moonlight Holly (Holly Walk, W; 13407).

Largest *I. a.* 'Latispina' (Holly Walk, NE; 13424).

Largest *I. a.* 'Recurva' (Holly Walk, W; 13424).

Largest American Holly (Holly Walk, W; 13516).

Largest Texan Walnut (Pagoda, SE; 10501).

Largest *Juniperus chinensis* 'Pendula' (Boathouse Walk/nursery, mid; 10314).

Largest Tamarack (Larches, 10630).

Largest *Ligustrum compactum* (back of ruined arch mound).

Largest *Liriodendron tulipifera* 'Integrifolium' (Temple of Bellona, 17551).

Tallest Tanbark Oak (Oaks, mid N; 801).

Largest *Magnolia* 'Kewensis' (Magnolias, 18379).

Largest Kobushi (Azalea Garden/Ashes, 2101).

Largest Star Magnolia (Temple of Bellona, 11006).

Largest *M.* x *veitchii* 'Alba' (Azalea Garden, 12708).

Largest *Malus baccata* var. *himalaica* (Apples, 15503).

Largest *M. b.* 'Lady Northcliffe' (S of Palm House).

Largest *M.* 'Laxton's Red' (Broadwalk/Bell Lawn; 5901).

Tallest *M.* x *purpurea* 'Aldenhamensis' (Lion Gate).

Largest *M. rockii* (N of Pagoda, 61408).

Largest *M.* 'Royalty' (N of Water Lily House, 34201).

Largest Weeping Mulberry (NE of King William's Temple, 11548).

Largest *Morus cathayana* (N of King William's Temple, 42204).

Largest *Nothofagus menziesii* x *obliqua* (Bluebell Woods, 3099).

Largest Lenga (Bluebell Woods, 1305).

Largest Ironwood (Duke's Garden, 14189).

Largest *Paulownia taiwaniana* (Woodland Glade/Cedar Avenue, 6141).

Largest Amur Cork Tree (Bamboo Garden, 18676).

Largest Colorado Spruce (Boathouse Walk, mid; 10648).

Tallest *Pinus ayacahuite* var. *veitchii* (Pines near dam, 6701).

Largest and tallest Calabrian (Pines W of Cherry Walk, 18392, and Pines below Lily Pond, 10698).

Largest Lace-bark Pine (Crab Mound, 13232).

Largest *P. cembroides* ssp. *orizabensis* (Pines near dam, 67001).

Largest *P. eldarica* (Boathouse Walk, W; 6249).

Largest Limber Pine (Pines near dam, 16455).

Largest Gregg Pine (Pines below Lily Pond, 13699).

Largest and tallest Aleppo Pines (Pines below Lily Pond, 10697 and 10696).

Largest Masson Pine (Pines near Lily Pond, 32505).

Largest Pond Pine (Pines near dam, 18414).

Largest and tallest Yunnan Pines (Pines, mid W, 65021 and 16555).

Largest Chinese Pistachio (N of Tea Pavilion, 51886).

Tallest *Platanus* x *hispanica* 'Augustine Henry' (Azalea Garden, 10001).

Largest Oriental Thuja (Cypresses, 16075).

Largest *Populus adenopoda* (Poplars, W of Lilac Garden; 8203).

Largest *P. nigra* 'Lombardy Gold' (N of Ice House, 2380).

Largest *P.* 'Rasumowskyana' (Brentford Gate toilets, 12820).

Largest *Prunus alabamensis* (Cherries, 19015).

Largest *P.* 'Ariake' (Broadwalk cherry group, 16006).

Largest *P. avium* 'Adiana' (Cherries, 11301).

Largest Naples Plum (Cherries, 11301).

Largest Flag Cherry (Japanese Gateway, 1105).

Largest *P. hirtipes* 'Semiplena' (Bluebell Woods/Woodland Glade, 42206).

Largest Black Cherry (S of Princess of Wales Conservatory).

Largest *P.* 'Umineko' (Cherry Walk, 14278).

Largest *P.* 'Yae-beni-oshima' (W of Rose Garden, 1128).

Tallest Hybrid Wingnut (behind Water Lily House, 66303).

Largest Chinese Wingnut (N of Rose Garden, 51249).

Largest *Pyrus bretschneideri* (Hawthorns, 1303).

Largest *P. communis* 'Beech Hill' (SE of Broadwalk, 70801).

Largest Plymouth Pear (Apples, 44301).

Largest Snow Pear (N of Water Lily House, 11530).

Largest Ussurian Pear (Apples, 62408).

Largest *Quercus afares* (Oaks, off Syon Vista; 44602).

Largest Encina (Mount Pleasant, 13450).

Largest *Q. aliena* (Oaks, N end; 15949).

Largest *Q. a.* var. *acuteserrata* (Oaks, N end; 15683).

Largest *Q. arkansana* (Oaks, N; 66406).

Tallest Swamp White Oak (S edge of Oaks, 3604).

Largest *Q. boissieri* (Oaks, N extension; 6595).

Largest Chestnut-leaved Oak (N of Palm House).

Largest Californian Live Oak (Oaks, far N; 45802).

Largest *Q. crassifolia* (Cypress glade, 93302).

Largest Spanish Oak (Oaks, N end; ?; 32807).

Largest *Q. glabrescens* (Cypress glade; 16298).

Largest *Q. gravesii* (Oaks, N extension; 3975).

Largest *Q. hartwissiana* (W of Holly Walk, 12402).

Largest *Q.* x *heterophylla* (Oaks, S; 61801).

Largest *Q.* x *kewensis* (Oaks, N; 16301).

Largest Valley Oak (Bluebell Wood, 85801).

Largest Ludwig's Oak (Oaks, N end tree; 12903).

Largest *Q. mongolica* ssp. *crispula* var. *grosseserrata* (Oaks by dell, mid; 13001).

Largest Water Oak (Isleworth Gate, 207).

Largest *Q. petraea* 'Cochleata' (Oaks, S end; 40107).

Largest Willow Oak (Oaks, N; 204).

Largest Ubame Oak (Secluded Garden border, 16028).

Largest Armenian Oak (Oaks, mid N; 23703).

Largest *Q. robur* var. *brutia* (Oaks, N; 32702).

Largest *Q. r.* 'Thomasii' (Oaks, N; 101).

Largest *Q. serrata* (Oaks, N; 56702).

Largest Shumard Oak (Oaks, S; 3502).

Largest Macedonian Oak (Oaks, N; 7302).

Largest Turner's Oak (NW of Princess of Wales Conservatory).

Largest Pink Robinia (Acacia Avenue, W side, mid; 13382).

Largest *Robinia luxurians* (Acacia Avenue, W side, S; 11923).

Tallest False Acacia (Robinias/Kew Road wall; 11932).

Largest and tallest trees of *R. pseudoacacia* 'Monophylla Fastigiata' (Acacia Avenue, W side, S, 22606, and Robinias near Pagoda, 22604).

Largest Fastigiate Robinia (Acacia Avenue near Tea Pavilion, W side; 11933).

Largest *R. p.* 'Rehderi' (Robinias, mid; 11936).

Largest *R. p.* 'Tortuosa' (N of Tea Pavilion; 11937).

Largest *Salix* x *calodendron* (Boathouse Walk, W; 20082).

Largest *Sophora affinis* (Robinias near Pagoda, 18102).

Largest *S. japonica* var. *pubescens* (Robinias, S; 44504).

Tallest Variegated Pagoda Tree (Robinias, S; 18312).

Largest *S. pachycarpa* (Robinias, S; 35901).

Largest *Sorbus alnifolia* x *aria* (Cherries, 51801).

Largest *S. commixta* var. *rufoferruginea* (S of Nursery, Woodland Glade; 38701).

Largest Mexican Swamp Cypress (Lake, NW; 49801).

Largest White Basswood (Limes, S; 12742).

Largest *Tilia insularis* (Limes, by Flagstaff; 11580).

Largest and tallest Mongolian Limes (Limes, 23801 and 86).

Largest *T. platyphyllos* 'Tortuosa' (Limes, mid; 12987).

Largest Vine-leaved Lime (Limes, N; 12980).

Largest *T. tomentosa* 'Spectabilis' (Limes, N; 1207).

Largest *Tsuga canadensis* 'Albospica' (E end of Boathouse Walk, 28504).

Largest *T. c.* 'Macrophylla' (Boathouse Walk, E; 12236).

Largest *Ulmus bergmanniana* (Elms, 11708).

Largest *U. castaneifolia* (SW from Japanese gateway, 11726).

Largest and tallest trees of *Zelkova schneideriana* (Brentwood Gate, 6615 and 6614).

Largest Chinese Zelkova (Brentford Gate, 21402).

Ruskin Park, Denmark Hill, Peckham. Public park. Largest Elder (SE, by Palladian shelter).

St James' Park, Westminster. The Royal Parks. Largest *Fraxinus excelsior* 'Verrucosa' (N of lake, mid E; 12026).

St John's Gardens, St John's Road, Isleworth. Recreation ground. Largest Cut-leaved Silver Maple (mid NW).

St Margaret's Pleasure Grounds, Twickenham. Residents' garden. Tallest Yellow Buckeye (lakeside).

St Mark's church, Battersea Rise, Wandsworth. Tallest Salamon's Weeping Willow.

St Michael's Community Centre, Wrotham Road, East Wickham. Largest *Prunus* 'Accolade'.

Shrubbery Road, Southall. Largest Schmitt's Cherry (street tree, by 2).

Southall Park, High Street, Southall. Public park. Largest Golden Weeping Ash (centre).

South Ealing Cemetery, South Ealing Road. Largest and tallest trees of *Acer platanoides* 'Drummondii' (E Cemetery, S).

Southgate Cemetery, Waterfall Road, Arnos Grove. Largest Hybrid Tansy-leaved Thorn (mid W).

South Park, South Park Road, Ilford. Public park. Largest Double Gean (mid NW) and *Tilia* 'Moltkei' (E edge, mid N).

South Park Gardens, Trinity Road, Wimbledon. Small public park. Largest *Ulmus* x *hollandica* 'Dampieri Aurea' (SE).

Sydenham Wells Park, Wells Park Road, Sydenham. Public park. Largest Bolle's Poplar (SE corner); largest *Prunus padus* 'Albertii' (E edge).

**Syon Park, London Road, Brentford. Most of the gardens open daily. A notable tree collection since the 16th century.

Tallest Zoeschen Maple (N of Flora).

Largest Cut-leaved Alder (Duke's Garden, public path).

Largest Turkish Hazel (N of lake; mid W; 2.30-36).

Largest *Fagus sylvatica* 'Purpurea Tricolor' (near lake, E from Flora's lawn).

Largest Raywood Ash (E from Flora's lawn).

Largest Afghan Ash (SE of Conservatory; 2.10-51).

Tallest Mandshurian Walnut (N of lake, mid; 2.30-100).

Largest Golden Rain Tree (N side of Conservatory; 2.20-62).

Tallest Sweet Gum (N of lake, mid; 2.30-123).

Largest *Pinus densiflora* 'Umbraculifera' (rockery W of Flora's lawn).

Largest Korean Hill Cherry (Flora's lawn, SE, labelled *P. sargentii*; 2.40-189).

Largest *Quercus glauca* (Duke's Walk; 2.20-6).

Tallest Shingle Oak (N of Flora; W tree).

Largest *Q. infectoria* (Church Walk – Rose Garden end; 425).

Largest Burr Oak (N of Flora; W edge, labelled *Q. dentata*).

Largest Chinquapin Oak (N of Lake, E. bridge).

Largest *Q. pagoda* (Duke's Garden, E corner).

One of the largest Swamp Cypresses (North park, by outer lake).

Teddington Cemetery, Shacklegate Lane, Teddington. Largest Mop-head Acacia (SW).

*Terrace Gardens, Petersham Road, Richmond. Public park. Largest *Populus* 'Rochester' (N).

Valentines Park, Cranbrook Road, Ilford. Historic public park. Tallest Hybrid Cockspur Thorn (S border).

*Victoria Park, South Hackney. Public park; many uncommon trees. One of the largest Figs (Old English Gardens, S edge); largest Narrow-leaved Ash (N of Lake, labelled *F. excelsior*); tallest *Gleditsia triacanthos* 'Nana' (W edge).

The Watergardens, Coombe Road, Kingston Hill. Residents' garden; NGS open days. Woodland garden on the site of Veitch's Coombe Wood nurseries. Largest *Chamaecyparis obtusa* 'Nana Gracilis' (NW flats back lawn; labelled 'Nana').

Waterlow Park, High Street, Highgate. Historic public park. Largest *Crataegus laevigata* 'Masekii' (SE edge) and *C. l.* 'Punicea' (W – top of sloping lawn).

Watling Park, Watling Avenue, Burnt Oak. Public park. Largest *Crataegus laevigata* 'Plena' (Watling Avenue gate).

Wembley parish church, Wembley High Road. Largest *Acer negundo* var. *violaceum*.

West Ham Cemetery, Cemetery Road, Forest Gate. Largest *Malus* x *gloriosa* 'Oekonomierat Echtermeyer' (mid NE).

West Ham Park, Portway, West Ham. Historic public park. Largest *Prunus* 'Kursar' (gardens, NE).

Westminster College Garden, Westminster Abbey. Open lunchtimes. One of the largest Figs.

*Woodcock Park, Shaftesbury Avenue, Kenton. Public park on site of large old garden; many rare trees. Largest Oriental Alder (W edge) and Oleaster (Brookside Close edge).

Woodford. Largest Fastigiate Rain Tree (front garden of 79, St Anthony's Avenue).

York House, Richmond Road, Twickenham. Historic public park. Largest Golden Hazel (rose gardens); tallest Chinese Tree Privet (N; SE tree in group).

Norfolk

The county's exceptional trees are largely confined to big old estates, and have yet to be extensively studied. The climate is dry and often chilly, while soils are varied: Lynford Arboretum occupies the light sands of the Breckland, while Ryston Hall lies above fertile greensand on the fringe of the Fens.

*Bradenham Hall, West Bradenham, Thetford. Occasionally open. Large young arboretum.

Earlham Cemetery. Largest Whitebeam (1990).

Fulmodeston Severals, Fulmodestone, Fakenham. Largest Bornmuller's Fir (1992).

Haveringland Hall, Cawston, Aylesham. One of the largest Small-leaved Limes (1991).

Hethel, Wymondham. The Hethel Old Thorn, once the largest Hawthorn, in field near church (Norfolk Wildlife Trust nature reserve).

*Holkham Hall, Wells-next-the-Sea. Public access to the gardens in summer. Huge historic parkland; many rare trees. Tallest Pencil Cedar (1973).

*Lynford Arboretum, Mundford, Brandon. FC. Extensive arboretum developed since 1949. Tallest Sargent's Cherry (1990).

Ryston Hall, Downham Market. A large private Edwardian collection (1995).

Tallest Eagle-claw Maple.

Largest *Acer pseudoplatanus* 'Brilliantissimum'.

Largest *A. sterculiaceum*.

Largest *Alnus glutinosa* 'Imperialis' (?).

Largest Grey Alder.

Largest *A. japonica*.

Largest Weeping Single-leaved Ash.

Largest Maries' Ash (East Garden).

Largest and tallest Red Ashes.

Largest *Fraxinus pennsylvanica* 'Variegata'.

Tallest Sentry Ginkgo.

Tallest Berlin Poplar.

Tallest Eugene's Poplar.

Largest *Populus nigra* 'Afghanica'.

Tallest Lombardy Poplar.

Largest *P.* 'Petrowskyana'.

Talbot Manor, Fincham. Many rare trees planted since the 1940s (1978). Tallest Weeping Grey Alder; tallest *Alnus sibirica*; largest *Gleditsia japonica* var. *koraiensis*; tallest *Malus* x *soulardii*; largest Parasol de St Julien; largest Grey Cherry (1973); largest *Tilia tomentosa* f. *fastigiata*.

Weasenham Woods, Weasenham All Saints, Castle Acre. A long-standing experiment in continuous cover forestry, with many unusual trees reaching great sizes. Tallest Japanese Big-leaved Magnolia (1990).

Northamptonshire

The less sticky soils of the higher ground grow some fine trees, concentrated particularly in the old estates of Rockingham Forest in the north.

Abington Park, Northampton. Public park. Tallest Indian Bean Tree.

Althorp House, Weedon, Harleston. (Pronounced

The Royal Botanic Gardens at Kew remain our largest collection of very rare trees (*Zelkova schneideriana*).

'Altrop'.) Open daily except in winter. Largest Santa Lucia Fir (1983).

Boughton House, Weekley. The park opens most afternoons in summer. Tallest Musk Willow (1987).

Bozeat, Northampton. One of the largest Hybrid Elms (Dychurch Lane – Back Lane opposite playing field in hedgerow, at SP911592; 2000).

Byeways, Grange Lane, Pitsford, Northampton. Largest Portugal Laurel (1994; ?).

*Castle Ashby Gardens, Castle Ashby. Open daily. A range of rare trees. Largest *Acer platanoides* 'Cucullatum' (park).

Courteenhall, Roade, Northampton. Largest *Alnus incana* 'Laciniata' and Huntingdon Elm.

*Deene Park, Corby. Regularly open. Many rare trees. Tallest Spaeth's Ash.

Kettering Crematorium. Largest Foxglove Tree.

Little Addington, Kettering. Largest Black Mulberry (garden of 2, Evergreen Drive, 1994).

Milton Malsor. One of the largest Sweet Chestnuts (in old parkland near the village, 1987).

Northampton. One of the largest Copper Beeches (rear of 47 Sheep Street).

'The Old Elm Tree', Higham Ferrers, Wellingborough. Largest Huntingdon Elm (front garden).

Salcey Forest, Hartwell. (One of the largest English Oaks, 1825.)

Sudborough Old Rectory, Kettering. NGS open days. Largest False Acacia.

Thenford House, Middleton Cheney. Young private arboretum. One of the largest Sweet Chestnuts (1986).

Northumberland

The widely spaced old estates of the eastern lowlands and Tynedale have often grown fine and rare trees; cool summers and the shelter of the Cheviots means that (northwards from the industrial pollution of Newcastle) conifers grow better than anywhere in England.

Alnwick Castle, Alnwick. Open most days (pronounced 'Annick'). Largest *Ilex aquifolium* 'Golden Milkmaid' (1977).

Beaufront Castle, Corbridge. One of the tallest Beeches (W of house); largest Blue Colorado Spruce (1982); tallest Bristlecone Pine.

*Cragside, Rothbury. NT; open most days. The limestone gorge of the river Debden grows some of the tallest conifers in England. Tallest Caucasian Fir (Rustic Bridge, 4242); Douglas Fir – tallest tree in England (bottom of pinetum, toward gorge path).

Etal, Lowick. Largest *Juniperus chinensis* 'Keteleeri' (1991).

Falloden Hall, Alnwick. Largest Sea Buckthorn (1992).

*Howick Hall, Alnwick. Open daily through summer. A garden close to the sea with many rare and some tender trees. Largest Wilson's Magnolia.

Kyloe Wood, Beal. Rare trees planted among the forestry plantations. Largest X *Cupressocyparis leylandii* 'Haggerston Grey' (121); tallest Western Larch; tallest Shore Pine (sawmill, 1991).

Painshawfield Park, Stocksfield, Corbridge. Tallest Foxtail Pine (edge of field).

Wallington, Cambo, Morpeth. NT; open daily. Largest *Sorbus reticulata* ssp. *pekinensis* (Walled Garden, 1992).

Nottinghamshire

The 'Dukeries' on the sandy soils of Sherwood Forest in the north-east retain large areas of old parkland, but few species grow really well here and there has been very little planting of rarities. However, the county's trees remains under-studied.

Sherwood Forest, Edwinstone. National Nature Reserve. One of the largest English Oaks, 'The Major Oak' (Birklands, at SK665615).

Oxfordshire

A county of rich, intensively-farmed soils and many big estates, whose notable trees have in general been under-recorded for many years. The soils most conducive to tree-growth are along the skirts of the Cotswolds to the north-west, on the Chilterns in the south-east, and on isolated Greensand hills near Oxford.

Buscot Park, Faringdon. NT; open most days except in winter. Tallest Pyrenean Pine (house; N edge).

Crowsley Park, Henley. A range of rare trees. Largest *Juniperus chinensis* 'Albospica' and tallest Red Oak (park, mid) in 1978.

Ducklington. One of the largest Hawthorns (in hedge, 1988).

Faringdon church. Largest Golden Box (1986).

Kingston Bagpuize House, Kingston Bagpuize. Frequent open days. Many rare plants. Largest *Ilex macrocarpa* (161; 1996).

Magdalen College, Oxford. (Largest Hybrid Elm, blown 1911.)

Norham End, Oxford. Largest Trident Maple (garden on site of Norham House, visible from road).

Nuneham Park, Nuneham Courtenay. The pinetum is open most days as the Harcourt Arboretum. One of the largest Persian Ironwoods (estate near house, 1993).

*Oxford Botanic Garden, Rose Lane, Oxford. Open daily. Britain's oldest botanic garden: 2ha in the city cultivated since 1621. Largest Western Redbud (CO1900); largest *Malus bhutanica* (MTG46); largest *M.* x *schiedeckeri* 'Hillieri' (MH46); largest White Mulberry (MA1800); largest *Salix babylonica* var. *pekinensis* 'Tortuosa' (SMT50); tallest Bollwyller Pear (SA50).

Rycote Park, Thame. One of the largest Oriental Planes (mound behind house, 1983).

Witney Cemetery. Largest Young's Golden Juniper (chapel, 1988).

Wychwood, Charlbury. Large ancient woodland, inaccessible to the public. Tallest Orchard Apple hybrid (1984).

Rutland

Lyndon Hall, Oakham. Largest Buttonwood Plane (?) and largest Valonia Oak (1984).

The largest Rowans are often found in harsh, upland conditions. Brook Vessons Nature Reserve on the Stiperstones, Shropshire.

Shropshire

The finest recorded trees are largely confined to the south and west, where, in the shelter of high hills, soils derived from the Old Red Sandstone grow huge oaks and churchyard Yews. There are rather few notable collections.

Bitterley. One of the largest English Oaks, 'the Crowleasowes Oak'.

Brook Vessons (Shropshire Wildlife Trust nature reserve), Pontesbury. One of the largest Rowans (boundary, by/on old wall).

Broome, Craven Arms. Largest Wild Pear (The Old Smithy, 1993).

Clun church. One of the largest Yews (N of church).

Hawkstone Park, Weston-under-Redcastle. The park with its historic follies is open daily through summer; the house is a hotel. Largest Sugar Pine (1992); tallest *Taxus baccata* 'Adpressa' (1978).

Leaton Knolls, Shrewsbury. (Tallest Cedar of Lebanon, blown 1993.)

Longnor Hall, Longnor, Church Stretton. Tallest Wild Black Poplar (streamside behind house); one of the largest Broad-leaved Limes.

Loughton church. One of the largest Yews (E of church).

Lydham Manor, Lydham, Bishop's Castle. One of the largest English Oaks, 'The Lydham Manor Oak'.

Norbury church. One of the largest Yews (S of church).

Oakly Park, Ludlow. Largest Eastern Hemlock (drive, E, 1995).

Pitchford Hall, Pitchford, Shrewsbury. Largest Broad-leaved Lime.

Quarry Park, Shrewsbury. Public park. Largest Cut-leaved Hornbeam (near river, by swimming baths and bus shelter).

*Walcot Hall, Lydbury North, Bishops Castle. NGS open days. Large and rare trees. Largest Variegated Nootka Cypress (reverting; 1995).

West Felton, Oswestry. Original West Felton Yew (preserved in open area in housing estate).

Somerset

A county with a particularly wide variety of growth conditions. Humid valleys under Exmoor shelter some of England's tallest conifers, while the hot summers and rich limestone of Bath have made the city's parks ideal for many broadleaves. The central levels are almost treeless, but many fine specimens grow in the old estates on the hills along the Dorset border.

Ashbrittle church, Wiveliscombe. One of the largest Yews (SE of church).

*Bath Botanic Gardens, Bath. Public gardens, within Royal Victoria Park (qv); founded in 1887 to house the tree collection of C E Broome. Largest Variegated Incense

Cedar (W of Great Dell); largest *Cotoneaster glaucophyllus* f. *serotinus* (pond); largest Hybrid Cockspur Thorn (mid E); tallest *Ehretia acuminata* var. *obovata* (N, mid); largest *Photinia serratifolia* (mid); tallest Chinese Necklace Poplar (mid S); tallest Silver Pendent Lime (SW corner).

Bitton Vicarage, Bath. (Largest Exeter Elm in 1960.)

Brooklands, Blackheath, Langport. Tallest Scotch Laburnum (1982).

Cannington. One of the largest Wild Black Poplars (public park by re-aligned A39).

Chapel Knap Gardens, Porlock Weir. Plant collection developed by Norman Hadden through the the mid 20th century. Largest Veitch's Magnolia and *Ternstroemia gymnanthera*.

Clapton Court, Clapton-by-Crewkerne. One of the largest Ashes (valley NE of house).

Clarence Park, Weston-super-mare. Public park. Largest Musk Willow (617; 1995).

Creech St Michael church, Taunton. Tallest Pissard's Plum (1986).

Dillington House, Ilminster. One of the largest Cork Oaks (1988).

*Dunster Castle, Dunster. NT; gardens and park open daily; National Collection of *Arbutus*. Tallest Pond Cypress (lower garden, 1991).

Greencombe, Porlock. Regularly open. A remarkable garden created on poor soils and a steep north-facing slope. Two of the largest Hollies.

Green Park, Charles Street, Bath. Public park. Largest and tallest Double Horse Chestnuts (W side); largest *Platanus* x *hispanica* 'Pyramidalis' (E side).

Hazlegrove (King's Bruton Preparatory School), Sparkford, Yeovil. One of the largest English Oaks, 'the King's Oak' (park).

Hedgemead Park, London Road, Bath. Public park. Largest Double Horse Chestnut (mid).

Henrietta Park, Henrietta Street, Bath. Public park. Largest Purple Sycamore (mid); tallest Purple Crab (mid N).

Kilve Priory, Kilve, Nether Stowey. One of the largest Wild Black Poplars in 1970.

Leigh Woods, Abbots Leigh, Bristol. FC. Tallest Wild Cherry (nature trail at ST555740; 1988).

Mallet Court Nursery, Curry Mallet, Taunton. Rare young trees. Tallest *Crataegus monogyna* 'Multiplex' (1989).

Nettlecombe Court Field Studies Centre, Williton. Largest West Himalayan Cypress in 1984.

Royal Bath & West Showground, Shepton Mallett. Largest *Ulmus* 'Urban' (FC Elm trial, plot 1; 1997).

*Royal Victoria Park, Upper Bristol Road, Bath. Public park (see also Bath Botanic Gardens); a variety of rare trees. Largest Kentucky Coffee Tree (under Royal Avenue, E).

Sydney Gardens, Sydney Place, Bath. Public park. Largest Golden Cappadocian Maple (NW) and Yellow Catalpa (pavilion).

Tetton House, Kingston St Mary, Yeovil. Largest Austrian Pine (1995).

*Wayford Manor, Crewkerne. NGS open days. Tallest *Acer palmatum* 'Shishigashira', Monarch Birch and Stone Pine.

Staffordshire

Ex-industrial sprawl alternates with fragments of rolling countryside with old estates, where the notable trees had for long to contend with some of the highest levels of pollution in Britain.

Field, Uttoxeter. Largest Wych Elm (felled by 1636).

Hanchurch Yews, Hanchurch. The garden includes a grove of ancient Yews. Largest Pacific Dogwood (1995).

*Trentham Gardens, Stone Road, Trentham. Open daily through summer. Fine and rare trees in the gardens along the banks of the Trent. Tallest Manna Ash (1994).

*Weston Park, Weston-under-Lizard, Shifnal. Regularly open; a grand estate with many unusual trees. Largest Variegated Sycamore (Big Lawn) and Sweet Bay (Temple Pool).

Suffolk

An intensively farmed county with warm, dry summers, notable for huge old oaks and the survival of elm trees in great variety. Its trees have been rather poorly recorded.

*Abbey Garden, Mustow Street, Bury St Edmunds. Public park (on the site of early Victorian botanic gardens). Largest *Acer grosseri* (Cloister Garden, labelled var. *hersii*) and Turkish Hazel.

Boxted Hall, Bury St. Edmunds. Largest and one of the tallest Walnuts.

Chelsworth, Hadleigh. One of the largest Ashes (near Poplar); largest Black Italian Poplar (River Brett below village bridge).

East Bergholt. (Largest English Elm in 1942.)

*East Bergholt Place, East Bergholt. Open daily through summer; large gardens with many plants brought back from China early in the 20th century. Largest Golden Oak of Cyprus.

George Street, Ipswich. Largest *Prunus* x *yedoensis* 'Ivensii' (1995).

Hawstead Place Farm, Bury St. Edmunds. Three of the largest Oriental Planes (field).

Hengrave Hall, Mildenhall Road, Hengrave, Bury St. Edmunds. Open by appointment. Largest Chinese Juniper (drive, 30m from lodge gates).

Henham Hall, Beccles. Open days. Largest *Larix* x *pendula* 'Repens' (near walled garden, viewable from footpath).

Huntingfield Hall Farm, Huntingfield. Fragments remain of one of the largest English Oaks, the 'Queen Elizabeth Oak'.

Ickworth Park & Gardens, Horringer, Bury St Edmund. NT; open daily; enormous historic park. National Collection of *Buxus*. Largest Downy Oak (park by fence); one of the largest English Oaks, 'the Tea Party Oak'.

New Bells Farm, Haughley Green. One of the largest English Oaks, 'the Haughley Oak'.

Notcutt's Nursery, 74 Cumberland Street, Woodbridge. Largest Golden Honey Locust (1994).

Park Drive, Worlingham, Beccles. Largest Caucasian Elm (retained on verge).

Sotterley Hall, Sotterley, Beccles. Large pinetum. Tallest Blue Colorado Fir and largest Blue Douglas Fir (1985).

Staverton Park, Eyke, Woodbridge. One of the country's best preserved medieval deer-parks, with many ancient oak pollards and huge hollies in the wooded Thicks. Tallest Hollies.

Stonham Aspal church. Largest *Platycladus orientalis* 'Elegantissima' (by E window).

Woodbridge. Tallest Raywood Ash (public land on Kyson Hill, once part of Notcutt's nursery; 1994).

Surrey

Britain's most wooded area; sandy soils predominate and, in the west, conifers prevail in the landscape more than in any other southern county. In the north, the Bagshot Sands are light and prone to summer droughts, but the Lower Greensand, which creates a band of high hills in the south, forms perhaps the best of all soils for all-round tree-growth. With London so near, there are many rich estates and a wealth of old gardens. Only the sticky clays of the Weald and the high downs lack concentrations of champions.

*Albury Park and House, Shere, Albury. The gardens across the river from the mansion, designed by John Evelyn, are regularly open in summer; the residents' garden opens for the NGS. The picturesque Tillingbourne valley provides ideal conditions for many trees. Original Albury Walnut (house lawn); tallest Cucumber Tree (garden; valley floor, E); largest Japanese Hop Hornbeam (garden; valley floor, E); tallest *Quercus castaneifolia* x *cerris* (garden; valley floor, W); largest *Q.* 'Pyrami' (garden; valley floor, W end); tallest Black Oak (garden; valley floor, mid).

Alderbrook Park, Cranleigh. NGS open days. Edwardian gardens with rare trees. Tallest Variegated Sweet Chestnut (N drive); largest Pillar Apples (NE).

Ashtead church, Leatherhead. Largest Austrian Pine.

Bagshot Park, Bagshot. Largest Red Maples; largest *Ilex* x *beanii*; one of the largest Cypress Oaks.

Brookwood Cemetery, Cemetery Pales, Brookwood. Largest White Cypress (S of St Chad's Avenue).

Burford Lodge, Westhumble, Dorking. NT; residents' garden. Largest *Carpinus turczaninowii* var. *ovalifolia* (S end tree in arboretum).

Burwood Park estate, Walton-on-Thames. One of the largest Swamp Cypresses (residents' garden; W end of Heart Pond, at TQ100639).

*Busbridge Lakes, Godalming. NGS open days. Fine and old trees. Largest *Aesculus* x *carnea* 'Briotii' (field to S); one of the tallest Horse Chestnuts (S line, mid).

Camberley. Tallest Saucer Magnolia (garden of 26, Heatherdale Road; 1996).

Chobham Place Wood, Chobham. Tallest Strawberry Tree (SU963640).

Coldharbour, Dorking. Largest Hazel (lower side of Broomehall Road just below church, at TQ148436).

Coverwood House, Peaslake Road, Ewhurst. Coverwood Lakes, below, opens under the NGS. Tallest Kobushi and Chinese Quince (1986).

Crowhurst church. One of the largest Yews.

Dogflud Way, Farnham. Largest *Populus tremula* 'Fastigiata' (street tree, opposite Sports Centre).

Dorking. Largest *Prunus sargentii* 'Fastigiata' (flats in Hampstead Road, by church).

Epsom Cemetery, Ashley Road, Epsom. Tallest X *Cupressocyparis leylandii* 'Castlewellan Gold'.

Esher. Largest Lilac (garden of 19, Esher Place Avenue).

Esher Place, Esher Avenue, Esher. Largest Tulip Tree (back garden).

Ewell Court Park, Ewell Court Avenue, West Ewell. Public park. Largest Salamon's Weeping Willow (in scrub S of stream at W end; ?).

Frensham Hall estate, Shottermill, Haslemere. The grounds have long been sub-divided but some exceptional trees survive on a sheltered slope on greensand soils. Largest Monarch Birch (Deer Wood, near top, N); tallest *Chamaecyparis lawsoniana* 'Wisselii' (Deer Wood, bottom edge); tallest Dove Tree (top of Deer Wood, N); largest *Taxus baccata* 'Adpressa Variegata' (S of Hall garden); largest Golden Yew (just E of Hall garden).

Gatton Hall (The Royal Alexandra and Albert School), Rocky Lane, Redhill. The historic gardens are regularly open. Tallest *Ilex aquifolium* 'Aurea Marginata' (S side of drive approaching mansion); one of the largest Rowans (NE corner of mansion).

Glebe House, Leigh Place Lane, Godstone. Tallest *Chamaecyparis lawsoniana* 'Columnaris'.

Godalming. Largest Sour Cherry (Tuesley Lane, in hedge at SU965420; ?).

Grayswood Hill, Highercombe Road, Haslemere. One of the most extensive private tree collections in Britain. Largest Lime-Leafed Maple (W side of vista lawn, mid). One of the largest Italian Maples (S of drive by house). Largest *Chamaecyparis lawsoniana* 'Grayswood Pillar' (Lodge). Largest *C. l.* 'Hillieri' (below S terrace in lawn). Largest *C. l.* 'Naberi' (W of tennis court). Largest *C. l.* 'Winston Churchill' (E of vista lawn). Largest Big-leaved Cornel (SE corner of garden). Largest *Cupressus macrocarpa* 'Goldcrest' (W of house). Largest Skyrocket Juniper (S of drive, mid). Largest Bishop Pine (E from vista lawn). Largest Lebanon Oak (S beds, SW boundary). Largest Black Oak (field to S). Tallest *Thuja occidentalis* 'Holmstrup' (Vista lawn, near front).

Guildford Cemetery The Mount, Guildford. Tallest *Chamaecyparis lawsoniana* 'Ellwoodii' (top of upper cemetery).

Hale, Farnham. Largest Spire Cherry (Alma Way/Elm Road street tree, outside 39).

Hambledon church. One of the largest Yews (SE).

Hannah Peschar Sculpture Garden, Okewood, Ockley. Regularly open. Part of the Leith Vale estate, a once-famous garden with many rare plantings. Tallest Hubei Crab (drive).

Heath Cottage, Puttenham, Guildford. (Largest Variegated Plane; blown 1987.)

Horton, Epsom. Largest Manna Ash (one of many fine trees on the since-developed Long Grove Hospital site, 1995).

Huntswood, Weydown Road, Haslemere. Largest Japanese Rowan.

*Hydon Nurseries, Clock Barn Lane, Hydon Heath, Godalming. Many rare trees in the nursery garden. Largest Joseph Rock's Rowan (garden; fence by greenhouses).

The original (and largest) Albury Walnut, at Albury Park, Surrey.

Kitlands, Coldharbour, Dorking. Outstanding trees in the shelter of Leith Hill. Largest *Cryptomeria japonica* 'Pygmaea'; one of the largest Tulip Trees; largest *Nothofagus betuloides*.

*Knaphill and Slocock Nursery, Barrs Lane, Woking. The old nursery gardens with many rare trees are open weekdays. Original Weeping Beech (E of Waterer's Walk, S); largest Weeping Pagoda Tree (N from garden centre, by outbuildings); largest Pond Cypress (E of Waterer's Walk, N).

Leatherhead. Largest Yellow Catalpa (war memorial garden in North Street).

*Leith Hill, Dorking. NT (open access). One of the largest Tulip Trees (Leith Hill Place paddock, by Rhododendron Wood, at TQ132424).

Little Bookham, Leatherhead. Largest *Populus* x *jackii* 'Aurora' (N end tree in Little Bookham Street, outside Mansard House).

Lythe Hill Park, Haste Hill, Haslemere. Residents' garden. Tallest Castor Aralia (E), *Sorbus aria* 'Majestica' (SE, above tennis court) and *Thuja occidentalis* 'Spiralis' (S side of drive, labelled *Chamaecyparis lawsoniana*).

*Nonsuch Park, Ewell. Historic public park. Largest Pyrenean Pine (gardens, S).

Norney Grange, Shackleford, Godalming. Largest *Halesia carolina*; largest and tallest trees of *Sorbus mougeotii*.

Oatlands Hotel, Oatlands Drive, Weybridge. Some historic plantings. Largest Red Oak (back lawn).

Old Kiln Museum, Reeds Road, Tilford, Farnham. Open most days; Rural Life museum with a young arboretum. Largest *Acer rubrum* 'Armstrong'; tallest *A. r.* 'Scanlon' (30).

*Painshill Park Landscape Garden, Cobham. Open most days. Some old and unusual trees. Largest Cut-leaved Alder (lake bank, SW); one of the largest Cedars of Lebanon (W side of lake); largest Pencil Cedar (N of lake).

Peper Harow, Guildford. Largest *Populus* 'Balsam Spire' and Railway Poplar (private gardens by river).

Priory Park, Reigate. Public park; some very tall tree in the woods on the greensand ridge S of the lake. Largest Downy Birch (ridge near Greensand Way, TQ245495); tallest Hornbeam (SSE of Priory Pond).

Pyrford church, Woking. Largest *Prunus* x *yedoensis* 'Tsubame'.

*Ramster, Chiddingfold. Open daily through spring; mature woodland garden. Tallest Big-leaved Storax (1994).

Reigate Town Hall. Largest Fastigiate Robinia (carpark, Castlefield Road edge).

Royal Holloway & Bedford College, Englefield Green. London University. Extensive arboretum developed in the 1960s. Largest *Nothofagus nitida* (old arboretum, SW), Buttonwood Plane (W from Theatre), White Oak (old arboretum, N of bog) and Algerian Oak (behind block 2 of Highfield Court, by A31).

Snowdenham Hall, Snowdenham Lane, Bramley. Victorian pinetum. Tallest *Thuja plicata* 'Pyramidalis' (N drive).

South Road, Horsell, Woking. Largest River Birch (street tree outside 'Birchwood'; 2000).

Sunbury. Largest Tamarisk (front garden of 19, Landwater Road).

Sunbury Park, Thames Street, Sunbury. Historic public park. Tallest Encina (outside S corner of walled garden).

*Surrey University Campus, Guildford. Open access. Extensive and ongoing plantings of rare trees. Largest *Fraxinus sogdiana* (N from Senate) and *Salix* x *sericans* (lake, E bank).

Sutton Place, Sutton Green, Guildford (1996). NGS open days. Largest *Ilex* x *altaclarensis* 'Camelliifolia' and *Pinus sylvestris* 'Watereri' (Wild Garden), in 1996.

Tandridge church. One of the largest Yews.

Tandridge Court, Oxted. Residents' garden. Largest Yellow Buckeye.

Templemere, Oatlands Drive, Weybridge. Largest Golden Robinia (private verge).

Tilgates, Little Common Lane, Bletchingley. Many young rare trees, planted by David Clulow. Largest *Morus alba* 'Laciniata'.

Virginia Water (town). Largest Variegated Ash (back garden abutting onto Christchurch Road, at SU987685).

Waterer's Nursery, 150, London Road, Bagshot. Now a Notcutt's wholesale nursery. Largest All Saints' Cherry (nursery beds, S).

West Hall, West Byfleet. One of the largest London Planes (by canal).

Weybridge parish church. Largest Hybrid Buckeye and Strawberry Tree.

**Windsor Great Park. Surrey's corner of the Park encompasses the Savill Garden (open daily), and the eastern half of the Valley Gardens (open access): woodland gardens developed since the 1930s, with a vast range of rare trees. National Collection of *Magnolia*. (See also Berkshire.)

Largest Uri Maple (Savill Garden; E edge, N).

Largest *Acer franchettii* (Savill Garden; N woodland garden; 82190).

Largest Fastigiate Alder (N of Savill Garden; E, by depot).

Largest *Betula celtiberica* (Valley Gardens; Elcock's Way, S). One of the largest Silver Birches (Savill Garden; NW corner).

Largest Cyprus Cedar (Valley Gardens; E of Botany Bay ride).

Tallest X *Cupressocyparis leylandii* 'Robinson's Gold' (Valley Gardens; just above Dick's Bog).

Largest X *C. l.* 'Silver Dust' (Valley Gardens; Heather Garden, mid/NE).

Tallest *Ilex* x *altaclarensis* 'Camelliifolia' (Savill Garden; N woodland garden).

Largest *Juglans hindsii* (Valley Gardens, above Dick's Bog).

Largest *Larix* x *czekanowski* (Valley Gardens; above Dick's Bog/Botany Bay; WGP7735; ?).

Largest Siberian Larch (Valley Gardens; above Dick's Bog). Largest Fastigiate Tulip Tree (Valley Gardens; Runway/ Azalea Valley).

Largest *M.* 'Princess Margaret' (Valley Gardens; in magnolia group above Oxshed fir plantation; WGP82009).

Largest *M. sargentiana* var. *robusta* (Savill Garden; N, woodland edge).

Largest *M.* x *soulangiana* x *campbellii* (Savill Garden; N woodland garden, S).

Largest *M.* 'Spectrum' (Valley Gardens; crest of Badger's Bank; USN82113).

Largest *Malus* 'Frettingham Victoria' (Savill Garden; SW edge of N woodland garden).

Tallest *Meliosma pinnata* var. *oldhamii* (Savill Garden; N, mid).

Largest *Pinus strobus* 'Pendula' (Valley Gardens; Heather Garden, mid).

Largest *P. s.* 'Nivea' (Valley Gardens; Heather Garden, mid).

Tallest Double Gean (Savill Garden; N fence by locked gate).

Largest Dawyck Cherry (Savill Garden – NE corner by glasshouse).

Largest and tallest Purple Bird Cherries (Savill Garden: SW edge behind WC, and in Spring Wood S of formal gardens).

Largest Oshima Cherry (Valley Gardens; Badger's Bank – S edge of garden slope; ?).

Tallest Yoshino Cherry (Valley Gardens; Plunket Memorial valley, W side, lower mid).

Tallest Chanticleer Pear (Savill Garden; S corner).

Largest *Rhododendron* 'Polar Bear' (Savill Garden; woodland garden, N fence).

Largest *R. ponticum* (Rhododendron Ride; 200m N of Cow Pond on W side).

Weeping White Willow (Savill Garden; NE, behind glasshouse).

Largest *Sorbus aria* 'Lutescens' (E of Cumberland Lodge, by track from Smith's Lawn to Empire Oaks).

Tallest *S. aucuparia* 'Sheerwater Seedling' (Valley Gardens; Queen's Corner/Plunket Memorial glade).

Tallest *Sorbus hedlundii* (Valley Gardens; road above punchbowl).

Largest Joseph Rock's Rowan (Valley Gardens; Badger's Bank towards Plunket Memorial glade).

Largest *S. oligodonta* 'Rosea' (Valley Gardens; above Dick's Bog).

Largest *S.* 'Savill Orange' (Valley Gardens; Heather Garden, E).

Largest Hemsley's Storax (Valley Gardens; Queen's Corner, mid).

Largest *Thuja plicata* 'Aurea' (Valley Gardens; Heather Garden, mid/NE; HIL77774).

Largest *T. plicata* x *standishii* (Valley Gardens; Botany Bay ride, lower, W).

Largest *Tilia cordata* 'Greenspire' (Savill Garden; far S).

Largest *Tsuga heterophylla* 'Greenmantle' (Savill Garden; NW).

**Winkworth Arboretum, Hascombe Road, Godalming. NT; open daily. The arboretum was developed by Wilfrid Fox in a spectacular hillside setting from the 1930s and specialises in maples and *Sorbus*.

Tallest Red Snake-bark Maple (Bowl).

Tallest *Acer davidii* 'Madeline Spitta' (Bowl).

Largest Amur Maple (Bowl).

Largest *Fagus sylvatica* 'Rohanii' (far S).

Largest *Halesia monticola* var. *vestita* (top path, mid).

Tallest *Magnolia* 'Kewensis' (Magnolia Wood, SW).

Tallest Turkish Apple (above Bowl).

Tallest Laurel Oak (Oak bank).

Largest Savernake Oak (Foliage Glade).

Tallest *Quercus* x *schochiana* (Oak bank).

Largest *Sorbus caloneura* (Sorbus Hill).

Largest *S. hedlundii* (below Foliage Glade).

Largest *S. umbellata* (Sorbus Hill; ?; 19601).

**Wisley RHS Garden, Ripley, Byfleet. Open daily (RHS members only on Sundays). The RHS' flagship garden since 1903: pinetum, woodland garden and a large young arboretum.

Largest Plantier's Chestnut (restaurant side of Seven Acres pond; 962958A).

Largest *Alnus* x *pubescens* (Battleston Hill, S).

Largest *Betula schmidttii* (Howard's Field, SW).

Largest Chonosuki's Hornbeam (Howard's Field, NE).

Largest Katsura (Battleston Hill, N, near Broadwalk).

Tallest *Chamaecyparis lawsoniana* 'Fletcheri' (South Pinetum, W).

Tallest *C. l.* 'Lanei Aurea' (North Pinetum).

Largest *C. obtusa* 'Tetragona Aurea' (Alpine Meadow).

Largest *Cladrastis wilsonii* (Seven Acres/restaurant lawn).

Largest X *Cupressocyparis leylandii* 'Naylors Blue' (South Pinetum, W).

Largest and tallest Tingiringi Gums (Battleston Hill Gum group, N side, mid, and SW of Trials Field).

Largest Jounama Snow Gum (Howard's Field, mid).

Largest *Euonymus hamiltonianus* ssp. *sieboldianus* (Seven Acres, SW).

Largest Golden Honey Locust (Rose Garden lawns).

Largest *Hippophae rhamnoides* ssp. *yunnanense* (entrance/formal gardens; LSE15724).

Tallest Lace-bark Pine (North Pinetum, SW).

Largest Big-Cone Pine (NW of Trials Grounds).

Largest Japanese Red Pine (North Pinetum, E).

Largest Holford's Pine (South Pinetum, NE).

Largest Mountain Pine (Seven Acres lawn)

Largest *Pinus ponderosa* ssp. *scopulorum* (South Pinetum, NE).

Largest Chinese Red Pine (North Pinetum, SW).

Largest *Populus* x *generosa* (Seven Acres, river boundary).

Largest trees of *P.* 'Oxford' (river N of Pinetum).

Largest *P.* 'Rumford' (Arboretum, SW).

Largest Weeping Aspen (Arboretum, mid E).

Largest *Prunus* 'Hilling's Weeping' (Rose Garden lawns).

Largest Judd's Cherry (Howard's Field, N).

Largest *P. pendula* 'Pendula Plena Rosea' (Seven Acres, SW).

Largest *Pyrus pashia* (Seven Acres by Pinetum, W).

Largest Variegated Turkey Oak (restaurant lawn/Seven Acres).

Largest *Rhododendron auriculatum* (Wild Garden).

Largest *Salix kinuyanagi* (Arboretum, S fence, mid).

Largest *Ulmus* 'Sapporo Autumn Gold' (Arboretum, S side, mid W).

Woking Park, Kingfield Road, Woking. Public park.

Largest Dawn Redwood (SW corner of swimming pool).

Wotton House, Wotton, Dorking. (Pronounced 'Wootton'.) John Evelyn's country home in the 17th century.

Largest True Service.

Warwickshire

An agricultural county with singularly few plantings of rare trees, though more may await discovery. Only Leamington Spa has a rich tradition in municipal arboriculture.

*Jephson Gardens, Newbold Terrace, Leamington Spa.

Public park with many fine and rare trees. Largest Golden Alder (1989).

West Midlands

Birmingham has some fine town parks, though soils and climate do not really favour tree-growth; the whole area has been under-recorded to date.

Woodbrook College, 1046, Bristol Road, Edgbaston. (Tallest White Willow in 1975.)

West Sussex

In the north east, among the wooded, sandstone valleys of the High Weald, a remarkable concentration of Edwardian 'wild gardens' pioneered the cultivation of many Chinese introductions; their trees are now in their prime. The clay vale of the Low Weald grows few notable specimens, but the Lower Greensand hills in the north-west provide very special conditions. Tender trees thrive in the coastal plain around Chichester.

Amberley Wild Brooks, Amberley. Largest White Willow (Drewitts Farm; dyke at TQ037134).
Architectural Plants Nursery, Bridge Farm, Nuthurst. Largest Grey Gum.
Beech Hurst Gardens, Cuckfield Road, Haywards Heath. Public park. Largest Naden (NW corner, by railway).
Beechwood House, Beechwood Lane, East Lavington. Largest Willow-leaved Bay (gate).
Birdham church, Chichester. Largest Italian Cypress (S side).
Bishop's Palace, Chichester. Public park. Largest Virginian Buckeye (NE) and Box (W bank).
**Borde Hill, Borde Hill Lane, Haywards Heath. Open daily. The trees were planted in unrivalled variety all across the estate by Col. Stevenson Clarke between 1893 and his death in 1946. About a third of these are now accessible to the public along the often muddy trails through Warren Wood, Little Bentley Wood and Stephanie's Glade, and via Lullings Gill, Stonepit Wood and the old Kitchen Gardens.
Largest *Acer erianthum* (W of Stonepit Wood, 19853).
Largest *A. longipes* (North Park near roadside, 19441).
Largest *A. l.* ssp. *amplum* (North Park; roadside pond).
Largest Cut-leaved Silver Maple (North Park by brick barn).
Largest Black Maple (North Park behind cottages, 19447).
Largest and tallest trees of *Alnus hirsuta* (Stonepit Wood, NE).
Largest Spaeth's Alder (Stonepit Wood, N edge).
Largest *Carpinus laxiflora* (South Roadside Plantation).
Largest Big Shellbark Hickory (South Park near Lullings Farm, 19704).
Largest *Castanea seguinii* (The Tolls).
Largest *Celtis labilis* (The Gorse, NW; ?).
Largest *Crataegus henryi* (South Roadside Plantation, 10288).
Largest *Cunninghamia konishii* (Gores Wood, SW).
Tallest Mexican Cypress (Stonepit Wood, 26093).
Tallest Rostrevor Eucryphia (Gores Wood, S).

This gigantic but relatively youthful Sweet Chestnut grows in the same field at Cowdray Park, W Sussex, as the well-known Queen Elizabeth Oak.

Largest Engler's Beech (Lullings Ghyll, by drive bridge; 19931).
Largest Black Ash (Stephanie's Glade, SW; 18982).
Largest Spaeth's Ash (North Park above Little Bentley's Wood, 19068).
Largest *Ilex pedunculosa* (below Kitchen Garden, 20170).
Largest Spanish Juniper (Warren Wood, NE; 22405).
Tallest *Juniperus virginiana* 'Glauca' (Gores Wood, E; 22616).
Tallest *Larix gmelinii* var. *japonica* (Stonepit Wood, N).
Largest Prince Rupert's Larch (Stonepit Wood, N; 26104).
Largest *Lindera megaphylla* (Kitchen Garden, S wall; 20148).
Largest Chinese Tulip Tree (Garden of Allah, 19240).
Largest White Campbell's Magnolia (The Tolls).
Tallest *Magnolia campbellii* ssp. *mollicomata* (The Tolls, 18763).
Largest Chinese Evergreen Magnolia (Kitchen Garden back wall, 20153).
Tallest *M. sargentiana* var. *robusta* (The Tolls, 18778).
Tallest Sprenger's Magnolia (The Tolls, 18762).
Largest *Malus baccata* 'Jackii' (Stephanie's Glade, 18959).
Largest *M. prattii* (below Lake, 20268).

Largest *Phellodendron chinense* (Stephanie's Glade, 18968).
Tallest *P. lavallei* (Warren Wood, mid; 19126).
Largest Schrenk's Spruce (North Park by road, 26060).
Tallest Japanese Black Pine (Azalea Ring, 26056).
Tallest Schmitt's Cherry (Pinetum).
Tallest Callery Pear (Warren Wood, S edge; 19189).
Tallest *Pyrus pyrifolia* 'Chojura' (Warren Wood, mid; 19129).
Largest Ussurian Pear (South Roadside Plantation, 20281).
Largest and tallest Kermes Oaks (Stonepit Wood, SW, and above Kitchen Garden, 20126).
Largest Northern Pin Oak (Stonepit Wood, NE, 20039).
Largest *Quercus floribunda* (Gores Wood, NE).
Tallest *Q. glauca* (Gores Wood, E; 18487).
Tallest Lebanon Oak (Peartree Wood, 19552).
Tallest Ludwig's Oak (Stonepit Wood, W; 20048).
Largest *Q.* x *moreha* (Stonepit Wood, mid).
Largest *Q. petraea* 'Acutifolia' (N end of line of trees over Borde Hill Lane; ?).
Largest *Q. spathulata* (Gores Wood, NW).
Tallest Pink Robinia (Garden of Allah, 19246).
Largest *Robinia hartwegii* (Stephanie's Glade, 18938).
Largest *R.* x *slavinii* (Stephanie's Glade, 18907; ?).
Tallest Cut-leaved Rowan (Gores Wood, S; 18505).
Largest True Service (North Park, S of Stephanie's Glade).
Largest *Sorbus glabrescens* (Garden of Allah, 19253).
Tallest *S. oligodonta* 'Rosea' (Warren Wood, E, 19220).
Tallest *S. pallescens* (Gores Wood memorial, 18423).
Tallest *S. pohuashanensis* (Gores Wood, S, 18424; ?).
Largest and tallest Ladder-leaf Rowans (Gores Wood, 18474 and 18410).
Largest Himalayan Whitebeam (below Kitchen Garden).
Largest Japanese Yew (Warren Wood, NW; 22455).
Largest Manchurian Lime (NW in Little Bentley Plantation, 19024).
Borden Wood, Milland. A late Victorian tree collection in exceptionally fine growing conditions on a sheltered greensand slope. Tallest Sawara Cypress (drive, mid) and 'Squarrosa' (below lake), Cherry Laurel (drive near house, N side), Epaulette Tree (back drive near house) and Scarlet Oak (drive, mid).
Chichester. Largest Tree of Heaven (back garden of 27, Westgate).
Christ's Hospital (The Bluecoat School), Horsham. Tallest Silver Maple (in group behind Barnes House).
Clock House, Lindfield, Haywards Heath. Largest Chinese Quince (1987).
Coates Manor, Coates Lane, Fittleworth. NGS open days. Largest *Betula papyrifera* x *utilis* var. *jacquemontii*.
Coldwaltham church. One of the largest Yews (NW of church).
*Cowdray Park, Midhurst. Footpaths cross the old deer park with its huge oaks and chestnuts, where a new arboretum is also being developed. The garden, with many fine conifers, opens under the NGS. Largest Sweet Chestnut (field E of Oaters Wood, far NE, at SU916228); largest *Chamaecyparis obtusa* 'Aurea' (garden pond); tallest *C. pisifera* 'Plumosa' (garden E of Giant Sequoia avenue); largest Hall's Crab (garden, by tennis court); two of the largest Sessile Oaks, 'the Queen Elizabeth Oak' (field E of Oaters Wood, at SU913226), and the burry tree next to it;

tallest Red Oak (garden; bank W of pond).
Crawley. Imaginative street plantings in the older parts of the new town. Largest *Prunus* 'Taoyame' (Ashdown Drive, Tilgate, on the corner of Titmus Drive).
Cuckfield church. Largest *Prunus cerasus* 'Rhexii' (1996).
Cumberland House, Thakeham, Pulborough. Largest Sentry Ginkgos.
Dangstein, Rogate, Petersfield. Largest *Cryptomeria japonica* 'Compacta'.
Duckyls, Vowels Lane, Turners Hill. The garden opens under the NGS, while many rare trees grow in the private woods below. Tallest Summit Cedar (mid) and Hill Cherry (sloping path).
Duncton Mill House, Dye House Lane, Duncton. Tallest *Populus* x *jackii* 'Aurora' (under Fountains Copse).
Fair Oak, Rogate. Tallest Monkey Puzzle (SW of house).
Funtington church, Chichester. Largest *Prunus serrulata* 'Albi-plena' (S side).
Goodwood, Chichester. Open access to much of the historic grounds. One of the largest Cedars of Lebanon (S side of cricket field).
Handcross Park School, Handcross. National Collection of Japanese Cherries. Largest *Ilex aquifolium* 'Ciliata Major' (above lake).
*High Beeches Garden, Handcross. Regularly open; large woodland garden with immaculate labelling. National Collection of *Stuartia*. Largest Shirasawa's Maple (behind glade, 25636), *Malus* 'John Downie' (below entrance, 15059), *Quercus wislizenii* (roadside, 25036) and *Stuartia monadelpha* (below pond).
*Highdown, Goring. Worthing Borough Council; open access. Established by Sir Frederick Stearn on a windswept chalk hill overlooking the sea, but growing many rare trees. Largest Turczaninow's Hornbeam (Middle Garden, W); largest *Cercis racemosa* (Middle Garden); largest *Fagus sylvatica* 'Rotundifolia' (Lower Garden, W).
*Hollycombe, Liss. The gardens of the Steam Collection are open most days and contain several of this large estate's remarkable trees. More are visible from the railwaylines through the woods.
Largest Purple Japanese Maple (Gardener's Cottage bank).
Tallest Red Maple (Liphook Road, N of Steam Collection entrance).
Largest Sugar Maple (Gardener's Cottage bank, W group).
Largest *Alnus firma* (Steam Collection, Lime Walk).
Largest trees of *Betula ermanii* x *pubescens* (Steam Collection, S of Lime Walk).
Tallest Bitternut (Steam Collection, Lime Walk).
Tallest Pignut (Steam Collection, Lime Walk).
Tallest Shagbark Hickory (Steam Collection, Lime Walk).
Largest *Daphniphyllum macropodum* (Steam Collection garden).
Largest *Prunus laurocerasus* 'Latifolia' (Steam Collection, Lime Walk).
Largest Lea's Oak (Steam Collection garden, S).
Largest Chinese Cork Oak (Steam Collections, S of gardens).
Largest Carolina Hemlock (Steam Collection garden, N.)
Hurst Mill, Harting, Petersfield. NGS open days. Largest *Prunus* 'Itokukuri' (millrace; 1997).

Oriental Beech at Wakehurst Place, W Sussex – a giant tree which only dates from around 1915.

The Hyde, Handcross. Edwardian gardens. Largest *Prunus* 'Yedo Zakura' (1996).

Kingley Vale, West Stoke, Chichester. National Nature Reserve. Ancient Yew grove, including one of the most spreading trees (N end tree on trail).

**Leonardslee, Lower Beeding. Open daily through summer. The most spectacular of all the High Weald's old woodland gardens, and one of the richest in rare trees. Largest *Acer palmatum* 'Albomarginatum' (poolside below Cross Paths, 2790).

Largest *A. p.* 'Kagiri Nishiki' (by pond below Cross Paths).

Largest *A. p.* 'Linearilobum Atropurpureum' (Loderi Garden, N).

Largest *A. p.* 'Reticulatum' (by pond below Cross Paths).

Largest *A. pseudoplatanus* 'Prinz Handjery' (Daffodil Lawn).

Tallest *Cornus kousa* (NE of Dell).

Largest Himalayan Holly (Lower Walk).

Tallest Campbell's Magnolia (Dell, 1042).

Largest Fishtail Magnolia (head of Dell).

Tallest Dawn Redwood (Dell).

Largest Sargent's Cherry (below mansion, 1848).

Largest *P.* 'Ukon' (Wallaby Pen, cut back).

Lower Sherriff Farmhouse, Station Approach, Horsted Keynes. Largest Keaki.

*Malt House, Chithurst, Rogate. NGS open days. The Victorian pinetum was originally part of the Borden Wood estate (qv). Largest *Prunus* 'Mikuruma-gaeshi' (drive); tallest Swedish Whitebeam (pinetum, E edge).

The Mens, Pulborough. Sussex Wildlife Trust nature reserve. An ancient wooded common. Tallest Wild Crab (The Cut, at TQ022231; 1993).

**Nymans, Handcross. NT; open most days. Many fine and rare trees.

Largest *Chamaecyparis lawsoniana* 'Pottenii' (Wild Garden).

Largest *Magnolia* 'Micheal Rosse' (Top Garden, 6627).

Largest Sargent's Magnolia (Walled Garden, S; 6731).

Largest *M.* 'Thomas Messel' (glasshouses, 6559).

Largest *M.* x *wieseneri* (drive opposite glasshouses, 6679).

Tallest Veitch's Meliosma (Top Garden, 6609).

Largest Silver Beech (Top Garden, 6611).

Largest *Phellodendron lavallei* (Gardener's Cottage, 6552).

Largest *Prunus pendula* 'Pendula Rosea' (Walled Garden, SE; 6779).

Largest *Robinia pseudoacacia* 'Rozynskyana' (North Park, mid; 7223).

Largest *R. p.* 'Semperflorens' (North Park, mid; 7263).

Tallest *Tilia americana* var. *vestita* (North Park, N; 7273).

Orchards, Wallage Lane, Crawley Down. Regularly open; established by the gardening writer Arthur Hellyer. Tallest *Malus* x *robusta* (NW of nursery beds).

*Petworth Park, Petworth. NT; open access to the deer park; the Pleasure Grounds are open most days through summer. Many outstanding trees. Tallest Sweet Chestnut (park; foot of bank S of Upperton at SU961226); largest Hop Hornbeam (Pleasure Grounds, town edge); largest Cambridge Oak (Pleasure Grounds, by cottage).

Red Oaks, Henfield. Gardeners' Benevolent Home. One of the largest Lucombe Oaks.

Rowfant, Crawley. Largest Silver Maple (woodland just N of Wallage Lane, at TQ328370).

St Cuthman's School, Stedham, Midhurst. Some outstanding trees along the bridlepath running under the bank north of the School: largest Single-leaved Robinia; tallest Silver Lime.

*St Roche's Arboretum, West Dean, Chichester. Open daily through summer. A 1km walk across the old park from West Dean House (qv); rare trees have been planted in this sheltered downland coomb since the 17th century. National Collection of *Aesculus*. Tallest Italian Maple (SE, edge of lawns); largest *Chamaecyparis lawsoniana* 'Intertexta' (S side, mid/W); tallest Cypress Oak (valley path; N side, mid).

Screens Wood, Arundel. Tallest Horse Chestnut (S end of line in valley N of footpath, at TQ004080).

Sedgewick Park, Nuthurst, Horsham. Edwardian gardens. Largest Weeping Gean (E of White Sea) and Shingle Oak (park by house).

Selehurst, Lower Beeding. NGS open days. One of the tallest Cider Gums.

*South Lodge Hotel, Lower Beeding, Horsham. Gardens created by Frederick Godman from 1883; many rare trees. Tallest Purple Japanese Maple (Rock Garden); largest *Quercus glauca* (towards Lake).

Stable Cottage, Binsted, Arundel. Largest Phillyrea.

Staplefield church. Largest *Juniperus chinensis* 'Kaizuka' (?).

Staplefield Place (Brantridge School), Staplefield. One of the largest Cider Gums (middle of 'wilderness').

*Tilgate Park, Titmus Drive, Crawley. Public park, on the site of Edwardian gardens and maintained to exceptional standards, with many younger plantings. Largest Yellow Birch (garden, mid S); largest *Chamaecyparis obtusa* 'Crippsii' (lawn below walled garden); tallest Yellow-wood (garden, mid S); largest *Cornus kousa* (garden, mid S); tallest Sweet Bay (garden, mid S; 1996); largest *Malus* x *hartwigii* (W of Inn; ?); Coast Redwood – fastest tree to x120cm (S of Inn); largest Chinese Stuartia (garden, mid S).

**Wakehurst Place, Ardingly. Open daily. Kew RBG's country outstation, with a framework of rare trees and rhododendrons planted by Gerald Loder in the early 20th century. National Collections of *Betula* and *Nothofagus*.

Largest Downy Japanese Maple (E of Pinetum, 32156).

Largest *Acer japonicum* 'Aconitifolium' (Coates Wood, 1992-1339).

Largest Golden Sycamore (head of Bloomers Valley, 32782).

Largest *Alnus inokumae* (Coates Wood, 42805).

Tallest Jacquemont's Birch (Coates Wood, 33662).

Largest *Carpinus viminea* (Sands/Pheasantry, in S corner).

Tallest Cyprus Cedar (Pinetum, 20958).

Tallest *C. pisifera* 'Aurea' (Westwood Valley, N side; 4580).

Largest and tallest trees of *Cornus walteri* (W of Mansion Pond, 30811, and Entrance Grounds, SE, 32780).

Largest *Cupressus macrocarpa* 'Donard Gold' (E of Pinetum, 7701).

Largest Sargent Cypress (Pinetum, E; 73016).

Tallest *Eucalyptus chapmaniana* (Coates Wood, 8094).

Largest Oriental Beech (below the Slips, labelled *Fagus sylvatica*, 32167).

to explain the high proportion of the champions of common trees found in Ireland's old parks. These parks are most numerous in the more 'civilised' Leinster, while the especially mild conditions of Cork and Kerry attracted many gentleman gardeners.

A high proportion of the trees featured here were first noted during the course of the Tree Register of Ireland project in 1999-2000; more will await discovery.

Antrim
St MacNissi's College (Garron Tower), Garron Point. Largest Blue Gum.

Armagh
Derrymore House, Bessbrook. NT; park open daily through summer. Largest Italian Alder (park).
*Gosford Castle Forest Park, Markethill. Largest Himalayan Fir (arboretum); tallest *Chamaecyparis lawsoniana* 'Gracilis Pendula' (1976).
Parkanaur Forest Park. Largest *Fagus sylvatica* f. *tortuosa* (lawn).

Carlow
Ballydarton House, Fenagh. Largest and tallest trees of *Ilex aquifolium* 'Argenteomarginata'.
Ballykealy House, Ballon. Largest Deodar (garden).
Fenagh House, Muine Bheag. Large Victorian pinetum. Largest *Picea asperata* var. *retroflexa* (S pinetum, 1995) and *Quercus robur* 'Atropurpurea' (drive, 1975).
Killinane, Bagnelstown. One of the largest Lombardy Poplars.
Lisnavagh Gardens, Lisnavagh, Rathvilly. Open by appointment. Largest Himalayan Tree Cotoneaster.
Myshall. One of the largest Sycamores (park, beside Community Hall).
Pollacton, Carlow. One of the largest Lucombe Oaks (park).
Springfield House, Bennekerry. One of the largest Hawthorns (roadside).

Cavan
Kilmore Cathedral. One of the largest Sycamores – 'Bishop Bedell's Tree'.

Clare
Caher House, Lough Graney. Largest Japanese Red Cedar (centre of lawn).

Cork
Historic gardens cluster along the very mild but also quite warm and sunny south coast; shelter is at a premium towards the west.

*Annes Grove, Castletownroche. Open daily through summer. Wild garden with many rare and tender trees. (Tallest *Azara microphylla* in 1968.)
Ardnagashel, Ballylickey, Bantry. Largest Chilean Myrtle; largest Willow Podocarp.
*Ashbourne House Hotel, Cork. Largest Kashmir Cypress (top of W drive); largest Alpine Ash (SE lawn); largest Silver Top (SE lawn); tallest Snow Gum; largest Roblé Beech; tallest Mountain Beech (top of drive); largest Chilean Plum Yew; largest *Viburnum cylindricum* (big bush in upper E area).
Bantry House, Bantry. The magnificent gardens (being restored) are open daily through summer. Largest *Lomatia ferruginea*.
Belgrove, Cobh. Rare and old trees. Largest Eagle-claw Maple, Japanese Walnut and Campbell's Magnolia.
Castlefreke, Roscarberry. Coillte; open access. Largest Chilean Myrtle (woods).
Eccles Hotel, Glengarriff. Two of the largest Blue Gums.
Fitzgerald Park, Cork. Tallest *Acer pseudoplatanus* 'Prinz Handjery'.
**Fota Arboretum, Carrigtohill, Cork. Duchas; open daily through summer. A great range of exceptional trees; the garden was narrowly saved from development into a leisure park in the 1990s.
Largest Taiwan Cypress.
Tallest *Chamaecyparis pisifera* 'Plumosa Argentea' (406, labelled 'Plumosa').
Largest Golden Tree Fern.
Largest Yellow Stringybark.
Tallest Small-leaved Gum.
Largest Lacebark.
Largest Bull Bay.
Largest Maiten.
Largest *Phyllocladus trichomanoides* (11142).
Tallest Sikkim Spruce.
Largest Armand's Pine.
Tallest *Pittosporum tenuifolium* 'Silver Queen' (19; 1987).
Largest *Podocarpus totara* var. *hallii*.
Largest Californian Nutmeg.
Glengarriff. Largest Bentham's Cornel (Church of Ireland churchyard).
*Ilnacullin (Garinish Island), Glengarriff. Duchas; open daily through summer. One of Ireland's most famous gardens, filling an island in Bantry Bay; many rare and tender trees. (Largest Taiwan Pine in 1966.)
Innishannon, Bandon. One of the largest Monterey Cypresses (garden).
Lisalene Gardens, Clonakilty. Open sometimes. Largest Monterey Pine (drive).
Mount Leader, Millstreet. Largest *Salix myrsinifolia* and one of the largest Rowans, in rough upland pasture.

Derry
Drenagh, Limavady. Tallest Cox's Juniper and Nootka Cypress (1983).

Donegal
Ardnamona House Hotel, Lough Eske. Largest Momi and Nikko Firs (garden).
Ards Priory, Creeslough. One of the largest Monterey Cypresses (park).
Ballyconnell House, Falcarragh. Udaras na Gaelige. Largest Golden Monterey Cypress (drive) and Papauma (woods).
Rathmullen House, Rathmullan. Largest *Ulmus glabra* 'Horizontalis' (garden).

Rossylongan, Donegal. Coillte; open access. Tallest King Boris's Fir (?; woods).

Down

Ballywalter Park, Ballywalter, Newtownards. Regularly open. Largest Kowhai (by wall; 1985).

*Castle Ward, Strangford, Downpatrick. NT; landscaped park open daily through summer. Largest *Ilex* x *altaclarensis* 'Lawsoniana' (1982).

**Castlewellan National Arboretum, Castlewellan, Newcastle. Forest Service; open daily. Great range of mature trees in the walled 9-acre Annesley Garden; large younger arboretum extends into the surrounding Forest Park.
Largest *Abies delavayi* var. *smithii* (1991).
Largest *A. fargesii* (1994).
Largest and tallest trees of X *Cupressocyparis leylandii* 'Rostrevor' (1982).
Largest Tecate Cypress (1994).
Largest *Cupressus guadalupensis* var. *forbesii* (1994).
Tallest Golden Monterey Cypress (1994).
Largest Urn Gum (1994).
Tallest Tasmanian Yellow Gum (1994).
Tallest Ulmo (1994).
Largest Tasmanian Eucryphia (1994).
Tallest Himalayan Weeping Juniper (1994).
Tallest *Lomatia ferruginea* (1994).
Largest Red Beech (1994).
Largest Golden Norway Spruce (Cypress Pond; 1994).
Largest Golden Scots Pine (13-H; 1994).
Largest Kohuhu (1994).
Largest *Podocarpus acutifolius* (1991).
Largest Prince Albert's Yew (1982).
Tallest *Schima wallichii* ssp. *wallichii* var. *khasiana* (1994).
Largest Tasmanian Waratah (1994).
Largest Himalayan Hemlock (1994).
Largest Golden Nootka Cypresses (Cypress Pond and garden, 1983).

Clandeboye estate. Occasionally open. Tallest *Cupressus macrocarpa* f. *fastigiata*; largest Chilean Firebush (private woodland garden).

Larchfield, Lisburn. Largest Golden Cedar of Lebanon (park); tallest Smooth-leaved Elm (woods).

*Mount Stewart, Greyabbey, Newtownards. NT; open daily through summer. One of Ireland's finest gardens, with many rare trees. Largest *Eucalyptus regnans* (31485).

Ringdufferin House, Killyleagh. One of the largest Monterey Cypresses; largest *Hoheria sexstylosa*.

*Rowallane, Saintfield, Ballynahinch. NT; open most days. A garden most celebrated for its rhododendrons. Largest Paper-bark Birch (Trio Hill, 32538); largest *Cupressus duclouxiana* (The Hospital, 32755); tallest Black Gum (Holly Rock, 32717); largest Myrtle Beech (The Hospital, 32761); largest *Paulownia tomentosa* 'Lilacina' (The Hospital, 32767); tallest *Prunus* 'Shirotae' (The Paddock, 32843); largest Yunnan Hemlock (Trio Hill, 32532).

Seaforde, Downspatrick. Open daily. Fine trees in the wooded Pheasantry valley; National Collection of *Eucryphia*. Largest *Quercus robur* f. *purpurascens*.

Champion MacNab Cypress (*Cupressus macnabiana*) in the National Botanic Gardens, Dublin.

Dublin

*Earlscliffe (Baron's Brae), Ceanchor Road, Baily. Open by appointment. A great range of tender plants.

Esso Ireland HQ, Stillorgan, Dublin 4. Largest Red Buckeye (garden).

Finnstown, Lucan. Tallest Myrobalan Plum.

Luttrellstown Castle Hotel, Castleknock. One of the tallest Yews (glen).

**The National Botanic Gardens, Glasnevin, Botanic Road, Dublin. Duchas; open access. A great range of trees, growing on alkaline soils.
Largest *Acer macrophyllum* 'Aureum' (Maple Collection, top path).
Largest *Acer mono* 'Marmoratum' (Maple Collection).
Largest *A. m.* var. *tricuspis* (Maple Collection).
Largest *Carpinus betulus* 'Quercifolia Aureus' (1993).
Largest Weeping Blue Atlas Cedar.
Largest *Chamaecyparis lawsoniana* 'Depkenii' (1992).
Largest MacNab Cypress (Lawson Cypresses).
Largest Persimmon (below Pine Hill).
Largest Utah Ash (Ash Collection).
Largest *Fraxinus texensis* (Ash Collection).
Largest *Ilex aquifolium* 'Crispa' (Yew Walk/pond).

Largest Maiten (wall by Oak Collection).
Largest *Picea abies* 'Finedonensis' (1980).
Tallest Calabrian Pine (1980).
Largest Digger Pine (1992).
Largest Variegated Plane (river below hollies).
Largest *Poliothyrsis sinensis* (1992).
Largest Callery Pear (Oaks border; 1993).
Largest *Quercus baronii* (1992).
Largest *Q. dalechampii* (Oak Collection).
Largest *Q. texana* (1992).
Largest *Robinia* x *holdtii* 'Britzensis' (1992).
Tallest *R. pseudoacacia* 'Bessoniana' (1987).
Tallest *Tilia* 'Moltkei' (Limes).
Largest Chinese Cedar (1992).
Trinity College, College Green, Dublin. Open access. Large range of trees across the 18-ha campus. One of the largest Oregon Maples (Library Square).

Fermanagh

*Florence Court, Florencecourt, Enniskillen. NT; Forest Park and Pleasure Gardens open daily. Largest Common Lime (park).

Galway

Gort na mona, Ballinasloe. One of the largest Beeches (park).

Kerry

Areas of natural woodland remain around Killarney, include pure Yew woods and thickets of wild Strawberry Tree. The limestone valleys which lie between the Old Red Sandstone mountains of the west coast tend to face into the prevailing wind, so that the gardens established to take advantage of the almost frost-free conditions cling to pockets of shelter and tall conifers do not feature prominently.

Caragh Lodge Hotel, Killorglin. Largest Kauri Pine.
Cloghfune, Killarney National Park. Duchas. Two of the largest Hollies and Grey Sallows.
*Derreen, Lauragh, Kenmare. Open daily in summer; many unusual trees. Largest *Chamaecyparis lawsoniana* 'Gracilis Pendula' (in 1966).
Dinis Cottage, Muckross. Duchas. Largest Strawberry Tree (woods).
*Dunloe Castle Hotel, Beaufort, Killarney. Open access in summer. Many rare trees planted since 1920. Tallest Chinese Swamp Cypress and *Prunus dielsiana*.
Garinish Island, Parknasilla, Sneem. Not to be confused with the better-known 'Garinish Island' garden (Ilnacullin) in Bantry Bay, Cork (qv). Largest *Leptospermum scoparium*.
Glan Leam, Valentia. Largest and tallest trees of *Clethra arborea*; tallest Cabbage Palm.
Glendalough House Hotel, Killorglin. Largest Cabbage Palm.
Kells House, Kells, Killorglin. Largest Silver Wattle.
Parknasilla Hotel, Sneem. Tallest Blackwood Acacia.
Queens Drive, Muckross. Duchas. Tallest Monterey Pine (woods).
Reenadinna, Muckross. Duchas. One of the largest Alders (woods).
Rossdohan, Sneem. Late Victorian garden created on a tiny island, with many tender trees. (Tallest Blackwood Acacia and largest *Olearia argophylla* in 1966.)
Tomies Wood, Killarney National Park. Duchas. One of the largest Downy Birches.
Uragh Woods, Inchiquin. Office of Public Works. A surviving fragment of West Ireland's original Sessile Oak woodland. Largest Grey Alder (lake).

Kildare

Ballindoolin, Edenderry. Largest Irish Yew.
K Club, Straffan. Country club. Largest Deodar and *Chamaecyparis pisifera* 'Aurea' (garden).
Kildangan, Kildare. Many rare trees. Largest *Meliosma pinnata* var. *oldhamii*, Veitch's Meliosma, and *Prunus sargentii* 'Rancho' – all 1990.
Naas. One of the largest Wild Crabs (in hedge near the town).
The National Stud, Tully. The Japanese Garden (probably the finest in Europe) is open daily except winter. Largest *Acer campestre* 'Pulverulentum' (mound near exit from Japanese Garden); largest Van Volxem's Maple.
St Patrick's College, Maynooth. Largest Oriental Sweet-gum (garden).

Kilkenny

Coolmore House, Thomastown. Largest Scots Pine (garden).
Kilfane Glebe, Thomastown. One of the largest Holm Oaks (park).
Kilfane House, Thomastown. Largest Norway Maples (garden).
Kilkenny Castle, Kilkenny. Duchas. Largest Copper Beech (park).
Mount Juilliet, Thomastown. Golf club and hotel; the gardens are sometimes open. One of the largest White Willows (riverbank).
Threecastles House, Kilkenny. One of the largest Turkey Oaks (park).
*Woodstock, Inistioge. Regularly open. Many of the largest conifers in Ireland. One of the largest Monkey Puzzles (house end of avenue, E side); largest *Cryptomeria japonica* 'Elegans'; largest Mexican Cypress (by avenue); largest *Cupressus lindleyi* var. *benthamii* (by avenue); tallest Hartweg's Pine; tallest Endlicher Pine; largest Coast Redwood; largest *Thuja plicata* 'Zebrina'; tallest Himalayan Hemlock.

Laois

Abbeyleix, Leix. An outstanding private arboretum.
Largest Siberian Fir (Island).
Largest Zoeschen Maple (lakeside).
Largest *Castanea henryi* (park).
Largest *Chamaecyparis lawsoniana* 'New Silver' (1985).
Largest West Himalayan Cypress (garden).
Largest *Fraxinus platypoda* (garden).
Largest Antarctic Beech (Pleasure Grounds).
Largest Persian Ironwood (garden).
Largest *Picea abies* 'Clanbrassiliana' (park).

Largest Black Spruce (island).
One of the largest Scots Pines (woods).
Largest *Thuja occidentalis* 'Aurea'.
Blandsfort, Abbeyleix. (Largest *Azara microphylla* in 1968.)
Quakers Field, Killeshin. One of the largest Wild Crabs.
Stradbally. One of the largest English Oaks (near the village).
Stradbally Hall, Stradbally. One of the largest Beeches (1990).

Louth
Clermount Park, Dundalk. Largest *Ilex aquifolium* 'Silver Queen' (park).
Oriel Temple, Dundalk. Largest Yellow Birch in 1980.

Meath
Ardmullchan, Navan. One of the largest Wild Cherries.
Balrath, Kells. One of the largest Small-leaved Limes (park).
Bloomsbury House, Kells. Largest Tulip Tree in Ireland (garden).
Gormanstown College, Gormanstown. One of the largest Sycamores (park).
Headfort School, Kells. Huge Victorian pinetum on two islands (1980).
Largest Balsam Fir.
Tallest *Abies delavayi* var. *smithii* (Large Island).
Largest Taiwan Fir (NE).
Largest *A. pardei*.
Largest Miyabe's Maple (Large Island).
Largest *Keteleeria davidiana*.
Largest Chinese Larch (Small Island).
Largest Pahautea (NE).
Largest Umbrella Pine (Small Island, 1990).
Largest Korean Thuja (gate).
Lismullen House, Navan. Largest Variegated Sycamore (garden).
Newstone House, Navan. One of the largest Common Limes.

Monaghan
Castle Leslie, Glaslough. Largest Incense Cedar, Thread Cypress, *Fagus sylvatica* 'Albovariegata' and Arolla Pine (gardens).
Lough Fea, Carrickmacross. Largest Monkey Puzzle (garden).

Offaly
**Birr Castle, Birr. Demesne open daily. Probably Ireland's largest collection of rare trees (many collected in central China in the 1930s).
Tallest Père David's Maple (Bothy).
Largest Montpelier Maple (1990).
One of the largest Italian Maples (woods).
Largest *Acer platanoides* 'Stollii' (farm road at Killean, 1990).
Largest Wilson's Maple (bamboos).
Largest *Aesculus* x *mutabilis* 'Induta' (garden).
Tallest *Alnus incana* 'Aurea' (River Garden, 1989).
Largest *Carrierea calycina* (River Garden by bamboos).
Largest American Sweet Chestnut (Log Hut walk).

Largest *Crataegus champlainensis* (garden).
Largest *C. chrysocarpa* var. *phoenicea* (garden).
Largest *C. macracantha* (park, 1988).
Tallest Ehret Tree (garden).
Largest *Fagus lucida* (Michael's Walk, 1990).
Tallest Oriental Beech (garden).
Largest *Fagus sylvatica* 'Aurea Pendula'.
Original *F. s.* 'Birr Zebra' (garden).
Tallest Manna Ash.
Largest *F. pennsylvanica* 'Aucubifolia' (park).
Largest *F. sieboldiana* (garden).
Tallest Arizona Ash (Fore Park).
Largest Himalayan Weeping Juniper (River Garden).
Largest Black Juniper (tennis court).
Largest Dawson's Magnolia (River Garden).
Largest *Magnolia sprengeri* var. *elongata* (garden).
Tallest *Malus bhutanica* (Mount Palmer).
Largest *Meliosma dilleniifolia* ssp. *cuneifolia* (River Garden, 3153).
Largest *M. flexuosa* (Bothy).
Largest *Picea morrisonicola* (River Walk).
Largest Wilson's Spruce (High Walk).
Tallest Bishop Pine (garden).
Largest Grey Poplar (riverbank).
Largest Chilean Plum Yew (Gate/castle).
Tallest Fuji Cherry (garden).
Largest *Prunus* 'Jo-nioi' (formal garden).
Largest *Pyrus glabra* (Lower Walk, 1987).
Largest *Quercus robur* 'Fennessii' (drive; 'b25').
Tallest Coral-bark Willow (lakeside).
Largest *Sorbus hybrida* (garden).
Largest *S. subcuneata* (High Walk, 1990).
Largest *Tilia chingiana* (Mount Palmer, 3524).
Largest *T. dasystyla* ssp. *caucasica* (Lilac Walk by Upper Walk, 454).
Largest *T. henryana* (Mount Palmer).
Largest *T. miqueliana* (park).
Largest *Ulmus glabra* 'Crispa' (Mount Palmer).
Coalraine, Tullamore. One of the largest Ashes (park).

Roscommon
Lough Key Forest Park, Rockingham. Coillte. Historic park, largely planted with conifers. One of the largest Horse Chestnuts.
Strokestown Park, Strokestown. Formal gardens and National Famine Museum open daily through summer. One of the largest Common Limes (park).

Sligo
Temple House Hotel, Ballymote. Largest Cut-leaved Lime (garden).

Tipperary
Ardfort House, Thurles. Largest Ash (park).
Cahemahallia, Cappagh White. Two of the largest Cherry Laurels and Elders (hedge).
Castle Lough, Portroe. One of the largest Portugal Laurels.
Glenleigh, Clogheen. Largest Bird Cherry.
Grove House, Fethard. Tallest Broad-leaved Lime

The biggest Grey Poplar grows on the bank of the Camcor at Birr Castle, Offaly.

Original Glencormac Cypress at Glencormac, Wicklow.

(garden).

Killaloan Lodge, Clonmel. Largest Wild Black Poplar in Ireland (garden).

*Knocklofty House Hotel, Clonmel. Many fine trees. Tallest Vine-leafed Maple (garden); largest *Acer platanoides* 'Goldsworth Purple' (garden); largest Fortune's Plum Yew (park); largest Bay (garden); tallest Medlar (garden).

Marlfield, Clonmel. Largest Oregon Maple in 1968.

Tyrone

Caledon Castle, Caledon. Largest *Chamaecyparis lawsoniana* 'Triomf van Boskoop' (1983); Sitka Spruce – tallest tree in Northern Ireland.

Waterford

Cappoquin House, Cappoquin. Regularly open. Largest Cabbage Palm (gardens).

*Mount Congreve, Kilmeaden. Open by appointment. Immense collection of rhododendrons and magnolias; many other rare trees. Largest Big-leaved Magnolia and *Photinia glabra*.

Tourin, Cappoquin. Largest London Plane in Ireland.

Westmeath

Ballinlough Castle Gardens, Clonmellon. Regularly open in summer. Largest Walnut in Ireland (garden); largest Aspens (lake).

*Belvedere, Mullingar. Open daily; extensive gardens along the shores of Lough Ennell. Tallest Fortune's Plum Yew and largest Japanese Balsam Poplar (woods).

Castlepollard estate, Castlepollard. One of the largest Ashes (park).

Charleville, Tullamore. The most spreading English Oak (the King Oak).

Lake House, Crookedwood. Largest Spindle (drive).

Tullynally Castle, Castlepollard. Grounds open daily through summer, and by appointment. Eighteenth century landscaped parkland with recent plantings of rare trees. One of the largest Common Silver Firs (park, right of entrance drive).

Wexford

Along with Kilkenny and Carlow, the richly farmed countryside of Wexford has many woods and hedgerow trees and is the most 'English-looking' part of Ireland. Winters are mild but summers relatively warm and sunny.

Ballyrahan, Gorey. One of the largest Turkey Oaks (park).

Courtown estate, Courtown. Largest Holm Oak.

Huntington Castle, Clonegal. Open by appointment. Tallest Chilean Plum Yew (by river, 1991).

**John F. Kennedy Arboretum, New Ross. Duchas. Open daily. A vast arboretum – at least 4500 taxa – laid out geographically since the 1960s near the site of President Kennedy's ancestral home. Largest Argyle Apple; tallest Weeping Sally; largest Smithton Peppermint; largest Messmate Stringybark; largest and tallest Swamp Gums; largest Black Sally (by 1989).

*Johnstown Castle, Wexford. State Agricultural College;

open access to the grounds. Largest Golden Monterey Cypress (W lawn, 1989).

Monksgrange, Kiltealy. One of the largest Winter's Barks.

Ramsfort, Gorey. Tallest Hiba (garden).

Wells House, Kilmuckridge. Largest Cockspur Thorn (garden; ?); Largest Service Tree of Fontainebleau (drive).

Woodbrooke, Kiltealy. Largest Japanese Angelica Tree and Nootka Cypress.

Wicklow

'The garden of Ireland'; many large gardens were established in the shelter of the mountains, within convenient range of Dublin. This is the best part of the country for towering conifers, while very tender trees also do well near the coast.

Annamoe. Tallest *Chamaecyparis obtusa* 'Filicoides' and *Cupressus lusitanica* 'Glauca Pendula' (private estate near the village).

*Avondale, Rathdrum. Forest Park; the house is a museum. Many huge and rare trees (1991). Largest *Chamaecyparis lawsoniana* 'Wisselii' (bank below house); largest Rough Arizona Cypress (1980); tallest Modoc Cypress; tallest Mount Wellington Peppermint (1974); largest *Pseudotsuga menziesii* 'Fretsii' (below house); largest Umbrella Pine (E of house); largest American White Elm (ride, E of House).

*Charleville, Enniskerry, Bray. Open days. Many outstanding conifers. Largest *Abies amabilis*; largest Algerian Fir (SW); one of the largest Sycamores.

Clonmannon, Ashford. Largest Pyrenean Oak (in 1991).

Coollattin, Carnew. Outstanding conifers. Largest Lawson Cypress.

Dunganstown Castle, Kilbride. Largest Hornbeam (garden).

Fassaroe, Bray. Largest Blackwood Acacia.

Fortgranite, Kiltegan. Largest Western Red Cedar (garden).

Glencormac, Bray. Historic gardens. Largest *Chamaecyparis lawsoniana* 'Pendula Vera' (lawn above dell, 1991); largest Patagua (garden); largest Glencormac Cypress (lawn); largest Brooker's Gum (1991); tallest Blue Gum (across stream, in park); tallest Akiraho (garden; ?); largest Southern Pitch Pine.

Gyles Quay, Ferrybank. One of the largest Monterey Cypresses.

Killruddery, Bray. Gardens open daily through summer. Largest Bhutan Pine (1989).

**Kilmacurragh, Kilbride, Rathdrum. Duchas; regularly open. An adjunct to Glasnevin NBG; magnificent mature trees (1990).
Tallest Himalayan Fir (1992).
Tallest and largest Smooth Tasmanian Cedars (E of house, 1980, and S of house).
Largest King William Pine.
Largest *Chamaecyparis obtusa* 'Crippsii' (1980).
Largest Mourning Cypress.
Largest trees of *Cupressus lusitanica* 'Glauca Pendula' (SW and SE).

Largest Winter's Bark.
Largest Mount Wellington Peppermint.
Largest Silver-leafed Mountain Gum.
Largest Patagonian Cypress.
Tallest Papauma (1980).
Largest Peruvian Nutmeg.
Largest *Pilgerodendron uviferum* (1980).
Largest Hartweg's Pine.
Largest Tarata.
Largest Chilean Totara (W).
One of the largest Keakis.

Magheramore (retreat centre), Magheramore. Tallest *Photinia serratifolia*; largest Snake-bark Spruce (road to Wall Garden, 1994).

Money House, Coolkenna. Tallest Weeping Ash (park).

**Mount Usher, Ashford. Open daily through summer. A garden with many rare and tender trees along the banks of the Vartry; notable Eucalyptus grove.
Tallest King William's Pine.
Largest Chilean Incense Cedar.
Largest Cherry Birch (entrance).
Largest *Chamaecyparis lawsoniana* 'Kilmacurragh'.
Largest Golden Chestnut (N).
Tallest Bentham's Cornel.
Largest Chinese Fir.
Largest Eurabbie (river, W).
Tallest and largest trees of *Eucalyptus bridgesiana* (labelled *E. stuartiana*; ?).
Largest *E. dalrympleana*.
Tallest Alpine Ash.
Largest Cabbage Gum (?).
Tallest Black Sally (Lime Walk).
Tallest Urn Gum (below bridge).
Largest Tasmanian Yellow Gum.
Largest and tallest Ribbon Gums.
Tallest *Eucryphia moorei*.
Largest Cox's Juniper (entrance).
Largest *Lomatia ferruginea* (river/woodland).
Largest Coigue.
Largest Australian Beech (wall).
Tallest Rauli.
Largest Canary Island Pine.
Tallest Endlicher Pine.
Largest *Pittosporum tenuifolium* 'Silver Queen'.
Largest and tallest Yunnan Poplars.
Largest *Sophora microphylla* (S).
Largest Californian Bay.

**Powerscourt, Enniskerry. Open daily. Formal gardens with magnificent vistas; many rare and big conifers.
Tallest Himalayan Fir (Giant's Grove, 1980).
Largest Vilmorin's Fir (garden; ?).
Largest Italian Maple (terrace, E).
Largest *Chamaecyparis pisifera* 'Plumosa Argentea' (garden; ?).
Largest *C. p.* 'Plumosa Aurea' (Pepperpot garden).
Largest Smooth Arizona Cypress (Trident Pool).
Tallest Monterey Cypress (woods).
Tallest Winter's Bark (Pepperpot valley, 1989).
Largest *Euonymus lucidus* (Dolphin Terrace, 1989).
Largest Western Larch (garden).
Largest Likiang Spruce (Pepperpot garden).

Tallest Corsican Pine (riverbank).
Tallest Austrian Pine (woods).
Tallest Chinese Red Pine (below Pepperpot).
Largest Torrey Pine (below Pepperpot garden).
Tallest Willow Podocarp (Rhododendron walk, 1992).
Douglas Fir – tallest tree in Eire.
Tallest Japanese Thuja (Rhododendron walk below Dolphin garden).
One of the largest Keakis (1990).

Rossanagh, Ashford. Largest Sweet Chestnut in Ireland (1989).

Tulfaris, Blessington. One of the largest Broad-leaved Limes (park).

ISLE OF MAN

Species can be grown on Man which are too tender to survive on mainland Britain, though tall trees are confined to the shelter of the steep glens in the east.

Glen Mooar, Glen Mooar Road, St. Johns. Tallest *Ulmus glabra* 'Horizontalis'.

SCOTLAND

Britain's champion conifers have become increasingly concentrated in the Highlands, where the cool, humid conditions allow them to thrive for longest. Some prefer the east's cold dry winters, while others need the constantly mild, wet climate of the west coast. Most of these champions stand in private estates where the use of non-native conifers for forestry was pioneered in the 18th and 19th centuries; many have not been revisited in recent years.

Aberdeenshire

The driest and one of the coldest but sunnier corners of Scotland. The fine conifers are concentrated in the Dee valley in the south-west, under the shelter of the Grampians.

Ballogie estate, Potarch Bridge, Aboyne. Tallest Scots Pine (drive).

*Crathes Castle, Banchory. NTS; gardens open daily; a range of rare trees. Largest *Zelkova* x *verschaffeltii* (park just above Castle).

Durris estate, Banchory. An important, sprawling botanic collection; part of the estate has now been developed. Largest *Abies beissneriana* (estate; ?); largest Low's White Fir (glen, by bridge); largest *A. gamblei*; largest Flaky Fir (Keeper's Lodge); largest *Kalopanax septemlobus* var. *maximowiczii* (estate, near Banchory); tallest Camperdown Elm (House) – all 1987.

Fasque House, Fasque, Laurencekirk. House open daily in summer. One of the largest Giant Sequoias (1990).

Glen Tanar House, Glen Tanar, Aboyne. Largest *Picea meyeri* and Siberian Spruce (1980).

Inchmarlo, Banchory. Largest Pindrow Fir (1987).

*Kildrummy Castle Gardens, Alford. Open daily through summer; the house is a hotel. Many rare trees

growing in a deep ravine. Tallest Silver Birch (1985).

Mar Lodge, Braemar. NTS. Largest Scots Pine (the Mar Lodge Pine, in the Caledonian pine forest).

Rie Crathie, Crathie, Ballater. One of the largest Goat Willows (on an abandoned sheiling at NO266992).

*Tillypronie, Tarland, Aboyne. Open days. Wide range of conifers growing at a height of more than 300m. Largest *Thuja plicata* 'Cuprea' (1991).

Angus

Strathmore provides a pocket of excellent tree-growing conditions: sheltered by hills on most sides, humid but quite warm in summer, and with excellent soils derived from the Old Red Sandstone. The coast is drier and more windswept.

Burnside, Kirriemuir. Extensive pinetum. Tallest *Abies fargesii* (1990).

*Camperdown Park, Coupar Angus Road, Dundee. Historic public park, with many notable trees. Tallest Oriental Spruce and Hungarian Oak (pinetum) in 1985.

*Cortachy Castle, Kirriemuir. Woodland walks and gardens open sometimes. Many fine and big trees. Largest and tallest Forrest's Firs (riverside walk and graveyard); largest Brewer Spruce (riverside, S); largest Oriental Spruce (American Garden); largest *Pseudotsuga menziesii* 'Stairii' (roadside, Ballfield Bank).

*Dundee University Botanic Garden, Dundee. Open most days; 10ha established in 1971. Tallest *Salix* x *sericans* (bed E01, 10/72?).

*Glamis Castle, Glamis. Open daily through summer; Victorian pinetum. (Pronounced 'Glahmz'.) Tallest trees of *Chamaecyparis lawsoniana* 'Allumii' and 'Pendula Vera' (1981).

Gray House, Dundee. One of the largest Cedars of Lebanon (1986).

Kinnettles House, Glamis. Tallest Field Maple and largest Colorado Spruce (1986).

Logie Lodge, Kirriemuir. Tallest Grey Alder (1986).

Tannadyce, Tannadice, Forfar. Extensive tree collection. Largest Salween Fir, Manchurian Fir (arboretum), and Shore Pine (bank below house, 1990).

Argyll & Bute

The west coast receives up to 5m of rain a year and most perfectly mimics the natural habitat of the giant conifers of British Columbia and Washington. Glens sheltering very tall trees are largely found in the south-east towards Clydeside; further west, the country is wilder but enjoys very mild winters, and has long attracted adventurous gardeners keen to grow Himalayan rhododendrons and southern-hemisphere trees.

Achamore, Gigha. Open daily. Island garden created by Sir James Horlick since 1944; most notable for its rhododendrons. Largest Dahurian Larch (S side of main lawn by drive).

*Ardanaiseig Hotel, Kilchrenan. Gardens open daily. Largest and tallest trees of *Nothofagus* x *blairii* and largest *Rhododendron vernicosum* (1994).

**Ardkinglas Woodland Garden, Cairndow. Open daily (Ardkinglas House opens under the SGS). Many of the tallest conifers in Britain; National Collections of *Abies* and *Picea*. Largest Common Silver Fir (pinetum); tallest Grand Fir (pinetum); tallest Noble Fir (across burn); tallest Lawson Cypress (bridge, 1989); largest Hinoki Cypress (pinetum, 1991); tallest *Chamaecyparis pisifera* 'Plumosa Aurea' (1991); tallest Patagonian Cypress (pinetum, 1991); tallest Dunkeld Larch (bottom of group, 1985); tallest Western Red Cedar (1988).

*Arduaine, Oban. NTS; open daily. A very mild garden on the shores of Loch Melfort, noted for its rhododendrons. (Often pronouced 'Ardoonie'.) Largest *Eucryphia glutinosa* (1991); largest *Hoheria lyallii* (6001/1009); tallest Fastigiate Tulip Tree (3714); largest Antarctic Beech (?; 3336); largest *Rhododendron zeylanicum* (1991); largest *Thujopsis dolabrata* var. *hondae* (bank; 6629); largest *Trochodendron aralioides* (3942).

Auchengavin Farm, Luss. One of the largest Alders (Stron an Laoigh Burn, at NS335923).

**Benmore, Dunoon. The Younger Botanic Garden (an outstation of Edinburgh RBG) is open daily through summer, with many rare conifers and magnolias; there are many very tall trees in the Glen Massan arboretum (FC). One of the tallest Common Silver Firs; largest *Abies densa* (361; 588088); largest Faber Fir (588029); largest Sikkim Crab (578594, lower tree); tallest *Nothofagus betuloides*; largest Black Beech (578610); largest Hondo Spruce (319; 558582); one of the tallest Douglas Firs (Pucks Glen Walk, S side of river, at NS151842); largest *Rhododendron campanulatum* (BG); tallest Western Hemlock – all 1991.

*Crarae, Minard. NTS; regularly open. Woodland garden with many rare trees; National Collection of *Nothofagus*. Tallest Taiwan Fir (1C 040?); largest *Chamaecyparis lawsoniana* 'Lanei Aurea'; largest Chilean Hazel; tallest Korean Pine; largest Vilmorin's Rowan.

Drymsynie Hotel, Lochgoilhead. One of the largest Sycamores (1989).

Gareloch House, Gareloch. Tallest *Chamaecyparis lawsoniana* 'Albovariegata' in 1979.

Glenarn, Rhu, Helensburgh. Open daily through summer; mature woodland garden. Largest Rostrevor Eucryphia (1986).

The Hyslop Arboretum, Dunans, Glendaruel. Joint-tallest Douglas Fir (best viewed from the Dunans Hotel).

Inveraray Castle, Inveraray. Open daily in summer. Largest Northern Pitch Pine (garden) and tallest Weeping Giant Sequoia (1982).

Islay House, Islay. Largest *Plagianthus regius*.

Kilbryde, Inveraray. (Largest Common Silver Fir, blown 1975.)

Kilmalie (or Kimallie). (Largest Ash, by stream in the churchyard, burnt down in 1746.)

*Kilmory Castle, Knapdale. Open access. Largest Chinese Red Cedar; tallest *Prunus pendula*; largest *Rhododendron arboreum* 'Album' (by triangle) – all 1986.

*Kilmun Forest Garden, Dunoon. FC; a wide range of forest plots (1994). Largest *Eucalyptus archeri* x *delegatensis* (G171); largest *E. delegatensis* x *gunnii* (G263); largest Weeping Sally (P50/G190); tallest Spinning Gum (1978); largest and tallest trees of *E. simmondsii* (P50/G158, P52/G276, and

Britain and Ireland's equal tallest tree: Douglas Fir at the Hyslop Arboretum, Argyll

P50/G269); largest *E. vernicosa* (?; G264).

*Mount Stuart, Rothesay, Bute. Open most days in summer. Old pinetum, now being extended as a reservoir for rare conifers from around the world.

Rossdhu, Luss. Largest *Fagus sylvatica* 'Albovariegata' (on golf course; 1985).

*Stonefield House Hotel, Tarbert, Knapdale. Largest King Boris's Fir (drive, labelled *A. nordmanniana*); largest *Chamaecyparis lawsoniana* 'Albovariegata' (1981); largest *C. obtusa* 'Lycopodioides' (1991); largest Urn Gum (1986); tallest Myrtle Beech (1991); largest *Rhododendron arboreum* (W garden, 1991); largest *R. falconeri* (1991).

Strachur, Loch Fyne. (Largest Golden Norway Maple in 1969.)

Ayrshire

Most of the notable trees are in the more rural south, where mild and sheltered valleys run down to the coast.

*Blairquhan, Straiton, Maybole. Open in high summer (except Mondays). Notable pinetum. Largest Chinese Hazel (orchard), Sakhalin Spruce (Long Approach), Koyama's Spruce (orchard) and Jack Pine (orchard).

*Brodick Castle, Brodick, Arran. NTS; gardens and Country Park open daily. Many rare and tender trees. Largest *Acer taronense* (3101; area 33); tallest Chilean Firebush (3252; area 35); largest *Euonymus tingens* (5865; area 13); tallest *Hoheria lyallii* (3469; area 37); largest Rauli (5866; area 50).

*Culzean Castle, Maybole. NTS; Country Park and garden open daily through summer. A great range of trees. (The 'z' is silent.) Tallest Kohuhu (1989); tallest Irish Yew (Happy Valley); tallest Southern Japanese Hemlock (Castle/carpark).

Glenapp Castle Hotel, Ballantrae. Tallest Cilician Fir (on estate, 1989).

Rozelle Park, Ayr. Public park. Tallest *Populus* x *generosa* (drive, 1989).

Dumfries & Galloway
Widely-spaced old estates; fine trees in the valleys which run down to the mild coast.

Capenoch, Penpont, Thornhill. Tallest Oak-leaved Beech (lawn).

*Castle Kennedy and Lochinch Gardens, Stranraer. Open daily through summer. A magnificent coastal gardens with many tender trees. Tallest Cider Gum (S of Castle by Loch); largest Ulmo (S of Castle by Loch); largest Papauma (Walled Garden wall); tallest *Rhododendron arboreum* (Giant's Grave); largest Camperdown Elm (Castle Green).

Drumlanrig Castle, Thornhill. Gardens and Country Park open daily through summer. One of the largest Sycamores (park).

Glenlee Park, New Galloway. Tallest European Larch.

Jardine Hall, Lockerbie. Largest Cut-leaved Lime (1984).

Lochanhead Hotel, Dumfries. Largest Grand Fir (1993).

*Logan House, Port Logan, Stranraer. Open daily except in winter. (The adjacent Botanic Gardens are an outstation of Edinburgh RBG, specialising in tender southern-hemisphere plants.) Largest *Olearia traversii*; Largest *Rhododendron decorum*; largest *R. fortunei* ssp. *discolor* (Henknow Wood); largest *R. grande*.

Monreith, Whithorn. Tallest *Ilex aquifolium* 'Golden Queen' in 1979.

Munches, New Abbey. Tallest Cappadocian Maple (path to wood, N; 1985); tallest Silver Maple (Farm Garden, H6; 1996); tallest *Pseudotsuga menziesii* 'Stairii' (drive, 1985); tallest Golden Wych Elm (Wagon Wood, 1985).

Raehills, Moffat. One of the largest Common Silver Firs (Dark Bend, 1984).

*Threave Garden, Stewartry, Castle Douglas. NTS; open daily. Extensive arboretum. Largest *Populus koreana* (1984), *P. tremula* 'Gigas' (1984) and *Ulmus* x *hollandica* 'Dampieri' (1991).

Dunbartonshire
Auchincruive, Dumbarton. Largest *Phellodendron japonicum* (1979).

*Balloch Castle Country Park, Balloch, Dumbarton. Open access; some unusual trees. Tallest *Chamaecyparis pisifera* 'Plumosa' (Mystery Garden, 1985).

East Lothian
Carberry Tower, Musselburgh. The Church of Scotland; fine and rare trees. Largest *Sorbus* x *kewensis* (?; 1985).

Glenorchy, 15, Glenorchy Road, North Berwick. Largest Swedish Whitebeam.

Lennoxlove, Haddington. House regularly open in summer. Tallest Sycamore (avenue, mid; 1985).

Saltoun House, Pencaitland, Ormiston. (Largest Balsam Fir, swept away by a flood in 1891.)

Seton Collegiate Church, Port Seton. Historic Scotland. Largest Bastard Service.

*Smeaton House, East Linton. SGS open days. Many rarities. Tallest Cut-leaved Hornbeam (reverting) and Cut-leaved Oak (park) in 1986.

*Tyninghame House, Tyninghame, East Linton. SGS open days. A variety of unusual trees. One of the largest Sycamores (by old church).

Whittingehame Tower, Stenton, Dunbar. Largest Whittingehame Gum (1996) and *Thuja plicata* 'Semperaurescens' (1987).

Edinburgh
The New Town has good populations of street trees, while elms in great variety were largely killed by disease in the early 1990s.

Castle Terrace. Largest *Ulmus glabra* 'Luteovariegata' (in 1989).

The Murray Home, 470, Gilmerton Road. Largest Double Gean (front).

**The Royal Botanic Garden, Edinburgh, Inverleith Row. Open daily. The arboretum extends along the southern edge of the historic gardens.
Largest *Acer multiserratum* (1985).
Tallest Black Maple (A01; 19687061A).
Largest *Alnus maritima* var. *formosana* (19260059A).
Largest *Betula pendula* 'Tristis' (M01; 19687193).
Largest *B. raddeana* (K02; 19621696A).
Largest Jacquemont's Birch hybrid (687236, 1991).
Largest Jacquemont's Hazel (J01; 19784163A).
Tallest Alpine Cider Gum (705307, 1991).
Largest *Euonymus bungeanus* (C07?; 19687512A).
Largest *E. hupehensis* (1985).
Tallest Golden Beech (734007, 1991).
Largest Japanese Walnut (061011, 1991).
Largest Tanbark Oak (C01; 19687759A).
Largest Siebold's Crab (A01; 19051019A).
Largest *Malus* x *zumi* (A01; 19171011A).
Tallest *Meliosma beaniana* (Acer collection, 1985).
Largest *Phellodendron japonicum* (980041, 1991).
Tallest Big-Cone Pine (698168, 1991).
Tallest *Populus* 'Androscoggin' (580318, 1991).
Tallest Himalayan Bird Cherry (M01; 19041003A).
Largest *Prunus maximowiczii* (M01; 19698237A).
Tallest Tibetan Cherry (1991).
Largest *Pyrus amygdaliformis* var. *persica* (980068; 1991).
Largest *P. balansae* (A01; 18980011A).
Largest *Quercus* x *hickelii*.
Largest *Q. lyrata* (C01; 19350109A).
Tallest *Q.* 'Pyrami' (1985).
Tallest *Robinia pseudoacacia* 'Tortuosa' (1985).
Largest Bollwyller Pear (A01; 19031004A).
Largest *Sorbus japonica* var. *calocarpa* (A01; 19151008A).
Largest *S. pohuashanensis* (?, 1985).
Largest *S.* x *vagensis* (698281, 1991).

Many conifers are happiest in the cool humidity of the north-east Highlands. One champion Western Red Cedar grows at Belladrum, near Beauly.

Largest Spur-leaf (051020, 1991).
Largest *Tilia laetevirens* (151018, 1991).
Largest *T. platyphyllos* 'Glauca' (A01; 19699330A).
Tallest Yunnan Hemlock (B01; 19699353A).
Largest Wentworth Elm (744388, 1991).
Largest *Ulmus turkestanica* (C07; 19021007A).
Tallest *Zelkova* x *verschaffeltii* (531019, 1991).

Fife

Inzievar House, Oakley, Dunfermline. Tallest Hybrid Strawberry Tree (dying 2001).
*St Andrew's Botanic Garden, Canongate, St Andrews. Fife Council; open daily. Developed since 1960, with a good collection of *Sorbus*. Largest *Betula forrestii* (8).
St Andrews University, St Andrews. One of the largest Hawthorns (St Mary's Quad, 1992).
Tulliallan Castle, Kinkardine. Largest *Juniperus virginiana* 'Glauca' (1990).

Glasgow

The city has some fine public parks, whose trees have been little-studied. Until recently, industrial pollution prevented the growth of the conifers which would otherwise thrive in Clydesdale.

Kelvingrove Park, Kelvingrove. Public park. (Tallest Willow-leafed Pear in 1974.)

Highland

The west coast is bleak and wet, but winters are mild: a few gardens specialising in tender trees have been created in the wilderness. On the other side of the mountains, the sheltered glens running down to the Beauly and Cromarty Firths contain a concentration of Britain's tallest trees, growing on Old Red Sandstone soils, with more in the Findhorn valley on the Moray boundary.

Achnacarry, Fort William. Largest *Picea orientalis* 'Aurea' (1982); tallest Arolla Pine (drive, 1986); largest Bird Cherry (1986); one of the tallest Giant Sequoias.
Aldourie Castle, Loch Ness. Tallest Pindrow Fir (1992).
Ardross Castle, Dingwall. Tall and uncommon conifers. Largest *Chamaecyparis lawsoniana* 'Youngii' (Japanese Garden); one of the tallest Grey Poplars (river); largest Goat Willows (W garden/river); largest Hybrid Sallow.
Armadale Castle, Armadale, Sleat. Gardens open daily; on the sheltered side of Skye. One of the largest Common Silver Firs (Laundry Road corner, 1988); largest Common Juniper (1978).
Balmacaan, Drumnadrochit, Loch Ness. The Woodland Trust. Many of Britain's largest conifers. Largest Grand Fir; tallest Spanish Fir (Arboretum, S); tallest Giant Sequoia (N of house); largest Western Red Cedars.
Beaufort Castle, Beauly, Inverness. Open days. Largest and tallest Crimean Pines (1983).
Belladrum, Beauly, Inverness. One of the largest Western Red Cedars (1993).
Brahan, Conon Bridge. Largest trees of *Chamaecyparis lawsoniana* 'Allumii' and 'Lutea' (1989); largest Wych Elm (field below arboretum).
*Castle Leod, Strathpeffer. Open occasionally. One of the largest Giant Sequoias; Sweet Chestnut with the earliest confirmed planting date.
*Cawdor Castle, Cawdor, Nairn. Open daily through summer. Wild garden and woodland trails. Tallest Gamble Fir (Big Wood, 1994); largest *Chamaecyparis lawsoniana* 'Glauca Pendula' (Big Wood, 1980).
Dalvey, Alness. Tallest *Ilex aquifolium* 'Argenteomarginata' (1989).
*Dochfour, Loch Ness. Regularly open; extensive pinetum. Largest Veitch's Fir (1992); largest and tallest trees of *Chamaecyparis lawsoniana* 'Stewartii' (1992); largest *Thuja occidentalis* 'Lutea' (pinetum, 1982).
The Doune of Rothiemurchus, Aviemore. Grounds open Mondays in summer. Tallest Sitka Spruce ('280' in grove).
Dundonnell, Ullapool. One of the largest Alders (in ancient woodland, 1986).
Dundonnell House, Ullapool. SGS open days. A number of rare trees in one of Scotland's most northerly big gardens. Largest *Eucalyptus coriacea*; largest Snow Gum (start of laurels); one of the largest Hollies.
Fairburn House, Muir of Ord. Rare and very big conifers. Largest *Chamaecyparis lawsoniana* 'Silver Queen' (Pinetum); tallest *C. l.* 'Triomf van Boskoop' (Pinetum);

largest *C. l.* 'Westermannii' (Pinetum); tallest Mountain Hemlock (old garden); tallest Blue Engelmann Spruce; two of the largest Sitka and Morinda Spruces.

Flowerdale House, Gairloch. (Largest Himalayan Larch (past graveyard, 1991).)

Glenferness, Nairn. Largest Noble Fir (Prince's Stone, 1987).

*****Inverewe Garden**, Poolewe. NTS; open daily. Created on a peninsular in Loch Ewe from 1865 by Sir Osgood Mackenzie; many tender species. Tallest Heart-leaved Silver Gum and tallest Chilean Hazel (Bambooselem).

*****Kilravock Castle**, Croy, Nairn. Kilravock Castle Christian Trust; open daily in summer (except Sundays); pronounced 'Killrock'. One of the largest Sitka Spruces (lawn).

Kinloch Hourn, Loch Hourn. A remote late Victorian garden. Tallest Whittingehame Gum in 1978.

*****Leckmelm Shrubbery and Arboretum**, Little Leckmelm House, Ullapool. Open daily through summer. Victorian gardens and arboretum. Tallest *Abies amabilis* (lower edge; ?; 1986); largest Sawara Cypress (1991); tallest Vilmorin's Rowan (1991).

Logie House, Grantown-on-Spey. Largest Eastern White Cedar (1992).

*****Reelig Glen Wood**, Moniack, Beauly. FC. Many of Britain's tallest trees in a sheltered glen. Tallest Norway Spruce (W entance, by burn, 1986); joint-tallest Douglas Fir; tallest Goat Willow (gate, 1987).

Wester Downie, Ardgay, Bonar Bridge. Largest Aspen (1993).

Wester Elchies, Strathnairn. Tallest Western Balsam Poplar (1989).

Midlothian

Arniston House, Gorebridge. Regularly open in summer. Largest *Sorbus aucuparia* 'Dirkenii' (1987); one of the largest Small-leaved Limes (end tree in Common Lime avenue).

Moray

Sheltered valleys with tall conifers run down to the North Sea, though the climate is cold and relatively dry.

Cullen House, Cullen. Largest Single-leafed Ash in 1980.

Darnaway, Forres. Large pinetum; the Meads of St John, by the Findhorn, are accessible on foot. Largest Hokkaido Spruce (1989); largest Sessile Oak in Scotland (Meads of St John).

*****Innes House**, Elgin. Open by appointment; a range of rarities. Largest Red Buckeye; tallest Paper-bark Birch; tallest Sorbus 'Wilfrid Fox'.

Park Hotel, Forres. Largest trees of *Ilex* x *altaclarensis* 'Hendersonii' (1989).

Randolph's Leap, Forres. Open access. One of the tallest Sitka Spruces (bank of Findhorn at NH998493).

Perth & Kinross

Strathearn and Strathtay have some of the densest concentrations of champions in Britain, and some of the tallest stands of common trees: there are many old estates, the Old Red Sandstone soils are conductive to tree-growth,

the summers are quite warm but humid, and the mountains to the west provide deep shelter.

Abercairney, Crieff. One of the tallest Common Silver Firs (park); one of the largest Sycamores (park); largest Variegated Red Oak (Stables Road) – all 1986.

Ballathie House Hotel, Kinclaven, Stanley. Largest *Chamaecyparis lawsoniana* 'Pendula Vera' (1984).

Ballindean, Carse of Gowrie. Tallest Norway Maple (1987).

Birnam, Dunkeld. One of the largest Sycamores (second of the 'Birnam Oaks', by the river in the park behind the Birnam Hotel).

*****Blair Castle**, Blair Atholl, Pitlochry. Open daily through summer. Diana's Grove is a remarkable 1ha grove of tall conifers planted in the 1860s. Largest Red Fir (St Bride's, 171?, 1995); largest Jeffrey's Hemlock (drive, S; sixth in avenue, 1989); largest Dunkeld Larch (Gunroom Bridge, 1983); tallest Japanese Larch (Diana's Grove, 1989).

Castle Menzies, Perth. Giant Sequoia – fastest tree to x250cm (died 1931).

*****Cluny Castle Garden**, Aberfeldy. Open daily through summer. Rare younger trees under huge Victorian conifers. Largest Giant Sequoia.

Colquhalzie, Auchterarder. Largest Chinese Juniper (1997).

Comrie. One of the largest Scots Pines (private estate near the town, 1990).

Craighall, Rattray. Largest *Larix decidua* 'Pendula' (1986).

Dalguise House, Dalguise, Dunkeld. Tallest Variegated Sycamore and Copper Beech.

Drumkilbo, Meigle. Open days. Tallest Cut-leaved Lime.

Dunira, Comrie, Crieff. Edwardian gardens; open access. Largest Korean Fir; largest Veitch's Fir; largest *Picea abies* 'Inversa'; largest and tallest Northern Japanese Hemlocks.

*****Dunkeld Cathedral**. Historic Scotland. Very big conifers in the Cathedral Grove: one of the largest European Larches; tallest Alcock's Spruce; one of the largest Douglas Firs.

Dunkeld House Hotel, Dunkeld. Tallest Dunkeld Larch (Bishop's Walk, 1983); largest Japanese Larch (drive, 12; 1990).

Dupplin Castle, Forteviot. (Largest Variegated English Oak (Pinetum, N; 1983).)

Errol House, Errol, Carse of Gowrie. Largest *Cornus controversa* 'Variegata' (1986).

Fortingall church, Glen Lyon. Fragments of the oldest and largest surviving Yew.

Garth House, Aberfeldy. Tallest Walnut (1988).

*****Glendoick Gardens**, Glendoick, Glencarse. Open days in May. Many rare trees, collected largely in W China by the Cox family. Largest Birch-leaved Maple and Euodia (Den).

Gourdie, Mains of Gourdie, Dunkeld. Tallest Turner's Oak.

The Hermitage, Dunkeld. One of the tallest Douglas Firs (across the Braan Burn from the viewpoint, in FC woodland).

Invermay Castle, Forteviot, Perth. Largest Subalpine Fir and Blue Engelmann Spruce (1988).

Sycamore is the ugly duckling of the maple genus. Conservationists and gardeners uproot it by the million; it is familiar to most people as a weedy gangling plant of railway embankments and waste ground, its leaves blackened by Tar-spot fungus. But its shelter in coastal and upland regions is indispensable, while a few lucky areas, such as the Southern Uplands of Scotland and east Kent, grow ancient trees of immense stature and majesty. Why it should thrive here, and remain so disreputable elsewhere, remains one of the puzzles of dendrology. The champion was discovered in a field near Posso House, Peebles, by Jim Paterson in 1992.

Keltie, Crieff. Grand Fir – fastest tree to 50m (in plantation near village, blown 1953).

Kinfauns Castle Hotel, Perth (1985). Largest Silver Hedgehog Holly (1985).

Lude House, Blair Atholl. Largest Western White Pine (drive, 1991).

Megginch Castle, Errol, Carse of Gowrie. Open daily through summer. Largest Japanese Maple and Scotch Laburnum.

Moncrieffe House, Bridge of Earn. Largest Corstorphine Plane and tallest Golden Ash (1982).

Monzie Castle, Crieff. Open days. (The 'z' is silent.) Largest European Larch.

Murthly Castle, Murthly. Many very big conifers. One of the largest Grand Firs (E Drive, third tree, 1993); tallest *Chamaecyparis lawsoniana* 'Lutea' (1983); largest Mountain Hemlock (lower terrace, 1988); tallest Sakhalin Spruce (1989); largest and tallest Serbian Spruces (Jubilee Terrace, 1990); largest *Picea omorika* x *sitchensis* (1989).

North Inch, Perth. Public park. (Tallest Belgian Elm in 1983.)

Ochtertyre Hotel, Crieff. Largest Southern Japanese Hemlock (1987).

Pitcarmick, Strathardle. Largest Cork Fir (1986).

Princeland, Coupar Angus. One of the largest Giant Sequoias (1985).

*Rossie Priory, Dundee. SGS open days. Many notable trees. Tallest Ash (woods), and Wych Elm (group below drive) in 1985.

*Scone Palace, Perth. Pleasure Grounds open daily through summer; Victorian pinetum, the trees spaced in lines. Largest Alcock's Spruce (E Pinetum); largest Jeffrey Pine; one of the largest Scots Pines, 'The King of the Forest' (woodland at Lynedoch); largest Western Hemlock (Pinetum).

Snaigow House, Dunkeld. Largest *Chamaecyparis lawsoniana* 'Erecta Viridis' (657).

Taymouth Castle, Kenmore, Loch Tay. Open access to the grounds; many outstanding conifers. Largest Nikko Fir; tallest Red Fir (E); largest Noble Fir; largest *A. spectabilis* var. *brevifolia* (W end of conifers by Loch Tay); largest Morinda Spruce (W); one of the largest Coast Redwoods – all 1990.

Scottish Borders

The widely-spread old estates lie mostly in the relatively sheltered valley of the Tweed, as it winds through the bleak Southern Uplands.

**Dawyck Botanic Garden, Stobo, Peebles. Outstation of the Royal Botanic Gardens, Edinburgh; open daily through summer. The arboretum has 300 years of planting. Tallest *Abies fabri* ssp. *minensis* (Policy Bank, W; V10; 1997). Largest Maries' Fir (Policy Bank, 1992).
Largest *Acer nipponicum* (V06; 19795193; 1997).
Largest *Fagus crenata* (E Policy Bank, 19795168b; 1997).
Tallest Dawyck Beech (1992).
Largest *Larix gmelinii* var. *japonica* (V01; 1992).
Tallest *Phellodendron chinense* (Dynamo House, V06; 1979-5022; 1997).

Largest Engelmann Spruce (Herons Wood, 1992).
Largest and tallest Balfour's Spruces (Shaw Brae, 19795293 and 19795296, 1997).
Largest *Picea maximowiczii* (V43; 1979-5115; 1995).
Largest *Sorbus alnifolia* (Sargent's Garden, V08; 1979-5257; 1997).
Largest *Tilia americana* var. *vestita* (Chapel Wood; ?; 1982).

Dryburgh Abbey Hotel, St Boswells. Largest Atlas Cedar (in 1992) and Fastigiate Scots Pine (drive) ; Yew with one of the earliest known planting dates.

Harestanes Country Centre, Jedburgh. Largest Spanish Fir (drive to Country Park).

The Hirsel, Coldstream. Grounds open daily. One of the largest Tulip Trees (private walled garden).

*Monteviot, Jedburgh. Open daily through summer. Historic 'Pinery'. Tallest *Chamaecyparis lawsoniana* 'Albomaculata' (1983).

Posso House, Peebles. Largest Sycamore (in field, 1992).

The Yair, Galashiels. Largest Cock's Comb Beech (in 1984).

Stirling

Airthrey Castle, Stirling. Stirling University; open access. Largest Arolla Pine.

Ardgomery, Kippen. Largest West Felton Yew (1988).

Blair Drummond, Doune. Largest White Spruce in 1974.

Culcreuch Castle Hotel, Fintry. Largest Grecian Fir (above pinetum); tallest Single-leafed Ash (back drive); tallest Lodgepole Pine – all 1984.

Doune Castle, Dunblane. Largest Incense Cedar and Western Hemlock (private garden).

Gartmore House, Aberfoyle. Largest *Ilex aquifolium* 'Golden Queen' (1984).

*Keir House, Dunblane. Open days. Many rare trees. Sweet Chestnut – largest in Scotland (1970).

Kippenross House, Dunblane. Tallest Amur Maple (1986).

Quinloch Wood, Strathblane. Largest Hazel (S edge at NS520814, 1985).

Watson House, Gargunnock. Open access to grounds. Largest Golden Red Oak (1988).

West Lothian

Hopetoun House, South Queensferry. Scotland's grandest stately home, open daily. Tallest Veitch's Fir (Pinetum, 1984).

Preston House, Linlithgow. Fine and rare trees. Largest Exeter Elm in 1987.

WALES

Most of the finest trees are in the populous south-east, and along the Marches where the shelter of the mountains combines with good soils derived from the Old Red Sandstone to grow huge oaks, an abundance of ancient churchyard Yews, and some of Britain's tallest trees. Conifers thrive best in the lea of Snowdonia in the wet north. The rural west is mild but often exposed to Atlantic gales; some notable trees here probably await discovery.

Golden Grove, in the Gelli Aur Country Park in Carmarthenshire, is one of Wales' oldest arboreta. Exceptional trees include this unmeasurable Western Red Cedar.

Anglesey
Plas Newydd, Llanfair PG. NT; open most days through summer. One of the largest Sycamores; tallest *Viburnum cylindricum* (17777).

Carmarthenshire
*Golden Grove, Gelli Aur Country Park, Llandeilo. Small historic arboretum; open access. Largest *Chamaecyparis pisifera* 'Plumosa'; tallest Young's Golden Juniper; one of the largest Tulip Trees (Wall Garden); largest Turner's Oak – all 1993.
Pantglas Hall, Llanfynydd, Carmarthen. Largest Weeping Beech.
Talley Abbey, Llandeilo. One of the largest Ashes (hedge).

Ceredigion
Trawsgoed, Aberystwyth. Open by appointment. Tallest *Juniperus chinensis* 'Albospica'.

Conwy
**Bodnant, Tal-y-Cafn, Colwyn. NT. Open daily through summer. A spectacular garden with a ravine of tall conifers and many rarities. National Collections of *Eucryphia* and *Magnolia*.
Tallest Yellow Birch (1990).
Tallest *Chamaecyparis lawsoniana* 'Erecta Viridis' (Dell Garden, W; 1990).
Largest *Cupressus arizonica* var. *bonita* (1990).
Tallest Black Juniper (1990).
Tallest *Magnolia sprengeri* var. *elongata* (1984).
Largest Hubei Crab (Chapel Walk, 1990).
Largest Mexican White Pine (Pinetum bank, 1990).
Largest *Prunus* 'Amanogawa' (N Garden; 1981).
Largest Tibetan Cherry (by lawn, 1990).
Tallest Coast Redwood (Dell Garden, 1984).
Largest Weeping Giant Sequoia (1990).
Largest Chinese Hemlock (upper cascade, 1990).

Coed Coch, Abergele. Tallest Bhutan Pine (1984).

Hafodunos, Llangernyw, Llanwrst. Many rare conifers. One of the largest Norway Maples (drive, 1990); largest Irish Juniper (1984); tallest Himalayan Weeping Juniper (1990); largest *Prunus cerasifera* 'Nigra' (1984).

Llangernyw church, Llanwrst. One of the largest Yews.

Denbighshire

Three Sisters, Llanrhaeadr, Ruthin. One of the largest Sweet Chestnuts.

*Vivod, Llangollen. A Forest Garden was developed when the FC owned part of the estate in the 1940s and 50s. Largest Fraser Fir (206); largest *Picea jezoensis* ssp. *hondoensis* x *sitchensis* (302); largest *P.* x *lutzii* (210) – all 1988.

Glamorgan

Cardiff and Swansea both rival London in their traditions of municipal arboriculture. Winters along the coast are mild but summers sunny and quite warm, so that a number of heat-loving trees have done surprisingly well. Were it not for a history of industrial pollution, the steep valleys running south from the Brecons would also be a good area for tall conifers.

Brynmill Park, Brynmill Lane, Swansea. Public park. Largest X *Crataemespilus grandiflora* (NW gate).

*Bute Park, Cardiff. Public park; a range of rare trees. Largest *Acer palmatum* 'Shishigashira', Fastigiate Thorn, Idesia and Foxglove Tree (NW).

*Cathays Park, Cardiff. Public park. Largest *Prunus* 'Geraldinae' and tallest *Prunus* 'Hokusai' (in 1985).

*Cefn Onn Park, Cardiff. Public park – notable for magnolias and rhododendrons. Tallest *Thuja plicata* 'Zebrina' (1990).

*Clyne Gardens, Black Pill, Swansea. Historic public park, and one of the most magnificent in Britain; ravine with giant rhododendrons and rare trees. Tallest White Campbell's Magnolia (N of bog garden, up slope); largest *Malus* x *robusta* (S of top pond); largest *Rhododendron decorum* ssp. *diaprepes* (lower/mid valley).

Coedarhyddglyn, Cyntwell, Cardiff. Pinetum planted in the 1940s. Largest Tupelo (60) and largest Siberian Stone Pine (Pinetum) in 1991.

**Dyffryn Gardens, St Nicholas, Cardiff. Open daily. Edwardian gardens extended in 1960s to make Wales' most extensive tree collection.
Largest Paperbark Maple (Arboretum, S; 975).
Largest *Chamaecyparis lawsoniana* 'Filifera' (Arboretum, W; 805).
Largest *Crataegus arkansana* (Arboretum, 109).
Largest *C. jonesiae* (Arboretum, 327).
Tallest Fastigiate Thorn (Arboretum, 3814).
Tallest *C. punctata* (Arboretum, 478).
Largest and tallest Southern Cucumber Trees (Arboretum, 777 and 922).
Largest *Prunus lusitanica* 'Myrtifolia' (Arboretum, W, 895).
Largest Chinese Wingnut (West Garden, 2093).
Tallest Almond-leaved Pear (Arboretum, 286).
Largest Lebanon Oak (Arboretum, 303).
Tallest *Sorbus glabrescens* (Arboretum, 398).

Tallest Chinese Elm (behind Rockery, 3883).

Garwnant Visitor Centre, Merthyr Tydfil. Largest Ley's Whitebeam (outside rangers' office).

Margam Park, Margam, Port Talbot. Gardens and Forest Park open most days; fine old trees. Tallest Bays (1985).

Merthyr Mawr, Bridgend. Rare trees. Largest Swamp Chestnut Oak.

Newcastle House, West Road, Bridgend. Collection established by the late Fraser Jenkins; parts have since been built on. Tallest Chinese Yellow-wood (Kitchen garden); largest Wolgan Snow Gum (W Garden); largest *Eucalyptus kitsoniana* (W Garden); largest *Prunus* 'Okame' (W Garden) – all 1990.

*Roath Park, Cardiff. Public park; a great range of rare trees. Largest Green Alder (Roath Mill Gardens; 1990); tallest Oleaster (Botanic Garden); largest *Emmenopterys henryi* (Botanic Garden); largest Weeping Ginkgo (Botanic Garden); tallest Osage Orange (Botanic Garden); largest Basford Willow (Pleasure Grounds).

*St Fagans Castle Gardens and Museum of Welsh Life, St Fagans, Cardiff. National Museum of Wales; open daily. Historic gardens with many fine trees. (Pronounced 'Faggans'.) Largest Sorrel Tree (?; 1992).

*Singleton Park, Swansea. Historic public park (Singleton Abbey itself is now part of the University of Cardiff); many rare trees concentrated in the Botanic and Ornamental Gardens. Tallest Hybrid Buckeye (N of Ornamental Gardens); largest *Crataegus submollis* (Botanic Garden, labelled *C. laciniata*); largest Japanese Raisin Tree (Botanic Garden, N border); largest *Photinia beauverdiana* (Ornamental Gardens, E); largest Japanese Wingnut (Ornamental Gardens, NW); largest *Viburnum odoratissimum* (Ornamental Gardens, W gate).

Tal-y-Garn, Cowbridge. Small pinetum. Tallest Hondo Spruce (1986).

Gwynedd

Mallwyd church. One of the largest Yews (E of church).

*Penrhyn Castle, Bangor. NT; open most days; grand old conifers. Largest Big-leaved Storax (1989).

Portmeirion, Penrhyndeudraeth. Open daily. Some rare and tender trees in the woodlands above Clough Williams-Ellis' Italianate village. Tallest *Cryptomeria japonica* 'Elegans' and Mayten.

Monmouthshire

Bettws Newydd church, Usk. One of the largest Yews (W of church).

Mamhilad church. One of the largest Yews.

Penrhos Farm, Llantilio Crossenny. One of the largest English Oaks.

Pembrokeshire

Ffynone, Boncath. NGS open days; historic woodland garden. One of the largest Common Limes.

Powys

The sheltered valleys of the headwaters of the Severn have long vied with the Scottish Highlands in growing the islands' tallest trees. Summers are also warm enough for many other trees to grow well.

Abercynrig, Llanfrynach. (Largest Common Laburnum in 1988.)

Buckland Hall, Llangynick, Brecon. One of the largest Beeches (house) and largest Silver Lime (lake) in 1988.

Buttington church, Welshpool. Yew with the earliest known planting date.

Christ's College, Brecon. One of the largest Wild Black Poplars (E edge of playing field near Usk, viewable from path to Llanfrynach).

Crickhowell. Largest Wild Black Poplar (Usk Bridge at SO214183, 1988).

Defynnog church, Sennybridge. One of the largest Yews (N of church).

Discoed church. One of the largest Yews (N of church).

Garthmyl House, Garthmyl. One of the largest English Oaks (1984).

*Gliffaes Country House Hotel, Crickhowell. Many big old trees. Largest *Chamaecyparis lawsoniana* 'Erecta Viridis', and Yellow-berried Holly (1995).

Gregynog, Tregynon, Newtown. University of Wales; open access. One of the largest Lawson Cypresses.

Lake Vyrnwy (Llyn Efyrnwy), Llanwddyn, Welshpool. FC. One of the tallest Douglas Firs (E bank, at SH998215).

Leighton Hall, Welshpool. The 1857 Ackers Memorial redwood grove and the historic pinetum are owned by the Royal Forestry Society; Park Wood (separate ownership) has a plantation of some of the tallest Grand Firs (1994). Largest X *Cupressocyparis leylandii* 'Leighton Green' (Ackers Memorial); tallest Wild Black Poplar (1984); largest and tallest Plantier's Lombardy Poplars (in 1964).

Llanafan Fawr church. One of the largest Yews (E of church).

Llanfaredd church, Builth Wells. One of the largest Yews.

Llanfeugan church. One of the largest Yews (N of pair at E end of church).

Llangattock, Crickhowell. One of the largest Giant Sequoias, 'The Courting Tree' (in Llangattock Park, just N of canal near bridge 13).

Llangoed Hall Hotel, Llyswen. Largest Mountain Snowdrop Tree (1993).

Maesllwch Castle, Glasbury-on-Wye (1989). NGS open days. One of the largest Maidenhair Trees (1989).

Portmarr, Crickhowell. Largest Stone Pine.

*Powis Castle, Welshpool. NT; open most days. A range of rare trees. Largest Henry's Maple (below terraces, 17127); tallest Japanese Angelica Tree (woodland garden near icehouse, 17270); tallest True Service (S corner of woodland garden, 16913). Other champions on currently inaccessible private land near Welshpool include the tallest Manchurian Fir (1981); largest Arolla Pine (1989); largest and tallest Western Yellow Pines (1989); one of the largest Sessile Oaks, 'The Giant' (viewable from the Castle drive); one of the largest English Oaks; and one of the largest Giant Sequoias.

Stanage Park, Knighton. Many rare trees.
Largest *Acer giraldii* (Knighton drive).
Tallest Birch-leaved Maple (dam).
Tallest *Alnus japonica* (Wood Garden).
Tallest River Birch (wood bank).
Largest and tallest Yunnan Crabs (on dam, and road from house to cave).
Tallest Koyama's Spruce (Wood Garden).
Tallest Corsican Pine (Knighton drive).
Largest American Aspen (E drive).
Largest Laurel Oak (Oak Avenue).
Largest *Rhus potaninii* (by walled garden).

Tretower Court, Tretower, Crickhowell. Cadw; open daily through summer. One of the largest Alders (1995).

Ystradfellte church. One of the largest Yews (E end tree of three NW of church).

Wrexham

Pontfadog, Chirk. One of the largest Sessile Oaks (field boundary near church).

How to Record and Measure Trees

Tree-hunting

The study of trees is a constantly rewarding activity. Where trees grow well, the best way to 'hunt' champions is often to explore on foot, focusing on pockets of good soil, sheltered valleys, or the banks of lakes and rivers, and using binoculars to spot interesting foliage and tell-tale crown shapes at a distance.

Identification

The biggest challenge lies in the correct identification of the 2-3,000 taxa which can be met with, almost anywhere: flowering trees, present in such diversity in most townscapes, are regularly under-recorded because of the difficulty of separating them out of season. It must also be remembered that any labels found on garden trees can not infrequently be wrong.

Locating the tree

The tree you are recording may still be there in a hundred years' time. For the record to be meaningful, people then will need to be able to find where it is. Six-figure Ornance Survey grid references or GPS co-ordinates are often essential.

Accuracy

To record a tree's height as 28 metres is unavoidably to claim that it is neither 27 nor 29 metres, and any such claim needs to be backed up by the painstaking pursuit of accuracy. A number of pitfalls exist when measuring trees.

Trunk thickness

The most valuable record is usually the trunk's thickness. A tape-measure is run horizontally round the stem to give its girth. The 'thickness' (i.e. how broad the trunk would look from an 'average' viewpoint; *not* an 'average' thickness) is the girth divided by pi (3.14159). This is often termed the 'diameter' (a word that denotes the thickness of a perfect circle, which tree-trunks in cross-section never are). It is customarily given in centimetres, since to obtain uniformity with the metres used for denoting the height would be to introduce a decimal point and with it an increased chance of misprints. The standard height at which to take the girth is 1.5m (from ground level on the upper side if the tree is on a slope).

Measuring trees with irregular trunks

If the tree in the photograph was taped at 1.5m it might be 160cm thick, but if the tape were to stray upwards or downwards a few centimetres, 170cm or 150cm could be recorded. Any such trunk is best taped *at the narrowest accessible point*. (If a measurer applying the same principle 20 years later records 7cm of growth, this becomes significant evidence in estimating such trees' ages.) If you have to record a girth at anything other than 1.5m, you

must however make this clear, since a forking trunk 250cm thick at 0.4m from the ground differs widely in appearance and volume from a clean stem of the same thickness.

Sometimes the tape needs to be run round the tree at an angle, and should be recorded as at, for example, 0.2-0.9m. (If the trunk leans, the lowest recordable value will nearly always be with a slanting tape – ideally at an average 1.5m.)

Steve Young measures the champion Silver Birch at Rookery Wood, Penshurst, Kent.

Measuring multi-stemmed trees

This tree (below) is best measured both around the single stem at the base and around the 'main stem' plus the 'additional stems' at chest height. (But take clear not to write it as '250cm@0.2m, and 120cm+120cm'. This gives the impression not of a two-stemmed tree but of one with three stems, the first much larger and shorter than the others.)

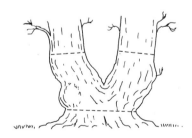

Measuring heights

A stick cut to half the length of your arm from the fingers to your eye, and held vertically at arm's length so that the top and bottom seem to coincide with the top and bottom of the tree, can help you to estimate heights: the height of the tree will be half the distance between yourself and the trunk (see diagram overleaf).

Most tree recorders use a hypsometer – or clinometer – this works on a trigonometrical principle to convert an angle into units of height, depending on the length of a baseline (see diagram overleaf).

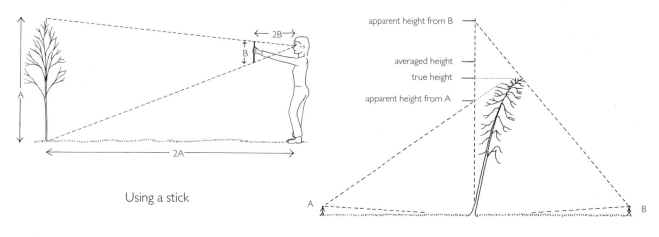

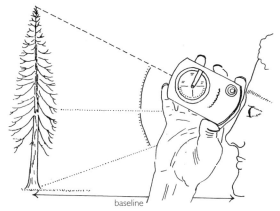

Using a stick

Using a hypsometer

Various errors can creep into height measurements. They usually combine to make the tree seem taller than it is.

Aiming at the apparent top of this tree (below) from a 30m baseline will over-estimate its height by more than 40%; to hit the true top you must aim at a point only half way up the near side of foliage. From a 40m baseline, the over-estimation has decreased to about 20%, and from 60m, it is only 8%. For a tree the shape of a Cedar of Lebanon, such errors become proportionately greater. There is an almost overwhelming temptation to aim above the true top of a broad crown: this is by far the largest source of errors when heighting trees. The best safeguards are to use long baselines (60-80 metres), always to sight from a point which is above rather than below the level of the tree's base, and to take the height off baselines in more than one direction.

Baselines in different directions from this leaning tree (above) will give different heights. Note that the true height will always be *less* than the average of the readings. (Most straight-stemmed conifers start vertical, but have developed a slant away from the prevailing wind by maturity.) Many hypsometers have a mark at 90° on their rotating scale which shows what is directly above your head (otherwise surprisingly difficult to estimate), and it is best to utilise this when measuring any tree so that your baseline starts underneath what seems likely to be its tip, rather than automatically next to its trunk.

It can be impossible to differentiate the tree's crown from its neighbours'. In such cases there is no substitute for experience, but it can help to wait until winter and to shine a bright torch vertically into the crown while measuring it.

If the baseline is on a slope, the horizontal distance between you and the tree is less than the measured distance along the ground. A 12% slope creates a 1% over-estimation of height, and a 20% slope a 2% over-estimation.

Using a laser range-finder

Use the range-finder to measure the distance from yourself to the tree's top (B), and to its bottom (C), then use a hypsometer's scale to calculate the angles (D and E). This method automatically compensates for any lean, and 'virtual' baselines can be established which, for example, cross rivers or valleys. However, the laser can only be used

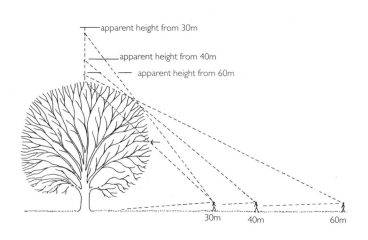

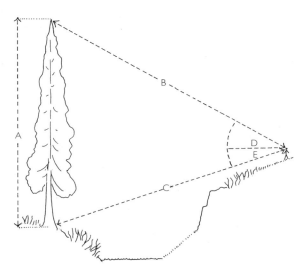

if the true top of the tree is clearly visible.

Most accurate of all is to climb the tree and dangle a tape; understandably, this has been reserved for only a select few of our tallest trees. The length of a windblown tree along the ground tends to be greater than its height was, because of the displacement into one plane of long, broken branches which previously grew at wide angles.

When a tree has died back, it is the height to the highest live growth that is customarily measured; leaves (which add more than a metre to the 'height' of a palm tree) should be excluded.

Measuring crown spreads

The tree's spread is seldom recorded as it is directly dependent on any other trees around it. Spreads recorded in this book are maxima, unless stated.

Bibliography

Alderman, David and **Stevenson**, Pamela *Champion Trees of Bedfordshire* (Bedfordshire County Council, 1993).

Bean, W J *Trees and Shrubs Hardy in the British Isles* (John Murray; eighth edition 1970).

Bevan-Jones, Robert *The Ancient Yew* (Windgather Press, 2002). Includes a gazetteer of ancient Yews in Britain.

Browne, Dinah and **Hartwell**, Mike *Our Remarkable Trees* (Trees of Time and Place, 2000). Illustrated introduction to the trees of Northern Ireland.

Chittenden, F J *Conifers in Cultivation* (Royal Horticultural Society, 1932). Comprehensive study of the growth of conifers.

Cornish, Vaughan *The Churchyard Yew and Immortality* (Muller, 1946).

Elwes, H J and **Henry**, A H *The Trees of Great Britain and Ireland* (Edinburgh, 1906-13).

Hillier and Sons *Hilliers' Manual of Trees and Shrubs* (revised 2002 by Allen Coombes).

Howard, A L *Trees in Britain and their Timbers* (Country Life, 1947). Includes details of many individual specimen trees.

Hudson, Norman (ed). *Hudson's Historic Houses and Gardens* (Norman Hudson). Annual guide to public attractions.

Johnson, Owen *The Sussex Tree Book* (Pomegranate, 1998). Introduction and guide including Sussex's county champions.

King, Peter (ed.) *The Good Gardens Guide* (Bloomsbury). Annual guide to the best gardens in Britain and Ireland open to the public.

Lowe, John *The Yew-Trees of Great Britain and Ireland* (Macmillan, 1897).

Mabey, Richard *Flora Britannica* (Sinclair-Stevenson, 1996). A cultural history of plants in Britain.

Marren, Peter *The Wild Woods* (David and Charles, 1992). A regional guide to Britain's ancient woodland.

Miles, Archie *Sylva* (Ebury Press, 1999). A natural history of trees and woodlands in Britain.

Miller, John *Trees of the Northern Highlands* (John Miller, Alness; revised edition 2002).

Mitchell, Alan *Alan Mitchell's Trees of Britain* (HarperCollins, 1996). Encyclopaedic introduction to the best examples then known of 150 kinds of tree.

Mitchell, Alan *Conifers in the British Isles* (Forestry Commission, 1972). Comprehensive study of the growth of conifers.

Morton, Andrew *Tree Heritage of Britain and Ireland* (Swan Hill, 1998). A geographical guide to famous and historic trees.

Morton, Andrew *Trees of Shropshire* (Airlife, 1986).

National Gardens Scheme *Gardens of England Wales and Scotland Open for Charity* (East Clandon, Surrey). 'The Yellow Book': annual guide to gardens opening for charity.

Pakenham, Thomas *Meetings with Remarkable Trees* (Weidenfeld and Nicolson, 1996). Photographs of many of the oldest and largest trees in Britain and Ireland.

Rackham, Oliver *Trees and Woodland in the British Landscape* (J M Dent; revised edition 1990).

Royal Horticultural Society *The Plant Finder* (Dorling Kindersley). Annual directory of all the plants in commerce in Great Britain.

Rushforth, Keith *Trees of Britain & Europe* (HarperCollins 1999). A field guide to 1200 species.

Scott, Alistair *A Pleasure in Scottish Trees* (Mainstream, 2002). A personal introduction to many of Scotland's finest trees and woodlands.

Swanton, E W *The Yew Trees of England* (Farnham Herald, 1958).

The Tree Council *Great British Trees* (2002). Portraits of 50 remarkable trees selected by Parish Tree Wardens.

Webster, A D *London Trees* (1920).

White, J E J *Estimating the Age of Large Trees in Britain* (Forestry Commission; revised 1998).

Glossary

Ancient Woodland Land (in Britain) which has been continuously covered by trees since at least 1600.

Bundle planting Several trees of the same taxon planted in the same hole to create a large-looking, bushy specimen quickly.

Chimaera Plant originating in the non-sexual fusion of two species' tissues.

Clone All the plants propagated vegetatively from an individual.

Coppice To fell a tree so that the base sprouts to make new trees; a stump treated in this way; to regrow like this.

Crown All of a tree above its trunk.

Cultivar A '*culti*vated *vari*ety' or mutant clone, nursery-distributed.

DED Dutch Elm Disease: fungal pathogen of plants in the Elm family (researched largely in Holland).

Fastigiate Growing nearly vertical branches and/or shoots.

Forma (plural formae) Scientifically-described sport or minor variant of a species.

Genus (plural genera) Scientific grouping of species, into which families are divided.

Graft To fuse a shoot of one kind of tree onto roots of another; a tree fused in this way.

Hybrid The offspring of different species, subspecies or varieties.

Layer A branch touching the ground and rooting; the secondary trunk that results.

Microspecies A species that is usually local and produces fertile seed without pollination.

Original The first tree of a taxon in cultivation in a country.

Pleacher A stem cut and bent horizontally in a laid hedge.

Pollard To cut a tree at 2-4m so that is grows new limbs; a tree cut in this way.

Sport A genetic freak (of independent occurrence).

Stool The persistent stump of a coppiced tree.

Subspecies A scientifically recognised (regional) variant of a species.

Taxon (plural taxa) A single discrete nomenclatural unit.

Type The usual form of a species (as opposed to a variety or clone); the individual on which a taxon's scientific description was based.

Variegated With leaves consistently lacking green colouration in patches.

Variety A scientifically-recognised (morphological) variant of a species.

Veteran tree A tree old enough to be of special historical and ecological value.

Index to the Directory: common tree names

Index to the Gazetteer: place names